JOURNALISTS AT WAR
The Dynamics of News Reporting during the Falklands Conflict

by

David E. Morrison and Howard Tumber

SAGE Publications
London · Newbury Park · Beverly Hills · New Delhi

First published 1988 by Sage Publications Ltd
for the Broadcasting Research Unit
Chairman: Richard Hoggart
Head of Research: Michael Tracey

SAGE Publications Ltd
28 Banner Street
London EC1Y 8QE

SAGE Publications Inc
2111 West Hillcrest Drive
Newbury Park, California 91320
and 275 South Beverly Drive
Beverly Hills, California 90212

SAGE Publications India Pvt Ltd
C-236 Defence Colony
New Delhi 110 024

British Library Cataloguing in Publication Data

Morrison, David E.
    Journalists at war: the dynamics of news
    reporting during the Falklands conflict.
    1. Falklands Islands War. Reporting by mass
    media in Great Britain
    I. Title   II. Tumber, Howard
    997'.11
        ISBN 0-8039-8057-4
        ISBN 0-8039-8058-2 Pbk

Library of Congress catalog card number 88-060146

Publishing services by Ponting–Green, London
Photoset by Parker Typesetting Service, Leicester
Printed in Great Britain at the Alden Press, Oxford

Contents

Acknowledgements

We are indebted to the Broadcasting Research Unit which financed this whole study. But money apart, this book would not have appeared had it not been for the Executive Committee of the Unit. It was they who originated the idea for such a study and saw that out of the unhappy circumstances of war the understanding of broadcasting might be advanced, in this instance, by an investigation of the reporting of the Falklands Conflict. We are grateful for, and acknowledge our debt to, their imaginative decision. At a more personal level, since such large-scale study requires constant support, we would like to thank them for their sustained encouragement of the whole project.

Our special thanks go to Dr Richard Hoggart, Chairman of the Executive Committee, for his careful reading and perceptive observations on substantive points. To Anthony Smith, Director of the British Film Institute, for his reading of an early draft of the manuscript and his helpful comments and suggestions. To Stephen Hearst, for his reading and comments on broadcasting points, and to Kenneth Lamb for his general enthusiasm and personal encouragement throughout the life of the project.

One of the most exciting aspects of writing *Journalists at War* was interviewing the journalists who accompanied the Task Force. All had their own stories to tell and we are extremely grateful that they gave their accounts to us. Without their cooperation the book could not have been written. They were generous with their time, and patient with our questioning about events, happenings and situations. As much as anyone's this book is theirs and we hope that any disagreements they might have with the way we have interpreted their experiences are not taken as indicating disregard for their occupations or for the difficulties they faced.

Ministry of Defence officials, or 'minders' as they were most commonly known, have come in for much severe criticism for the way in which they handled the flow of information from the Task Force. Their agreement to talk with us therefore, and their openness in answering our questions, contributed enormously to our general understanding of the reporting of the Falklands operation. Their job was not an easy one and we would like to thank them for telling us the details of their lives with the Task Force and recounting events which they clearly felt have been the subject of much misunderstanding.

We would also like to thank those on the 'home front': editors of ITN news, BBC Television News, BBC Radio News, BBC World Service News, BBC Television's *Newsnight*, BBC Television's *Panorama*, journalists from BBC Television News, BBC Television's *Newsnight*, television executives, defence correspondents from the press, the Press Association and television, foreign editors of press and television, engineers from ITN and BBC; and some who would wish, out of personal preference, to remain anonymous.

We would also like to thank the senior but 'unattributable' voices of the Ministry of Defence, Members of Parliament and the Prime Minister's Press Secretary, who agreed to talk with us.

For material assistance with the study we would like to thank Piers Hoare-Temple. For his generous and invaluable technical help in relation to broadcasting engineering, our special gratitude goes to Peter Heaps of ITN.

Dr Janet Morgan's contribution to the book must be singled out for special mention. Her professionalism in editing our very lengthy report to the Executive Committee of the BRU into publishable proportion along with her general editorial skill in making the whole manuscript more readable cannot be praised enough. More than any other single person we are indebted to her for the cooperation, energy and hard work expended in the many months of editorial discussion.

We would like to thank NOP, the market research company, which undertook the field-work side to our national audience survey, for its efficiency. Nick Moon, a director of the company, was singularly helpful, far beyond that which might be expected from a commercial arrangement. His intelligence was much appreciated as was his humour which helped relieve the frustration of the survey stage of our work.

For the statistical computation of the content analysis we wish to thank Paul Croll. Any help with content analysis is always appreciated and this particular operation was no exception. We would also like to thank our coders for their diligence and painstaking efforts at watching and coding hours of television news bulletins: Louise Donald, Neil McCartney, Walter Mason, Alex Sutherland, and Graham Whybrow.

With over seventy interviews conducted, some lasting as long as six hours, an enormous amount of material was generated which had to be transcribed. For this task we wish to offer special thanks to Lille Coppin for giving us hours of her valuable time, which she did with amazing equanimity. For typing the various manuscript drafts our thanks go Shivaun Meehan, Anna Noble, Kate Pluck and Olivia Stewart, for their efficiency and organization.

Special thanks are owed to our colleague Dr David Docherty for his friendship and help; Kirstie Morrison for her support and encouragement, and to Hila and Michal Tumber for their patience and understanding.

Finally, we wish to express our appreciation to the Head of the BRU, Dr Michael Tracey, for his administrative help, editorial assistance and suggestions for improvement. Simply to say 'thank you' does not capture the amount of time and effort which he gave throughout the study nor the part that his support played in guiding this book to completion.

Introduction

It is strange to find journalists, whose business is to enquire into the occupations and lives of others, so frequently making the comment that it is impossible to understand their occupation unless one has oneself been a journalist. Yet journalism as a practice, and journalists as an occupational group, perhaps more than any other, have been the subject of intensive enquiry; in American schools of journalism, the findings of such studies form part of journalists' own professional training and education.

Reading the academic literature one cannot help but feel sympathy with the journalists' claim that the 'outsider' has failed to get inside the trade: it is all too formalistic, too sterile, too serious; and it is not surprising, therefore, that working journalists fail to recognize the world they are supposed to inhabit. To begin with, there are not many laughs in the academic literature, but anyone who has spent time with journalists knows how amusing they often are. Journalists are individuals whose work and working conditions involve the unpredictable, and their attempts at control and management of events and people are, especially as told by themselves, often hilarious. Journalists, as could be expected from the nature of their trade, are good story-tellers, which, generally, social scientists are not. What we have done therefore, in the first eight chapters of this book, is to let the journalists tell their own story. (In doing so we hope to have corrected the outsider's failure to deliver the inside workings of a journalist's world.)

The setting for the book is, of course, the conflict between Britain and Argentina over the Falkland Islands; but the main purpose of the study is not war reportage as such, or that war in particular, but to understand journalists through the unique facility offered by events in the South Atlantic. The advantage of using the conflict as the stage upon which the story is set is that it offers near-perfect vision, a kind of bell-jar condition, for observing journalists going about being journalists.

It has another advantage. The stage was such that the actors themselves were forced to confront the role they were playing, reflect on habits, practices and procedures that in other more normal circumstances would be taken for granted. Not only, therefore, did the Falklands Conflict offer a clear view to the outsider of journalistic procedures, it also opened the eyes of the journalists themselves, turning them into reflective witnesses of their occupation.

While the principal method of the research was the ethnographic one of having the journalists recount their experiences and comment on their approach and practices, the stories the journalists told have at times been used in the same way that an anthropologist might use stories and myths of some primitive tribe to explain the culture out of which the stories have emerged. The accuracy of some stories is not always, therefore, an essential condition of their usefulness, especially those in which journalists referred to the behaviour of their colleagues. A readiness to scorn the performance of others appeared to us, leaving aside the genuine dislike that some journalists developed towards their colleagues, to function as a technique by which to highlight their own abilities without having to name them: a silent boasting by omission. So common was this characteristic that it appeared to be an occupational one, the roots of which no doubt rest in the tendency towards insecurity that afflicts journalists in general; one which is perhaps not too surprising in an occupation that combines scholarship with showmanship, promoting the writer through the by-line to the status of a personality but denying him outright editorial control of his product. Yet by understanding this tendency towards insecurity it becomes that much easier to understand the type of behaviour engaged in by the journalists which upset and shocked the military: the internecine bickering; the hostility towards those who clogged up the signal system with over-long despatches or those who filed for foreign newspapers; the complaints that the military were unfairly dispensing favours to some journalists; the collective agreement by one group to block another group getting ashore quickly and thus robbing it of equal reporting opportunities. Compared to their own disciplined men, the military saw the journalists as childishly irresponsible, referring to them as the 'fourth form'.

Thus while we have allowed the journalists to tell their own story, we have not allowed the story to go unstructured. What we have attempted is to develop the coverage of the Falklands hostilities as a general treatise on journalism: other journalists in less dramatic situations which might not so easily be observed, would show similar patterns of behaviour. Furthermore, the behaviour exhibited by the journalists in our case study of the coverage of the Falklands would be recognizable to other journalists who have never covered a foreign story let alone a war. Although the possibility of death and the sheer physical hardship was new to some of them who were, to quote one of the journalists, 'office and bar-room trained', the manner of gathering the news was not. The situation presented new twists and turns to basic patterns of reporting: being bombed may have been new, but being lied to was not.

Too often studies of news concentrate either on the formal editorial control of content or on the informal control whereby the
journalist is socialized into the news values and procedures of his
organization. What is missing is any notion of the 'journalist as
person'. That is, he is first and foremost regarded as a performer of
a specific role with certain attributes rather than an individual with
his own biography of sensibilities; for example, following the fall of
Port Stanley, Ian Bruce of the *Glasgow Herald* was talking by phone
to his editor, who complained that Bruce's stories sounded very
bitter, to which Bruce replied: 'That's because I am fucking bitter'.

A soldier Bruce had known well and with whom he had shared a
drink on many occasions failed to make it to Stanley having been
badly wounded, possibly crippled, at the very close of the war.
Bruce was upset, it affected him, and in doing so moulded the mood
of his copy.

Of course it would be sociological madness to deny the vital
importance of structural factors influencing the manner in which
journalists report; the journalist does not, after all, write for himself, but for an organization. Nevertheless, insufficient attention has
been paid to how the journalist as an individual exercises his own
judgement in negotiating his role, and more than that, the critical
politicizing of research in the area of mass communications has
meant that the journalist as news gatherer has been pushed out of
sight. He no longer fits, or rather researchers cannot find a place for
him, in the grand indictment of the news as the reproduction of
dominant ideology. If nothing else, a study such as this which
examines journalists at work under the difficult conditions of the
Falklands Conflict is a reminder that there is something called
journalism as opposed to 'information oppression'.

This is not to deny the value and contribution to mass communications research of the 'critical' tradition, but there is a need alongside this for a more humanistically inclined individual perspective.
One needs to know how those at the cutting surface of news collec-
tion operate before making statements drawn from general understanding of social processes. Content analysis can help, but even
then its major benefit is in determining values; it cannot go beyond
its own methodology to explain how the picture was arrived at. The
values say something in that they do not appear by chance; indeed
they represent the workings of social relationships which go beyond
even the news industry itself and into social formation. Yet to
understand the creation of news, as distinct from social relationships
as demonstrated by the news, it is essential to get to grips with
people as operatives within a system rather than operators of a
system. The latter too easily leads to notions of conspiracy on the

one hand and on the other to give social structures a life of their own.

We see our focus on journalists themselves in the first eight chapters of the book as a method of bringing home the complexities and difficulties involved in any interpretation of happenings. It may be convenient to say that journalists got this or that wrong without defining what 'wrong' could mean; does it mean a wrong perspective; does it mean a wrong understanding in some historical sense of social movement and distribution of power within society; does it mean wrong in the sense of factually wrong?

All we can expect from journalists is a reasonable amount of accuracy and a rounded presentation of the facts. Unfortunately, however, facts are provisional upon wider understandings than that which is observed; but a factual account can be taken to be what a community accepts as reasonably accurate, given the limitations and difficulties of observing events. A correspondent for *Pravda* may have been capable of filing a factually accurate account for the *Morning Star*, but not for readers of the *Daily Star*. Facts, as we said, are provisional, but we will see how the Task Force journalists working within community-structured definitions of what is factual struggled to decide what constituted a fact and what counted as an accurate factual account.

Illustrating how the journalists operated gives a sense of reality to proceedings rather than some imagined account of what the journalists ought to have been doing and how they should have viewed events according to, let's say, some creed of abhorrence of war. Was, for example, the firing on British troops after the Argentinians surrendered at Goose Green to be taken as fact, and were the reports of the bayoneting of surrendered Argentinian soldiers by the British to be accepted as fact and, if so, given the contextual meaning of war, where death in all its forms loses the meaning that it has in civilian life, reported as fact?

These were difficult questions and not all the journalists arrived at the same conclusions, but the point is that one cannot treat journalists, any more than any observer, as if they are simply pairs of eyes. They must be seen as active, thinking human beings who make judgements, but at the same time it would be wrong to take the journalist's account of what he was doing as the account of what was going on: what he thought he was doing and what he was actually doing, if the same, would presume perfect knowledge of events. Consequently, the accounts the journalists gave us (and given their lengthy reproduction in the book they are open to inspection and interpretation by the reader) have been set within our own occupational understanding, as sociologists, of social behaviour and social organization.

The journalists, then, have not been regarded as passive observers of something called facts, but as active witnesses of happenings which called for judgements on their part. The judgements journalists make, however, take place within professional codes and set standards of accuracy which allow them to evaluate the level of interpretation present in their reports. The fact that we can see those codes and standards tested to the limits in the Falklands is one of the benefits of the study, but the holding of codes and professional standards of accuracy is no guarantee against systematic distortion since journalists may operate within an occupational ideology that prejudices them in ways they are barely aware of. That is, their accounts are not the same accounts that members of the public would give had they been present. Distortion might take place, in other words, not because of a lack of shared agreement about facts, but because of practices of collecting facts peculiar to journalism. But again, an advantage of the situation in the Falklands was that for most of the journalists, faced by events that threatened their own lives and the deaths of soldiers they had become fond of, the basis for their own activities was opened for self-inspection to an unusual degree. Tony Snow of the *Sun* may not have slept with the light on after writing 'Up yours, Galtieri' on a Sidewinder Missile, but he could not escape reflecting, as our interview shows, on the nature of popular journalism and his procedures as a reporter. What he could not do in his copy, which included the Sidewinder episode, was to explain the basis of his judgement, and it is that basis which requires examination: it cannot be read backwards from a content analysis of his story.

Although the individual is not the object of sociological study it does not mean there is no room in sociological explanation for biographical placement, especially when the subject of investigation (the news) is constructed in the first instance by individual investment of meaning. The observer must be observed. Non-participant observation is a well accepted technique for examining the workings of journalism; most typically conducted in the formal setting of the newsroom where the observer is attempting to distinguish patterns of behaviour or judgements made in deciding what is newsworthy. Occasionally the observer will accompany the journalists on assignment. Whether those observed behave differently under the outsider's eye is open to question. In the busy confines of the newsroom, probably not. The news must be produced and routines cannot be altered to massage the image for the watchful eye of the observer. The situation of the assignment is somewhat different. One sometimes has the feeling that the behaviour is promoted for the benefit of the observer, indeed that one is even being 'taken for a ride'. It is not surprising, there is something slightly ludicrous about all observation situations where significance is looked for in every act.

Most observational work, however, whether in the formal setting of the newsroom or the more fluid assignment situation, do not allow much insight into the personalities of those who are being observed. It is a pity, but to be expected from a trade that tends to pride itself on remaining removed from those it studies. There are some notable exceptions, and within sociology different approaches and different definitions of what constitutes correct procedure are necessary. Yet, mass communication research has been especially guided by the attempt at general description: it is the audience as the statistical average of responses, or the journalist as a 'role incumbant', or the news as the filtered expression of social arrangements, or within the tradition of political economy, the organization as a factor of production. The fact that at times, for example, within gratification studies or laboratory experiments, the numbers of people studied are small, does not mean they feature as individuals. They become statistical expressions of states of arousal or the incorporators of information.

The overall purpose is to understand journalism, or at least to gain greater insight into news-gathering than has hitherto been provided by abstract description or the attempt at formalizing procedure. Hopefully, the lengthy treatment of the journalists' accounts of what went on in the Falklands, and their differing perceptions of events will allow the reader to establish the journalists as distinct individuals and by so doing frame the activities with a measure of some understanding of the people involved. Thus Max Hastings becomes, not only the reporter from the *Evening Standard* or the *Express*, but someone with his own individualistic approach and even foibles. But, equally, Ian Bruce, from the *Glasgow Herald*, is seen not as a man just filled with hatred for Hastings, but as someone tired of the trials of obtaining the news in a situation that worked against all efforts without, as he held, the help of Mr Hastings.

What we arrive at by this method is not only an understanding of the individual journalists, but an understanding of the context within which the individuals operated and how they acted in gathering the news. However, while we lay claim for greater focus on journalists as individuals in understanding the production of news, it must be recognized that they are only one part of news production. The whole world is not open to inspection through the individual, only parts, and even those parts can resist full understanding without wider placement in the world from which the individuals have been drawn.

Thus, while the major part of the book deals almost exclusively with the Task Force journalists, the following three chapters examine the handling of the news in London, including the political controversy that resulted from the manner in which the Ministry of Defence released the news and the political attacks made on the media for the way in which the war was reported. This part of the story takes us directly into wider issues and into questions about the role of information in liberal democratic societies.

It is at this point that the study comes to questions, not of individual behaviour, but of power and power arrangements, the role of ideology and the value structure of society. In other words, it is one thing to give a detailed account and advance understanding of journalists as practitioners, but it is quite another to understand how the product of those practices surfaces as meaning, and even more so, how the meanings of events presented for popular consumption are digested. Chapter 11 therefore gives the result of our content analysis of news during the Falklands Conflict. Chapter 12 gives the results of our national survey of public opinion about the news people saw and their attitudes towards the media both during crisis and non-crisis times.

To have the press we deserve is an old adage, but it pays no attention to the press the public might want or at least it pays no attention to the type of news and reporting the public might want. The answers come at the end, but first, the journalists, then the politics, then the public.

1

The media prepare

It wasn't a news war, it's as simple as that.
It was in the wrong place. (Martin Cleaver, PA Photographer)

The routine of a leisurely spring weekend was destroyed by the invasion of the Falklands by Argentinian forces on Friday, 2 April 1982. On Saturday morning the House of Commons met (the last Saturday sitting had been at the time of the Suez crisis) and on the same day the United Nations Security Council called for the end of hostilities, the withdrawal of Argentinian troops and the peaceful resolution of the dispute. The Government's proposal to send the Task Force was overwhelmingly supported by Parliament; the first ships were to sail on Monday.

The assembly of the journalists who were to sail with the Task Force was, if anything, even more frantic. In the rush of events, the press was obliged to scramble for places. When most of those who wished to go discovered that they would not have a place, they were astonished, angry and panicky. With hindsight, the way in which the choice was made was typical of the haphazardness and improvization which, in the view of broadcasters and journalists, characterized the entire expedition.

A Ministry of Defence official hastily telephoned John le Page, the Director of the Newspaper Publishers' Association (NPA), at lunchtime on Sunday, 4 April to ask him to choose within two hours representatives of four national newspapers to sail with the Task Force. When we asked the Ministry why the selection was left to the NPA, we were told by an official that this was 'normal custom', but he knew of no good reason for it.

There was an almighty clamour for places, not just in Britain but world-wide. (Roger Goodwin, the press officer on duty at the Ministry at 2 a.m. on Thursday, 1 April, when news of the Argentinian invasion first broke, took a call from, among others, the *Rocky Mountain News*.) Since it was clearly impossible to satisfy more than a handful, le Page simply asked his wife to draw four lucky names out of a hat. These were the *Daily Mirror*, the *Daily Express*, the *Daily Telegraph* and the *Daily Mail*. There was also a photographer from the *Daily Express*, with two representatives from the Press Association (PA). One correspondent was to go from BBC Television and another from ITN; they were to share one cameraman and one soundman, a crew, chosen by the toss of a coin, from the BBC.

Understandably the losers refused to accept the result of this raffle.

According to Tony Snow of the *Sun*:

> . . . our editor said 'That's ridiculous, bloody great Task Force – it's crazy, you know, and we're going to lose the media war hands down again.' . . . So various other editors, including ours, went spare and got in touch with John Nott and Maggie Thatcher and other people and put the pressure on.

The editor of *The Times*, Charles Douglas Home, who telephoned Downing Street, eventually heard from the Ministry of Defence. According to the *Times* correspondent, John Witherow,

> . . . he couldn't do anything . . . but then, I think, about nine o'clock that Sunday night they called back and said 'OK! We've got a place for you.' They didn't say which ship. I think all they said was 'Make sure you bring a dark suit' which sounded bizarre . . .

The instruction was clearly intended to make sure the press conformed to the standards of dress expected in the wardroom and is indicative of the Navy's apprehension that those about to join it came from another world with different cultural behaviour.

Since Downing Street was also concerned that so few places had been allocated to the media, the editors had a powerful ally, although it appears that the Prime Minister's Press Secretary, Bernard Ingham, decided without further consultation that the number should be increased and gave instructions to that effect. In all, nineteen news organizations were to be represented by twenty-nine people (see Appendix I), some of whom joined ships that left later. Apart from the Press Association, the only non-national organizations to be allocated places were the *Glasgow Herald* and the *Wolverhampton Express and Star* (replaced subsequently by the *Yorkshire Post*).

For those who sailed immediately, the departure was chaotic. Gareth Parry of the *Guardian*, for example, was telephoned at home and given only twenty minutes to prepare:

> The train was going from Waterloo to Portsmouth – the last train on a Sunday night . . . I packed very hurriedly, ridiculous things like a swimming costume . . . It's 'see you next Wednesday' or whatever, you can't bloody well start discussing [it]. It's a really good story, so you go.

John Witherow 'went home and threw some things into a suitcase'; Tony Snow's preparations were even more informal. Fed up with hanging about the *Sun*'s offices on Saturday night, as he waited to hear if the paper had a place with the Task Force, he left for home. Then:

> About nine o'clock I got a call from the office and they said 'Go towards Portsmouth . . . you may be sailing tonight.' . . . so I just put some things in a bag, put it on the back of my motorbike and drove . . . And about ten miles from Portsmouth I went in a phone-box and said 'Hello. How's it going?' And they said: 'You're on. Go to HMS *Nelson* and ask for a certain person . . . We don't know anything about it, just go there.' . . . I had to put my motorbike in one of their long-term Navy car parks . . . in fact, it stayed there for three months in the open.

As for Mick Seamark of the *Star*, ' . . . two pairs of trousers, two pairs of underpants and shaving gear was what I took with me, basically'.

Those who embarked later, in the P & O liner *Canberra*, took advantage of the delay. Kim Sabido of Independent Radio News (IRN), for example, bought 'a whole lot of little Antarctic equipment from the Alpine sport shop', before boarding, while, according to Charles Lawrence of the *Sunday Telegraph*, others were fitted out as thoroughly as the intrepid William Boot, the hero of Evelyn Waugh's *Scoop*:

> It was the cleft-stick routine. Alastair McQueen from the *Mirror* was by far the best equipped. He turned up with the whole lot, including his own water bottle, mug and camping stove.

In fact, it was those in *Canberra* who needed such equipment the least. They were to be kitted out by the Army, whose knowledge of equipment required was based on a bit more than the amateur's perusal of camping catalogues. It was those in *Invincible*, or the *Invincible* Five as they came to be known, who in the end were stuck without any proper equipment or clothing to withstand the freezing cold of the Falklands and went ashore literally with a suitcase, oddments of naval attire and a packet of cheese and pickle sandwiches which Tony Snow had the presence of mind to bring along.

It was the speed of events, especially the despatch of the Task Force, that chiefly caught the press by surprise. But interestingly, some had already warned their organizations of tension in the region. Reuters, for instance, had received material from their 'stringer' in the Falklands, while Bob McGowan of the *Express* had asked to be sent there:

> It was just a question of listening to the news and reading newspapers. I mean, we knew what was going on in South Georgia and people were banging drums and it seemed quite likely that something might happen. I put my name down for it then. We'd made a decision here apparently not to bother . . . Then of course the

invasion came on the Friday morning, of the same week that I'm talking about, and I was off.

Jeremy Hands of ITN also saw the storm-clouds gathering some three months before the actual invasion took place.

> I saw a paragraph in the *Telegraph* saying that the Argentinians had rejected the British negotiations [at the UN] and someone had said 'We are going to have to do something positive.' So I went upstairs and said, 'Look,' very optimistically, 'why don't we go down to the Falklands and do some background stuff on what it's all about. Go to Argentina as well.' And got absolutely no reply at all. After that happened, it started building up, and I sent more and more memos and got more and more rejections, and two days before the Argentinians invaded South Georgia or Stanley, I was told . . . 'Even if World War Three breaks out we can't afford to go down to the Falklands.' To which I said 'Fine, that's up to you. I think you're mad.' A day after the Falklands were invaded a reporter was sent to Buenos Aires, and the day the Task Force sailed another reporter was sent with the *Hermes,* at which point I felt like resigning.

It is interesting to speculate that, if Hands had managed to persuade ITN to release him and a crew some three months before the actual invasion occurred to go to the Falklands and Argentina, ITN might have saved themselves a lot of money and the military a lot of lives. Although history's alternatives are forever unknowable, it is not beyond imagination to consider that the public airing of the Falklands as an issue, and Argentinian designs as plans, might have caused the parliamentary gaze to fall upon the private understandings of the Foreign Office and thus at least place the Falklands on a more visible agenda.

The type of journalist sent

As Tony Snow put it, 'I am not a war correspondent. I had never done this sort of thing before.' He was not alone in his inexperience. Martin Cleaver, the Press Association's photographer, had only been abroad once, to cover the monitoring of the ceasefire of the Rhodesian civil war. In his case, admittedly, this was not unusual, since the Press Association, being a national agency, relies for foreign coverage on the photo service of Associated Press, the American agency. Now, however, on an occasion of such undoubted national interest, there was no question of the Press Association's not wishing to be represented.

Because the media have regular production cycles and production deadlines, one of the major organizational goals is the regulating of uncertainty. Quite apart from the internal organizational arrangements, the major factor in achieving this goal is the regulation of the news itself. News does not exist independently of someone defining it as news, and it is the media's collective consensus of what news is that allows the efficient budgeting of scarce resources.

Thus, news is made more predictable by defining in advance areas of likely news, such as parliament, industry, sport, defence and so on. The allocating of specialists to such areas means that events within those domains require less visibility than areas which do not qualify for such attention. In other words, it is the journalist who makes the news, and not simply the occurrence of the events themselves. Only by making news predictable in such a way can the media organization operate at all.

Not only does the relative importance of different specialisms change over time but, at any one moment, the boundaries of several specialisms may overlap. All this complicated matters when it became necessary for news organizations to decide which of their correspondents should be sent with the Task Force. There were those, for instance, who believed that, over the years, the quality of defence correspondents had declined. (Simon Jenkins, of *The Economist*, attributes this to the absence in recent times of a major war.) As a story, however, the Falklands expedition was not easy to classify; it fell into not one but several categories. Was it a war story, a diplomatic story, or a straightforward 'pageant and colour' story? In a sense it was all of these: how much of each? Editors had to decide whether to send a feature writer, a hard-news man, a defence correspondent, someone old but experienced in reporting trouble, or someone young and fit. They did not know whether the story would be 'out there' and so deserve a 'star' reporter, or 'back here' in London, where the appropriate specialists could handle it. To what degree was it a political as opposed to a military story? How, indeed, did the Government see it?

Brigadier Ramsbotham, Deputy Public Relations Officer of the Army at the Ministry of Defence, told us how disappointed he had been by Fleet Street's decisions:

> When we saw the list on Monday the feeling was what the hell do they know about war. I mean, [it] appeared to be the journalist who was on duty at that particular paper that got a nomination to go and so [was] told to pack [his] bags . . . we felt that we ought to have somebody who at least understood the jargon, because you don't understand the imperatives of what people are doing unless you've actually worked with us before.

The first correspondents to be chosen were nominated by Ian McDonald, Acting Chief of Public Relations at the Ministry of Defence in consultation with Jack Gee, Chief Press Officer. In the week that followed, however, there was some lobbying for places in *Canberra* for certain specified journalists. Ramsbotham continued:

We had a chance then, the Army and the RAF, to suggest that other people went, including Max Hastings, who I must admit I put on because we had known him in Northern Ireland and it seemed absurd that he, as the only well-known military correspondent, should not be going.

In fact, Hastings was so highly regarded that Ramsbotham admitted that, had Hastings not put himself forward, he would 'certainly have contacted him anyway'. By and large, however, the Ministry of Defence kept to the principle that the news organizations themselves would select their correspondents. In the words of one senior Ministry of Defence official:

I certainly would not subscribe myself to the view that the selection procedure should give us any entitlement to say Mr X can go but Mr Y can't. If you are referring to the war photographer McCullen, who claims he was refused, well, yes he was, but . . . not because of who he was, or because he was a war photographer. We had room for two photographers and it was agreed that one . . . should be [from] the *Daily Express*. Now the *Daily Express* could have sent who the hell they liked to represent them, and ditto the Press Association.

The *Express* has about twenty photographers in its London office, four of whom who would tend to do the kind of work involved in this assignment. Tom Smith was selected, according to him, because: 'I was lucky, it was Sunday afternoon and I had to get to the MoD by six o'clock and down to Portsmouth by eight, and I live in St Katherine's Dock.'

Though the Ministry did not put names forward, some correspondents proposed themselves. As Ramsbotham described it:

People would ring us up saying, 'Please will you represent my case,' and so one did represent it to Ian McDonald, saying 'Look, we've been rung up by the Germans, by the Americans, and what are you going to do about it?' 'You must leave it to me,' he said. But we were not included in the decision process because at that time it did look terribly like a naval exercise.

Such calls came mainly from editors, but Max Hastings was one who acted as his own lobbyist: 'I fought very vigorously on the telephone with Bernard Ingham,' he told us. (It could in fact be said that Hastings qualified for a place more on the strength of his standing as a journalist than as a 'representative'. A contracted, rather than a staff writer, he was to send back reports for the *Express* (already represented by McGowan), for the *Spectator* (hardly a national paper), and for the London *Standard*, by whom he was officially despatched to the Falklands.

It is not surprising that Brigadier Ramsbotham was disappointed. Only three of the twenty-nine accompanying the Task Force were defence correspondents: Derek Hudson, of the *Yorkshire Post*; Ian

Bruce, of the *Glasgow Herald*; and, stretching a point, Alastair McQueen, of the *Mirror,* who had been a defence correspondent some years before. Hudson, though interested in defence, actually enjoyed the title of Chief Reporter at the *Post,* while Bruce doubled at the *Herald* as Industrial Correspondent. In the main, therefore, the journalists who went with the Task Force were neither military minded nor experienced in military matters. As David Norris of the *Daily Mail* informed us: 'My ignorance was such that I didn't even realize the Royal Marines were attached to the Royal Navy and not the Army'.

More surprising than the absence of defence correspondents was the status of many of the journalists. Few organizations sent their big guns. Brian Hanrahan, of BBC Television News, was, for instance, a most unlikely candidate: inexperienced, a remote choice for such an assignment, a reporter for only three or four years.

According to Robert Fox, of BBC Radio, the Corporation had toyed with the idea of sending a defence correspondent but thought better of it. Various people were considered – Martin Bell, for instance, the experienced Washington correspondent; John Humphries, who was on holiday in Wales; Brian Barron, who was in Northern Ireland and out of contact. Keith Graves could not be released since he was needed for diplomatic coverage, and Kate Adie, as a woman, was ruled out, largely, it appears, because Peter Woon, editor of BBC News, assumed that, as he put it: 'If we'd said our reporter was a woman, [the Navy] would have said no'.

As for Hanrahan:

I'd just got back from being on holiday and I rang the office and said I was back if they needed anybody. And they said OK, we need somebody . . . The night it all happened I sat and watched it on the news and thought they would need an extra pair of hands over the weekend. I wasn't angling, because I didn't know who was going at the time. It was a big story and I was saying 'I'm here and I would like a finger in it.' I think you always do when there's a big story going on, it's human nature.

Bernard Hesketh of the BBC, one of the most experienced and highly respected cameramen, told us that he was concerned because he knew that the inexperienced Hanrahan would be up against Mike Nicholson, the veteran ITN reporter. 'With hindsight', however, Hesketh admitted that Hanrahan was 'probably the right man for the job in every way'. Nicholson himself generously described Hanrahan as having done 'marvellously well':

It was his first biggie. I can remember him doing the Stanstead hi-jacking on the screen and wasn't too impressed, professionally. But the guy was incredible. Absolutely bloody incredible. That one phrase, it will be knocked onto my bloody tombstone, you know, 'I counted them all out and I counted them back.' It's the only phrase people remember out of the millions of words that were sent out.

Lack of experience was, therefore, not always a disadvantage. In fact, as Nicholson himself confessed: 'When I got down there I found myself floundering around as much as the new boys.' For even the experienced war correspondents had only covered land wars and knew very little about the Royal Navy. In some ways, as Cleaver put it afterwards, things were more difficult for the experienced man than for a novice like himself:

> Nicholson is . . . too experienced in a way. He knows what he'd done before, he knew what the Israelis let him do in '68 and all the rest of it and he tries to apply it to the British Navy. And they won't have it, it caused a bit of aggravation. But since it was my first war, as it were, I took it as it came. I asked for what I wanted to do and, if I wasn't allowed to do it, I didn't throw a tantrum. Whereas the more experienced blokes crawled up the wall and round the ceilings a few times. 'They let me do this in Vietnam; and if I wanted a helicopter in Vietnam' and all this sort of thing. I thought: Great, go to Vietnam.

In journalism there is in any case a long tradition of being thrown in at the deep end and learning on the job. It was, for example, young and relatively inexperienced American foreign correspondents who performed well in Vietnam. In the Falklands, men like Hanrahan were not only, in Hesketh's words, very much on their mettle, they were also obliged, like their more experienced colleagues, to grasp the essentials of each situation very quickly. As for the Ministry of Defence's contention that, had the journalists been less new, relations between press and officialdom would have been better, this seems disproved by the fact that for the most part the more experienced journalists were the ones who most vehemently complained. Some were not at all surprised by the selection. As Bob McGowan put it: 'There is one thing about this particular profession: nothing surprises you. The most unlikely people turn up.' Furthermore, according to Gareth Parry: 'You don't make value judgements on colleagues. I don't mean that pompously, you just don't, you know, you just go along on a story and do your bit.' McIlroy, however, admitted that he was slightly perplexed by the *type* of experience his companions seemed to have had: 'Quite a few sent just ordinary reporters based on ordinary Fleet Street experience . . . There were some who had never actually been overseas before.' (As a *Telegraph* 'fireman' McIlroy himself would spend eight or nine months of the year abroad.)

The situation all the journalists faced was different from anything they had previously come up against. Hesketh, a former combat soldier, wounded in the last war, said he thought it was closer to his experience in the Second World War. He continued:

> I think the worst part was the uncomfortableness of it. You know you haven't got a bath, you know you can't have a shave, you know the water is cold, if there is water at all. You know you are going to sleep on a hard floor or in a hole in the ground and you think, oh fuck, not another day like yesterday.

What must not be overlooked, therefore, is that performance in such situations is very closely tied to personality factors which allow the individual not to be ground down by the sheer force of depressing circumstances, and that such personality factors, required to report well from the Falklands, are not necessarily represented by virtue of an existing career position. They had to be discovered and tested in the difficult circumstances of the Falklands. As Max Hastings told us, describing the usual rivalry between 'news' and 'feature' people:

> There were a lot of tough young news desk reporters, and [some] in fact not so young, who felt all this sort of traditional antipathy, bullshitting all the way down: 'All you middle class ponces will get sorted out when the rough part starts.' One of them didn't walk a yard from the day he arrived at San Carlos onwards. The broadcasters had a good war. They were a competent bunch. I admit I have never been in a situation where the newspaper coverage has been so one-sided and I honestly believe that to be a reflection of the competence of the other people who were sent. If you had the usual people who cover these things, Robert Fisk, John Edwards, John Pilger, all the rest of it . . . the whole level would have been far higher.

Hastings' colleagues and rivals were afterwards obliged to admit, not always grudgingly, that his coverage was outstanding and that he made a personal success of the war. As for Pilger, whose style is one of radical criticism of the received or 'establishment' line, he might have found the Falklands unstimulating, for here, unlike, say, Vietnam, there was no 'other war' to report. John Shirley was another who specifically mentioned the absence of reporters of Pilger's stature. Shirley himself was very much the *Sunday Times'* second choice, for Simon Winchester, a more likely candidate to sail with the Task Force, was already in the South Atlantic (and was shortly to be gaoled by the Argentinians). In recent years the *Sunday Times* foreign staff has been much depleted; the choice of Shirley, however, owed as much to the paper's view of the importance of the issue as to shortage of staff. In Shirley's own words:

> It actually tells you how big they anticipated the thing would be. I think the *Sunday Times* regards me as a good solid reporter, but I'm not one of their jewel wordsmiths . . . and that's the level on which they sent them in. Indeed, that's what the papers mostly sent, you have to offset the fact that they might just as well have sailed round the ocean for six weeks with nothing to do . . .

And the absence of the war photographer, Donald McCullen? According to Shirley: 'I don't think any paper seriously thought the thing would come to a conflict, so nobody sent their best men.'

And Hastings?

> It was not so much the Standard sending him as Hastings sending himself. He is much more of a freelance journalist . . . and was therefore in a much looser position to decide his own interests . . . For Hastings, a writer of military books, to go with the Task Force was important, even if there was only a one in six chance of something happening.

Charles Lawrence, of the *Sunday Telegraph*, explained his own presence in these words:

> I should think the editor decided on me because I am more expendable . . . The editor is more prepared to have a news hack spend five or six weeks floating around the Atlantic than one of his favourite feature writers.

Anyhow, Lawrence added:

> Editors think we're better equipped to survive a job like that than feature writers. We've got more experience of being patient and living in different circumstances . . . If you look at . . . the CVs of the feature writers, they are sort of gentlemen scholars, but they are not necessarily hard-trained reporters, which I am, more or less.

Moreover, as Mick Seamark asked us, 'Would you want your best people locked on board a ship?'

The assembly of journalists to sail with the Task Force was, to quote Lawrence, who was used to travelling abroad alone on self-initiated assignments, 'the return of the big-pack job', but before they sailed members of the pack were mostly unacquainted. Each journalist knew at most three or four of the others; by the end of the conflict they were to know each other extremely well. From this experience there grew in some cases close friendships, in others active dislike and even, in one or two cases, hatred. 'I'd expected', said Gareth Parry, 'a good bunch of fun . . . In fact I found a lot of sort of scholarly feature writers which rather surprised me.' Why did they think they were there?

Would there be a war?

Hardly a journalist seriously thought war was likely. Robert Fox believed the whole affair would come to nothing, that it was no more than an exercise in gunboat diplomacy. As he told us:

I had a Churchill fellowship to go and look at community radio and TV in the remoter parts of Canada and the wilder parts of southern Italy, and I thought that sounded much more like fun . . . You see, the Director-General of the Churchill Trust is a former General Commandant of Berlin, and he assured me that the bloody ships would go down to Ascension and go round and round, which they did, and the whole thing would be settled, as it so nearly could have been. It seemed to me a tedious waste of time.

In some Fleet Street offices the venture was seen as no more than a joy-ride, and, as John Shirley recalled it: 'The general attitude was one of hilarity. Everybody thought it was ridiculous . . . I don't think anybody wanted to go on the *Canberra* except me.'

John Witherow had mixed feelings: 'It seemed such an exaggerated response'. Nevertheless, he saw its professional potential:

I remember thinking at the time: This could mean going into a war . . . It was only after a couple of days at sea, I think, that we began to realize it, as the issue of sovereignty became paramount.

As the Task Force sailed, even Jeremy Hands of ITN, who three months earlier had seen the Falklands as a developing tension spot, did not see it as a possible war story. At that stage, he believed: 'It was going to be two weeks out in the Atlantic, and it would all be settled at the United Nations and we'd all come sailing home again – but even that was going to be fun'. To Kim Sabido, the excursion seemed even more unreal. A reporter with IRN, he had been given a screen test for ITN just before the Falklands crisis broke and, on the day he departed on *Canberra*, he heard he had been successful.

It was a bit confusing, you know, going out for IRN and being offered a job by ITN and having to resign a few days into the thing on board *Canberra*. I made my resignation in the middle of a taped report. I said it in a cassette and sent it back for the attention of the editor and said I'd been offered a job by ITN.

Photographers and radio and television correspondents, who needed technical equipment, had to prepare on the assumption that there would be a war, however much they disbelieved it. Bernard Hesketh left Portsmouth aboard the carrier *Hermes* 'properly provided to go to war' with more videotapes and film than usual and 'more batteries, because we knew that if it came to a shooting war on the Falklands one of the problems would be power supply'.

Martin Cleaver, the Press Association photographer, hurriedly 'broke into the film cupboard, smashed the lock off the door to get my hands on some film . . .'.

Some journalists harboured a suspicion that there might be war. McIlroy, for example, thought when he looked at the size of the battle-fleet that it would have to be used for something: 'We would have had to have gone and zapped the Channel Islands, or sunk Southern Ireland or done something; there was just no way we could have gone back.'

Tony Snow, too, had a premonition:

> I'm one of these sorts of people unfortunately that, you know the sort, when I get involved everything sort of happens . . . At the back of my mind I thought it wouldn't surprise me at all if we got all the way down there and then started shooting.

As the Task Force moved south, the air of unreality about the venture gave way to a sense of foreboding. According to John Shirley:

> After we left Ascension Island . . . it gradually became clear that we were landing. You got this sense that it was actually quite extraordinary and quite unique to be going to war with the British Army. You get those kind of moments just occasionally when you are an observer on the notes of history; it sounds very pompous, but you know what I mean. It's one of the privileges of the job in a way . . . Max Hastings was very aware of it historically, too. When we were going to these intelligence briefings before the landing and all the preparations for the landing he kept on saying to the MoD official: 'Look, don't you realize this is a very historic moment? This doesn't happen very often. These guys are really going in; it's not West Germany, it's not an exercise, it's not Norway, they're actually going to war and you should be taking pictures of this and should be recording it. You should be taking note of it.' And I don't think they appreciated it. Max had a kind of sense of history about the thing. I know the thing's a tinpot little war really, but in terms of the British Army it was quite a remarkable event.

There was increasing pressure on the journalists to do well. As Jeremy Hands put it: 'Everybody knew that if they fucked this one up they might as well give up journalism'.

'Where do I sign on and for how long?': preparation and accreditation

The journalists were not the only participants to need time to adjust to the likelihood of war. Brigadier Ramsbotham himself admitted that when the Task Force sailed: 'It did look seriously like a naval excercise that might well turn round without getting even as far as Ascension'. That, and the haste of preparation, accounted for much of the muddle in which arrangements were made. A senior civilian official who confessed that the Ministry had been caught off guard, emphasized that: 'Even among the military I think there was a feeling . . . as they went down [there], that it would be called off because diplomacy would take over'. He continued:

> One can say that was pretty stupid, but nevertheless that was a fact of life that

during the early stage ... there was no guarantee ever that we were actually sailing to war. We were sailing to prepare for war. A lot of people – it was a necessary posture – thought the whole thing would be called off, pulled back, solved on the way.

Once the Task Force had sailed, the Ministry of Defence official told us, there was little chance that anyone could be added to, or subtracted from, the party.

While, according to Brigadier Ramsbotham, the Navy was 'quite keen that there should be a facility to fly people out to Ascension Island and put them on board', such arrangements were never forthcoming. As the Ministry official explained:

Rushing it together, we hadn't thought it through. We were told that the reason people could not be flown to Ascension was because there was no space on the aircraft and also ... the airport is leased to the Americans ... Nobody really wanted to let the world know what help the Americans were giving us and of course, if you put journalists aboard, you can't keep that quiet.

At that time the Americans were still acting as brokers between Britain and Argentina, so the situation was obviously sensitive. The journalists were frustrated at being forbidden to stretch their legs and have a swim; more important, they were profoundly annoyed by this evidence of lack of trust. As Ian Bruce emphasized:

The troops all [went] ashore; the press [was] not allowed ... They said the Americans would object, which turned out to be bollocks. So we went up to the monkey deck to sunbathe – everyone was desperate to get on land after six weeks. We came back down with a pair of binoculars and said: 'Is it for the reason there are nine Victor tankers and two Vulcans sitting on Wideawake airfield?' They hummed and said: 'Well, basically, yes,' and we said: 'Well, we've seen them. You vet the copy, there's no way we can report that, there's no way that we would. All we want to do, a very human reaction, is put our feet on dry land.' They said: 'No, sorry. You can't go ashore'.

Although they were allowed ashore later for an afternoon, it was the first example of what was to be the underlying philosophy: if in doubt, *ban*. Military priorities were seen as vastly outweighing journalistic needs. The stakes were, admittedly, high. Security was, however, only one reason why, with a single exception, no journalist could be flown out to join the expedition at Ascension. The chief obstacle was the lack of available transport. The sole journalist to be carried was Derek Hudson who was flown from Brize Norton in an RAF VC10 to Wideawake airport, to replace the provincial press's representative from the *Wolverhampton Star*. When asked about this, he told us:

I was accompanied by an MoD press officer. I don't know whether he was just there to guard me on the way or not ... I was the only one, I think, who actually saw the airport, and I had to swear a special oath that I wouldn't discuss at all what I'd seen. In fact they were refuelling the Vulcans.

Hastings considered that this was Fleet Street's 'big miscalculation'. As he said:

In every situation of this kind ever in history that I can remember, there's always been a second chance . . . You send somebody to sort of put your marker down, and you can usually reinforce . . . when the going gets rough. And of course they all knew that the fleet was going to stop at Ascension, and . . . I don't think that they were geared to the idea that this was the one chance to get a correspondent in.

Indeed, Hastings believed that the editors did not initially appreciate the importance of the story.

An awful lot of copy that was sent in the first week or two from the Task Force, including a lot of mine, was spiked because again, instinctively, most of the papers for whom we were writing all thought that this was a bit of theatre, . . . a circus.

Caught as much by events as were the Fleet Street editors, the Ministry of Defence faced many of the same problems. It, too, had no time to consider whom to send. It also faced the problem of authority. Whereas even a young, relatively inexperienced journalist can challenge the statements of senior military personnel because he represents *The Times*, the BBC, or the *Sun*, a service public relations officer stands within the same organization as the military and to challenge a statement is to challenge the authority not of the statement, but of the person making it. Thus one very senior Ministry official involved with organizing the public relations team said:

First of all there was no question of sending any of the service PROs because their rank alone would have meant that you'd chosen a Navy man, a captain. And if we'd sent the Army man you'd have had a brigadier landing on the Falklands with a brigadier in charge of the operation. So we decided to go for [civilian] PR staff.

Civilian 'minders', it was thought, would work more effectively with the military. This decision, however, produced another difficulty. Civilians, especially civilians of lowly bureaucratic status, not only lacked the respect of the military but were eyed askance, as non-uniformed 'foreign bodies'. The 'minders' sent by the Ministry of Defence were too junior to do their job effectively and the military, keenly aware of rank and insignia, or the lack of them, knew it. It was an unenviable situation. Unloved by the journalists, helots to the military, the civilian PR staff were under intolerable strain. Like the journalists, they too would be judged by their performance.

According to a senior Ministry of Defence official, the selection of the minders was made in close consultation with the naval director of PR, C in C Fleet at Northwood, because they were his team. Once they had sailed they were part of the Task Force, under its commander.

As for briefing and accreditation, the Ministry was equally unprepared. Brigadier Ramsbotham explained why:

> We were always accused of having three reasons for everything. I think there are three reasons for this. I think the first reason is that it was essentially a naval operation and since the war the Navy has not had the same experience as the other armed forces of working with journalists. I think the second reason, and this is in a way the Army experience, has been Northern Ireland, where they don't go through this process because Northern Ireland is part of the UK, or watching exercises in Germany, where . . . what you are talking about is a NATO environment, so that any correspondent coming to watch the British forces must have the same rights with the German, the French, the Dutch and the Belgian, the Americans, or whoever happens to be around. I think the third thing was that, for one reason and another, the Ministry of Defence had not done contingency planning for PR for a very, very long time – certainly not since 1977.

Ramsbotham and some of his colleagues had hoped to fly the correspondents out to Ascension before they joined the ships. This would have given an opportunity for more thorough briefing; as Ramsbotham emphasized:

> Accreditation is not just an editor saying 'I want somebody to go' and we say 'OK, here's your pass'; the briefing that goes with it explains the parameters of what he may report and what he may not, whether he is or is not subject to military law, whether or not he is subject to the Geneva Convention, the conditions of his employment, if you like, the bills he is going to be asked to pay, what his communications are likely to be.

We told Ramsbotham that our conversations with the journalists indicated that there was some confusion as to whether or not they had signed the Official Secrets Act. Some knew they had done so, some, since they had signed nothing, knew that they definitely had not, while others knew they had signed something but not exactly what. Ramsbotham explained:

> The whole procedure consists basically of the editor saying 'We want to send somebody'. He is then brought round and briefed and given various documents, which include documents for him to take back for his editor to sign to say that he accepts editorial responsibility . . . It does include the Official Secrets Act and his rights are absolutely there. A copy is held by his paper and a copy is held here.

Ramsbotham, who is much respected amongst defence journalists for his helpfulness, quickly added, however, that these procedures were not followed on this occasion. It was, he said, 'totally haphazard . . . there wasn't time to do it'. Nor was there time for the journalists. Bernard Hesketh described the process:

> So the documents came. Now the editor, Peter Woon, and the foreign editor sat and read them and I said, 'Look, for Christ's sake, will somebody read them, because I haven't got time to do it.' So they read the documents and to this day I don't know what I signed. It's stupid, but there was no alternative.

Ramsbotham made two further important points:

> First, hindsight shows that a properly briefed and assembled press corps is much more effective than one rather hastily gathered together and just chucked away without proper preparation; second, that one of the lessons one learns from all these modern conflicts, not just this one, but the Arab–Israeli or whatever, is that if you haven't got your act together on the day it's too late.

Not only was the act not got together; plainly the Ministry had a great deal of difficulty simply getting the show on the road.

'Stand up when I call your name. You've won a cruise'

Not only did journalists depart without proper Ministry briefing, they also left without time to brief themselves fully.

Although practice varies, most journalists would not expect to be formally briefed by their organization: it is assumed that they know what is expected of them. At BBC Television, for example, according to Brian Hanrahan:

> There wasn't any briefing, . . . I heard nothing for about two days and one was simply told that it was Portsmouth and seawards. I had the Ministry of Defence papers thrust at me as I was setting off with the crew and there was a phone call from Peter Woon to say good luck, and that was it.

Robert Fox told us much the same of BBC Radio:

> I thought by the way I was despatched I would just play it by ear as I have done in so many big disasters . . . Nobody really tells you specifically: 'We want you to do this, that or the other'.

Kim Sabido of IRN said, 'I think they more or less assumed that you knew how to handle the story in certain respects', and Jeremy Hands of ITN said he was told to 'just go down and cover it. Whatever happens, cover it'. Instructions were slightly more complex for those newspapers whose various desks requested material. For example, according to the *Observer*'s correspondent, Patrick Bishop, they saw it as 'a joint operation' between the home and foreign editors. Although 'abroad', 'it was very much a home story – it was the Falklands and British troops, and all the rest of it'. Since Bishop sailed in *Canberra*, which did not leave until the Friday, he considered that he had 'quite a lot of time really' in which to prepare. But he had only 'the flimsiest of instructions':

What they said was, 'We want a piece for this weekend'. The *New York Times* did a deal with us [to] take my stuff if it came to anything, so they said, for the duration of the voyage, do a piece for the *New York Times*, one piece a week for us and also something for the syndication service; just whatever you feel like, kind of thing. And they said there might be periods where there might not be anything happening, so don't bother to file anything. They were really rather subdued.

John Shirley of the *Sunday Times* had to deal with a more complicated set of expectations:

It was the measure of the confusion, I think, that before I went I was given four sets of briefings. The news desk asked me to file certainly a story for that first week and then news stories on a weekly basis. The foreign desk asked me to file a serious think-piece – a speculative military sort of thing. The features department asked me for colour pieces of my own choosing. And 'Insight' asked me for a day-to-day calendar.

As he explained:

It's quite impossible to fill all those requests. Some of them were for specific types of copy – not specific interviews or directed material because you don't get that at the *Sunday Times*. You are very much left to determine the shape of the piece yourself. The strongest direction you get is in terms of probable wordage . . . but obviously during the week that changes . . . By and large it's fairly flexible.

For Derek Hudson of the *Yorkshire Post* and Ian Bruce of the *Glasgow Herald*, life was even more complicated. Hudson had to file for all the English and Welsh provincial papers, sending copy to his own paper and then responding when he could to specific requests from other papers, generally those in the South-West of England and Cardiff area asking for material on Welsh soldiers. (One journalist told us how skilfully Hudson had inserted the word 'Yorkshire' in practically all his copy, to supply 'local interest'.)

Bruce represented the outraged voice of Scotland, for the Ministry of Defence had told the *Glasgow Herald* that 'the PA will cover for all you regional people'. There followed, in Bruce's words, 'a small dispute'. Three Scottish MPs from different parties were recruited to raise the matter in the House, and this, with lobbying from the editors, led to Bruce's selection as representing all the Scottish papers. His instructions were to file a daily story for the evening papers and another for the dailies, plus a weekly story for the Sundays 'and some features, if you can'. His own editor at the Herald assumed that he would be gone for three or four weeks, would sail around Ascension and return. He told Bruce to 'get a good sun tan' and he departed, after 'grabbing as many cuttings as possible from the library, photocopying them and sticking them in a bag'. His editor next heard from him three and a half months later, in a telephone call from Port Stanley.

David Norris set off:

> Completely clueless ... until the invasion I didn't know the capital was Port Stanley. I knew the basic details: that it was mainly sheep farming and that the Argentinians had this sort of claim to them, but that's about all really.

He added wistfully: 'Usually in other countries there's an embassy you can go to and get the background.'

John Shirley had a little briefing from the *Sunday Times* defence correspondent:

> ... but the only thing he said was: 'I think that the personalities of the commanders are very important, and I think you should try to find out as much as you can about that, and I think we could do with a lot of colour on the individuals, on people like Woodward and Jeremy Moore and various people like that.'

Rear Admiral Sandy Woodward went with the *Hermes*, the Task Force flagship, which, though older than *Invincible*, had better communications facilities for Woodward and his support staff. At the last minute, some of the journalists – Peter Archer of the Press Association, Michael Nicholson from ITN and Brian Hanrahan from the BBC, found themselves switched to *Hermes* from *Invincible*. At the time the explanation given by the Ministry of Defence was that the move was to protect the privacy of Prince Andrew, who was travelling as a helicopter pilot on *Invincible*. This story was pretty thin, since the correspondents of the two most avid 'Royal watching' papers, the *Daily Star* and the *Sun*, were, to their glee, assigned to *Invincible*. Other reasons were given for the move to *Hermes*. First, according to Nicholson, that Woodward 'loves cameras', and, according to Archer, that the Rear Admiral appreciated the value of 'the widest possible coverage, for propaganda purposes'. The second reason, according to a well-placed informant in the Ministry of Defence, was more crudely political. It was intended that *Invincible* should be sold to the Australians after hostilities had ceased, a sale which was being resisted by the Navy high command. The Minister of Defence, John Nott, did not want *Invincible* to be covered in televized glory, which might rally the public to the Navy's cause, and it was on his express orders that the PA and television correspondents were therefore moved to *Hermes*.

Despite the complications of the move, Archer did manage to have 'a brief session with the editor-in-chief ... and with the PA's defence correspondent', and there was 'enough time to rush around getting a few cuttings together, background on the Falklands [and photocopies of] a few bits and pieces from *Jane's Fighting Ships* to see what the Argies had'. The editor-in-chief gave a last, optimistic piece of advice: 'If you think censorship is unreasonable, say so'.

Accompanying the forms, about which many of the correspondents were so vague, was a green booklet, a kind of journalistic guide to operations. Patrick Bishop, who clearly read it carefully, considered it 'a very full description of how the MoD see the journalist's job, and how they see the Army's job'. 'In fact', he went so far as to say, 'it's very specific. It doesn't leave you any illusions about what you will be allowed to say and what you won't.' However, Bishop could not remember having signed anything to the effect that he had seen the booklet and agreed to abide by rules and regulations. Those who had, found the booklet amusing. It was subtitled in Arabic and had originally been prepared for the Suez venture.

Some did not receive a copy. 'I don't think Charlie Lawrence ever got one', said John Shirley, 'They ran out of copies'. Others, too, failed to see the booklet. According to Bishop, 'When I showed them to the MoD guys on the *Canberra* they'd never seen them before. They simply didn't know the stuff existed.' It seems surprising, but Shirley simply took it as evidence of their lack of preparation. 'I suppose', he acknowledged, 'you could posit a conspiracy theory about it, but in my mind it's more of a cock-up than a conspiracy.'

If there is any truly single event to act as a mark by which to understand the Ministry of Defence's inability to plan sophisticated news control, then it must be the despatch of Tony Snow of the *Sun* and Mick Seamark of the *Daily Star* to the carrier *Invincible* to become 'shipmates' of Prince Andrew. Such selection is not planning but muddled performance. Because his paper occupies a special place in the market, Gareth Parry of the *Guardian* was the least concerned amongst the journalists about the antics of his competitors, but even he was more than a little surprised on first going aboard *Invincible* to discover who his fellow-journalists and travelling companions were. 'I was puzzled because, if you remember, a couple of weeks previously there had been an enormous row between Buckingham Palace and the *Star* and the *Sun* over the publication of [a picture of] Princess Diana in a bikini.'

If Parry's reaction was one of puzzled surprise, Seamark's was one of uncontrollable delight at being allocated to the same ship as the sub-lieutenant HRH Prince Andrew. 'When I got to Portsmouth and discovered I was going to be sailing with Prince Andrew, I phoned the office in the morning and it was like manna. Whoever dreamt of me and Tony Snow of the *Sun* to get on *Invincible* with Andrew – an MoD decision?'

Thus if the journalists did not know or, indeed, found it difficult on embarkation to believe that they were actually going to do battle with the Argentinians, they were certain of one thing right from the beginning: that the Ministry of Defence, in terms of its information planning, was in disarray. Such thoughts were hardly cheering, but on meeting the minders foreboding turned to certainty that impediments and trouble lay ahead. Asked when this realization dawned, Gareth Parry replied in no uncertain terms, 'Immediately. When our eyes met.'

2

Welcome aboard

Hastily assembled, badly briefed, poorly prepared and in some cases bizarrely equipped, the journalists set sail to cover a war that hardly any of them thought would happen. Ian Bruce observed:

> I think after we left Ascension attitudes began to harden, to realize this could potentially be a shooting war and when the *Sheffield* was hit that was the night of the deepest depression I remember. The word had come through in the middle of a party in the wardroom on the *Canberra*, and that changed the atmosphere of the entire trip.

Sheffield had been hit on Tuesday, 4 May with the loss of twenty lives. The missile attack introduced a new word into the public conversation: Exocet. Three days earlier the Port Stanley airfield had been bombed by a force of Harrier fighters and a Vulcan bomber. Three Argentinian aircraft had been shot down. The next day, 2 May, the Argentine cruiser *General Belgrano*, had been sunk by torpedoes fired from the nuclear submarine *Conqueror* with the loss of over 300 lives. The party was certainly over.

The journalists on board *Canberra* were lucky that they remained there since their complaints had infuriated the Navy. According to Ian Bruce: 'The Navy tried to send all of us back at Ascension. They said, if the press were so browned off with the way things were going, then facilities would be made to put them all ashore to go home. That was a genuine threat, but Number 10 settled that one.' Certainly, the Captain of *Canberra*, Chris Burne, was not overjoyed at having to accommodate so many journalists. He originally refused to take more than four, and even that was too many for his liking. In Sabido's opinion the Navy did not even welcome the presence of Paratroopers aboard, 'but they had to have them, though they didn't think they had to have us'. Captain Black, on *Invincible*, also found it uncomfortable to have journalists on his ship and, to quote Seamark, 'He offered in the nicest possible way to throw us off at Ascension.' It was a question, Seamark thought, of saying 'Get off or toe the line'. In this case the journalists had embarrassed Captain Black, who was not only liked by the correspondents but also adored by his crew. He had obtained for his men the overseas allowance to which, strictly speaking, they were not entitled. Press stories had brought this to the attention of the

Ministry of Defence and Captain Black's knuckles were rapped. Seamark added: 'I think he was a bit peeved and realized that we could be quite dangerous to him'. There was another problem. According to Witherow:

> Captain Black is quite a decent guy – very quotable . . . He gave us a lot of stuff and put it on the record. Then he realized that he was in danger of being the only senior officer being quoted and started going off the record and after a while stopped being 'the senior officer' and became just 'an officer', and his comments became increasingly noncommittal and uninformative. We used to get daily briefings from him, but really they told us very little. At least he was seeing us, which is better than Middleton. [Captain of *Hermes*]

Snow described *Invincible* as having a 'very good atmosphere' and, according to Archer, it had 'a much more relaxed regime. The Captain used to give daily press conferences on the bridge. He would sit and drink coffee out of a mug saying 'Boss' on it. He was much more tuned into PR'.

Obviously a great many briefings must be 'off the record' in such a situation, especially with regard to operational discussions, but the requirement that quotations should not be attributed, nor ships, units or individuals named, made life difficult for the journalists, particularly for the agency men from Reuters and the Press Association. Peter Archer said that the ban on giving the names and addresses of troops interviewed was 'death to an agency like the PA'. While the Press Association does not especially seek stories with 'local interest', it nevertheless follows general reporting practice of taking 'all the details: the town they come from, the street-name' in order to 'bring out all the local colour you can get'. The provincial papers, which in part own the Press Association, can then, if they wish, follow up a story – which was, of course, exactly what the military did not want, lest, as Archer put it, 'the news desk decided to buzz up and get an interview with the wife or parent'. Moreover, the inability to name units, unit commanders, or individuals undermined one strong principle by which agencies in particular protect their reputation for accuracy: 'sourcing' material. Understandably, neither Reuters nor the Press Association was happy to depart from this principle.

Security was not the only – nor even the chief – reason for the reporters being obliged to take briefing off the record, or more accurately, on a non-attributable basis. As Jeremy Hands explained it:

> One of the major problems we had was that stuff was being cut out, not on security grounds, but because it would reflect badly. We could all understand why we should not say 'Tomorrow HMS *Hermes* will arrive in the Falklands Sound',

because that would give the Argies twenty-four hours to prepare a welcome. But they were banning interviews with people and saying 'He's been interviewed before and he's becoming a bit of a showbiz personality'.

There was a good deal of competition between ships and between units, particularly between the Marines and the Paratroopers, for press coverage. They wanted publicity for their ventures, not least because public attention now might undermine proposed defence economies later. Some officers realized this and turned the correspondents' presence to advantage. Martin Cleaver told us about the attitude on *Invincible*:

> They'd got a slightly more PR-conscious captain, [who] realized the value of the press on board. He could, in the nicest possible way, manipulate them, get stories out about . . . how *Invincible* was floating about doing wonderful things, and that keeps everyone happy back home. Whereas, initially, the hierarchy on *Hermes* were not so keen; they saw us as more of a threat. Later on they realized the value of stories about people doing things on *Hermes* – if for nothing more than morale back home.

Cleaver's description of Captain Black as 'slightly more PR-conscious' – particularly in comparison with Captain Middleton of the flagship *Hermes* – is corroborated by Michael Nicholson. 'There were', according to Nicholson, 'bad scenes on the *Hermes* . . . and they came from the Captain'. Captain Middleton, he thought,

> hated the press . . . And we got on like a duck and a fox. I just couldn't bear to look at the man in the end . . . We had a lot of problems; we had arguments with the senior men. I remember on one occasion the senior naval officer said, 'You guys are as good as Argentinian intelligence officers'. And Bernard [Hesketh] ripped his trousers back to show the scars on his leg and said: 'I got these scars at Arnhem.' He was an artillery captain in the Second World War, and he said: 'Don't call me an Argentinian spy.' He was furious, shaking with anger.

Peter Archer corroborated Nicholson's account of the unhappy trip south on *Hermes*: 'We also had access to the bridge; overheard a few things we shouldn't have done. We knew exactly how they felt about us. We were at best a nuisance, at worst Argentinian spies.'

Just before Ascension, Rear Admiral Woodward came aboard *Hermes,* the flagship. From that point the journalists by-passed Middleton, channelling copy through Woodward's office not only because 'he had his own communications set-up' but also because, as Archer pointed out, 'we found out pretty quickly that he was more interested in the PR side, the propaganda side or, as it turned out, the misinformation side'.

It is true that the relationship between Middleton and Nicholson was one of special, and open, hostility. The two men seemed to voice the underlying tension that the journalists felt existed between themselves and the Navy (less so, they believed, on the part of the officers commanding smaller ships). Max Hastings spoke of this:

> The hardest thing in a way of the whole expedition was to suddenly go and spend three months in which you're treated, even by the humblest sub-lieutenant or whatever, as a pain in the neck to have around.

Gareth Parry described the Navy's attitude as 'a sense of awe that these men from Mars had suddenly arrived in their own private world'. Once on board, however, the closed world was open. As Parry put it: 'You can't have banned, cordon sanitaire places. You're waiting about, seeing things touching things. It's impossible to keep secrets on a ship.'

Comparisons have been made between the attitude to the press taken by the Navy, on this occasion, and by the Army, in Northern Ireland. Such a parallel is mistaken. When we asked a senior Ministry of Defence official about this, he said:

> It's misleading to say that the Army was much better at all of this because of its Northern Ireland experience. It's unfair on the Navy because the attitude of the Navy to the press was coloured by the fact that the Navy had in its ships correspondents living for six weeks and in many cases longer, with them day and night, hearing everything that went on on board that ship. For instance, the commanding officer addresses the ship's company and says, 'Right lads, tonight we are going in within half a mile of the coastline . . .' If you've got journalists on board . . . he can't very easily switch the intercom off in the one part of the ship where two of them are, so they are trusted to be part of the ship's company . . . Now, the Army does not have that problem in Northern Ireland. The press do not live in the barracks, they do not live with the troops. When they go out to Northern Ireland they are given briefings . . . they are only given what the Army wants to tell them.

Captain Middleton's attempt to cut off information rebounded on him. 'Even the ship's company', Archer told us, 'complained at one stage that there were not even the usual situation reports being tannoyed to them . . . because we were on board'.

For the duration of the expedition the journalists had been given the rank of captain, as their Army equivalent, and lieutenant, as their Navy equivalent. This enabled them to eat in the officers' mess. There, though Parry might claim that attitudes 'were very pointed', there was no open hostility; 'we were tolerated'. The men, however, were more friendly:

> We were a bit of a novelty. We were invited just about everywhere. The voyage south was a bit of a jolly affair as far as Ascension Island. The chief petty officers had had us in their mess to get the press boys drunk and humiliate us, and remind us who runs the ship. Then the petty officers had us in, then the junior ratings had us round. They all wanted to get you drunk, basically. They all wanted to share

their can of beer with you. And also they seemed to think we'd bring cans of beer with us, too, that we had access to beer – which we did, I suppose.

It emerged later that the officers had briefed the lower ranks, warning them that they should be careful about what, and how much, they said.

Once ashore in the Falklands the general view among the journalists was that the Army was more expert at public relations. One whom they praised most highly was David Nichols, Public Relations Officer of 3 Commando Brigade. Hastings, an especially strident critic of both the Navy and the civilian minders, said: 'He actually did a super job, and I think Bob Fox thinks so, too.'

John Shirley made an interesting observation about the differences in the Marine's and Navy's approach to public relations:

[The Marines] have a different sort of perception of the world . . . at Ascension Island we had a briefing from Commodore Michael Clapp, the Navy's head of amphibious warfare . . . Woodward's job was to get us down there, Clapp's job was to get us onto the Islands and . . . Thompson was in charge of the land campaign. But Clapp is a sailor and Julian Thompson is a Marine, and Clapp could quite easily direct battles from over the horizon and say that he didn't need to see the other ships involved in the campaign. He could speak to them on the radio, he could tell them what to do when they were a hundred miles away. He didn't need to generate any sense of personal loyalty among his sailors. He did to some extent, but he didn't have to . . . There's nowhere you can go if you are on a ship. You can't run away. And this sense of personal loyalty and personal dealing, I think, is rather alien to the Navy; they don't think like that. Whereas Julian Thompson was very concerned about the morale of his troops – his personal relationship with the troops. Every time he came on *Canberra* he went straight down to the sergeants' mess, he ate with the men, he went running with them all the time and he would talk to them. He was very, very aware of establishing personal loyalty . . . He said to me when we were on the Islands: 'Look, I've got to command these people, because if they don't like it they can always run away.'

With regard to Northern Ireland, Shirley said:

My only experience of the British Army previously has been in Northern Ireland, and I've never been very impressed by them. The press officers are appalling, they oil around the Europa Hotel – they *are* oily. And most of the blokes I haven't much time for. They never seemed to me to be very bright; they seemed to be thoughtless and clearly contemptuous of the IRA, and they don't consider any political dimension of the Provos at all – whether you agree with the Provos or not is irrelevant – but there is actually a fairly serious political situation in Ireland as well as the military one. Of course, they are very closely related, but these guys never seem to see it at all. I think in their favour it must be said that they clearly loathe going to Northern Ireland. I can see for a professional soldier it must be an appalling place to be, because the rules of the game are so different – I mean, it's not like what you are taught war is like. You don't know who the enemy is, and everybody wears civilian clothes, and the civilian population insults you in English – they're not wogs you can go and beat up. They make a fuss. I was expecting, frankly, the officers to be effete and stupid, too. By and large they weren't. A lot of them were very bright and I was impressed by them.

Shirley raises some important points, but the real question is why his view of the military, based on his experiences in Northern Ireland, changed during the campaign. They were not a different breed; indeed, some had served in Northern Ireland. He repeated the point he made about the military's lack of political appreciation. For example, when we asked whether there was any debate about British policy, he replied: 'Not with the military. It was the one subject you simply couldn't talk to them about.' This is, however, hardly surprising. The military profession emphasizes the importance of loyalty and obedience, the subordination of individual opinion to a collective purpose.

Military life is a rather peculiar occupation in that it is both premised, and structured around, violence. It may be that at officer level it is disguised as a ritual insistence on courtesy and respect for authority. These qualities, however, are no more than the veneer for a particular setting: change this and it is quite clear that such qualities lie loosely over others, such as toughness, aggressiveness and determination of purpose. What Shirley witnessed therefore, was the same type of officer albeit operating in a different setting. He was also able to study the military much more closely than was ever possible in Northern Ireland.

Close living and working with the troops forced some journalists to reconsider their opinions of the military. Hastings admitted that one reason for his successful coverage of the venture was that he 'spoke the same language'. 'I like soldiers', he told us. 'I get on well with them, and I spend a lot of my working life with them.' He compared this with the attitude of Pat Bishop who, Hastings said, 'conceded from day one that he doesn't like soldiers and he doesn't like the Services'. They were therefore unlikely 'to pull a finger out for him . . .'. Most of the journalists came to admire the military; some even made friends. Gareth Parry said:

> I felt a terrific kind of admiration for them. I could put aside the fact that it was ridiculous that we should be doing this. I was terrifically impressed by these guys, and the spirit of friendship as well. It sounds bloody corny now, but I tell you, you could leave a quid on your bunk and it would still be there two days later.

The sheer intensity of living and working so closely together forced the journalists to re-evaluate opinions which had been formed in the very different conditions of Northern Ireland. Nonetheless, there was friction. Archer was understandably annoyed when Captain Middleton took a hard line on how much copy might be transmitted. He complained: 'I was getting a fraction of the words which the people on the *Invincible* were allowed to send. I mean, they were sending literally l000–2000 words a day.' Middleton's reason for such tight restrictions was that 'his signal office was too busy'; certainly *Hermes*, as the flagship, began battle preparations earlier and produced more traffic than the other carriers. Transmission of copy was not therefore given the desired priority, an attitude which made matters very difficult for the minder who acted as inter-mediary, Robin Barrett. He was obliged to say to Archer: 'Look, it's no good you flooding me with copy, because I can't get it off the ship'. In fact, the pressure was so wearing that at Ascension Barrett left the ship and returned to London. With hindsight, Archer sym-pathized: 'I think physically he found it a bit hard . . . Don't forget all the way down we were literally from dawn to dusk at action stations, rushing around on exercises. He had a very difficult task. The minders really were up against it as much as we were.'

Of all the journalists aboard *Hermes* (the others were Nicholson, Hanrahan and Cleaver of the Press Association), Archer had the most contact with the unfortunate Barrett:

> Brian and Martin would be filing their film [but] I had to try and get stuff off daily . . . Barrett kept clearing me out of the signal room saying: 'You will not go in there; that's out of bounds for you. No, you can't go and bang on the Admiral's door. No, you can't go and see the Captain.'

He came to be seen by Archer and the others as a barrier. Caught between wrathful journalists and displeased officers, Barrett began to feel the strain. Unlike the journalists, he had no colleagues to turn to for support. Later, Archer appreciated how uncomfortable his life must have been:

> Of course you tried to keep your professional cool, and I personally bear no grudge towards him. I understand that he had a difficult job to do. And it's obvious now, perhaps it was obvious at the time, that he had doors slammed in his face so that he couldn't act as a liaison.

Seeing Barrett as an obstacle, Archer tried to circumvent him: 'you had to try and go round him and go direct'. The minder thus became ever more irritated and irritating.

It would be fair to say that the Navy's unhappiness had a lot to do with the differences between life on board ship and on land. Sir Geoffrey Johnson Smith, former Parliamentary Under-Secretary of State for the Army, talked about this to us:

> Once at sea the psychology is different. When you are a journalist and you're on a ship, you're a guest, but, if you are on dry land with the Army, it is no more their land than yours and I think you are much more equal . . . The commanding

officers are in charge at sea in the way that the colonel on the ground isn't. He's in charge of his men but he isn't in charge of the ambience.

We asked each journalist whether he was aware of any way in which he had annoyed or upset the military. John Shirley recalled one incident:

It was the night the *Belgrano* went down. I was in the bar with Kim Sabido, the IRN reporter, and Kim was going round getting reactions in the bar on tape with a microphone . . . Two or three officers objected and said that we were guests in the wardroom, and that we shouldn't behave like this; and Kim said we weren't guests, we were there of right, and an argument developed. In the end they threatened to throw him over the side of the ship. It all got a bit nasty.

Some journalists, however, felt that they had been too compliant. Jeremy Hands, for instance, believed that from the beginning he and his colleagues had conceded too much:

The biggest mistake the press made on *Canberra* was allowing [the minders] to call the shots. They called a meeting every day at 9.30 and we all went to it, and that immediately gave them the upper hand because people sit round in a semicircle and they stand up and address us and tell us what's going on, what we could do and what we couldn't. If we'd told them to get stuffed in the first place, I think we would probably have got a bit further.

Gareth Parry agreed:

You see, we were there initially at the grace and favour of the Navy and, because the only critical thing is getting the story back, we became manageable, and even malleable to some extent. It was said to us very early on that the press was not in any way a high priority, to which the Ministry of Defence men nodded sagely.

There was one particularly sensitive moment on board, when Argentinian bombs dropped on the British ships failed to explode because of faulty fusing. This, interestingly, was the only occasion when a serious breakdown of collective control of copy occurred. Snow recalled: 'They didn't tell us not to mention the unexploded bombs until there had been about six or seven of them, and then they suddenly said: "Don't mention them".' Had the Argentines learnt that their bombs were not exploding and remedied the fault, damage to the Task Force would have been considerable. The omission was odd, but provides a very good case for not leaving control of copy to the journalists' own discretion or self-censorship, since it was clearly in their own interests not to broadcast and no doubt they would not have done so had they understood the reason. They were as vulnerable as everyone else. This fact was not lost on Captain Black of *Invincible*, who made it quite clear that the journalists were responsible for their own preservation. According to Snow, he reminded them:

You're sending out stuff; obviously it's got to be censored, but bear in mind if you send out anything that is of assistance to the enemy, remember that you're on here as well as we are, and if the ship gets sunk you go down the same way. You're not quite an observer, you know, an independent observer.

The point went home.

The moment when the troops and ratings realized that the journalists intended to stay with them, even to face death with them, was an important turning point. As McIlroy explained:

We were going through times which drew everybody together anyway, so whatever happened the very fact that we were there was enough to tell the people on the ship that they had five civilians with them all the way through. They were always expecting us to be taken off at some point. When they realized we weren't, they obviously realized we were prepared to sink with them if necessary. And that really made us part of the ship, more than we would be normally.

The troops were clearly puzzled by any civilian's readiness to risk life and limb on such a venture, 'even a journalist'. This, and the way the correspondents chose to live and behave, produced reactions of affectionate amusement. 'They were as fascinated by us', observed Patrick Bishop, 'as we were by them.' Bishop himself bore special responsibility for this. According to Ian Bruce:

[He] couldn't use an iron, so all of his shirts after so many weeks at sea looked like an electric storm because they had been washed, crumpled up in a bag, then spun dry and the creases were in there for ever: perma-creased shirts. And he'd turn up on occasion in his bare feet and perma-creased shirts, and a dim view of that was taken by some of the more staid officers in the wardroom.

Most of the journalists' social habits and lifestyles, let alone their comparative ages, hardly equipped them for the rigours of life with the troops. McGowan, for example, lost two stone. As Ian Bruce, now McGowan's close friend, remarked, 'the soldiers were parade and battleground trained, we were office and bar-room trained'. Consequently the sight of struggling journalists making the best of the conditions ashore was a kind of comic relief for the troops. Charles Lawrence, having been heard over the World Service describing the troops as looking like 'dirty tramps' after his exhausting 'yomp' with them, said: 'They took the piss out of me saying, "Morning, Fleet Street", as they passed the trench while you were trying to make a cup of tea'.

Perhaps there is no better illustration of the difference between the troops and the press corps than the journalists' refusal to accept the accommodation allotted them aboard ship. Not the type of people to take discomfort lying down, the obvious unsuitability of their sleeping arrangements, based on an acquired taste for the better class of hotel, produced a knee-jerk reaction to secure better arrangements. The method of procurement was one not unknown to journalists. As Kim Sabido delicately put it: 'I believe money changed hands'. Heliopter pilots were offered similar inducements later but, to the disappointment of some, could not be bribed. Sabido went on:

> The one big thing was the changing of cabins. That was thought of as a classic example of how journalists operate . . . didn't care about the orderly running of the ship. They should have the best, and if they could buy the best, then they would buy the best. The rules were there to be broken as far as the journalists were concerned.

The democratization of arrangements by money may well have gone against the grain of the Navy's authoritarian ideas of distribution, but it was effective.

Nevertheless, as Sabido said:

> We were totally alien to them. They are used to rules and regulations and paying attention and people doing what they are told and people turning up on time and things like that. And journalists, they never turned up on time, we never did what we were told, we never paid any attention to rules and regulations and disciplined life that they led. It was a complete anathema to us.

Altogether, the voyage to the Falklands was, for journalists, minders and naval officers alike, a protracted trauma. John Shirley believed that it was then that the seeds of later trouble were sown:

> I think the whole censorship argument, the whole of the conflict between the reporters and the Ministry of Defence officials, is really a result of bad feeling that developed on the way down on the *Canberra* and other ships, too, and the general difficulties and frustrations that we all had with the situation.

3

War clouds gather

By now the journalists were beginning to wonder what the future held. According to Charles Lawrence, they were not the only ones to do so. He overheard a senior officer saying one evening in the Crow's Nest bar on *Canberra*: 'It's one thing to die for Queen and country but quite another to die for Mrs Thatcher'. John Shirley talked to us about his doubts:

I just began to think, this is really rather serious . . ., men were putting live ammunition in their guns. After Ascension, we started going to intelligence briefings laid on by Mike Norman, the Major, who had been in charge of the people who were in the Falklands when the Argentinians invaded. He organized a series of first-aid classes for us so we were told how to patch each other up if we got injured. We went to a series of unarmed combat lectures where I was taught how to tear a man's ear off, punch his eyes out and twist his bollocks off . . . And we were issued with these dog-tags. I think that was the key moment . . . Mine just had 'J Shirley, Press' on it, but they had the religion of those who were religious. You had two of these little plastic tags. One hangs immediately round your neck and the other hangs below it – there's a green tag and a brown tag. The idea is that if you're killed whoever finds you cuts the brown tag off to report you as dead; they leave the green one on so that you can be identified. Yes, I was frightened and I just began to wonder if I fancied dying (a) so far away and (b) for such a silly assignment.

Pat Bishop, like several of his colleagues, began to think about practical matters:

. . . Everyone started getting very worried about their insurance cover . . . The *Observer* being the *Observer*, I was covered for about 7/6d and there's the *Mirror* bloke covered for half a million and their wife gets £200,000 a year or something, so the lot of us cabled back and demanded higher insurance rates. And they were genuinely surprised. Because we were all scared shitless. I sent a cable off saying, 'I'm the least valued member of the press corps and can you do something about it?' I got a telex back saying, 'What a gloomy message'. Then you realized that people back [home] thought that the landing was a long way away.

Charles Lawrence talked about the mood on *Canberra*:

. . . a few people, unexpected people, were windy . . . Some of the officers were quite nervous, people started talking about how many casualties there'd be. And this of course was accompanied by the wonderful South Atlantic that was closing in on us, and it was no longer sunshine and sunbathing but rain and storms and albatrosses. There was one wonderful night when I think a Force 9 was blowing and they decided to test out the machine guns. It was an incredible scene. It was just as it was getting dark and these guys with duffel coats on up on the bridge and guys shooting away, it was like something out of the Second World War. I think we all got more excited. Some of the journalists, I suppose, got nervous. There were various different reactions, like McGowan, he was very experienced [at] this sort of thing, he takes it out on his equipment. He had the best-equipped survival jacket on the entire troopships . . . It weighed about 35lb. It was a combat jacket with spare woollies, Mars bars, torches, you know, everything needed. Other guys were going around writing out wills . . . But I wouldn't say it was gloomy or pessimistic at any point.

Rumour spreads fast on a ship, fed by superstition. This was a mixture of ancient and modern. *Canberra*, for example, which was known as 'the Great White Whale', sliced through a whale near Ascension, turning the sea blood-red. That, and the ship's postal code number, 666, shook sailors and troops alike, whether they knew the Devil's sign from the Bible or the film, *The Omen*. Farewell letters were written home. Lawrence, who had his own taboos, told us:

That's the other great habit servicemen have got . . . they like to write last letters to be posted if they get killed . . . All this stuff, frankly, I don't go near because I have a kind of superstition about it.

Ritual became important. John Shirley described how they passed the time:

People did get frightened and anxious and a bit worried and confused – certainly in those first two or three weeks because we were surrounded by two and a half thousand blokes who were, if they weren't directly hostile they were sceptical, and that was a fairly strange position to be in. There were about fifteen of us reporters, civilians, the only other civilians on the ship were the P & O crew. We had to be quite supportive of each other. People did have little panics and got upset and you had to go and kind of talk to people and the way we solved it really was just to throw ourselves into the military routine. Some of us started doing this PT and running round the deck. I lost a stone and a half – it was terrific, but it was hard work to start with . . . Kim took a Berlitz course with him – tape recordings – and started learning Spanish. Bob Fox started running a little class for us . . . and we got this chart of silhouettes and we started identifying ships . . . testing each other on weapons . . . It was all quite good fun. But it was all really designed to support each other. We had this first-aid class which was very very good indeed. We had military supervision for it . . . In a sense, we were forming our own little unit. It was quite fun really.

The PT was Fox's idea, Shirley told us:

He was the person encouraging all of us . . . because he said that he'd been stuck on a ship during the Cod War for something like six weeks and he had put on a stone in weight because he got no exercise. And he said we'd all got to go and do some PT 'cause otherwise we'd just get huge and fat and gross. It was a very good idea.

The journalists had no illusions about the destructive capability of the Argentinian air force. Peter Archer said that at one point 'I didn't think we were going to be able to make the landing, I really didn't; I mean, look at the rate that ships were being hit'. It is certainly the case that the air cover was not sufficient to provide the kind of security the amphibious forces would have preferred. Archer, on *Hermes*, claimed that everyone was frightened:

> Not just the journalists . . . I think it's a natural reaction when you're up against people firing missiles at you; missile warfare at sea was something nobody had experience of before.

The loss of *Sheffield* was a sad moment, not only because it seemed that *Hermes* might share her fate but also because Archer and his shipmates began to think that Britain was not necessarily invincible. He continued:

> When the *Sheffield* was hit there were two Exocets fired and the other one was coming for us – this is all censored from copy – . . . Within seconds the observer on the bridge rushed across the room, barging people out of the way and it was obvious that he'd seen something, and the commanders of the Task Force, the Captain and the commanders on the bridge were all ducking, going down with hands on the floor. And that frightened me because at that stage still I thought: Well, these blokes know what they're doing, they're in charge of the situation. I realized then that they were as vulnerable and as frightened as everybody else.

According to Gareth Parry, some officers were privately saying, 'We really are in it; we could be in trouble'. Such conversation was naturally not encouraged. As Archer described it:

> It was almost taboo, because sailors are very superstitious . . . And one evening the chap who was Number Two on the ship, said to me: 'Well, Peter, what do you think of missile warfare at sea?' And I said: 'Well, I'm afraid you're asking the wrong person. What do I know about it?' And he said: 'Dear chap, you know as much about it as anybody else does, as much as I do'. It was very worrying, and on top of that you had the pressure of having to sleep with your clothes on, not having regular meals, regular wash and shave, the uncertainty of being at sea and what happens if they hit and you survive the blast? All these things go through your mind. Will you survive the sea?

Gareth Parry was angered by the officers' refusal to admit openly that people were afraid. We asked him whether he had tried to report the reactions of the men to attack by Exocets. 'No,' he replied, 'I knew there would be unnecessary hassle. They would say: "I don't think this happened".' He gave an example of an earlier attempt he had made:

> I remember a particular event. You try to do it not in snidey ways, but more subtly. During action stations – very tense – there was a kid next to me crying . . . and well, it happened, and I thought this demonstrates how people feel, real

bloody fear, which the Navy call 'anxiety'. And I filed this, . . . it was looked at and the Captain said: 'I find this extremely hard to believe'. Which is his gentlemanly way of saying 'You've made it up'. That really disgusted me . . . There was no acknowledgement that that sort of thing could happen. While at one point they'd say: 'Well, we're all sailors and we're all very sorry for the *Belgrano,* we all wear life jackets', they weren't prepared to admit that they were also human beings.

The military must neither openly recognize that such emotion exists nor allow it to be publicly expressed. The journalists, however, did recognize it in others and in themselves and, what is more, wished to write about it. There was no way in which they could do so. Parry admitted as much when he discussed a moment when the façade did crumble:

We'd been in action a couple of days and *Sheffield* had been hit, and we had no defences at all against this Exocet thing and the padré on the *Invincible* was asked to write a special prayer. This is significant . . . So what's so special? Tell you what's special – you're going to die. That was the implication. The prayer went down like any ship I'd seen, you know; it said 'for those of us who might not make it today . . .' That's the kind of story I was anxious to file when I got back, because you can imagine it, people are to pretend you are going to survive and the padré comes on and says 'those who may well die today' . . . that's terrific for morale. He never said it again, interestingly.

The attempt to offer spiritual comfort by the promise of death clearly did not impress Parry, added to which, professionally, he was deeply frustrated. 'What's the point of seeing things,' he asked us, 'if you can't file them?' Just before the landing, he was moved to the Royal Fleet Auxiliary ship, *Sir Geraint*, moored in San Carlos water; there, after sailing some 8000 miles to report a war, the futility of what he was being obliged to do struck him with full force: 'she was completely empty, just sailing around, and we were acting in fact as an Exocet foil'.

'God,' he added, 'I'm begining to sound like the Navy'. Parry now felt he was 'so bloody behind in the story, it was fucking dismaying, actually'. He went on, 'It's bloody important to get the story before people get very bored with it . . .' Shortly after they landed, according to Seamark: 'Gareth left me, I think it was one morning at Darwin, to say he was going back to San Carlos to see if he could get some more kit for us . . . and that was the last I saw of him. And about four days later somebody said, "Oh, he's gone".'

This came as no shock to Seamark:

. . . because Gareth wasn't that keen on war. He had seen Vietnam and the horrors of war. He came back and he wrote some very long pieces on the war and the futility of it and all the rest, and I think the *Guardian*, they were delighted.

A month after the Task Force sailed, there was a particularly revealing incident. By this time South Georgia had been retaken, Port Stanley airfield attacked by Harriers and a Vulcan, Argentinian aircraft brought down, the *General Belgrano* sunk and the *Sheffield* hit by an Exocet. A yellow, four-sided stencilled, unofficial ship's newspaper, *The Screws* of 6 May, was distributed on board *Invincible*. Its style was that of a school magazine: small titbits of humour and information about life on board. Page 2 was the letters page, and in this issue were two letters, one serious and angry. It ran for fourteen lines; we give it in full:

Dear Screws,

I discovered today that one of our guests on board has been sending some interesting copy to London. I refer to the 'Sponsor a Sidewinder' campaign which I believe is being run by the *Sun*.

As a senior maintainer on the 801 Fighter Squadron I wish to put on record that I think the idea as a whole is a disgusting piece of sensationalism. Furthermore, I find the suggestion that any member of the Squadron would be associated with this both insulting and a slur on our professional dedication. To suggest that we would be prepared to kill on a 'bonus scheme' is scandalous: it compromises the pride and traditions that separate our Squadron from mercenaries.

I would sincerely ask him, in the name of truth, that the paper concerned, via the journalist, prints a retraction of the whole idea that we are involved and stating our feelings. If he wants real copy he should join us on the flight deck during action stations . . . he would get some real quotes then. He might even get his name on a Sidewinder. At the moment the way the Squadron feels, he might get the whole Sidewinder.

CAEMN Bob Smith
SMR 801 NAS

The letter referred to an article in the *Sun*, announcing the paper's 'sponsoring' of a Sidewinder missile, with the indelicate inscription, 'Up yours, Galtieri'. It made Tony Snow, the paper's correspondent, an unpopular man aboard. The *Sun* may have boasted that it was the paper 'that supports our boys'; quite the opposite, the boys did not support the *Sun*. The paper was vilified for crude and insensitive jingoism. Some of the journalists were themselves embarrassed by the *Sun*'s coverage: the issue, for instance, published after the *Belgrano*'s sinking, headlined 'Gotcha!' Those in *Canberra* sent off a message to the *Sun*'s offices asking for more copies, which were 'urgently needed for lavatory paper'. Officers and men were hungry for newspapers; even so, they were selective. According to John Shirley, 'the *Mirror* reporter on the *Canberra*, Alastair McQueen, specifically asked his office to send 100 copies every day for the troops. The *Sun* was doing the same thing.' The papers were flown to Ascension Island and then dropped in the postbag, which meant that, by the time they were read, the contents had dated. Shirley described their reactions:

> I was very impressed by the level of discrimination of the Marines and the Paratroopers anyway. Most of them were contemptuous of the *Sun*. They thought it was rubbish. The key moment when that showed was when the *Belgrano* went down, and when the *Sun* arrived with that headline 'Gotcha!' people were throwing the paper over the side of the ship because they felt that the guys who had gone down on the *Belgrano* could have been them. It's totally different from the experience I have had with the British Army in Northern Ireland. Their attitude towards the IRA is very different. They regard them as sort of cheats because they don't fight in a straightforward way. Whereas the Argentinians were another army and, OK, you've got to go and kill them, but . . . there was a sort of undercurrent of respect for them.

A Sidewinder is rather a small missile and the *Sun* added insult to injury by using a picture of a much larger weapon. McIlroy, of the *Telegraph,* spoke of the effect produced by the *Sun*:

> The others suffered from their material being trivialised . . . If you work for the *Sun* and *Star* . . . you have to expect that, and that was reflected often in the attitudes of the people on board ship to them, but it was just a natural reaction to the newspapers as you'd find them in the street. You'll find some people who think the *Telegraph, Times* and *Guardian* are something that's for special people and not themselves, and so you'll find in the other messes that they'll be delighted at what we regard as trivial material. But . . . things like sponsoring a missile and so on didn't go down well at all, right across the ship.

Talking about the ordinary Marines and Paratroopers, Shirley said, 'generally, their attitude was one of contempt [for the *Sun*]. I mean contempt; that is a strong word, but I use it'.

Snow's colleagues may have universally disapproved of that episode but it was seen as Snow's own business, no concern of theirs, and no one sought either to prevent the incident or criticize it afterwards. 'There was,' according to McIlroy, 'the odd joking reference . . . but no serious conversation at all.' Witherow said: 'We just thought it was tasteless'. Comment at the time was inappropriate because, as journalists, Snow's colleagues appreciated the difference between his personal views and his paper's line. Like him, they were doing a job, whatever their own feelings about the enterprise. Seamark, whose paper, the *Star,* supported the British Government's line, talked about professionalism:

> I cannot understand the Services. I do not like soldiers and sailors and airmen because I just cannot comprehend what leads them to do what they do. So I found that on a personal level I had to mask my feelings totally . . . I think all of us . . . hated what was happening and hated the fact that we were going to war, but

because we had to get a story out and do the business we had to mask those true feelings and adopt the Service philosophy.

He continued:

As the incidents happened, as people died I kept thinking: God, great, this is it at last, in an awful way now the *Sheffield*'s gone down people will see the sense and stop. But say that to them on board *Invincible* and, God, no, 'We've got to hit them back,' revenge and all this sort of stuff. My feelings didn't change throughout. I thought it was futile and disgusting and despicable from the moment we sailed until the moment I got back. And I still feel that way.

As a journalist, however, he did what was required:

The *Star* was backing our boys, but not going over the top like the *Sun*. It didn't cause me any problems. I work for the *Star* because it's a national newspaper and it pays a lot of money. I never really gave any thought at all about what was going into the newspaper, what the editors were saying. I thought I knew how the *Star* would be presenting the war, so, we all work for different newspapers, we all know what that newspaper wants and as far as conscience and that sort of thing goes, we haven't got one, have we, if you see what I mean?

Snow was himself hurt to think that he was thought responsible for the *Sun*'s position and for its headlines, 'Gotcha!' especially. He explained that:

About halfway through there was a *What the Papers Say* about the war and it featured the *Sun* and 'Wallop!' and 'Gotcha!' and that sort of stuff. Now, that [programme] was supposed to be [made] by a professional journalist who knows that the reporter out there is not writing the headlines or taking a particular point of view. And basically the bloke said: 'If there was a prize this year for the worst journalist of the year, it must go to Tony Snow . . . And my friends and relations thought: Bloody hell, there he is out there getting shot at and back here he's getting bloody hammered as well.

Snow was responsible neither for the caption nor for his paper's policy. The story of how the Sidewinder came to be 'sponsored' is complicated. It was not Snow's own idea to sponsor the missile and he thought it in poor taste. He was well aware of the difference between attitudes at home, as his newspaper perceived them, and feeling on board ship. As he told us:

. . . Being 8000 miles away, it was very difficult for me to know what the mood was in Britain. And I got a lot of stick from the soldiers and the sailors that I met out there for the *Sun*'s stance . . . But when I came back I realized that the *Sun* had in fact . . . captured . . . the mood of the country perfectly . . . I mean this sort of gung-ho 'You can't pull the lion's tail' and 'We'll fight to the last drop of your blood' . . . When people are banging Exocets around and 50-calibre machine-guns . . . you've got a slightly different attitude to the whole thing, and particularly, I mean, the *Sun*'s coverage of things like the *Belgrano* – 'Gotcha!' and 'Wallop!' and that sort of thing. Now, a lot of people came up to me and . . . said 'What kind of people are the *Sun* . . . we don't take any delight in fellow sailors freezing to death out there.' . . . these blokes are all conscious that the *Belgrano* today, us tomorrow.

Snow's principle was to play the story in the style he thought the paper would want; this meant he had to guess how his editor would judge the mood of the country. Snow gave us his own account of the sponsorship incident:

> I was on board *Invincible* one night in the mess, and they said: 'Hey, you're from the *Sun*. Does the *Sun* want to sponsor a missile?' I said: 'That's a bit over the top.' They said: 'Well, in the last war, people wrote messages to Hitler on bombs to Germany.' Well, they were doing the same kind of thing there, with 1000lb bombs and everything. And they said: 'You put your money in and it's all for a big party at the end of the day.' And they [asked me] . . . because of the *Sun*'s . . . very gung-ho attitude . . . Anyway, a couple of days later I heard on the World Service that the *Sun* was accusing Michael Foot of being a traitor for daring to speak against Margaret Thatcher in Parliament and I thought to myself: That's funny. And they [i.e. the *Sun*] called the *Daily Mirror* traitors, the BBC traitors, Peter Snow [a] traitor. And I thought to myself: Well, if that's their attitude, this is right up their street . . . the missile bit, although personally I found it a bit distasteful . . . If I felt that strongly about it, I could quit, fair enough. But if I'm there as a representative of the *Sun* and they're paying my wages, I've actually got to act on their behalf in the way I think they'd want me to act . . . I thought, if I had the editor and held an editorial conference here, and said, 'Do you want to sponsor a missile?' they would say: 'Yeah, yeah.' . . . So I sponsored a missile. And then there was the difficulty of finding something to put on it, because all the things they put on the bombs were unprintable: 'Suck on this, Argie' and things like that. And so I thought to myself, [we need] something that was just slightly offensive: 'Up yours, Galtieri'. And that was just about as far as you could go and get into print.
>
> Now the funny thing was, I took a lot of stick about that as well . . .

He explained why it seemed that the idea had been his in the first place:

> I went and had a word with the bloke who got the first one – it was a Sidewinder missile from a Harrier – and I said: 'As the *Sun* are doing it, they would like the first one. Do you mind?' And he said, 'No, you have the first one and I'll have the second,' and that was it. You could sponsor anything down to a cannon-shell for 25p, or the odd thousand-pound bomb or whatever you see. And this was all just light-hearted . . . it's just one of those things. In fact, the bloke who fired the missile was a helluva nice fellow, and he [later] hit a bomber . . . and the whole thing blew up and the men who were on it were killed . . . and he was quite upset that they had died and hadn't had a chance to parachute out and be saved.

The pilot who carried the sponsored Sidewinder was killed when his Harrier collided with another in fog.

Snow was, as it happened, one of those who most vehemently objected to the Falklands venture, especially after the breakdown of negotiations which he thought could have produced a satisfactory peaceful settlement. 'As far as I was concerned, from that moment on, all the people who got killed, blinded and lost their legs and all the rest of it was a waste from our point of view. Personally, from my own point of view I would have found it easier to represent the *Guardian . . .*'

Snow however was still paying the price for his newspaper's stance as the expedition drew to an end. He recalled:

> After the surrender, I was on a ship in Port Stanley harbour waiting to . . . use the telephone in the wardroom and lying on the table was a photostat of the *Sun*'s front page, which said: 'Kill an Argie and Win a Mini Metro.' And . . . this person came up to me and said . . . 'They've gone over the top now. I don't like the way they've been doing it.' And . . . it said: 'Pictures of dead Argies on page 10.' And I thought to myself: What am I going to say to this fellow? And suddenly someone said: 'Don't be a twit. That's the front page of *Private Eye*.' And at the bottom it said: 'Is the Pope gay? Ten tell-tale signs,' and I thought . . . I get it now. But . . . for a fraction of a second, I believed it.

There is of course no evidence that the *Sun* had correctly gauged the nation's mood. Indeed, there is no evidence, as our readership surveys in Chapter Twelve show, that the *Sun* judged even its own readers' mood correctly. Although many factors can affect circulation, during the conflict the circulation of the *Sun* actually fell. It lost sales at the rate of 40,000 a day, while its main competitor, the 'treacherous' *Mirror*, added 95,000.

The journalists on *Invincible* were embarrassed to find their copy pinned on a noticeboard for officers and crew to read. Roger Goodwin, their minder, admitted that he thought this a mistake and offered to have it stopped. John Witherow explained why the practice was unfortunate:

> . . .[It] also played a very important part, actually, in the Captain's reaction to our stories . . . he was very conscious of morale and, if we were writing, say, after the *Sheffield* that the crew were alarmed and frightened he got very upset . . . and . . . thought it was undermining morale. Morale is very temperamental on a ship. The whole thing runs on buzzes and feelings . . . and so he actually accused us at one stage of lying . . .

Captain Black objected to two of Witherow's stories in particular:

> I wrote that a petty officer had told me [that] after *Sheffield* was hit he no longer thought that the Argies were a bunch of beaneaters and they were perhaps the best-equipped military forces in South America. The Captain's secretary asked me to change this, on the Captain's request to say instead . . . that they were *well* equipped – to soften it mainly because he knew the crew were reading it.

Witherow acceded to this request but:

I don't think it changed it dramatically. They didn't often ask us . . . but they
sometimes changed it without our knowledge, which made us very angry. There
was the case when I wrote about the second Vulcan attack, underlining the failure
of the first and that they had to go in again. And this was changed. I can't
remember the exact wording, but it was changed to read something like: 'The
second Vulcan attack was another successful raid on Stanley airfield.' I didn't see
that . . . until it was too late.

As for the reactions of the men, Witherow said:

I think it was read avidly for the first few weeks and less so after a while. You'd
often go down – it was in the NAAFI – and see groups of men reading it. They
didn't actually say 'I think it's a load of crap' but I think they thought it.

In any case, newspapers were dropped to the ships. As Seamark
said:

I think up until Ascension we used to see our newspaper two weeks late, and I saw
the *Star* a few times. Again, in the Navy they had lashings of *Telegraphs* and *Times*
for the officers. For the troops they certainly got the *Sun* and they got the *Star*
several times. The guy I felt sorry for was the *Guardian* because the *Guardian*
never found its way onto a Royal Navy ship.

Parry agreed: 'I never saw my copy. I never saw the *Guardian*; it
simply did not arrive on board the *Invincible*.'
This was odd because, as he explained:

There are, believe it or not, quite a few *Guardian*-readers in a warship . . . chief
petty officers [who] run the ship. Extremely wise and almost aloof people, and I
found it fascinating that there was a great core of *Guardian* readers.

Seamark knew where to find his readers:

The problem with *Invincible* first of all was that we were billeted with the officers
. . . but naval officers are not by and large *Sun* and *Star* readers. It was no problem
apart from that, personally they were fine. But all our readers were on the lower
decks so we had to go and find them, the boilermen and all that.

The *Star* and the *Sun* could, however, be useful to the officers. Snow
explained:

Captain Black used to talk to us quite a lot, not only to tell us what was going on
but [because] we had the ear of the 1000-man crew . . . He can't actually go round
and talk to the ordinary able seaman and the junior ratings, because they immediately clam up and say, 'Yes, sir. No sir,' . . . We would do stories sometimes on the
men and he would say: 'I can't believe that's true. Did they really say that? Did
they really feel that?'

McIlroy considered that he enjoyed certain advantages because he
wrote for the *Telegraph*:

The thing that endeared [them to] the *Telegraph* was the fact that they were
reporting every day, no matter what the content was, it reassured families . . .

They saw my name in the paper, on *Invincible*, they knew the ship was still afloat. And that was a big source of comfort. It established a confidence in us which we all benefited from. It was more of an advantage to be from the *Telegraph* than the *Guardian*, but it never materialised in favouritism . . . The advantage was that it was a regular news service, whereas often the pop papers or the others would miss a day or two because [copy] was rewritten in London. And *The Times* would miss their first edition . . .

The first or early editions were the ones which went to the provinces, where the men's families would see them. They would often comment on reports in letters to the ships, sometimes sending clippings. McIlroy said:

Eventually, after a couple of weeks of no mail, you'd get a mail-drop . . . and it would be letters saying 'Don't worry, we're not worried because we are reading the *Telegraph* every day and we know that you're all right'.

Brian Hanrahan considered that it was easier for the broadcasting journalists than the print journalists to establish their credentials. He said:

I think the broadcasters established their own individual identities because they got around so much more. They became quite familiar figures. I think the press corps were the 'press' and . . . there were actually too many of them because they tend to travel in packs . . . It was very hard to see them individually. When you meet four people . . . they virtually hold a press conference. Whereas a broadcaster tended to turn up individually, or at the most two of us. I suppose, also, we were well enough known figures, especially as . . . people kept hearing our stuff. Max Hastings . . . established an individual identity, but I don't think the rest of the press did.

According to Hanrahan, the World Service of the BBC was important in establishing the presence of the broadcasters among the military:

It helped enormously. Because it began, obviously, to dawn on them that I was, as far as they were concerned, their contact for information . . . anything they wanted out they would come and tell me. And when I got to meet up with the other troops . . . I had already an identity . . . and they were all willing to help out. The point was that I was trying very hard . . . to establish an identity of my own . . . I'd go out of my way to say I was the BBC, not media or press or anything else. That was my conscious effort to try to establish that there was a BBC and . . . that you only had to turn on the radio to see how responsible and sensible we were and wasn't that a good thing. And I could see a way of opening doors all over the place.

Each journalist discovered during the voyage those groups of shipmates with whom he felt comfortable. Shirley made an early mistake by arguing with some Royal Marine captains about the pointlessness of the whole operation:

It was a very foolish thing to have done. I was branded as a sort of Trotskyite after that. It took quite a bit of time to get round it. I never got rid of it, in the sense that people always thought that I was a convivial lefty . . .

Shirley was well aware of the subtleties of social relations on board:

I think [the journalists] tended to identify with their respective groups, or roles, or groups in the military, too. For example, . . . McQueen knew absolutely clearly that his readership – the *Mirror*'s readership – was in the sergeants' mess, and he went straight down there and that's where he got his stories from. McGowan and Smith [*Express*] tended to go down there, too. Bishop [*Observer*], myself [*Sunday Times*], Fox [BBC Radio], Hastings [*Standard*] and Kim [IRN] tended to mix more with the officers, though Kim, I think, got to know more ranks probably than anybody else . . . he's a very very good reporter indeed and a very diligent man. Ian Bruce of the *Glasgow Herald*, who's a tough little Glaswegian, was very much down there with the blokes. I was personally a little bit intimidated in talking to Julian Thompson, who's the Brigadier . . . he's a very impressive man. You could talk to him about all sorts of things . . . He was so clearly on top of the military situation and I was so clearly not. I tended to mix with the captains and lieutenants, which may say something about my self-perception. Whereas Max [Hastings] was straight up there; he fancied himself as the Brigade Commander.

Fox, like Hanrahan, benefited from being heard on the World Service, particularly, according to Sabido, 'with the senior people'. Sabido continued:

In a way, they thought he was doing a grand job in censoring himself, and he wasn't rocking the boat . . . It did help him a great deal . . . People like the Royal Navy Captain, Christopher Burne, treated him sort of as the representative of the press, invited him to dinner because he was on a sort of intellectual par with them as well.

The journalists knew they were being vetted on the way down to the Falklands. The impression they made was an important factor in the decision as to which units they would accompany ashore. As John Shirley told us:

No doubt at all that the most popular commanding officer of the unit commanders was a man called Lieutenant-Colonel Nick Vaux, who's the commander of 42 Commando. Extremely nice man, very urbane, bright, open, friendly. He also had a very good press officer, too, which, I think, made a difference, called Lieutenant Tom Maklinsky, . . . who was very keen to help us, but not bossy, not domineering. Three Para were very good as well. Lieutenant-Colonel Huw Pike and their press officer, Bob Derby. 40 Commando weren't so friendly; it wasn't that they were hostile, it's just that we weren't particularly impressed by the guys. And so we tended to associate more with 3 Para and 42 Commando. One or two of us tended to eat with Nick Vaux in the evening. He'd come to our cabin and we'd go back to his. You know, sort of relationships developed and I know that Vaux was quite keen to have me, Max Hastings, and I don't know who else. Three Para were quite keen to have Bishop and to have me, too, and they wanted Bob Fox as well. How the allocation was actually done I don't know, but it was obviously decided between the COs and these two MoD officials, who in fact became three because one other joined at Ascension Island.

This was the moment when the journalists were seen as individuals, rather than being lumped together as a general nuisance. Their popularity, educational and social skills were, they believed, all appraised. One senior officer, something of a snob, was anxious that representatives of the more popular papers should not accompany his command; such journalists were, he confided, 'a bit grubby'. As things turned out, the process of disembarkation was complicated and confused.

Despite the danger, those in the *Invincible* were 'up with the story'. As McIlroy emphasized: 'one had an incredibly good run on the *Invincible*. We had all the accounts of the *Sheffield*, we had the eye-witness account of South Georgia being retaken'. Furthermore, as we have noted, the *Invincible's* Captain was more cooperative than his colleague in *Hermes*. In fact, so badly were the others being serviced that the BBC asked Brian Hanrahan, on board *Hermes*, to ask Gareth Parry if he would file for the BBC from *Invincible*. Parry was also asked if he would file for the *Mail on Sunday*.

> When we had these complaints from Hanrahan and others, we suddenly realized how lucky we were to be on *Invincible* . . . I'd rather have been on the others, frankly, for safety [but] at least you were there when the story was happening and actually sharing those dreadful weeks when the Exocets were being sent your way.

The good news-run of 'the *Invincible* Five', as they were now called, eventually came to an end. Rear-Admiral Woodward, anxious to protect his carriers from the Argentinian air force, decided to lay as far out to sea as he could, earning thereby the unkind pun of 'Windy Woodward'. The journalists noticed longer delays in getting copy out and shorter tempers on the part of the Navy. John Witherow told us:

> There was much greater censorship, we were told less and less, and the frustration just grew constantly and we complained much harder . . . On occasions the Captain was dragged out of his bunk at night and he stopped stories of ours and we complained about certain things and he just considered us, I think, a bunch of prima donnas, which the Navy tends to if you don't behave in a Navy-like way.

Gareth Parry described a row between the journalists and Roger Goodwin, the minder on *Invincible*:

> We went to see Black in the end. God, it was bloody embarrassing actually . . . Captain Black was especially tired and so were we; we'd been at defence stations for a long time and there came a point when it's no longer possible in fact to be nice to this guy [the minder] and it was a story we had to file, I forget which, but

we raced in and asked the Captain of the ship, which could have sunk at any second, whether he would adjudicate . . . and to his credit he did.

We suggested to Parry that it was probably the last thing the Captain wanted to consider: 'Absolutely. Fucking captain of a ship and a thousand people could be sent to the bottom at any time. Ridiculous'. The journalists' behaviour now seemed entirely exasperating. Only one of the group thought, and then only briefly, that anything would be gained by remaining on *Invincible*. That was John Witherow:

> I knew that John Shirley would be covering for [*The Times* and *Sunday Times*] on land, so I was at one stage thinking: Well, I'll . . . cover the air war from *Invincible*, in case there were any attacks on the fleet; so we'd be covered on both fronts . . . I signalled the office and advised that that was a good idea and they signalled back . . . 'Yes, do it'. Then all the others were signalled by their offices to go ashore and I became concerned that I'd become stuck out there indefinitely. It would have been worthwhile being there for a week . . . covering the fleet as it came under attack and the landings. The problem was I could have been stuck there right to the end of the war . . . It was a very hard decision, but in the end I decided to go ashore as well.

The war with the carriers did not cease because action was moving to the land; it ceased only in the news sense of an absence of journalists, and news is where the newsmen are. Caught by competing claims for attention, events at sea went unrecorded because they were considered insufficiently news-worthy to deserve significance. The sighting of journalists by other journalists acts as an indicator where 'news' is expected. Clearly something was going to happen ashore and witnessing the rest make preparation to disembark fuelled the desperation of all on *Invincible*, not just Witherow, to follow their colleagues.

Captain Black was also determined to get them off his ship. He was assisted by a 'personal note' from McIlroy, who knew that those on *Canberra* were about to disembark, asking him to do his utmost, after having had the sea battle for so long, not to let them miss the landings. Seamark told us what happened next:

> On the evening of the landing of 20 May we were transferred from the *Invincible* under a black cloud, because we had our first and final row with the Captain, over the MoD guy as it happened. He transferred us onto a supply-ship which was allegedly going with the landing group of *Fearless*, *Intrepid* and *Canberra* inshore, so that we'd get straight off and straight in, because the carriers *Invincible* and *Hermes* would stay on. We got on to this ship [The *Resource*]; we were told it had satellite communication so that we could file.

The *Invincible* Five now found themselves, however, in an even worse predicament than before. They were told that, rather than being transferred ashore, they were to stay where they were, on the *Resource*. Seamark described their despair, as 'the helicopter takes off back to the *Invincible* and we were stranded . . . told [we] were going nowhere near inshore for two days'.

Worse, the *Resource*, they found, was carrying ammunition. Witherow spoke of their consternation:

> That was the big joke. They had taken no precautions on *Resource*. They knew that if it was hit the whole thing would go up. On a warship they would remove all the flammable material, curtains, carpets, pictures, but on *Resource* it was like sailing in a cocktail bar, pictures everywhere, wooden furniture, all these things that if you were hit, would just fly across the room and be lethal.

Seamark was able to telex his office for the first time since he had left Britain. His message was frantic:

> 'Do something. I'm stranded 400 yards from the Falklands, but not allowed to get off, me and four others.' They said, 'What are you on?' and I said, 'Well, I'm on . . .,' and the MoD minder who was standing next to me said, 'You can't tell them the name of the ship'. I just typed it as RFA *Resource* and I said 'ammunition ship'.

The London office's reply of 'Jesus Christ!' was as unhelpful as it was reassuring. The *Resource* was not in fact an ammunition ship, but a Royal Fleet Auxiliary vessel which was carrying ammunition as part of its cargo. For the journalists that was bad enough but there was another disadvantage. Goodwin, the minder, still marooned with his troublesome charges, broke the news. As Parry put it: 'His favourite phrase was, "Sorry, bad news, guys," and we said, "Yes," and he said, "No communication".' Parry seemed to consider such pleasure out of place: 'You'd think he'd have pretended a bit of concern, but "Sorry, bad news"!' The Marisat was eventually repaired but the *Invincible* Five, stuck on *Resource*, had little news of the landings. They were, however, able to report on the air attacks on British ships, news that in the circumstances they would have preferred to be without. McIlroy spent five days on *Resource* and his colleagues four days, although (we will explain why) it was nine days before they finally secured a firm footing on land. Meanwhile, as Seamark told us:

> We were going round kicking sailors' legs in; it was really dreadful, really dreadful times. The biggest news story in the world, and it wasn't your fault, but that's not the point. The editor wants you on the Islands. He knows it's not your fault. He knows it's an MoD cock-up, but that doesn't help you, and it certainly didn't help him.

He continued:

> It's very difficult to take the law into your own hands when you're fifty miles offshore in the middle of the Atlantic with the military. You can't buy naval or RAF helicopter pilots; we tried, but you just cannot bribe them to take us ashore.

Some blamed Captain Black and Roger Goodwin for their situation, though it was hardly a berth the minder would have chosen. According to the minders, the Five brought their own fate upon themselves; their behaviour had so soured their relations with Captain Black that he was not prepared to have them aboard a moment longer. By demanding to be moved, they gave him his chance.

The eyes of those in *Invincible* had been firmly fixed on their colleagues in *Canberra*. There the correspondents were trying to ensure – with 'lots of sneaky deaky stuff', according to Lawrence – that they would be assigned to units which would see some action. The intrigue was such that 'on a personal level' Lawrence was 'enormously relieved' when he was transferred to the *Stromness*. Until now, as Seamark put it: ' . . . the guys on *Canberra* [had] nothing to do because they were . . . just basically a ferry; they were not involved, they had got no Harriers, no anti-submarine helicopters, . . . nothing to write about . . .' Asked how he felt about this he said, 'We felt great'.

Parry, on *Invincible*, realized that those on *Canberra* would turn their circumstances to advantage when the time came:

> As soon as we knew they were coming down with the Paras and the Marines, we knew we were screwed . . . You can't have a long voyage down to war with journalists without a rapport being built up between them . . . We were Navy journalists and they were Army . . . I think that initially anyway the Army was pissed off with the great publicity the Navy was getting; if you can call an Exocet attack great. But they were coming down, literally on a cruise, on *Canberra* . . . I think the military had made private promises to the Army correspondents on *Canberra* such as 'When you get ashore it will be your kind of story; these buggers in blue jumping up and down on the ship, they can go and . . .'

Seamark, too, 'realized as the landings got nearer that we were the ones who were going to get stitched up'. This knowledge was not based on any observation at that stage but on a model of how journalists are likely to behave: 'We knew that they would do all in their power to stitch us up, just as we'd do the same for them.' Certainly the journalists made sure that the Army recognized that their – and the Army's – turn for publicity had now arrived. Kim Sabido described how a deal was struck:

> Brigadier Thompson and Commodore Michael Clapp . . . brought us all over to *Fearless* for a briefing. It was a very vague sort of thing about how they saw things. Then over the next week or so we had [daily briefings with] their guy – David Nichols, who was a sort of Royal Marine PR guy, . . . a sort of liaison between the

Brigade Headquarters, the Commodore and us. And we worked out that if we were going to go ashore we would all be allocated to units . . . and we were pressing to make sure that we were going to have the right gear to survive with and all that sort of thing. And then we said, 'Well, what about the people on *Hermes* and *Invincible*?' and we suggested . . . as a group that it seemed a bit . . . hard on us that they'd had all this stuff to report on the way down and now they were going to be allowed to go ashore at the same time . . . Who were they going ashore with? Were they going to come onto the *Canberra*? And they hadn't actually worked out anything for them, they had not got any equipment for them . . . and he conveyed our thoughts to the Brigadier and came back the next day and said: 'Yes, the Brigadier has agreed that they should not go ashore for about four days'.

Asked how the minders were persuaded that this was, in reporting terms, 'fair', Jeremy Hands said: 'We told the MoD we'd kill them if they let anybody from the *Hermes* or *Invincible* off first'.

It was accepted that the *Hermes* and *Invincible,* because they were ahead of us all the way down, and they had all the front-line stories . . . to themselves and we were chasing up to two weeks behind. Then we caught up and it was agreed – and we certainly did threaten that terrible things would happen – that the *Canberra* journalists who were with the soldiers would go with the soldiers and that the other journalists on *Invincible* and *Hermes* could sit and pick their noses the same as we had had to do until things changed. I think we had about a week's start on them. We told Martin Helm [the senior minder]. You don't ask Helm anything. You don't say, 'Please, Martin, can you arrange that we do this that and the other?', you just say, 'Look, mate, this is not going to happen. I'm telling you we are taking steps that this will happen'. And you tell your desks in London, 'For God's sake make sure that MoD London put the blocks on the others going ashore before us'. And in fact it was amicable as far as we were concerned. We were amazed when he said: 'Yes, that's the way it's going to be.'

Childish though this attitude may seem, for the journalists their professional reputations were at stake. As David Norris said: 'It sounds a bit callous to say it, but I think that if the whole thing could have ended there we would have ended up without a story. They'd have done all the sea-battles.'

Norris and the others in *Canberra* needed some glory but so too did those in *Hermes* who were also trailing, though slightly less far behind, after the *Invincible* journalists. The attempt by those on *Canberra* to stitch up the *Hermes* group with those from *Invincible* was, however, less successful. The *Hermes* journalists fought hard to free themselves from their imprisonment, as Hanrahan explained:

Canberra after all was that difficult ship where they didn't want press anyway . . . they'd literally been forbidden to send out anything, except the most nebulous type of copy . . . So when this came along they said: 'Look, we want to go ashore, and we don't want these other chaps . . . which was petty minded, I think. They persuaded the minders that this was a good thing . . . The minders went off to the military and, as the military didn't want anybody anyway, they were very happy to say they didn't want anybody else and somebody came up with this pack of lies about how it had all been agreed in London and telexed it off to the Admiral. I mean, they lied to us and they lied to the people who were running our bit of it . . . Nothing of this sort had been discussed, let alone agreed in London. I remember saying at the time 'I don't believe it' . . . The BBC doesn't agree that its only television reporter should sit on the battle fleet because he's already had a go at reporting things. It isn't [what] people do, strange though some of the agreements were at the time. So we were a bit surprised at that and in fact didn't take any notice of it, we just got on and set about getting there, regardless.

The *Invincible* journalists realized too late that they were stuck on *Resource*. Those from *Hermes* fared better, as Hanrahan explained:

We managed to get ourselves to the landing group, we did manage to make the transfer. When we got into San Carlos, we then got stuck on a ship and it took a bit more persuasion to get ourselves on the right ship, one which was going to stay there, and not one that was going to shove off. But we managed that as well.

Nicholson was having no arrangements made for him by other people. On moving from *Hermes* to *Canberra*, he met the minder, Martin Helm, who told him what was afoot:

'Well, you know, this is very embarrassing, because the war now belongs to these fellows on the *Canberra*. You've had all the exposure; now it's [their] turn.' I just said, 'Fuck off, Helm'.

He and his colleagues from *Hermes* were nonetheless transferred, first to *Stromness* and then to *Fearless*.

But Nicholson and the other *Hermes* people were fortunate. As he told us:

Of course we weren't allowed to go ashore [with] the *Canberra* people . . . They went ashore on the landing, on D-Day . . . Thank God we didn't, because we got all the pictures of 'Bomb Alley' and all the air attack, which was where the story was, because the troops didn't do anything.

Nicholson himself was particularly successful:

Mostly by luck, I think, and timing, which is luck, my report of the landing was the only one to get out that night, Friday night. Brian and I transmitted at the same time. Brian always went first, by the way, because the BBC have more bulletins than us and they're in the World Service, and there was never any argument, except on occasions when he'd obviously missed his bulletin and we were coming up to the *News at Ten* and then, right, I'd go in. When we had the PA man with us, he went last. It was Brian, then me, then him. That was the broadcasting priority. That night my report got out . . . And of course it was just in time for all the editions. So I got enormous coverage, almost every newspaper, including world-wide, had my account of the landing. Now, all those guys who had landed, of course, filed the same day, but gave it to people to take . . . It was one of the few occasions I don't blame them for not leaving the spot to come back, because they were with the Forces. Anyway . . . nothing at all got back to London that night, with the exception of my piece. So of course I got tremendous coverage and tremendous herograms from all the newspapers, from everywhere, and, when those guys came back a few days later expecting to hear that their stuff had made the front splash on every page and mine did, well, you can understand: 'Fucking hell, he didn't even land with the bastards, he wasn't even ashore'. Well, that's the way the cookie crumbles, that's the way it is.

Life on *Fearless* was infinitely preferable to that on *Hermes*. 'It was marvellous,' Nicholson told us, ' . . . a different ship with a different captain . . . liked the press and thought we had a . . . necessary job and couldn't help us enough'. Even here things nonetheless began to pall: 'It was something like ten days before we were allowed to go ashore,' according to Hanrahan. They did, however, recognize that they could well be 'a drain on limited resources' if permanently based on land and therefore requested that they be allowed ashore for day trips, coming back again in the evening. Hanrahan told the minders that he would be happy with such a facility: 'I certainly don't want to sleep in a nasty little wet trench; I'd be much happier in a comfortable bunk on board, but I'd like to go and see what's going on on shore'. He was told it was impossible. 'I just think,' he told us, 'it was nonsense.' The major obstacle to the *Hermes* correspondents getting ashore was Jeremy Moore, the land commander, who had come to think of the journalists as belonging either to amphibious or naval groups and had decided that only those who had trained with the troops and knew the officers, who had attended survival classes and were properly equipped, could be allowed to disembark. That is, those from *Canberra*. He felt the others would be a hindrance and a liability.

If the *Hermes* journalists were concerned about getting ashore, for those from *Invincible* life was a nightmare, 'stuck there', as Parry said, 'like dummies, for days'. Once the Marisat was working again, those in *Resource*, although incarcerated in a floating arsenal, did at least witness the sea strikes and could file. 'It was good stuff', Parry told us:

> I say that advisedly, but you know what I mean by good stuff . . . It was great. Argentinian air attacks every morning and we were able to file. That's typical, isn't it, to journalists: give them a typewriter and they're delighted.

The Five on *Resource* were delighted to have the Marisat. Parry told us, 'As soon as we knew where the radio shack was, we made discreet visits there'. For a time they even managed to file direct to their offices by telex, missing out the Ministry vetting procedures in London. Parry knew he was not to use 'privately' the Marisat to file direct to his office. On one occasion Parry was caught by a minder, who told him, 'You must never do it again'; as Parry said, 'We were always being told off like naughty children', but he added, 'It was too much of a temptation.' As well as the telex facilities it offers, a Marisat can also be used in the same way as an ordinary telephone link. Archer of the Press Association told us:

> I could in fact dial from the South Atlantic to be put through here [PA office, Fleet Street] and if the Editor-in-Chief wasn't here they could patch the call through to the Garrick Club.

We asked McIlroy whether this freedom from supervision meant that they sent a different type of copy, but he denied this:

> The quality of the stuff really is governed by what was actually happening anyway and anything else is superfluous in that kind of story. You don't want to try and dress up a story; there's no need to.

In other words, in a very tight place like Bomb Alley, it was quite enough simply to describe what was happening. This is interesting. On this occasion, at least, news from the Falklands was defined by the application of accepted news values to a set of objective circumstances and not by what a system of censorship allowed. The story was simply the drama that went on over the journalists' heads. As Parry recalled: 'I remember . . . there was an air attack in the middle of it and I had to cut off because I think one of the Mirages had . . . taken a bit of the aerial away'.

There were now four groups of journalists. One party was in *Stromness* and *Fearless*. The *Invincible* Five were in *Resource*, while the group from *Canberra* had divided, some disembarking with the troops on the morning of Friday, 21 May, the others – Shirley, Sabido and Bishop – waiting with 42 Commando and Colonel Vaux. (42 Commando was held back, in reserve, to help establish the critical bridgehead.) Shirley was particularly businesslike. When he heard they were about to leave *Canberra*, he put his affairs in order:

> I cabled the office [about] the conditions of my insurance policy, which was actually quite a sensible thing to do, because the NUJ Chapel Secretary cabled me back and said, 'You know, there's a hundred and twenty-five grand there, but you've got to make a will,' and I hadn't . . . So I made a will on *Canberra* . . . I gave one copy to the Captain of *Canberra*, one copy to these Ministry of Defence officials and I sent one back to the lawyer of the *Sunday Times*.

In the afternoon Shirley, Bishop and Sabido landed with 42 Commando. Once ashore, however, they began to worry that they might not be able to get their copy out, so in the early hours of Saturday, as Sabido told us: 'We just managed to con our way onto a landing-craft that took us back to the *Canberra* . . . Ten minutes later it sailed off to the edge of the Exclusion Zone.' Fearing to find themselves stuck out on the edge of action, on Sunday morning they transferred by helicopter to *Resource*, which was going into San Carlos Water to unload its cargo of ammunition. For the rest of that day, Sabido, Shirley and Bishop shared the discomfort and inconvenience of the *Invincible* Five (as, at that point, they still were). Sabido's account expresses their horror:

This guy suddenly turned round and said: 'Do you realize that you're sitting on twenty times the power of Hiroshima here?' Mirage jets were going over fifty feet away and bombs were landing fifty feet away; it didn't do our morale any good . . . All the other journalists on board from *Invincible* had been told they couldn't get off. The three of us were able to get a helicopter off, but I [left] last. I wanted to file a report on the attacks that day, and the Marisat on board only worked on telex . . . We tried to get a call through on the telex to London for them to put in a call to us . . . The Post Office in London refused to [do it] because they thought it was breaking military regulations or something, so IRN had to get permission from . . . the top of the MoD to tell the Post Office that it was quite all right. I was getting frustrated, I wanted to get off the ship, because the ship was sailing out again, so I went over to *Stromness* which was a hundred yards away on a helicopter and used their satellite, so I gave the cassette to Allan George (a minder) who was [there] with people like Mike Nicholson and Brian Hanrahan. And I said, 'Can you play that down to my people as soon as the phone's free?' I got to the helicopter-pad, it was getting dark and all the helicopters had gone. They managed to signal one down and it came and picked me up and took me back to *Resource*. I discovered that Shirley and Bishop had . . . buggered off and I just grabbed my pack and raced up to the flight deck . . . One guy . . . I knew, one of the helicopter coordinators, called down a helicopter and they winched me up . . . The helicopter dumped me in the middle of nowhere, where he had dumped Bishop and Shirley . . . in the middle of this field . . . So I had to walk to the Brigade Headquarters two miles away. It was getting dark and all you could see was this white house . . . It was the first time I'd done any real walking with all this kit . . . It was absolutely lousy, I was really getting pissed off by the time I got to this place. I was falling over and my ankles were going all over the place because I didn't have the strength to carry this back-pack which had everything in it – rations and sleeping bag on the top, clothes, boots, everything . . . two days' rations and water bottles . . . They took me down to this big wool-shed about half a mile away and Max Hastings was sitting on the top of this wool-sack striking his report and smoking a cigar and having a little shot of whisky and all the other hacks who were attached to 40 Commando were kitting down for the night. And we stayed there for the night . . . on these wool-sacks.

Sabido was thus reunited with Bishop and Shirley. As they watched first Bishop and Shirley, then Sabido, leaving *Resource*, the frustration of the *Invincible* Five reached breaking point. There, however, they were stuck.

In any case, the *Invincible* Five were ill-fitted to go ashore, as they realized when Shirley, Bishop and Sabido were deposited for their brief stay on *Resource*. As John Witherow described them: 'They came on board all kitted out, they had morphine jabs, the works, and we felt really miserable in comparison in our blue navy suits'.

On meeting the 'Miserable Five', Shirley was surprised at the contrast:

> They hadn't got any equipment, they were sitting around . . . soft shoes and sports jackets. You needed better stuff than that; apart from the fact that you needed a rucksack and a sleeping-bag, you needed . . . sweaters, thermal underwear, camouflage equipment.

Sabido, Shirley and Bishop, splendidly outfitted, took off. Those left in *Resource* were thoroughly dejected. They were now conscious that the Navy could not ensure the safety of those in the ships moored in San Carlos Water. Indeed, they had not only lost confidence in their hosts as protectors but also in the Navy's competence. Seamark spoke particularly scathingly:

> There was *Resource*, there were another three RFAs, *Fearless*, *Intrepid* and, I think, three frigates defending the water . . . You're talking about another foolhardy piece of naval planning. They'd not only got *Resource* but another ammunition-ship in San Carlos; they'd almost got them side by side right in the middle of the water. It was a beautiful target . . . The crew, were livid . . . They thought, as we thought, that it would be under the cover of darkness and away. But they kept *Resource* there for, I think, four days. A farce . . . When somebody says, 'How on earth did we win this war?' I sometimes wonder.

Understandably, the journalists complained even more vehemently:

> For two days we were being bombed and strafed by Mirages four times a day, which is hairy, I can tell you . . . We said, 'Where are our one-piece survival suits and where are the life jackets?' because every time we moved on the ship it was getting a bit chilly and a bit nasty, . . . and they said, 'Here's your one-piece survival-suit, but forget about life-jackets. We issue parachutes here . . . If *Resource* gets hit, we'll be blown sky high and the last thing you'll want is a life jacket'. I mean, these guys were really laid back about it.

After a bomb missed them by a mere fifty yards, the journalists' desire to abandon ship became overriding. Seamark again:

> On Tuesday, 24 May, we thought: Well, tomorrow's Argentina's National Day; there's no way we're staying here, 'cause if they've been trying to get us the last two days, then you can bet your bottom dollar they're really going to try and get us on the 25th. And we were genuinely frightened . . . So we eventually browbeat Goodwin . . . and we said: 'Look, we want to get off and, if you're not going to get us off, we're going to swim off'. And so we got him to write a letter saying 'This is Roger Goodwin, these are my charges; please look after them when they get ashore'.

One person was to file for all, attaching a memo to his editor asking him to distribute the material to the others' offices. McIlroy took up the story:

My main aim was to report Bomb Alley, and to that end I stayed on the ship . . .
So I insisted that, if we were going to divide our forces . . . someone should stay on
the ship . . . It was of course the day the *Atlantic Conveyor* went. In the end I
stayed . . . I had the Marisat to myself.

As predicted, Argentina's national day was celebrated with a ven-
geance. The *Atlantic Conveyor* was hit by an Exocet and abandoned
and HMS *Coventry* was lost. McIlroy was in the right place:

The MoD chappie by this time trusted me so much that any moment when we had
a break in the raids I'd be up on the Marisat, letting the office know. I had to
notify the other offices that their men were on shore and as a result my office
wouldn't use my copy as pool despatch; they used it purely and simply in my own
name, as the only one on board.

Despite the agreement to pool, McIlroy was the only one credited
when the reports were printed. We asked why. McIlroy's reply was
disarming: 'Because anyone who was daft enough to stay on board
ship on 25 May deserved to have [his] own story'.

On 25 May, therefore, the '*Resourceful* Four' finally came ashore,
armed with Goodwin's recommendation. It proved poor protection.
'We were given the bums rush by everybody,' said Seamark. Everything went wrong. According to Witherow:

We spent a day there sort of half-hiding, and then Major Norman found us . . .
told us, 'No, there's no kit for you here. You've got to go to HQ where there will
definitely be kit for you,' knowing full well, as he admitted later, that there wasn't
and that we would likely be sent back to the ship. They wanted to get rid of us
because they thought there were too many hacks. So we went over to HQ and
stumbled about midnight into this potting shed where we found Nichols and a
couple of his aides and Percival [minder] and all the others.

To Shirley, Bishop and the others, they presented a sorry picture.
Sabido sketched it for us:

All of them – John Witherow, Tony Snow, Gareth Parry and Mick Seamark – [in]
these rather peculiar boiler-suits the Navy issued them with which weren't warm at
all, and they had a great big suitcase which they said they had their clothes in and
they had a packet of cheese and pickle sandwiches which the chef had made up on
the ship as their rations.

Witherow described what happened next:

We had a tremendous row, saying: 'We insist you get us kit; you've taken us on
this entire venture . . . it's your responsibility. We're here to cover this war; not to
sit around on a ship'. And it looked quite hopeful. Percival was being helpful. We
spent that night with an Arctic warfare unit . . . We had . . . no sleeping-bags and
fortunately some really kind SAS blokes took pity on us. They'd requisitioned a
kelper's cottage and found a stove that worked with peat, and we spent the night
huddled between the sleeping bags and these SAS guys to keep warm . . . It was a
weird night.

They were woken at six with the instruction to be prepared for artillery. They were being bombarded. Otherwise, Witherow continued:

> Percival said he was going to try and get kit, and so we went down to this wool-shed where a lot of people were and went into semi-hiding hoping that they would forget about us and we would be able to borrow enough kit and stick it out.

Their optimism was misplaced. The Army told them that not only was there no kit for them but that nothing had been arranged. '*Canberra* journalists' had been assigned to units, with whom they would be marching forward, but the *Invincible* group were to wait a week until the arrival of the Scots and Welsh Guards.

Furious at the prospect of missing so much of the land war, the journalists took up the argument with their Ministry of Defence minders. Alan Percival did his best to help them but they got nowhere. Seamark begged the Army public relations officer at least to get them some kit: 'it was minus ten and going to get colder at night'. Parry was more philosophical: 'We would have made out somehow . . . At that time, you see, it was unusually warm during the day and it was only about six or seven o'clock at night that it was extremely cold, but you could always take cover in the shed or something . . .' Instead, Major Norman sent them back to Brigade Headquarters; from there they were returned to ship. The Five were outraged that having come so far, they were denied the opportunity to cover a major story. Tony Snow said angrily: 'They kept us on the ship at the height of the bloody war for eight days, right in the middle of everything. Five out of the eight national newspapers were kept on this bloody ship, in the middle of nowhere'. Snow went so far as to ask to be recalled: 'I sent a memo back to my office saying "How about sending a replacement, I'm a bit fed up".' The *Sun* agreed to send a replacement but, since the Ministry of Defence would only allow a substitute to be sent once Snow had returned to Bouverie Street, the scheme was too risky.

Even worse, during the night *Resource*, with its Marisat, had sailed out of the San Carlos Water. The four were put on another RFA, *Sir Geraint*, which had no such facility. At first the journalists refused to go aboard, demanding instead to be sent to *Fearless*.

> We said, 'No. If we're going to be put back on a ship, we want to stay in San Carlos where at least we will be able to send back stories about the air attack,' and they said, 'No, you can't go on *Fearless*. Nobody is allowed on *Fearless*'. We subsequently discovered that Hanrahan, Nicholson and the PA guys were on *Fearless* and all the other hacks were going off and on, so we were misled over that. We were put on the *Sir Geraint* and told we were going off to join the 5

Brigade, which was to arrive, as they said, in a day or so. So we went out of the TEZ [Total Exclusion Zone] and cruised around for nine days.

McIlroy, meanwhile, had left *Resource*. He too tried to go ashore but was quickly sent packing. At first he was fortunate, for he was sent to *Fearless*. Then he was 'cross-decked' to the *Sir Geraint*, bringing accounts of conditions aboard *Fearless* that made the Four the more bitter. As Witherow said:

> That really annoyed us because we were hearing about ... *Fearless* ... they're giving wonderful stuff over the intercom, you know what's going on there, and here we were on the *Sir Geraint*, the Captain didn't know very much, little access to signals, because it was an RFA, so we sat around in the TEZ playing cards, darts and reading Somerset Maugham.

Gareth Parry described life on board *Sir Geraint* as 'one of the most frustrating times of my life. To get ashore and to finally be sent back to sea simply because somebody somewhere had decided you were five too much or whatever'. He and his colleagues did manage to file a little copy, devised from briefings kindly given by the Captain from signal information, patched with intelligence from the BBC World Service, but this was small consolation. Their colleagues ashore were not only getting in information about events but were actually witnessing them as well.

The Five, eventually reunited, did get ashore. Seamark nearly lost his life. This was his story:

> I was hitching a lift from Bluff Cove to Fitzroy across the water and it was a dreadful day. I got on [this LCU] in the morning to get across to link up with ... *Galahad* and saw all the Welsh Guards there, itching to get off. But instead they took off, I think, three Landrovers and five trailers full of medical equipment for a mobile surgical unit and went back to land where ... [they] ... took off this lot. Then they went round to another part of the coast to pick up some oil-drums and then they went back to *Galahad* ... I was getting really bored because I had twice thought about getting off ... and getting a helicopter across the water, but I decided to stick it out on the LCU and went back to *Galahad*, empty finally, to take off these Welsh Guards, who I was going to go with to Fitzroy. And, as they were approaching, the big ramp that went down on the LCU locked. Failed ... so they tied up alongside it, while they tried to make hasty running repairs which would take about an hour, and of course as they were doing that bombs went whizzing past our heads into the side of the ship. So that was why I was there ... I shouldn't have been there.

Not only should Seamark not have been there; no one should have been there. It was a military blunder to have delayed the off-loading so long and exposed the Welsh Guards to attack. Pointing upwards, Seamark said:

Galahad was here and I was just this side and they were hit by two bombs; one went in and one bomb passed clean through, the hole literally no more than the top of the ceiling there, and just dug a bloody great hole, which was mind-blowing in the extreme.

It was the biggest single human disaster on the British side during the war. Seamark continued:

About a minute after it had been hit and all these people were coming over the side into the landing-craft with gross injuries, I took out my sleeping-jacket and put it round some guy's arms and gave him some water . . . everyone else was doing it. There was all this blood and gore and screaming and smoke, and for some reason, which I am almost ashamed of, I took out my notebook and started taking down notes. It was just an automatic reaction . . . I think it was probably just to save me from going round the bend . . . It's very odd this detachment, even then, really in the peak of war, you know, you've just been bombed, horrid, and people dying all around you, and I actually took out a notebook – strange.

Asked if it was good material, Seamark replied: 'Brilliant . . . You don't have to be good. I mean, you just stand there and look around and write down what you see. I was writing one-liners, just awful, a man running out of a shower with a bath towel, shampoo, naked, just things that you saw.' Shaken by the experience, he was lucky to escape with his life. We asked him how others reacted to his behaviour. He replied:

The astonishing thing was that the day after a guy came up to me and said: 'You got the story OK, you got the story OK' . . . They just wanted to make sure I'd got it. Not admiration at all, I don't think . . . they thought we were mad to volunteer to cover a war. That was probably the worst moment in my war, the *Galahad* being hit. But taking out a notebook, I don't know how to this day whether I should have done, but I did.

The memoirs of correspondents are full of accounts of such dilemmas. John Shirley, who like others became attached to the troops, described one incident:

I was at Ajax Bay one Saturday morning – I'd just delivered some copy and I was just moving around, getting a cup of tea or something, and a Sea King helicopter came. A general shout went up for people to go and help unload it. I went over because I had nothing else to do, and it was dead bodies of Paratroopers who had been killed in Goose Green . . . It was like the Burghers of Calais . . . There's a copy of it outside the House of Commons. It's a very dramatic statue of five men who are in some state of agony. There are limbs sticking out all over the place and it's a very grotesque statue. And that's what they looked like. They weren't all neat and tidy and done up in body-bags. They were all wrapped in sacking and there was blood everywhere and bits sticking out all over the place. I helped unload the helicopter and take the guys over to the hospital . . . I'm still affected by it. I went to have a look at the statue the other week and burst into tears . . .

And those are guys I'd known. I'd seen them in the bar on *Canberra*. You get very emotionally involved in it. And yet it's not my job to get emotionally involved.

Shirley was severely disturbed by having to handle the dead; Seamark, who witnessed the deaths themselves, was overcome. It was twenty minutes before he got ashore and according to him, he was in a poor condition, 'I was just walking round in an absolute daze, white-faced. I bumped into John Witherow and the guy from the PA, who grabbed me and took me inside'. He continued:

> The awful thing is, and I'm now talking professionally, that I got that story, which is perhaps one of the best stories of the war – actually being in the *Galahad*, the biggest single casualty incident. I got back to land and wrote what I thought was a fairly good piece and which everyone else said was a brilliant piece – not because I'm a brilliant writer but because when you witness something like that you only have to write what you see and it's fantastic. And so I handed it over to the Land Army PR guy, who read it and ticked it and put it into a helicopter and sent it back to Ajax Bay which was where the MoD were manning their satellite link. I went to bed that night thinking that my name was going to be splashed on every newspaper in the country, and on TV and radio around the world. Anyway, I got to Stanley several weeks later and had my first telephone conversation with the office and said: 'Have you been getting my stuff? Did you see the *Galahad* piece?' . . . They said: 'What *Galahad* piece?' It had been 'mislaid' by the Ministry of Defence which was astonishing.

In Seamark's words, his office 'went spare'. He therefore suggested that he write the story again, 'it's so embedded in my memory'. He did exactly that: 'I just wrote it again, and sent it, and the following day they did a big spread, saying, "this is what the MoD refused to let you read".'

To 'turn' the story like that is a classic example of giving what in effect was an old story 'new legs': it was not the 'runner' that it would originally have been, but it was still a finisher. Smarting with disappointment, Seamark confronted the minder he held responsible:

> I quizzed him at Port Stanley about it and, not realizing how upset about it I was professionally, he said 'We see so many stories, can't remember' . . . To this day nobody knows why it was mislaid.

Seamark's own view is that: 'presumably the last thing they wanted was to tell the British public that fifty had been burnt to death in a bomb attack, so that's presumably why it may have got mislaid. I don't know'. It is difficult to say what happened to Seamark's original story, as with much of the copy that vanished within the black hole of the Ministry of Defence. It may even be wrong to conclude that its disappearance was the Ministry's fault. There were so many links in the communication chain that it could have vanished at one of several points along the line. It may not even have reached the satellite link at Ajax Bay. As Max Hastings pointed out to us:

> Any war [produces] fantastic stories; the problem is getting them out ... Normally ... you spend about a quarter of the time looking at the fighting and three-quarters of the time commuting to and from the front trying to get despatches out, that's true of all war.

All the journalists came to appreciate this dictum. Our next chapter discusses why this was and how they coped.

4

What are we doing – competing or cooperating?

Unlike the military, schooled to cooperate, the journalists were trained to compete. Some went to extreme lengths, as Charles Lawrence explained:

> I discovered fairly early on that giving stuff in an official envelope to a helicopter was bloody unreliable. Nothing was going on one day so I got a little ammunition-chopper back to Teal Inlet . . . to find a minder who I thought would be there . . . He was living in a chicken-shed, definitely upper-class accommodation. He was a nice guy, Captain Mark Stephen, I think, was his name, and he was sitting in the doorway . . . reading through some copy, laughing his head off. I asked what the joke was and he replied that he had this neatly typed piece from one of the reporters who had got as far as Teal Inlet and no further which described how [the reporter] was watching the Argentines moving about Stanley from the top of the mountain – which he'd never been to. I [was] a bit peeved on the basis that I had actually walked to the top of Mount Kent . . . I should have been the first reporter to have seen Stanley . . . which would have made a nice story. As it happened, it was so fucking misty you couldn't see the town, so I end up writing a story saying that mist prevented me seeing Port Stanley. I then discovered that two days before some fanny sitting by a comfy stove had made the story up anyway.

Although annoyed by this episode, Lawrence, ruefully alluding to certain conventions of his profession, said: 'The tradition of the guy sitting in the hotel bar in Kabul and writing about the North is not unusual, so in a sense it conformed to that'.

Jeremy Hands was somewhat more strident in his complaint:

> It is beyond question that some very memorable reports were made by people who were taking it from secondhand information totally, who weren't there and used the words 'I saw' and 'I did' when it was absolutely bullshit, they just didn't see. They were sitting on a ship hearing other people's reports and then doing their own stuff.

Considering the risks and discomfort some of the journalists faced, it is not surprising that there were objections to this kind of behaviour. Yet Tom Smith, the *Express* photographer – described by one journalist as 'a tough little Eastender' – appeared not only surprised by the tricks journalists pulled on each other but also confused by their placid reaction to such activity: 'If photographers had behaved the way some of the journalists did, they would have come back as walking wounded'.

As a group photographers do perhaps have a greater tendency to settle scores physically, but violence was certainly in the *Glasgow Herald*'s man's mind when he caught one journalist in the signal room altering the sequence in which despatches were to be sent – the culprit had moved his to the top of the queue – and threatened dire consequences if, when he returned to the signal room, the despatches were not in their original order for transmission.

Whether one views such practices as trickery or tricks of the trade, such behaviour must be seen within the context of the journalists' working world. As Max Hastings put it, 'Some people's judgement about what was going on was appalling', and one reason why he did not wish for an anonymous pool. He continued:

> After the war was over, when I saw this story appear which was the description of a British attack that never happened, I said to the two people who had filed it: 'You must be absolutely crackers. This is the attack; it didn't happen for another week.' They said: 'Well, we just had this one chance to get the copy out the night before.' And I said: 'But you can't go filing accounts of attacks before they've happened,' and they replied: 'But you don't understand, Max. This was our one chance to get copy out.'

To file copy about something that can only be a 'racing certainty' is a dangerous practice, and therefore requires understanding. Asked if he was worried about how his performance might have been viewed by his office, Hanrahan replied:

> I think Fleet Street is actually more paranoic about things like that than television; we are a gentler organization. We are a much more understanding organization . . . I don't know whether Fleet Street editors are as awful as people make them out to be, but the reporters seem to live in fear of them.

There is, therefore, a pressure not to fail, and the desire not to be shown up by competitors who appear to be doing well is an incitement to cut corners. To file a story about an expected event whilst the communication system was available, when later it might not be, must have been a temptation too strong to resist.

By and large the pooling of copy by journalists in the field is designed to reduce pressure, but the pooling operation of the Falklands actually increased it. In effect, it was not so much a pool, as an enormous lake into which editors in London dipped. By doing so they could directly compare the performance of their man against everyone else's. The arrangement was that all editors could use any copy sent back to London; this in a sense turned each journalist into something of a news-agency operative.

This peculiar arrangement was the root cause of many of the difficulties, antagonisms, misunderstandings and recriminations by the journalists' home offices in London. Furthermore, because each news organization could raid the copy of others, there is a case to be made that there were too many journalists with the Task Force. As it was, each man still operated independently, duplicating the efforts of the others. Since all material could be shared at the London end, it might have been possible to move closer to a concept of *collective public service journalism* and away from one of *independent private enterprise.* The war would most certainly have been covered more fully, and after all competition only really flourished at the collecting point of information, not at the distribution end. Despite the fact that news organizations still liked to claim possession of 'our man with the Task Force', much of the condition for that boast lost its full meaning once exclusivity was not guaranteed; the possibility existed, or at least conditions were favourable, for a new approach based on the maximization of effort in the service of public information.

The fact that this did not happen owes as much to the industrial structure of news as to anything else, but what is amazing is that some of the journalists did not even know there was a pool, or only had vague ideas about its operation. For example, although Snow was part of the *Invincible* pool which still continued for a time when ashore, he operated in ignorance of the overall pool.

'I didn't realize', Snow told us, 'that the editors had said everyone can use everyone else's copy'. Gareth Parry, also on *Invincible*, said: 'I've no idea to this day when the pool was first employed; perhaps you could tell me . . .'

Bishop, in *Canberra*, had heard another version:

> The way it was told to us right until practically the landing was that there would be pool copy only for the first twenty-four hours and possibly the first two or three days. And even a day after the landing . . . we were saying 'When are they going to break the pool?' We thought it would only last another couple of days and we would all be back to writing individual stuff for our own individual newspapers.

Jeremy Hands, filing voice-pieces for ITN, heard nothing about a pool from his own office: 'The first time I knew about it was when a copy of the *Daily Mail* landed and there was my name by-lined on the front page, and I thought: Christ that's my name . . .'

We were told that at first the BBC refused to cooperate in the pool. Kim Sabido certainly knew of the scheme, even though, like others, he had been told that it would only be in force for the first twenty-four hours. He described the arrangements:

> It was pooled at this end, London. We all filed stuff. It wasn't put into one story and then sent back. Yes, we knew how it was going to operate because the conditions were set down at the beginning and all the way through. You'd get your report either on a tape and give it to somebody to take back and they'd play it out, or you'd come back to a ship and broadcast it . . . through the MoD. The first day I

remember coming back onto the *Canberra* to file the first reports of the landing. Three of us got back to the ship in the early hours of the morning, just ten minutes before it sailed off to the edge of the Exclusion Zone. I filed all my stuff and was told by my office that the BBC had refused the pooling arrangement, and we said: 'That's all right. We won't bother to give them your stuff.' So ITN had my stuff, BBC didn't. And then they agreed to pool everything after that, because they realized that if they didn't agree to pools they might lose out on quite a lot of stuff . . .

Max Hastings was none too pleased with the pool, even though, to the annoyance of his colleagues, it worked in his favour by providing him with many more outlets. Thinking as a freelancer, his own verdict was: 'It makes you think of all the money you could have got out of the bastards if it hadn't been for the pool'.

During the long journey south, small voluntary genuine pools were formed. One was between Bruce, for the Scottish press, and Martin Lowe, covering for the English regional press. When Lowe was replaced at Ascension by Hudson, the same scheme applied, for the representatives of the provincial press had too many clients to file for each unilaterally. Norris of the *Mail*, also on *Canberra*, said: 'There were occasions when there was such heavy traffic that we ran a pooling system on the ship. I used to do it with the *Mirror* and the *Express*. We thought it was better to stick in bunches of similar newspapers'.

It was on board *Invincible*, however, that the most firm system of pooling occurred. Tony Snow said:

For the first couple of days we were allowed to use the radio telephone, and then after that it had to be through the signals . . . Mack McIlroy . . . was one of those people who says that his job is to make his readers seem as if they're actually there. So he did some stories, literally what they had for breakfast: sausage, bacon. And some of his stuff got fairly lengthy, up to about 2000 words a day . . . And then you've got the fellow from *The Times* who's putting out quite a lot of stuff as well, and because of the difficulties in communication we would do a story that day . . . and then of course we'd have to cover whatever was happening during that day, which would go on maybe until ten o'clock at night. At one stage we were accounting for a third of the signal traffic . . .leaving the ship . . . and they said: 'You can't carry on like that. We'll have to limit the copy a bit. They did give us a certain wordage but I thought they were quite reasonable about it.

Snow described how the *Invincible* pool worked:

In . . . a closed situation in a ship, it's not an open competition, you've got to go and get some quotes from various seamen . . . If you were one person and had to run around getting all the different quotes, by the time [you get] all those quotes and do the story and bung it through the communications system, you might not get it into that day's paper. So we agreed on certain things for reaction stories . . . We would all rush around, one of us would get a couple of ratings, one of us would get one of the officers, etc., and then we would come back, do the story, and,

though we did separate stories, we would swap quotes from various people . . .
We'd have a sort of conference between each other fairly early in the morning and
say 'What's on today?' . . . and do a fairly early story, and then we'd cooperate
during the day.

It is not difficult to imagine that, with papers as different as the *Sun*,
Star, *Telegraph*, *Guardian* and *The Times*, this led to problems.
John Witherow of *The Times* explained:

When the Special Boat Squadron boarded the trawler that had been caught spying
in the Zone, we wrote a fairly straight news story about it. They (the pops) put,
'Please rewrite this in the style of pirates boarding, piratical endeavour,' just in
case they missed the point.

If Witherow did not care for the style of the popular papers they in
turn were not enchanted by the style of the 'heavies'. Snow, who
said 'we did have disagreement on a lot of points' told us:

. . . Mack [McIlroy] didn't agree that the fact that the second in line to the throne
had been put in the most dangerous position in the whole fleet was a news story
. . . He wouldn't have made it the intro; he would have included it in a paragraph
further down in the story. And I said, 'No way can you say that . . . It's a fantastic
news story . . . The Exocet is such an emotive word and he's sitting up there as the
Exocet decoy,' and he wouldn't have it . . . But we all got on very well together
really.

Cooperative though they may have been on board ship, once on
shore the *Invincible* Five were far from happy with these arrangements. Witherow was one who complained:

We pooled *Galahad* because we thought it was a big story, and we wanted to get it
off fast. We pooled that among ourselves, although the only people there were
Seamark, Saville (Press Association) and myself. Snow and McIlroy were up at
Bluff Cove and couldn't come back, so their names went on it although they
weren't there . . . I was very unhappy with that by then . . . I thought it was
ridiculous to take a risk . . . you go on writing and it's . . . going to all the papers,
so we stopped that and that caused ill feeling. McIlroy was unhappy about it.
Saville and I were quite adamant . . . There was another piece I wrote. Saville and
I spent a night in a trench with the Scots Guards, a very bad night, and we wrote a
pool piece, as if we'd all done it, and that was ridiculous. We said 'no more' after
that. This was immediately after *Galahad,* the night after it, and I saw [it] later in
the *Telegraph*; here it was with A. J. McIlroy and they were using 'I' . . . 'the rain
poured down on the Scots Guards', and that was just silly.

The others knew that Witherow was unhappy with the scheme and
wanted to end it. According to Snow, strains showed even before
the *Invincible* reached the Falklands:

We'd go . . . and get various bits of quotes and information and all exchange it. He
would be in among that exchange but at the same time he would go and talk to
various people around the ship and he would put nothing into the general talk, but

take out what we had already got, so he had everything we had plus what he'd got as well. Everybody would like to do that; they'd like to have four other reporters working on their behalf . . . He'd do that for about two days, and eventually we said: 'Go and jump in the lake. Either you want to chip in and work together; you can't just take everything we've got'.

The correspondents' difficulty was in seeing where their self-interest lay. Snow gave an example:

There was a very funny situation like that when we were on the Falklands; we were at Bluff Cove and we'd agreed, although we had split our forces, to pool our copy amongst the five of us, plus Richard Saville of the PA. We stayed at Bluff Cove and John Witherow and Richard Saville went back to Fitzroy . . . about six miles away. And we'd agreed to split our forces but bung all the stuff in each other's names so it would all go to all our papers. Now, one particular day when we were in Bluff Cove John Witherow and Richard Saville said, 'We've got to break the pool; we think it's gone on long enough . . .' Gareth Parry and Mick Seamark were in fact still in Fitzroy and we said: 'No, you can't break the pool, really, until you inform those people, because they are still working on your behalf not knowing that you're not working on their behalf.' So they said, 'Right, we'll send them a message by helicopter' . . . We said: 'No, you can't do that, because they may not get it. They'll still be working on your behalf and you'll not be working on their behalf. It's unfair.' And they said: 'Well, sorry about that. We'll send them a message, and if they don't get it that's hard luck; we're breaking the pool tomorrow, because my paper wants individual stuff from me and not from various people.' Well, at night we used to listen to the Falklands Islands broadcast coming from Britain and a couple of days earlier we had been in Darwin and we'd done another pooled story . . . And we . . . spoke to . . . the farmer at Darwin, who gave the first sort of independent account of the Darwin and Goose Green battle. And he'd been right in the middle of it in his house with his family lying on the floor, and the battle had gone right round him; I mean they'd fired shells right over him. Now, Mack McIlroy and I spoke to him and got this really quite hair-raising account and we bunged that over as well in everybody's name . . . On this particular Darwin/Goose Green story John Witherow had not spoken to this bloke and, in fact, when we were typing it he went and had a shower because it was the first place . . . where they had running water . . . This happened a couple of days before we were having this discussion about breaking the pool. We were all sitting there with about a dozen people from the Falkland Islands listening to the broadcast and on this broadcast was a review of the British newspapers, and it said: 'John Witherow of *The Times* has told the story today of the first independent report of Goose Green and Darwin battle.' It goes into fantastic quotes from this bloke about the machine-gun post and bullets going through his house and his family lying on the floor. And people were saying 'There's John Witherow over there'. Anyway, about ten minutes after this had all finished, he says, 'Perhaps we ought to keep the pool on a couple more days'. We just fell about laughing.

Pooling material is a form of journalistic cooperation, but lacks the development of any real corporate spirit. Asked if he was surprised by the charges the journalists subsequently made against each other, Michael Nicholson observed:

> Journalists are wolves by nature, aren't they? They hunt as a pack and then at the first sight of blood they turn on you. That's the way it is. I've lived with it and I'm one of the pack. I know just how uncharitable the people in the business can be.

He gave us an illustration:

> Witherow of *The Times* once had a marvellous bloody story, and we were at a helicopter base forty minutes from San Carlos and I said, 'I'm going back to transmit. Do you want me to take your copy?' And McIlroy was with him and they said 'No'. And I said: 'I'm going back, I'll get it on the telex.' But they said: 'No, it'll be all right.' They didn't trust me. I couldn't believe it. I said, 'You stupid shits' . . . so they gave it to a press officer. I then went into a little helicopter and as we took off there was something on the radio and the pilot then circled on another fjord . . . I got out to talk to another sergeant I knew in another helicopter and there was a brown paper package that had 'Press' on it. And I said: 'Where's that off to?' And he said: 'It's to go to San Carlos sometime today.' So I undid it and looked inside and there was Witherow's report and McIlroy's, all the reports I had wanted to take back. And I felt like 'sod them', but I took it back. Now, Max [Hastings] is a hard guy. Keith Graves [BBC] is a hard fellow, Martin Bell [BBC], John Humphries [BBC], they're all very hard workers and hard men in the field. And they don't give much. But I would give them a piece of my copy and be bloody certain that they would hand it over the other end as quickly as they could. But it was very odd, because the guys weren't used to it, they suspected everybody. And, whereas when you've been in the business a long time you suspect everybody, you know the guys you can trust.

McGowan and the photographer Tom Smith, both of the *Express*, admitted that distrust of their colleagues was part of the reason why they were not displeased when moved from *Sir Lancelot* to join up with other journalists on *Canberra*:

> . . . the MoD minders wanted us all together so they could keep an eye – that's point one and point two was, always being suspicious characters, we felt that while we're on this ship [*Sir Lancelot*] some bugger's getting away with murder on the other one . . . We were all happy to keep an eye on each other.

This suspicion led to strained relationships, as McGowan reported:

> A journalist is a very strange animal. If he thinks that somebody else is getting more copy out through Fleet Street than he is, he sweats, he smells a plot, which probably doesn't exist. Looking back on it now, I don't think there were any plots – it was just the circumstances of the way it was. But when . . . you listen to the World Service . . . and you know quite clearly that people are getting more stuff out than you, you get bloody angry. You think they're getting facilities that you're not getting. And sometimes when one unit would come through your unit, you'd see other journalists; yes, there would be an exchange of words.

The generally suspicious atmosphere meant it was very difficult for the minders to convince the journalists that conspiracies were not being hatched, and that events were not the result of plots. Patrick Bishop remembered the weariness of it all:

... all the professional things about nicking each other's stories. People getting on each other's nerves, you know, people always arguing that someone was screwing up the arrangements with the military and they were all putting the military's backs up, just constant arguments.

The success of Max Hastings made some of the others suspect that he was being dispensed favours, which made him an object of dislike. For example, a colleague held him responsible for the fact that at one point in the campaign *Fearless* was put out of bounds. According to his accuser, Hastings, who frequently visited *Fearless* to have his material vetted, 'swanned around' and provoked the ban. This was not so, according to Martin Helm, the MoD minder. Despite the establishment ashore of forward command posts, *Fearless* remained the main command centre; the need for secrecy at one particularly sensitive moment led to the ban. It had nothing to do with Hastings.

When matters went wrong, as they frequently did, anyone could attract blame, however remote his responsibility. John Shirley made an interesting point about the kind of animosity which developed:

> The most hostile person to Hastings was Bob McGowan of the *Express*. They were both filing stuff for the *Express*, and McGowan didn't like him at all. I don't think Ian Bruce of the *Glasgow Herald* liked him, but that was more of a class thing. Ian Bruce makes McGowan look like a softie. Very, very nice man – Glasgow tough. He's a strong Glasgow working-class. All to do with class . . . Max is Charterhouse and Oxford, smokes cigars and walked around with a stick all the time – rather pompous and quoting Homer and that sort of thing. But that's all part of the class war in journalism. I think Ian Bruce was pretty hostile towards Bishop and I as well. He thought we were both middle-class graduates from trendy papers . . . Bruce, McGowan and Derek Hudson from the *Yorkshire Post* were very hostile to Max. But Derek is a sort of Yorkshire backwoodsman really. He thinks the world begins and ends with Yorkshire. He managed, I think, to get Yorkshire into every single story he wrote . . . great colourful stories he wrote . . . a wonderful story he wrote in the week of the final battle saying, 'British troops are at the gates of Stanley. Young men eager with bullet and bayonet preparing to liberate these islands' . . . and it went on and on and all this colourful language. And right at the end he said, 'Two young men from Yorkshire sent regards home.' A little paragraph about someone from Leeds, nice stuff in a local paper sense. But I don't think he understood Max as an animal at all; he just thought he was bonkers.

McGowan and Hastings had a particularly prickly relationship, since McGowan's paper, the *Express*, also claimed Hastings, who supplied them with a column, as 'their man', to the fury of the *Standard*, to which Hastings had been accredited. McGowan was sensitive about the cost to his own reputation:

> Every paper wants to say 'by Robert McGowan; Max Hastings', as if to say 'my man is there' . . . it's called pride in the paper that wants to use your stuff. If every

day you keep seeing 'by David Norris [*Mail*]' instead of 'by Robert McGowan [*Express*]', they are going to get very pissed off. I know the way my office is, and every other journalist knows the way his office is, going to react in those circumstances, so you don't get lazy.

According to Hastings, McGowan was 'consumed with jealousy and resentment'. Hastings – Mad Max, or Commander Mad Max, to his colleagues – became the focus of tension and suspicion. This nonetheless provided amusement:

On *Canberra* someone . . . decided that Hastings was getting a bit loopy and wasn't very happy and was suffering the strain. So he called in the padré and told the padré that he'd better check out Hastings to see if he was all right. And the padré, bless his heart, came along and knocked on the cabin door and went in and said to Hastings, 'I gather you're having problems. If you'd like to talk about them,' etc., and Hastings got up – you know he's about six foot five and he said: 'I'm going out of this cabin now and I don't want to find you here when I come back.'

Hastings himself was not above playing such tricks on those whom he disliked. Pat Bishop told us of one:

We used to get these signals from the MoD coming through on the telex machine which were all stamped 'secret' . . . Max got hold of one and did a duplicate; he typed it up on the telex machine saying 'Essential that all MoD personnel accompany journalists ashore as high risk of hostilities. Vital that you are all issued with personal weapons immediately,' and stamped it 'secret' and shoved it under their door, and they were all walking around ashen-faced for about three hours.

The importance of both stories rests in what they demonstrate. To the non-participant, or outsider, both may appear self entertainment of a childish nature – the dormitory japes of mendacious schoolboys. Peter Archer's description of bunk life aboard *Hermes* with Michael Nicholson 'taking the ship very lightly and immediately electing himself mess president, scribbled it on his bunk', and the making of 'apple-pie beds and that sort of thing, all light relief', reinforces that imagery.

Any group of individuals living within total institutions, be it in prison, boarding school, hospital or on board ship for any length of time will develop an enclosed culture mystifying to those outside, but understood and known to those within. It may well be at variance with normal patterns of behaviour, in fact, one would expect it to be. One of the key indications of the development of an enclosed culture is the adoption of a specialized language, understood and used by the habituees. Another feature is the assumption of rights which on the outside would be the privileges of all, but which within the total institution, because they are unevenly distributed, operate as a means of social control. The cultural consequence of this, however, is institutionalized pettiness as jealousies develop. Viewed this way, the objections which many of the journalists harboured towards those of their colleagues whom they considered had been given favours or privileges can be seen not just as worries that the favoured might outperform them as professionals, but also as stabs of petty resentment. For example, when Jeremy Hands was asked about the press's relationships in *Canberra* he replied:

> You stick fifteen pressmen in a tin can for six weeks, you're going to get trouble, and there was trouble. Tempers flared, people didn't like each other, there were little cliques building up, little hatreds; it was all terribly petty and stupid.

Gareth Parry talked about one catalyst for quarrelling:

> . . . spending too long on the . . . Marisat. One person was Robert Fox from the BBC. There was a lot of acrimony because, as well as working for the Beeb, he was freelancing for an Italian paper and the *Financial Times*. So whenever he went to the Marisat he would be there for hours. He'd do his BBC voice-piece then a huge *Financial Times* piece and then some bloody piece in Italian. People were fuming, understandably. You know you've got deadlines coming up and you're going to miss [them]. And the *Daily Mirror* would only want to file about six paragraphs or so. It was that sort of unpleasant atmosphere.

Sabido, too, was doing freelance work, in his case for Australia and for ABC in America. Max Hastings had first arranged this but subcontracted when he discovered he had insufficient radio experience. It turned out to be less rewarding then Sabido had hoped:

> Max had told me there was a fee. When I came back and I didn't hear from ABC, I rang them up and they said, 'Send us the bill.' . . . The price Max had agreed was sixty dollars a time and they said, 'We only pay fifty dollars a time', so I didn't end up getting as much as I thought the whole thing was worth. And I'm not quite sure whether it was worth the sweat at times and the arguments.

Fox was also filing, via the BBC, for another American network, NBC. Sabido describes their difficulties:

> One time he was really getting uptight about me using the phone and I just waited about an hour and a half listening to him doing his stuff for America and everywhere else and of course at the BBC you don't just have to do one, you have to do half a dozen for all the different departments. They'd suddenly say, 'We'll hand you over to the *Today* programme to do something,' and then back and all this stuff, and then the shipping programme for the World Service and things. So I had to sit through all of that and, as soon as I started doing my stuff, he used to go bananas. But that was the only time I think we really had an argument.

Problems were real enough, especially those caused by pressure on communication facilities, but they were not helped by the hot-house atmosphere and the tempers of those involved as they failed to see beyond their own problems. Martin Cleaver for example, the Press Association photographer, complained that too many 'service personnel [were] running around with cameras trying to do news pictures and clogging up the wire back to the UK'. It was 'Salisbury Plain stuff' according to Cleaver. What really angered him was the discovery that a journalist was using 'his wire'.

Cleaver was asked if any journalists also took photographs:

> The only person, I think, who had the audacity to start sending pictures back was Max Hastings. And if I come across him there's going to be a row because Max Hastings was clogging the only picture circuit in the world that was getting pictures out of there . . . he's definitely out of order. He was using one of the transmitters; I don't know which one. If I'd seen him with the film, it would have gone straight in the bin. OK, if he wants to take happy snaps of himself to take home and play hero, great, but don't clog up my wires.

It was not egotism or the joy of taking 'happy snaps' that prompted Hastings to take pictures, but money – he sold them to a picture agency. Cleaver may have been unaware of this, but what his annoyance demonstrates is an occupational possessiveness. It was not 'his wire', but it is certainly true that, while others were transmitting, Cleaver's pictures had to wait. Although considered by the minders to be one of the most helpful and reasonable amongst the journalists, any move onto *his territory* would appear to have provoked the same kind of response seen in others. Cleaver was no more given to cooperation when it was not in his professional interest than were the writers or broadcasters. It is understandable, but since self-interest is not always obvious, it serves to underscore the difficulty of organizing a successful pool, especially when the whole principle of pooling is open to question.

To a person as individualistic as Hastings pools are repellent. His mentality is that of the freelance who sells himself and his stories:

> One thing I'm violently opposed to is consensus journalism, in that even before a pool was officially introduced a lot of those present were very keen on the idea of a pool and actually started pooling even sometimes when it wasn't necessary because they said: 'Since we are all sitting here with the same story, why bother to do individual stories, why not pool it?' I think that unless there are very exceptional circumstances, you should aim to go it alone.

Hastings was not one to apologise to his fellow-journalists for his success:

> What you always do in these situations – you just hustle from dawn to dusk. But it's part of the nature of journalism: you make friends with who you can, and you get out of them what you can. And the fact that, all right, you hustle to find a helicopter to get to Mount Kent or wherever – this is what we're all allegedly being paid to do 365 days a year. When everyone was getting hopping mad I just said:

'Well, you know, this is life, baby, this is what we are all at.' I mean I said . . . at the time . . . that, as far as I was concerned, we were not running a sort of commune here, that we all start level and that if one can't do it then the others don't. As far as I am concerned, we're in a competitive business.

We asked Hastings whether he attributed his colleagues' complaints to inexperience or to the particular circumstances of the Falklands. Rather than answering directly, he reflected on a different episode:

I remember very well one day in the Indo-Pakistan war when we all had a terrible time, nobody was getting near the front . . . At some point about thirty of us [were] all in a field about five miles behind the Indian line and an Indian general appeared and gives us a briefing and then he finishes up and says: 'Well, I suppose I'd better get back to the front now and see what the chaps are up to.' And Harold Jackson from the *Guardian* shot up his hand and said: 'Please, sir, may I come and represent the foreign press?' And the general said 'Yes'. And of course we were all frightfully pissed off and we were absolutely seething, but deep in your heart you think: Well, good for fucking Harold, if he's smart enough to pull a gag like that. You can't say that it's unfair that he did that, of course you're bloody furious and want to kill him or drive a bloody jeep over him, but if I'm absolutely honest, I think it's a matter of an approach to journalism.

Hasting's policy was the same in dealing with the Ministry officials:

The only way you actually made any impact on the minders was by heaping shit on them day and night, and this I sought to do . . . It's a question of what you expect to have done for you . . . I suppose I actually like these intensely competitive things. I started sort of chasing across Biafra in 1967 when sixty of us all set out from Lagos and fifty-eight of us were arrested and two of us by fluke got through the last roadblock because the police were taking the last lot who had tried off to prison . . . Either you respond to these things by actually liking the challenge of just struggling through and doing something, or you get thoroughly pissed off. I said when the minders laid down the rules: 'This is the biggest load of nonsense I've ever heard. And personally I'm going to say "Piss you all" as soon as we're ashore.'

And the broadcasters? One of the oddest features of the Falklands coverage was that Jeremy Hands of ITN was also working for the BBC. This came about when the Ministry decided there was space for a second television crew and, after the BBC and ITN tossed up, Hands was despatched. He told us how he worked:

Both news editors had equal claims on my time and my sign-off was British Television News . . . It made my job that much easier because I was my own competition . . .

Nicholson, on the other hand, was competing with Hanrahan, while sharing a crew. We asked Nicholson whether this gave them special problems:

When we landed, of course, or when we were under attack, it's quite common for me to just suddenly walk into camera and do a piece under fire. It's quite dramatic and people back here . . . love to see their men under bang-bangs, and it works very well. What I normally do, as the cameraman is filming, is go and whisper in his ear 'I'm going to do a piece to camera'. I know I have to stand six feet away, so he sees me coming and cuts in. The soundman's watching and he knows exactly what to do. It doesn't need 'stop camera', 'stand up', etc. But you couldn't do that with Bernard [Hesketh] simply because (1) he would have objected to it, and (2) it would have spoiled the BBC's coverage. Just as if Brian had walked in it would have spoiled our coverage of that stuff. Brian and I were hampered with one camera in not being able to do those sudden spontaneous things . . . In that respect the normal techniques that I've always employed in war reporting could not be used.

As Nicholson pointed out, the Falklands was really a radio war, with television taking very much second place. This made it all the easier to produce a vivid account of what was going on without leaving the communication-ship, simply by analysing information from other journalists' copy. Whereas video reports from Hanrahan and Nicholson were sent to Britain in the same packet as Cleaver's rolls of film, their voice cassettes were moved by Marisat.

When Nicholson realized that film was taking between ten days and three weeks to reach the Ministry of Defence, he abandoned television for radio:

I left Brian and Bernard for days. On one occasion I didn't see them for four days and they were off filming and shooting stuff and I wasn't part of it. I was more concerned with putting back the radio spots, because the BBC had Robert Fox who was putting back radio, but we didn't. We had Jeremy Hands, but he was working way up with the Marines and wasn't coming back for days on end. So I was the lone representative for our company. I was making more use of radio than I was of television. I cheated in that Brian would send back tapes from where he was filming – voice tapes, cassette tapes – with a little note saying 'Mike, will you get this played to London', so I would. I'd hear his stuff going out and I would take notes, so that when the film package came through I had already recorded my commentary from what I'd heard Brian saying, so I wasn't out of pocket in that way. It was a slight cheat, but I never said I was there. I've had a lot of flak recently. The *Daily Mail* were going to publish a story that I sent back three [eye-witness] reports on one day . . . [when] I couldn't possibly have covered all those stories . . . I said: 'Great, go ahead, mate, and I can retire tomorrow.' I knew the three stories they were referring to. One was the story about the telephone call Brigadier Wilson made – you know, 'Are there any Argentinians there?' and whatever his name said, 'No, there are not'. One was about *Monsoonan*, a little ship that he commandeered to take the Ghurkas and supplies up round Bluff Cove. I reported on both these stories, and the MoD held them up for four days and released [them] on the day of my report on the *Sir Galahad* thing. So ITN ran all three stories on the same evening.

We asked Brian Hanrahan what he thought about this:

If it was a feature item . . . it's not what I would do. If it was strategic, then I would do it, yes. If it was information about what was happening, then I would incorporate it because I would need that to fill in the whole picture.

Hanrahan felt that Nicholson's use of his material was legitimate, not simply because he understood the ground rules of the pool but also because:

Nicholson took a different attitude. He went back to the *Fearless* during that week because he wanted to do a radio piece, but I wanted to stay up and do television. I could write a feature and say what was happening as well in Goose Green as I could back in San Carlos Bay. Nicholson decided to go back to San Carlos Bay and do it there. He had the only access to the phone, but on the other hand I was with the camera team so, if you like, I thought I was better placed to do a television job and he thought he was better placed to do the radio part.

Nicholson was delighted in his new-found role:

This was the first time I'd done any extended radio reports and I enjoyed every minute of it. A television reporter is simply a caption writer, all we do is just write a few words over a picture and, if the cameraman has done his work, then the picture tells the story . . . For the first time in my life I could go out for a couple of days, scribbling notes, come back and write a story that was perhaps ten minutes long. The account of the *Galahad* thing apparently went for about ten to eleven minutes. I've never had a film that long on ITN. But there . . . you were painting pictures. It was an enormously exciting sensation . . . Suddenly I was back in journalism, actually writing.

Hanrahan, on the other hand, was emphatic about the benefits of being with the camera crew and witnessing events first-hand: 'If you've been there it shows through'. Asked if he had seen other journalists' copy and, if so, whether he could have used it, he replied:

In fact, I saw nearly all of it pass through. I suppose I could have used it if I had wanted to, but it . . . was stuff like 'How I waded ashore and I had now dug in and it was cold'. All it was telling me was some details about how people were living and what it was like, which I was getting anyway from people who were coming back. So I didn't want to know that Alastair McQueen [*Mirror*] was living in a fox-hole with three men, but no doubt from his point of view . . . it was a good story . . . There was nothing in it for me.

Hanrahan evidently thought he had the right to the others' material, an understanding of the pool which differed from that of his colleagues. We believe this was so because of his, and Nicholson's, special situation. As they shared a television crew, they developed closer coordination than the press journalists enjoyed, a connection, in fact, much nearer to the true meaning of 'a pool'.

John Shirley was in no doubt about the experience of the press:

The pool didn't work. [It] wasn't really thought through properly. When it was imposed [on us, we knew] that we were all going to separate units. But what happened – and I have this only from the MoD officials – was that . . . everybody tended to write the story which said . . . 'All over the Falklands they are doing this, that and the other.' 'General advances moving forward on fourteen fronts.' And everybody tried to write that story from the position of one unit, so . . . very repetitive material was coming back. Whereas, if we'd stuck absolutely strictly to reporting what was happening with our unit . . . more varied copy would have appeared.

The journalists were understandably torn. Professionally, they were required to report both the highlights – occasions of historical importance – and the everyday detail of the campaign. They were, moreover, professionally obliged to compete. To ask them to depart from the principles and to work together was to demand too much. They continued to compete for information and fought amongst themselves. This baffled the minders and the military, as Shirley reminded us:

As I say, the whole military were about cooperation and obeying orders and if the colonel said do something it was done. Whereas they suddenly came up against this group of probably the most anarchistic, competitive group of individuals you could meet. We found it difficult to cooperate.

The psychiatrist attached to the Task Force, Surgeon–Commander Morgan O'Connell, forecast that the journalists would suffer exceptional strain, their competitiveness and lack of cohesion making it harder for them to support the harsh conditions of the expedition. David Norris agreed:

It's a very good point, I think, because when you see the military people who are all in very tight-knit little groups and look after each other; they're all great mates and personal friends as well as colleagues . . . They have this state of mind and I think he's quite right that journalists tend to operate in cutting each other's throats.

As time went on, however, some of the journalists modified their behaviour. Ian Bruce told us that:

Initially there was great rivalry but it tailed off. When we got ashore cooperation increased . . . there was no point in cutting someone's throat for a story; he'd get his throat cut very easily by staying where he was, probably.

The patterns of cooperation or, at least, understanding – were interesting. It might be expected, for instance, that the *Sun* and the *Star* would be natural rivals but, as Seamark explained:

The battle between the two [papers] is largely on a higher level than us . . . it was quite pleasant to have somebody who you were familiar with alongside you, so the competition didn't actually materialise. I think we came to a sort of tacit agreement, we're both in this and it's going to get pretty hairy and hard work, so let's not make it difficult for each other, and in fact we didn't.

Shirley said of his relations with Bishop (with whom he had shared a cabin):

> I think the element of competition was reduced because we both had a fairly good idea of what our papers wanted and they were slightly different things. The *Observer* tends to play up its individual writers more. Pat's a very good colour writer – he's a better writer than I am. The *Sunday Times* wanted more information; they wanted probably harder stories. I knew I was feeding into the sort of 'Insight' gang bang, so in a sense we were writing for different markets . . .

To some extent the journalists were infected by the enforced mateyness of the voyage. As Shirley recalled, they got up at seven:

> You did half an hour's PT, you had a shower and then you had breakfast. And you then tried to create a routine for yourself . . . There were people who tended to sit around – hang around in the bar or, get a bit morose or try and get drunk or behave like it was El Vino's.

Asked whether he had ever seen this sort of supportive behaviour among his colleagues before, he admitted:

> No, actually I haven't . . . You get a level of cooperation, but nothing quite like that, no . . . I had lunch with Max last week and he said that there would just never be anything like it again.

By temperament Hastings was, as we have noted, the least inclined to cooperate. As the campaign came to an end, as its danger faded and the correspondents' difficulties ceased, their independence reasserted itself. According to Ian Bruce:

> I think once we reached Stanley and the cable and wireless offices reopened, friendships that had been formed disappeared. That's a good test of . . . old newspaper instincts, where people became rivals again. [It] didn't happen to the degree it probably would in Fleet Street or back here in Glasgow, but it happened anyway. Stories were still shared if someone got something half-decent, but there was a certain amount of rivalry when we had free communications again.

Some relationships did not cool even when the journalists came home. Jeremy Hands:

> I've got some enormously good friends out of it. Some of the blokes I was down there with I'd do anything for, I have the most enormous respect for. There's a couple I wouldn't spit on if they were on fire. I thought they behaved atrociously.

The experience was summed up by Pat Bishop:

> I only actually made one and a half friends there, which is quite surprising really. *I made more friends among the military than I did among the journalists*. I'm vaguely friendly with Max and John Shirley now and I'm friends with John Witherow, but

all the others . . . if I never saw them again it wouldn't upset me. I'm sure they feel the same about me. I'm sure most people feel the same about each other in that respect. On the day that Stanley fell we were talking and saying that we would have a big party when we got back and hire HMS *Belfast* and invite all the Army blokes up and all the rest of it. And after about five minutes somebody said: 'Fools, we will never do it; we'll never want to see each other again.'

5

Is this really
what we came for?

As we have seen, before they had landed the journalists had manoeuvred, with varying success, to ensure that they were attached to favoured units. Like the arrangements for pooling, these assignments were in some cases to be no more than temporary. Hastings told us that he warned his colleagues: 'I said quite clearly and Bob Fox said the same, "Well, this is fine for when we go ashore, but once ashore you've got to play it by ear as usual".'

Ian Bruce described what happened:

I think naively most of us hadn't been to a full-scale conflict at any time in the past. Hastings had. From the start he was determined to use the best means of communication possible once ashore, despite a gentlemen's agreement on the day we were all transhipped . . . that each guy would stay with the unit to which he was assigned no matter what, since a pooling system would operate and no one would lose out in the end. Hastings then used the old-school-tie system to some degree, also his record as a war correspondent, also his presence which is quite considerable, to cadge, cajole or force people to supply transport. The first indication we had that any change had been made in that agreement was in the march across East Falkland when Charles Lawrence and I saw a helicopter touch down. We had been marching for three or four days by that time and it debouched Hastings and Fox who stayed one night and departed by helicopter again to leave us to walk on. We had no choice.

Or, if they had a choice, they chose to stay with the group to which they had been assigned. At first, in any case, some simply seemed more fortunate than others. McGowan, for instance, felt that:

Hastings was in a sense lucky – it's not a criticism . . . and chaps like Hanrahan were lucky. Circumstances unfolded where he was. He was at San Carlos Water with 40 Commando. All the ships were there, so Hanrahan was still there, so they were seeing all these dramatic air raids and the *Atlantic Conveyor* . . . There were many times, I'll be completely honest with you, when I wished I wasn't with 3 Para, but was down there. We couldn't all start storming over the beach head and saying 'Sod it, forget the war, we want this'. It wouldn't have been fair to the pool. In other words we had a responsibility to people like Hastings and Hanrahan to do our reporting, because otherwise it would have been uncovered and, there would have been a major void in the war . . . But, I used to envy Hastings like hell, thinking, Christ, he's getting all this stuff in and I'm in a place where the advance has stopped. The highlight of my day is whether the chicken supreme is going to

come out all right . . . Then the major battles started. After Goose Green, there
was a change and there were the battles of Mount Longdon, Two Sisters, Harriet
. . .

It is difficult to believe that McGowan felt a responsibility towards
Hastings, but equally his reponsibility to the pool was misplaced.
Given the way it actually operated in London, to stick with the
demands for obedience to its rules made as much sense as a fox's
conniving in its own death by acceding to requests to run slower
because the hounds cannot keep up with the chase. Bruce, who
shared McGowan's sense of reponsibility, nevertheless had a grud-
ging respect for Hastings, who seemed to owe responsibility to no
one but himself. As Bruce informed us: '[He] made use of the only
available channels of communication, and for that I admire him. It
was unfair in the context of what had been agreed. But again, as he
told me later: "You never trust anyone in a war".'

Hastings was on occasion prepared to point out the benefits of
cooperation; although it seems a bit like believing in religion for
other people, he told us:

> There were about eighty different stories with the Task Force, there was the story
> about what the Harrier pilots were doing . . . what [the] helicopters were doing,
> the gunners . . . the engineers . . . and in fact a large number of those never got
> reported by anybody because of the way that things worked out. I said, quite late
> in the war, when three or four of us were gathered together, 'Somebody ought to
> be out with the carriers reporting on what the Harriers are doing'. It was terribly
> obvious that the Harriers' contribution to the war was decisive, to which there was
> a howl of people saying: 'Well, if you feel that strongly about it, you fucking well
> go out there, because we're not going to spend another minute on Hermes'.

He continued, disarmingly:

> It would have been in everybody's interest really if there had been a bit more
> direction of the correspondents, sensible direction, even if they drew lots for it and
> said: 'Somebody has got to cover what's happening out on the flat ship and what's
> happening there and somebody has got to do this that and the other.' There was
> no directing of the correspondents of any effective kind.

Hastings was well aware of his own strategy:

> I don't think one can make valid generalizations for other people. I can only say
> that this is how I perceived my job to be and on Mount Kent, you know, when I'd
> gone up with the SAS and 42 Commando, I stayed one night and in the end about
> two nights on Mount Kent, but I got down again as soon as I could and they said:
> 'Aren't you going to stick around because this is where it is all going to be at'. But
> since you've actually been there for two or three hours you've seen all you're
> going to see.

Bruce was, as we now know, over-optimistic in believing that,
because copy was pooled, no one would lose out. Since stories were

pooled not in the Falklands but in London, each reporter's material was, in general, individually by-lined. Their offices at home were thus asked to compare each man's performance with that of the others. It was almost impossible for editors in London to appreciate the difficulties under which their correspondents worked, not least the problems that they had in communicating copy. The choice was often not so much between staying with a unit or moving among them, rather, reporters had to decide whether to go with a unit or remain in a place from which they could file. McGowan made this point:

> I think in hindsight when you bear in mind that some people got a lot more copy out than I did because they were back at base, in terms of copy and in terms of making my mad masters happier, it would have been better. In terms of covering the war – which, after all, was why I was sent there – no, . . . because I wouldn't have seen half of what was going on . . . I don't know if you saw *The Task Force South* TV thing with Brian Hanrahan. Brian was with the ships and it was fantastic, but you did not see any fighting inland because he had to stay with his crew there and it was bloody good film, but you can't be everywhere. If you just stayed at the bridgehead area, yes, you could communicate, but what would you be communicating?

Charles Lawrence, on the other hand, felt some regret:

> To be frank, by the end of it I felt a bloody fool for all the hardship I'd had, because I did make a decision to stay at the front – partly at first, I admit, because I was enjoying it . . . but at the end of it I felt pretty sick – I could have done better by living in the comparative comfort of the Brigade sheep-shed along with the other hacks, or indeed on *Fearless*. A lot of them spent more nights on *Fearless* than they spent anywhere else, they could have wine and food and central heating.

Those who did not stay at Headquarters had a very difficult time of it.

The physical hardship and danger of the expedition were, not surprisingly, less of a shock to the troops. Their initial suspicion of the journalists derived in part from their belief that the correspondents would be a nuisance, that they would slow them down. The troops remained wary but, where the journalists showed that they could keep up, attitudes improved. McGowan described his experience:

> You would march with them as far as you were able or allowed . . . There were times when a company would be going ahead to do nasty things in the middle of the night, but they wouldn't let you go because physically you could not have kept up with them. They were very fit people. I lost two stone marching.

The training the journalists had done on the voyage had put some of them in better shape than they had enjoyed for years. Even so, McGowan admitted:

In fairness . . . the major advances through the night were slowed down because of us. I wouldn't say by very much, but we probably did. I don't think we got in the way as such, apart from that, because they gave us work to do and we had to do it. They don't dig your trench for you, they don't cook your food, they don't do anything for you, you've got to do it yourself. And also, since you've got nothing else to do, you've got to wade in and do things for them. We were carrying ammunition, not because we wanted to, but because they said: 'If you don't carry it, you can't come. We don't take passengers'.

The general attitude appears to have been that if the journalists could keep up, they could accompany the troops. Charles Lawrence and Ian Bruce were, according to Lawrence, 'by accident both sent to 45'.

Andrew Whitehead, . . . the Colonel . . . , is a really hard man. His attitude from the start, when we first went over to *Stromness* and had dinner with him, was 'bloody journalists . . . well, what do you want to do?' We said humbly, 'We just want to see it happen,' and he said, 'Fine, if you can keep up with us. You'd better go and see my quartermaster'. So we . . . got equipped and from that point on, to use a military phrase, his attitude was 'if we could hack it, we could be there' . . . as far as we knew, that was what a lot of other people were doing. But . . . the 3 Para, for instance, decided that the hacks they had weren't up to it and wouldn't let them join in. They made them very comfortable in the farmhouse at Port San Carlos and said 'Wait there'. Huw Pike, the Lieutenant Colonel, said: 'you stay where you are and I'll send a helicopter when I'm ready'.

Even Les Dowd, an extemely fit man, was refused permission to go with 3 Para. Some of the soldiers seem to have been prepared to deal firmly with stragglers. When Derek Hudson joined the Task Force at Ascension he noticed that all was not harmonious:

I was behind the TV crews and we'd just been to the lifeboat crew and briefing. I was shaven by then and I just had a camouflaged windproof on, so I was lost in the whirl of uniforms, but there were several of the troops making pistol-type gestures towards the TV crew who didn't notice the troops on the flight down. They were saying 'They look like Argentinians'.

'They probably thought,' Hudson explained, 'they would get in the way'. Ian Bruce said that attitudes varied but that antagonism could be perceived:

All the way through every echelon of the hierarchy of a battalion. There was hostility. There was friendliness. Some of the Marines reckoned the press . . . would be a liability, and if they went into action they didn't want their actions reported anyway. They changed their minds. There were death threats on board. Les Dowd was threatened and I was threatened: 'You get in the way and we'll shoot you'.

The death threats not only worried Bruce but also puzzled him:

It's surprising, after their involvement in Northern Ireland for so long, that the Marines, and the Army especially, hadn't come to some kind of living arrangement with the press. Some of them seemed to think that going into a shooting war the press would report incidents . . . which would possibly put them in a bad light. I think they felt that if they had to march a long way the press would get in the way and would be a problem.

The threats were made more plausible by explanations that since British and Argentinians used the same type of rifle, no one would know which side had hit any unfortunate journalist. This was not wholly true. The British used a self-loading rifle, the 'SLR', the Argentinians the Belgian-designed FN. They both, however, are 7.62 calibre weapons. Since the cause and likelihood of death in battle is so obvious as to make post-mortems unheard of, the troops' mentioning of the similarity of weapons can only mean that they were having fun making threats at the journalists' expense.

But when the fighting started, the journalists' presence was welcomed – particularly by the battle troops, who felt that there should be a record of even the most harrowing episodes. Because the journalists moved between units (especially after Bluff Cove), and because they could talk to senior officers, they were better informed than most of the combatants and so themselves became a source of news, giving bits of information about other units. Consequently the journalists occupied twin roles, one ancient, one modern. As local travellers they were story tellers dispensing broadsheets, describing events; as international reporters they gave news that kept the men's families informed of their progress and deeds. Relations could nonetheless be strained to breaking point by individual conduct that re-affirmed the military's original low estimate of the journalists as a group. The most serious incident was the discovery that Jeremy Hands had at Teal Inlet used a settler's telephone to contact McGowan at Ascansia, way up near Mount Longdon, to tell him that the Paratroopers were going to attack Mount Longdon.

I was at Teal and McGowan was at Ascansia . . . Bob asked the people at Ascansia if he could use the civilian phone line to phone me to ask me what I thought was going on at Teal Inlet, and he said to them, 'Is the line safe?' and they said: 'Yes, it's been pulled down the other side of Ascansia house . . . nobody else can hear.' So he phoned me and I wasn't there and he left a message for me to call him back. So I went to the phone at Teal Inlet and I said to the woman, 'Is this line safe?' not knowing that Bob had asked the same thing, and she said: 'Yes, it's totally safe because it's down in both directions. There's just one line from here, one secure phone line.' So I phoned McGowan and told him the whole bloody works, about everything, where the British were, where the Argies were, who was doing what, what the plans were, who was in charge, which soldiers were doing what, the whole works. You know, no question about it, if the Argentines had been listening we'd all be dead . . . But I was convinced that it was secure. Idiot though

I was, I didn't go to the General and ask if I could use the phone; he would probably have said 'No.' I said all this to McGowan, came out of the telephone and I was jumped on by a Marines officer, thrown in front of the Brigadier who was purple with rage, jumping up and down saying 'You've blown the whole bloody thing. This is going to cost lives. I'm seriously thinking of having you sent home.' He really went bonkers. And eventually, as he raged and raged, he said: 'Well, I'm not going to send you home. I'm going to give you one last chance. Be a good boy, fuck off and don't do it again.' So I felt suicidal because he said: 'Everything on that phone call was picked up in Port Stanley, and listened to by the Argentinians, and they will doubtless act on it.' I'd cost lives, I'd probably lost the war. I was ostracised by the other blokes on the press. Max Hastings was sticking a knife in every chance he could . . . I very nearly thought about doing a Captain Oates and walking out and saying I'd be a long time. Three days later, the Colonel of the SAS, Mike Rose, saw me on *Fearless*, skulking, avoiding people, and he said, 'Oh God, are you still in Purgatory?' and I said, 'Yes' and he said, 'Haven't they told you?' and I said, 'What?' and he said, 'They knew ten minutes later that the phone line had been secure and the Brigadier had specifically said, 'Let the bastard sweat.' So I went to the military minder, a bloke called Mark Stephens, and said, 'I hear it's all OK,' and he smiled and said, 'Yes' and I said, 'Well, why didn't you tell me?' and he said, 'Well, I had orders from the Brigadier not to put you out of your misery.' And I gave him a mouthful and, honestly, I went off and I cried, partly relief. That is the gospel truth. That is what happened. I don't mind that coming out because it's true. It's interesting, Hastings, Sir Hastings, said: 'No cooperation. Hands has fucked it. We'll never get any more help from the Ministry, or from the military at all. We've blown it. We've probably lost the war as well.'

According to Robert Fox, 'Julian Thompson was absolutely devastated on learning about the phone call' and the incident 'absolutely changed the whole atmosphere'. In reporting terms the outcome, so Fox said, was that 'I wasn't allowed to go to an O Group again'. None of the journalists were. An O Group, or Orders Group, is the meeting where the battalion commander gives his orders before battle; but not only were the journalists banned from these, Brigadier Julian Thompson wanted to stop all news-gathering ashore and, according to Shirley, 'Send us all back to the ship'. Thompson's angry and indiscriminate response of banning all O Group attendances and threatening to banish all the journalists back to ship is a very good example of the suspicious way in which the military considered journalism. If that had not been the case, then more individual discrimination would have resulted. In other words, had the journalists been accepted as a legitimate presence such general disapproval would not have occurred so readily.

For the journalists themselves, one of the more annoying reporting acts of the war was Hastings's privileged use of the SAS communications system to file a story direct to Britain about their exploits on Mount Kent. The background to the 'coup' however

provides very good insight into the Army's mystified understanding
of the journalists. For example, Hastings was asked whether his
helicopter-hopping between units did not make the Army look on
him as a 'carpetbagger'.

> I think I would be seen as a carpetbagger anyway. Journalists are odd people,
> especially in the eyes of soldiers; the funniest case was over this business of Mount
> Kent; it's one of these things that's funny with hindsight. What actually happened
> was that of course as soon as I knew there was going to be a landing on Mount
> Kent this was an obviously good thing to be in on. They had a helicopter lift to
> take one company of 42 Commando and three or four SAS – there was an SAS
> patrol already up there. And Shirley and Bishop and Sabido, who were all
> attached to 42 Commando, were all told it's going to be really tough up there and
> disagreeable, and you don't really want to go, do you? And they said 'No'. Well,
> then I went to Dave Nichols [Brigade Press Officer] and said, 'I'd very much like
> to go,' and after a bit of hassling they said: 'Well, it's going to cause a bit of upset
> with 42 journalists, so we'll send you with the SAS so nobody can say that you're
> attached to anybody.' But the whole idea was that none of the other correspon-
> dents were supposed to see me on the way up, to avoid any aggro with them. But
> then we had to stop on the way to refuel – in fact on the landing-zone where 42
> were joining us. And there on the landing-zone are bloody Shirley, Sabido and
> Bishop who said, 'Where the fuck are you going?' and I said, 'I'm going to Mount
> Kent,' and then there was the most appalling row. Now, the Marines at this point
> were actually very frightened. Because nobody actually knew what was on Mount
> Kent and nobody knew what the bloody hell was going to happen up there. And
> here were all these blackened Marines loaded with kit and four journalists fighting
> bloody tooth and nail. And eventually Sabido, Shirley and so on give up and stalk
> off into the night swearing that they'll murder me if it's the last thing they'll do.
> One of the Marine officers came over to me and he said: 'Are you surprised that
> we all think you're a right bunch of cunts, that here we are on the eve of the
> hairiest operation of the war, and all you buggers can fight about is who is going to
> come and report it?' And the idea that, whatever we did, that any of them were
> actually going to respect us is absolutely ridiculous. I suppose, I just took that for
> granted from day one. I thought, well, even if you charged out of bunkers hurling
> grenades you'll still be seen like that.

In the nervousness which precedes a battle in which you might die,
to watch the journalists squabble amongst themselves for the privilege of being there was so incomprehensible that it is not difficult
to understand the Marine officer's abusive dismissal and a good
indicator that, no matter how much the journalists began to identify
with the troops, there was a limit to the acceptance of them.

Despite fluctuations in the popularity of the journalists, one thing
was clear: the troops did not want passengers. The press had to
work their passage. McGowan described how exhausted he became:

> [It] wasn't like Vietnam or the Middle East where there was a clear-cut Army
> there and a clear-cut Army here; there was just fighting all over the place . . . I'd
> never dug a trench before, digging the garden was all I'd done . . . There was one

time when I was completely knackered . . . I thought: I can't go on any more. And the sergeant came up to me and said, 'Have you got a map?' and I did have [one] I'd stolen from one of the command posts, which had all the proper grid references, all the kilometres . . . So he said: 'You're there. It's going to be daylight in five hours. Stay there. If no one picks you up by daylight, don't worry: one of the snipers will find you'. It was amazing – like Superman changing in a telephone-box – suddenly I had a burst of energy and I caught up with him. But, yes, they would leave you . . . if they'd stopped and daylight came they would be in the open with high ground all round them and then they'd be in trouble. So they would not stop for you.

Bruce, who had collapsed completely, was encouraged to continue by a soldier who hit his legs with a rifle-butt. Though he did not appreciate this attention at the time, he was afterwards grateful; safety lay in sticking with the troops.

Each journalist knew that he was not immune from attack. Jeremy Hands said:

I could see planes coming towards me dropping bombs and that happened twice, three times, and I thought: 'That's it; I'm dead. Lie on the ground and suck your thumb.' I can remember thinking on the occasion when troops were pushing forward at night, 'They've certainly planned this wrong': [I] asked the guy in the same tent, 'What happens if they've done a flanker, and they've dropped thousands of paratroopers behind us and they're marching up behind us?' [He said] 'We're fucked'.

He continued:

Looking back, people remember Goose Green, H. Jones and people getting killed . . . In fact it was three weeks living ashore in holes in the ground and 95 percent of that time was cold miserable frustration, 5 percent was sheer stark terror, and it's the 5 percent people remember.

As we have noted, the psychiatrist with the Task Force, Surgeon–Commander Morgan O'Connell, estimated that because the journalists were not only unfit but also competitive they would suffer the strain and stress of war much more than the troops. This observation was frequently related to us by the journalists in almost joking fashion as if O'Connell was wide of the mark and the journalists did not live up to his diagnostic expectations. Nevertheless, some of the journalists did show signs of acute distress and at a level great enough to give rise to concern about their ability to continue. Whilst all personnel during a red alert and especially during an attack itself show signs of obvious fear and tenseness, once the danger has passed relief takes over, and normal posture, movement and expression quickly return. One of the key indications of a deteriorating mental state is that, for those in trouble, that does not occur. For them the anxiety created by the battle remains for a much longer time and this length of time increases with each attack until the person is in a state of permanent agitation, eventually reaching the point when he can no longer function normally or has a complete breakdown.

A number of the journalists reached such a state. They either no longer wanted to go on, and in some cases could not, or they started behaving strangely. We are not talking here of single events such as the fabled Bruce 'bayonet attack' on Hastings, which from the assailant's point of view was a rational although perhaps exaggerated action prompted by a particular clear-headed dislike but, rather, of the effect of 'layers' of stress gradually applied over a period of time with the result that the individual's own personality becomes distorted. One particular minder described how one of the journalists who was taking longer than most to regain his composure after a red alert approached him on one occasion with a very odd expression on his face. The journalist stood for some time looking at him strangely and then said in an accusing but also peculiar way: 'You've got better equipment than me.' The minder regarded this unnerving incident as an obvious sign of stress.

The journalists themselves were aware of the fact that some of them were finding it less easy to cope with the stress. The minders, however, provided the best source of information about this. Despite the antagonism the minders may have felt towards some of the journalists, their diaries plainly relate the facts and are not discursive. These diaries are clearly not medical records, but the entries do support the case that severe stress was occurring amongst the journalists, particularly when added to other known facts.

Given the conditions faced, it is not surprising that some of the journalists should suffer from stress. The main reason for raising the question of this kind of 'casualty' is to underscore not simply the difficulties faced but the fact that no journalist escaped such pressure entirely and that this pressure affected both the way they behaved and the way they saw things. All the minders interviewed emphasized that the journalists held to a very conspiratorial view of the world, seeing intrigues and plots where none existed. It was mentioned, for example, that Shirley, Bishop and Sabido went ashore in the afternoon of the landings because they were with a reserve brigade and, though it was understandable that they might worry about the advantages of those who did land in the morning, Shirley immediately felt that it was the result of a devious design rather than an unfortunate turn of events. He complained to Martin Helm that the minders were biased towards the tabloids because they were right-wing and pro-Tory papers. He even went so far as to suggest that had the *Express* and the *Mail* (who had gone ashore in the morning) been in his and Bishop's position they would have been able to buy their way out of it. In the end Shirley, who was considered one of the more reasonable journalists, accepted that Helm hadn't been 'nobbled', 'but only just'. One of Shirley's worries was that he thought McGowan and Smith of the *Express* would 'buy up a Falklander'.

All concerns and worries are bound to be exaggerated under stress, with half-thoughts becoming full truths; furthermore – and it is something which the minders found hurtful and difficult to understand – the savage insults that were heaped on them, during the day could then be followed by pleasantries over an evening drink as though nothing had been said. Journalists are probably more skilful than most in acting aggressively to get what they want; it is, however, also likely that these angry insults were on occasion the result of stress. As Shirley informed us: 'Those MoD minders were just the easiest people to kick'.

The minders themselves suffered from the strain of working under difficult and often frightening conditions. Thus, according to one of his colleagues, one minder became obsessed with the notion that one of the journalists had stolen his sleeping-bag. He would not leave the subject alone even though it was pointed out that, even if it was the case, he could easily obtain another one. Allan George, who travelled down with the main body of the press corps in *Canberra*, was subjected to more abuse than any of the minders and said that, pressed from all sides, he felt that to have remained in *Canberra* would have resulted in a nervous breakdown. He observed: 'My main overriding memory is of being constantly tired.'

The reporting background, therefore, the situation within which the journalists went about their work and the manner of their operations, is complicated by the factor of stress. It could not be escaped from and coloured practically all relationships and behaviour. Some, of course, faced up to the problems inherent in their situation and therefore fared better.

What bothered the journalists, however, was that given all the difficulties, particularly the element of danger, there was a poor return on risk.

For most, the main annoyance was not the physical risk but the overall difficult setting within which they were trapped and unable, as they saw it, to operate effectively as journalists.

Seamark attributed Parry's defection to his believing that the struggle wasn't worth the trouble: 'He'd had enough. The *Guardian* wasn't convinced about this war, he certainly wasn't and was very fed up with the way the MoD was messing him around, and he just got on a ship in San Carlos Bay and sailed north'. The most frustrating aspect of the enterprise was the difficulty of getting copy back. John Shirley described it to us:

> . . . the ship sailed away, so we didn't have [anywhere] to go . . . you could never find these damned people (the minders) when you wanted to . . . it took sometimes six to eight hours to get from your camp back to the satellite station – that's a bloody long time and it was freezing cold and it was raining . . . I went back with Ian Bruce . . . once. It took four helicopter rides and then we walked for six miles across the bloody islands. We then got a boat, and the boat nearly overturned. We got to *Fearless*, where the MoD official was . . . *Fearless* has a dock at the back and you just sail into the back of it normally. The dock was raised because *Fearless* was about to sail, so they put a rope ladder down to get us up . . . Ian got on to the ladder and fell off into the sea. Well, it's fucking cold in the Falklands – the military only give you fifteen minutes' survival-time in the water. We managed to get Ian out, but all his notebooks got lost, they all went down in the sea, so . . . his copy was lost and he had to re-do his copy. I know it's mundane stuff, but people aren't used to living like this. These are guys who are used to living in four-star hotels.

Bruce agreed: 'I may come from Glasgow but I'm not used to living in holes in the ground'. And Jeremy Hands:

> Normally you fight wars from the Commodore or the International or the Sheraton. You nip back and have a Scotch and you lie back and phone your piece over, or you pop across the road to the TV station and send down your cassette. Like in Beirut, you just sit in a hotel and pump stuff down the line. It wasn't my idea that the nearest phone box was going to be twenty-four hours away.

To reach a 'phone box', a Merchant Navy or Royal Fleet Auxiliary Ship with a Marisat, ship-hopping, or, as it was called, cross-decking, was usually necessary. Moreover, the vulnerability of the fleet to air attack meant that a journalist who stayed in one ship for more than a short time risked being catapulted hundreds of miles out to sea, as the ships ran for safety. McIlroy claimed that he 'did twenty-two Task Force ships . . . during the campaign'. Once aboard a communication ship, a journalist might find himself imprisoned there by fog.

There was another difficulty. as Charles Lawrence explained:

> Because there was no way you could communicate with the office privately, or there was no way they could get a message to you, you didn't know whether they wanted you to stay at Brigade and try and file an overall picture, or whether they wanted you to go and live in a trench for a week and see what it was like . . .

At the post-mortem in London, Lawrence's managing editor, Peter Eastwood, was reassuring:

> Eastwood said I'd made the right decision and, although on the surface it looked as if I was kicked to shit by Hastings, Eastwood's point of view wasn't that. It's very interesting how canny these guys are, because Eastwood said to me, not me

to him: 'The difference between you and Hastings is that Hastings didn't do it and you did'. For some reason a guy like that is canny enough to know that one man is filing it in comfort of HMS *Fearless* and the other guy is writing in a trench. So in fact he was pleased.

Hastings, as we know, had a firm view of what he should do and how he should use what resources there were. What is more, as a feature writer rather than a hard-news man, he was better able to adapt to the peculiar circumstances of the expedition; his copy had longer life and more easily survived the delays imposed by the deficiencies of communications and the censorship procedure.

The broadcasters had the advantage that they did get feedback from their offices. Hanrahan, Nicholson and Fox benefited most, as did those journalists who, from the beginning of the land campaign, despatched their material themselves, rather than entrusting it to intermediaries. Those who stayed 'in the field' often remained unaware of the inadequacies of the communications system until the end of the war. Jeremy Hands was one:

It's a very bitter lesson . . . I came out of the Falklands swearing that the next time I ever do anything like that I'll never go away from the phone box because the guys who came out of it as heroes on the press side were those who decided, rightly as far as providing news is concerned, that if you stay away from the action, unless you're guaranteed 100 percent that you're going to be near a phone box within a few minutes, you keep your own personal lines of communication open. It was more important than reporting the action. Where I made a mistake was to say, 'No, I'm here with this particular group of hooligans, I'm going to stick with them and cover their story even if it means I'm going to have problems getting my own material back'. Some of them spent the whole bloody time on ships.

Even so, Hands told us he did not regret going on with the troops. Few did. Some were proud, like Bruce and Lawrence who told us, 'Everyone thought Brucie and I were a bit lunatic'. Hastings only observed 'that there were no eagle scout badges for those who yomped the furthest'. Not that Hastings shirked. On the contrary, Lawrence said:

It was 80 percent good journalism and 20 percent a few deals and a bit of back-stabbing. But mainly Hastings just handles himself very well. And one of the reasons . . . was to make sure he got back to a communications channel. Fantastic energy. On several occasions I would just be too bloody exhausted to start bumming lifts on three different choppers back to a boat, taking a rowing boat out to a ship, climbing up a greasy ladder on the side, seeking out a typewriter, having an argument with the minder and taking another greasy rowing boat to another greasy ship . . . Hastings was right on top of it, and much credit to him.

Nicholson agreed:

Max got most of his reports back through sheer hard work . . . By going out, seeing it, getting a helicopter, coming back and transmitting. Whereas a number of times I saw a journalist give a piece of copy to some sergeant saying, 'Can you get that to a press officer, I want to get it to San Carlos,' and that was the end of it. Now, that's not the way you get stuff on the air. You do what Brian and I did, and what Max did, and that is working your arse off going there and getting back. The only way you can be certain of it getting back to London is to sit in front of a telephone transmitting. A lot of guys didn't know that. Basic, fundamental logistics of getting your copy physically, yourself, to the transmission-point.

It seemed an obvious strategy by the exact science of hindsight but to follow it was sometimes impossible for reporters who were exhausted and despairing. Jeremy Hands described what happened to his colleagues during one key engagement:

I begged to be allowed to go to Goose Green when we knew that 2 Para were on their way to take it . . . the two blokes who were there, Fox and Dave Norris – one of the most sensational guys in the world, very dry, marvellous guy, he was completely overridden by Fox's definitive, eloquent account . . . they were assigned to go with 2 Para and so they were the lucky ones . . . I said, 'We've got to go, we're the only film crew on the island', but they said 'No'.

(Hands believed this was 'because they didn't want the possibility of a British fuck-up being broadcast in any major way by the TV cameras'. In fact the real reason is that it was 'arranged' that Fox and Norris would have exclusivity.) He continued:

Dave suffered enormously during that battle. He was unfit, he's not terribly young, he's not terribly brave – although he acquitted himself magnificently on that particular occasion. At the end of it I saw him covered in sweat and wide-eyed. He said: 'I'm going for a fucking beer'. He'd had forty-eight hours of being shot at; I don't blame him. The fact that his own story didn't come back sooner was partly his own fault for not carrying his own momentum through. In other words, he didn't say, 'Right, now I've got to hurtle back,' but, 'I've just survived and to celebrate I'm going to have a beer'. To compound it, when he did get back there was a massive log jam, so although they had his story they didn't send it for about a day and half . . . so Dave's Goose Green account was held up and his paper has never forgiven him.

This, according to Hands, was why Fox's account was used by the *Mail*, rather than that of their own correspondent. Norris himself believed the piece was delayed at the London end:

Robert Fox got his piece – not a voice piece, but a telexed piece – to the BBC. We both went back to San Carlos on the Sunday . . . and his piece got back OK but mine didn't for some reason . . . That was the one piece I actually saw go from Ajax Bay and it got there three days later.

Norris assumed:

Some idiot at the Ministry of Defence had said, 'Well, we've seen one piece about this; we don't need two because they're operating a pool system,' not realizing . . .

that they were both individual pieces – two eye-witness accounts which would have been very useful seen through two pairs of eyes. [So the *Mail*] used Fox's [piece] and pretended it was mine. I think it was a fairly valid thing to do because Robert Fox and I knew the difficulties and we agreed to put each other's name in each of our pieces, so that if one didn't get there the BBC would know that he was there and we'd both reported this and the *Mail* would know it. So the *Mail* carried a rehash . . .

For Norris to have gone through a major battle, to have had an exclusive newspaper story and then to have lost it at the last hurdle was, as he put it, 'disappointing, not to say heartbreaking'. When his piece eventually turned up, the *Mail* ran it but in shortened form because the delay had devalued it. Norris was bitter, particularly because this was one occasion when he returned to San Carlos to send his copy on. But not far enough:

> On some occasions I could have been more careful, I could have taken it. It was a case of being so knackered some of the times, I just wanted to dig my trench and go to sleep, then I would entrust it to a helicopter.

Many journalists described how hard it was to keep going, let alone to write – though those who endured the exhausting journey back to a communications ship at least had somewhere comparatively comfortable to recuperate. McGowan talked about this:

> It was very difficult when you've got your portable typewriter to sit in a trench and type out a long and meaningful piece. For one thing you don't really have the time, because you've got all your duties to do, you've got to cook for yourself, clean yourself and dig a trench. You've got to trek over a hell of a lot of ground to get the material to write your stories. So you'd write a story of, say, 600–700 words a day. And the other guys who were with you would do the same and then it would go off in a helicopter. But if you were back near the bridgehead area . . . you could go back to a ship, have a shower . . . and you could sit down and because you don't have so far to go with that copy you have more time.

Sometimes even that was impossible. A ship, and with it the satellite terminal, might move, so there could be no filing at all. Kim Sabido told us of 'a whole week when there was no ship in San Carlos with a satellite'. All ships not required for a specific 'near-shore' task had been ordered out to sea for safety. Sabido described his situation:

> For five days I was out of touch, I couldn't actually send anything and I was just doing interviews and getting bits and pieces on tape, and then at the end of that period I compiled . . . two tapes of reports . . . I borrowed a Sony Walkman from one of the Marines and used it to play off onto another cassette on which I recorded little passages. I was sitting in a tent . . . with the wind blowing through at two o'clock in the morning with a candle to see by, doing these reports. There was John Shirley in a hut right next to the tent, in the loo, in the only loo actually. He was sitting on the loo typing away. All I could hear was him typing away and

all he could hear was me shouting into a tape recorder and recording all these pieces at two o'clock in the morning. It was quite funny.

It was. So was the moment, after one engagement, when the ITN soundman discovered the tall figure of Max Hastings, striding towards him, an old cap on his head, a stick over his shoulder, looking for all the world as if he were stalking grouse. As often as not, however, the journalists' situation was bleak and uncomfortable. Charles Lawrence and Ian Bruce had an especially distressing time. We asked Lawrence to what extent he felt part of the unit he grouped with. He replied:

> It was only after a while I realized I looked like these guys. There was quite a big bunch of Specials [SAS] at Teal Inlet, and because they don't wear a rank or insignia and they tend to have longer hair, etc. And because I was filthy dirty, wearing the same fatigues and sort of camouflaged, they thought that I was one of them. I remember one time, the first time we saw Hastings after we landed, which was at Teal Inlet, and he said: 'I must say, Charles, you look most warlike in your paint'.

Lawrence had, however, 'no illusions that we were part of the unit, although [we] spent the entire time with 45 till we got to the top of Mount Kent'. That was when his troubles really began:

> We were absolutely shattered and I had a blister . . . There was a ferocious storm coming in very quickly before we had time to get bivouacs up and I was absolutely soaked to the skin and it was just about to get dark and I suddenly knew I wasn't going to survive that night, you know, there was nowhere I could get shelter. My equipment wasn't even as good as the average booty [foot soldier] because I hadn't time to think about it and we hadn't been issued with all the equipment . . . Fortunately a bloke, one of the battery commanders who was with 45, knew that one of his sergeants [had] got an eight-man tent, set up near some rocks, so it was reasonably safe and he took me up there. I had exposure and so did Ian . . . it's amazing how good these guys are to you . . . they've got problems, but they make sure you've got a dry sleeping bag and if not they'll borrow one from a squaddie and they'll spend hours making you tea and meals and see you all right. I felt better the next day but my foot was throbbing like a beacon. It turned out that the blister had gone septic and had given me cellulitis, so I had to get sorted out. That was about the first time I left 45. After that I joined them occasionally, then didn't, and so on and so forth, because when we went back to *Fearless* we realized just the level of the cock-up on communications.

Lawrence's troubles were severe:

> When I got back to *Fearless* at first it was really bad news . . . you come all this way and you miss the big one, but fortunately they had a very, very nice surgeon on board *Fearless*, Douglas White, who was realistic and said: 'All I can do is shoot you full of penicillin and, if it goes down, you'll be all right and, if it doesn't go down in twenty-four hours, I've got to send you to *Uganda*, otherwise you'll lose your leg'. And I was very lucky because it worked. But I only waited about three days on *Fearless* . . . I'd been climbing over mountains, my foot was going bad

again. First of all I just felt very tired, but when I got to Stanley everything came back and I wrote a story which never got back, which I'll never forgive them for. Can you imagine it – a story of 1000 words about entering Stanley which was never sent back, which happened to a lot of other guys as well? I don't think Bob McGowan's feature ever got back, I don't think Ian Bruce's got back. This was the final chapter with Hastings incidentally, because people reckon that it was down to him. [The copy was given to him to take and transmit.] After doing the story and giving it to one of the PR staff and everybody was going off to the Upland Goose I suddenly thought: I can't make it to the Upland Goose. I got into my sleeping bag and I went to sleep for thirty-six hours. I eventually got to a ship and I had a temperature of 103 and this, that and the other, infected kidneys, bronchitis. I spent a couple of days on that ship before getting off and going back to the Goose, but I'd essentially retired. I was shattered. All I was really interested in doing was a couple of pieces, more reflective than investigative.

He was in such a state by the end that Brian Barton, one of the minders, failed to recognize him.

Shirley was more fortunate. He too was ill but in his case this enabled him to send his big story. He began to collapse while camping among the small group of mountains which dominate Port Stanley, to the west:

All the units were grouped around behind the mountains, and Brigade Head-quarters had moved up and was in the foothills of Mount Kent. So we pitched our bivouacs next to Brigade HQ and we slept in the open, got up early the next morning to see what was happening up the mountain. Bishop and I did a piece about the battle separately. I agreed to take the copy back to Ajax Bay. Got back to Ajax Bay and I was very ill. Three reporters had been taken off by that stage suffering from exposure and I had a fearful bronchial cough and I was actually peeing blood as well . . . something was wrong. I went to see the doctor on *Fearless* and he said: 'Look, just stay in bed.' So I stayed in bed over the weekend of the final battle and the march into Stanley, which I missed. On the other hand, I got some good stuff . . . On the Monday afternoon when Stanley fell, we got the news on *Fearless* and I knew what was happening from the commanders. I was the only journalist there and I knew that I was nearer the communications system than anybody else so I sat down and wrote this story: 'Falklands war is over. White flags have gone up. Surrender. Negotiations beginning'. And I thought: This is really my big moment. I got the splash lead in *The Times* the following day – I don't know what other papers used it. That was my big definitive story and I was very chuffed about it. I felt I was in a position to write a big story . . . it sounds very pompous to say that one felt a sort of sense of history about it. I mean, Fox and Dave Norris would, I'm sure, tell you the same about Goose Green. That was their moment. I think everybody was hoping for something like that.

Others were less lucky. Saville, Seamark and Witherow thought they would be 'first into Stanley', that, as Witherow put it, they would 'come storming in'. They knew 'there was some kind of ceasefire' and also that some of the Argentinians might not have agreed to it and they might get shot. Nonetheless, they set off. Witherow:

> It's a long road into Stanley, which had become a no-go area, so we threw all our kit off and walked in in jeans and pullovers and came to the football field where the helicopters were landing, bringing the negotiators to speak with Menendez at the settlement.

They turned a corner, ran into Tom Smith and Les Dowd, and learnt that Hastings had anticipated them. 'We thought, Fuck it. We weren't the first, which was damned annoying.'

The broadcasters may have been in closer touch with their offices but there were compensating disadvantages. We asked Michael Nicholson about the difficulty of getting action footage. He said 'it was difficult because it happened at night', and went on to tell us of one disappointing occasion:

> We were on Two Sisters looking down. It was a bit like the old Charge of the Light Brigade. Raglan sitting up there looking at the battle, it was that kind of feeling for us. We were under fire, too, shell fire, and we could see all the flares in the sky . . . all the tracers going up . . . the mines. It was quite graphic stuff and an ENG camera would have picked it up. Well, that was the only night that Bernard [Hesketh] was sick. We'd been up there for some days and it was very, very cold some of the time. Bernard's . . . an incredibly tough bugger – he wouldn't let anyone carry his camera in all the time I was with him and he's fifty-seven years old . . . he was a bloody rock of ages but he was just momentarily sick, he went a bit white and he went to sleep that night. He used some of his own clothes to keep his camera warm. That camera apparently came back to the BBC workshops in the same condition it left. Anyway, he went to sleep and he was snoring like a trooper. When we saw this happening Brian and I were side by side not too far away, we were recording it and making little commentaries and things . . . and we both said 'We really can't wake the fellow up because if we [do] he's useless tomorrow'. I don't think we lost much, just a few flares in the sky. But that was the only action we could have got.

We asked Hanrahan if they could have obtained more action footage:

> I don't think we would have had more action film. I was deliberately not placing us in the middle of the action. You can't see anything in the action; you're lying on the ground with bullets going over your head. You can't stand up and film in the middle of a battle. You can film bits of a battle and, if we'd been able to get into the Goose Green rear action undoubtedly we would have been very happy to have gone in and got something. One lot of it was going on at night. A lot of it was men charging up hillsides with bayonets in daylight, but you can't film that because you'll either get shot or you're too far away or you're behind a rock or you're being shelled or something . . . what we did was we put ourselves on a hill overlooking the action . . . the top of Two Sisters, we weren't very close, but we could actually see it and the fact that the pictures came back and do tell the story of people climbing up a mountain top and people shelling the hell out of the top of

a mountain and finally taking it and so on, yes, that's the sort of pictures we were aiming to get.

Hanrahan stressed his reasons for believing this the correct course:

I was reading somewhere recently about how the Germans went about getting pictures. After all, they did get some rather vivid action shots of the last war, and it was quite simply by signing up cameramen as soldiers, ordering them into every unit and sending them into the front line. They suffered the same casualties as the infantry. While I would not be totally keen to get involved in that professionally it's a complete bloody waste of time to get killed trying to assault a position, because there isn't another camera team to replace you. It's fine if you're running a propaganda corps and you see that your cameraman is dead so you send another one in, like if you lose a battalion, you send in another batallion. That's what wars are about, but if you happen to be the only camera team about there's no point in going and getting yourself shot.

Hesketh, the cameraman, and Jockell, the soundman, were also obliged to adapt their way of working to the demands of two journalists, Hanrahan and Nicholson, with different styles. We asked whether there had been any dispute. Hesketh told us:

on this particular trip, we had one problem . . . because the BBC wanted the BBC stamp to be put on their material and ITN wanted their stamp . . . and Mike Nicholson wanted his own stamp and he had his own ways of doing things. And I think he did a very good job, too. But for us there was always a bit of a tug because you know what you want and you know how you want to go and get it. Considering the confinement we were in and the conditions we were under, I think in any marriage like that you can have one or two slight differences.

As well as having to carry heavy equipment, the crew had another problem, shortage of light. It was scarce enough in the mountains and the days from the middle to the end of June were the shortest of the year. There was little time to prepare for filming. Hesketh:

The nights seemed very long. You woke up in the morning because you went to bed early at night and what can you do? You can't do anything, you can't even have a light – if you do, they'll have shells on you, so you go to bed frozen and eventually go to sleep. Then you wake up early and it's still dark. You look at your watch and it says six o'clock in the morning, and you've got three or four hours of total darkness ahead of you. There's no point in getting up, you might as well just lie there.

There were some quarrels, mainly from exhaustion. As Hesketh said:

When I reflect on the times we had, the ugly times, I remember one when we were up on Two Sisters . . . we were all bloody tired and said things which you normally wouldn't worry about and got very rude. But apart from that time, no, we had a very good time.

Tiredness, danger, discomfort, acrimonious wrangles with the minder, and the difficulty of living together cramped up with colleagues
competing for stories did not make it in the words of Tony Snow
'much of a plum assignment'. 'There were times,' he confessed,
'when I would have given my right arm to be away from it'. Nevertheless, every journalist would admit to its having been a 'big story'.
What made it worse for some therefore, is perhaps best described
by Charles Lawrence:

> After about two and a half weeks on shore we first saw the papers dealing with the
> landings. It was one of the most depressing days of my life, I can tell you – and
> everyone else was depressed, too. Stuff hadn't got through. We were naive
> enough to think that this system that had been set up on shore was going to work,
> and there hadn't been any mention of them sitting on our stories at home.
> Obviously we knew there was censorship and we expected that, but what we didn't
> expect was them to sit on our stories for twenty-four hours. I tell you, when you've
> been through all that, you've spent seven weeks on a ship sailing there, you get up
> in the middle of the night, I went over the side of a ship in a scramble net with a
> pack on my back into a landing-craft, the whole business of living like a soldier,
> and then after two and a half weeks you see the result of your work which is
> absolutely fuck all. It's very disheartening.

In the next chapter, we look more closely at the relationship which
developed between the press and the troops.

6

'It's all right; I am British, after all' — a theory of change and change in theory

Any social scientist who has engaged in biographical writing, come to know his subject well and, so to speak, lived with him, or any social scientist who has engaged in lengthy participant or even non-participant observation work of social groups, coming to understand their concerns and difficulties, finds it hard not to become sympathetically involved. To be *engagé* is no scholastic crime, but it can lead to problems of a particularly worrying nature.

To begin with, one is never really sure about the degree of influence which the subject or group has exerted, and especially so in cases where it is felt necessary to be critical. To recognize the problem, however, is not to solve it.

The academic is fortunate, however, in that his or her very occupational location and the timespan of production offer some protection against the worst ravages of identification. Usually there is a considerable time-lapse between the period of the research and the production of a report, paper or monograph, added to which the actual writing most commonly occurs within the setting of an academic institution removed both spacially and temporally from the setting of the research. Consequently, whilst the ghost of sympathy is never entirely exorcised, the main weight of the body is nevertheless removed. Academic production is also a matter of peer group reference, which means that colleagues who are not emotionally involved in the work can often as not offer detached comments before publication. In some cases it may also be that the actual writer has never personally come into contact with the group under observation, the bulk of such work having been conducted by assistants.

If the academic is exposed to the pressures which create partiality, he or she is nevertheless protected against their full force by virtue of his or her position in a way that a journalist, for whom the audience is also the subject, is not. At one level, as we have already argued, the Task Force personnel did see the journalists' copy but did not influence how it was written. In other ways, though, the journalists were highly vulnerable to the process of identifying with the military.

By and large journalists do not have peers to check their material. The only check is at the editorial level, and for the foreign correspondent even this is hardly workable. The reporter on the spot must be trusted by virtue of their exclusivity of knowledge. Also, unlike the academic, the journalist has hardly any time-span between the observation and the writing; copy, to use a good journalistic term, is 'pounded out'. Tight up against a deadline, there is little room for reflection, and with news agency men running a constant deadline no real time at all. More significantly, in the working conditions of the Falklands, copy was written amidst the very men reported on. There was no possible physical distancing, nor the psychological relief of trotting back to the luxurious camp of an Intercontinental or some other such watering-hole. Copy was often written actually in camp. Thus, the journalists not merely observed their subjects, but lived their lives and shared their experiences, and those experiences were of such emotional intensity that the form of prose which journalists use to take the reader into that experience – the 'I was there' form – provided not only a window for the reader, but also a door for partiality irrespective of any desire to remain the detached professional outsider.

We're with you all the way

A week before the troops disembarked from *Canberra*, the journalists, according to Ian Bruce: 'received a piece of paper saying "3 Commando. Don't shoot me; I die easily" . . . And it wasn't even in Spanish'. Bruce, like some other of his colleagues, decided, once ashore, to equip himself with a side-arm; taken, as he put it, either 'from dead Argies or heaps of weapons'. Asked whether that was for protection or as a souvenir, he answered: 'Both. I discovered after three nights that the slide in mine didn't work anyway so it was completely useless'. The journalists were given no formal instructions about arming themselves but, as Bruce told us:

> Everyone had some weapons training . . . but if you hold up a piece of paper saying 'Fleet [so and so], Commander [so and so], Brigade [so and so]' . . . or 'Take me to the nearest British Embassy', it's not going to do you too much good. No one was put in that position, so I don't know what anyone would have done. I had no wish to shoot anyone.

Undoubtedly, as Bruce makes clear, the journalists risked dismissal of a type about which even the National Union of Journalists could have done little. Their future was entwined with that of the troops; their mood, too, was the same. Bruce discussed their feeling at the beach-head on the first morning:

... The night before ... I think everyone had been given the same briefing ... that the carriers would be closing in with us, that we'd have their superiority for twenty-four hours to enable positions to be established ashore, get the rapier and gun batteries ashore, and then push the supplies in. We saw our first Argentine aircraft twenty minutes after we landed and then they came in in force. That day was incredible. It was like watching a movie, until a bomb landed fairly close. Then it became a problem. The second day they left us alone; I think the day after that we watched *Antelope* explode and sink. The evening before that happened, Charlie [Lawrence] and I had climbed to the top of the mountain; we'd seen the first ever Rapier operational; we'd also seen the Argentine aircraft still streaming in, and the Rapier battery ... trying to cope and failing. We counted nineteen ships in the anchorage and at a number of bays down San Carlos Water. The next morning when we woke up everyone was very, very depressed; they had headed back into the Exclusion Zone just to avoid being sitting targets for these raids ... At that stage life was very glum indeed.

Things which became important to the troops also mattered to the journalists. Bruce gave us one example:

Until just after we left Ascension papers would arrive periodically; afterwards it depended on air-drops and weather conditions. I think one of the saddest days of all was [one described by] Tony Snow. A Hercules from Ascension dropped a pack of mail into the sea; by that time mail assumed an importance you wouldn't believe back here, any contact with home was tremendous, it set you up for two days, morale was low just by being cooped up on board. And we'd watched this packet being carefully brought back on board *Fearless*, just being pulled on to the deck, and a helicopter landed and blew everything back into the sea again. Which dumped morale again.

It was not just a question of sharing the moods of the troops through shared experience, but of actively beginning to identify with them by being part of the whole exercise. Consequently, although some of the journalists disagreed with the decision to send the Task Force, once it was likely that there would be a battle, they felt an affinity with the troops, a shared determination to see the venture through to the end. It seemed clear that Argentina was wrong to have tried to stake a claim to the Islands by armed force. David Norris spoke about this:

We [the press and the troops] had some interesting debates about this ... you could say that the Falklands was a black and white issue, once it had started. But Northern Ireland, now, there's no way that's a black and white issue and they've [i.e. the troops] just got to accept that we do comment on it, we do criticize sometimes.

Kim Sabido thought the presence of foreign journalists would have been a corrective:

We'd have got a lot more idea, a different perspective, a more critical view of what was going on. You'd have got far more stories of what happened than actually came out. Just having British journalists, I don't think you were ever going to get too many critical stories . . . We were so close to the troops, . . . so close to the units, . . . involved with them and reliant on them. You never saw things that were in front of your nose, and . . . perhaps in fact you didn't feel the normal sort of desire to go out and find the truth. I think we are all to blame for that . . . It was all far too cosy for us, really. Obviously the military liked it that way; as far as they were concerned, they were doing a good job. Not in a devious way, they didn't think: Great, they're not seeing the truth. They probably thought that this is the way that journalists normally behave, isn't it quite decent, sort of thing. In fact, we said quite often to the MoD people and the military: 'You know, you should have some Americans here; they would soon sort you out'. I think we realized the failings in ourselves. We didn't do anything about them . . . To have had two or three Americans there would have provided an amazing difference to the way the whole thing was covered, and I think as British journalists we would have been provoked into doing our job a little bit better . . . I don't think overall we did a very good journalistic job.

There were no correspondents of other nationalities present and the journalists became involved in a way different to most reporting situations. It is very doubtful, however, whether the presence of foreign journalists would have made that much difference to the level of information obtained. Indeed, it is possible that less information would have been given by the military. Moreover, as Sabido suggests, the journalists were not innocents who failed to recognize that they were being seduced, but willing victims, to the point of self-seduction. For example, as Patrick Bishop observed:

The situation was that you were a propagandist; that's how it turned out. So there wasn't any need to put pressure on anyone to write gung-ho copy because everyone was doing it without any stimulus from the military. And that's how most of the reporters felt. They were all very patriotic and 'positive' about the whole thing. So the military didn't have to lean on them.

In fact, among the journalists a shift took place in the values that questioned the virtue of remaining untouched and unmoved towards those they lived with. There was simply no escaping the military's embrace. As Mick Seamark put it: 'On this occasion you were always part of it. You couldn't get off, you couldn't say at the end of one day: "Let's go and have a drink somewhere, away from the story". You were part of the story in that sense'. The journalists certainly began to feel that they belonged. Thus, David Norris said:

I found I was referring to 'us' collectively when we were on shore; not on the ships, [when] I still felt a little divorced from the whole thing because it still wasn't certain whether there was going to be a landing and it was still in my mind – was the whole thing really necessary? . . . But I think once they were on shore and fighting, and we were with them, I couldn't help but think of myself as part of the operation. I suppose people might say that that's a bad thing, you should still maintain some impartiality. It's very difficult. On shore I dressed like a soldier. I ate like them, I lived with them. I just began to feel a part of the whole thing.

And, in Bruce's words, 'I was starting to write stuff like . . . "then, like most of the filthy-faced Paras and Marines living around the beach-head, I hadn't had a chance to change my clothes for a week".'

Even Gareth Parry, of the liberal, often anti-establishment *Guardian*, mentioned that, with the approach of danger, his attitude changed.

> I noticed . . . that I began by saying 'the British' and within a few weeks I was calling 'us' or 'we', and don't forget we also looked like sailors by then as well. It made sense to wear naval clothing, because you were constantly sprawled on your face on the deck. It manifested itself in other ways as well, actually, because when a ship goes to action stations you sort out who you are going to save if you are able to.

The enmeshing, the identification, the whole process of involvement had nothing to do with each individual's private views, feelings about war, or the attitudes of his organization. The dynamics of the situation were so powerful that they overwhelmed all this. Not surprisingly, the degree to which each journalist sympathized with the military depended on his own personality and experience during the conflict.

The transformation began on the voyage south. Journalists normally fly to assignments abroad. Ships were therefore an unfamiliar world. To be down on the lower decks during an alert, sealed in by the bulkheads as by a tomb, was novel and frightening. Little wonder that Parry looked round for someone to save, or to save him. On shore the process continued, in Parry's case accelerated by an early adventure, which Ian Bruce told us 'affected him badly'. Bruce told us that Parry, ill-equipped to withstand the South Atlantic cold:

> Went ashore one night getting abandoned kit from the dead and wounded, trying to sort through it and find some stuff, and he heard the snick of a bolt going back in a self-loading rifle. And a voice asked him 'What's the password?' and he said, 'I'm terribly sorry, I don't know'. And he expected to die in about a second and a half and didn't.

In effect what was happening to the journalists was that their professional need to cover a story in a detached way was slowly being swamped by the very real, human need to belong, to be safe. The comradeship and closeness demonstrated by the troops, which the journalists so admired, were not just the random product that any occupational association throws up, but the response to having to work closely together especially during military exercises and having to solve tasks as a group. At the same time the enclosed world of a group of men living together means that the need for emotional expression, fulfilment and release, the talking over of worries, fears or any of a myriad small problems which beset individuals, became totàlly restricted to colleagues, thus giving a remarkable closeness in relationships.

McGowan observed: 'I think you'll find that most of the journalists made lifelong friends with some of the units. I certainly have'. What is more, if the setting is very dangerous, time spent in close proximity to others who are sharing the same experiences submerges the individual's personal characteristics. The other person becomes 'you': he knows what you are going through. There is a transparency to feelings and relationships not commonly found in civilian settings.

Troops and journalists shared the same fears, the same ailments, the same jokes. As Bruce recalled:

> The greatest pleasure in life at that point was a brew of hot tea . . . [Some] bright spark back at Whitehall obviously decided that, since we were close to the Antarctic, . . . arctic dehydrated rations would be the best fare to offer. Except that [they] need five pints of water to reconstitute. Water on the Falklands is undrinkable because of a bug called liverfluke; we were issued with a pint and a half a day each to cook, wash, shave, and you had to keep it for tea, coffee, hot drinks and some food. You couldn't cook your whole ration; you had to have plenty of water, otherwise it was just dry flakes, usually chicken supreme. The trail to Stanley is probably marked in both directions by tin-foil packets of chicken supreme . . .

As the journalists identified with the troops, so the troops' attitudes changed towards the journalists. Norris described how they behaved once people came ashore:

> As far as they could they would help. They had their jobs to do. Initially they'd show you how to dig a trench, and help you a bit, started it for you, but sometimes they just didn't have the time to help you in that way; you just had to do it yourself.

They helped Norris in other ways too. He told us that, before he joined the Task Force, he had believed that the Royal Marines were part of the Army. Gradually his ignorance diminished:

> I was in a fog, but it wasn't because the Paras weren't helping me and telling me what was going on, but [that] I'm just not very good at military strategy. The CO would show me . . . his Ordnance maps and tell me exactly where the other units were and what they were doing. But it was still all Greek to me. It's never been my interest.

His inexperience had a certain protective advantage:

> My worst fear was that we could have been bogged down, entrenched. I think it's probably more a childlike innocence, naivety, that led me to believe that we couldn't lose. From what I've heard since, it seems to have been a razor's edge,

but at the time I was so impressed with the performance of the troops – totally professional. Every move had obviously been practised a thousand times before.

John Shirley shared his admiration:

I had more to do with the Marines than I did with the Paras . . . They were enormously impressive. They were very serious blokes. The young guys . . . were wandering around with machine guns and plenty of kit to kill people. And they were terribly responsible about it; they were aware of the potential of the weapons they had. They looked after them, they were careful about them, they weren't going to kill people just idly . . . Obviously, they crossed that bridge that they were going to kill people if necessary, but they weren't going to do it in a wild gung-ho fashion. And they didn't actually look forward to it.

David Norris was to retain his new friends. He told us: 'I've become very friendly ever since. I've been to Aldershot a few times – had monumental piss-ups at Aldershot . . .'

The difficulties the journalists faced in performing their own professional duties obliged them to make allies of the military. This drove them further into cooperation. Bernard Hesketh described how he and the Captain of *Sheffield* collaborated in face of Ministry of Defence opposition:

We had an awful battle to get film of HMS *Sheffield* when she was being hit, and one of the factors which persuaded them to let us do it was the fact that it would get back to London in three weeks' time. We knew that *Sheffield* had been hit, we were up on the deck of *Hermes* and . . . we could see the smoke, that must have been five or six miles away . . . and it was broadcasting over the ship's system that this had happened and all sorts of orders were given for firefighting equipment and medics to be prepared to be helicopered out and the hospital to be got ready on ship to receive casualties, and we were there and able to observe and film all of this. And I thought at the time: 'I mustn't be silly . . . They're in the middle of a crisis; they don't want me in a helicopter . . .' I thought it would be unwise to ask at that time. I waited until late that afternoon before I asked, and I was told that . . . it would be impossible. Now, the next morning I was going from the ward-room to the area where we worked, which was on the top deck, and on the way you passed a place called 'CM flats' . . . it's the only open area on the ship, apart from the hangars, and any time you go through . . . there were always people sleeping . . . it's always very murky lighting, and there were all these people, you had to pick your way through them, and I suddenly realized these guys are . . . some of the survivors . . . Most of them seemed to be half-asleep, and I saw one guy who was awake and I said to him, 'Are you from *Sheffield*?' and he said, 'Yes'. And I said, 'Who is your senior officer here?,' thinking it would be a warrant officer or chief petty officer, and he said, 'Right here,' and he sort of jumped and stood to attention and it was the Captain, Sam Salt, who was lying on the deck asleep with the rest of his men. I introduced myself and asked him if we could interview him and he said, 'Yes'. Then I had to go and get Mike Nicholson, Brian Hanrahan and John [Jockell]. We then had to go to the other end of the ship to get our gear . . . I suppose it was a bit foolish, I was rushing a bit and Hammond [a minder] realized there was something cooking and he followed us and, when he realized that we were going to interview Sam Salt, he stopped us. And there was a long, long discussion between Sam Salt and Hammond and the Captain of *Hermes*, Middleton. This was all done, not in our presence, though eventually we did get to interview Sam Salt . . . After that I got to know him very well and got to know his engineer. The engineer told me he was going to board the ship that day . . . to see if there was any chance of saving it. And I said, 'Can I come with you?' and he said, 'Yes, of course'. So I said to Hammond, because I couldn't do anything without his permission, 'I've got permission from the engineering officer of *Sheffield* to go in a helicopter with him to see *Sheffield*' . . . He didn't know what to do about that, so it was agreed, but only one person could go because they were going to take other people as well to help the engineering officer and there would be no space in the helicopter. I got on the helicopter, the motors started and we were just about to take off and there was a great waving. So I got off and another guy came up and shouted that I was wanted, and the helicopter was gone. Twice I got on the helicopter and twice I was taken off. Once, the second time, I'm not sure but they said there was a fault on the helicopter and everybody got off, but then suddenly everybody got on and I was left behind. Subtle! Anyway, I got to know Sam Salt very well and I leant on him very heavily. Now he wanted to see the pictures of the ship, and I agreed, under considerable pressure, that the only way I'd get these pictures would be if I agreed to let the minders see the pictures and any officer who wanted to see them and that the tape would be sent in a separate package to the MoD in London. I had to tell them, incidentally, that I wasn't there to do PR films for the Royal Navy, I was there to cover a war and if they didn't allow me to go I would demand to be returned to the UK and there would be no television coverage and they would have to explain to Number 10 Downing Street exactly why. I did then go on a helicopter, flew there and got the pictures I wanted.

The important point about Hesketh's trials and tribulations is the accommodation he had to make to ensure that he filmed *Sheffield*. Hesketh clearly was not to be compromised into operating as the Navy's public relations cameraman, but the whole process is a classic demonstration of how the difficulties faced, the obstacles the journalists had to overcome, and did overcome, drove them in doing so further into cooperation with the military.

The tension implicit in the identification with the Task Force stemmed not from the question of whether an individual was or was not patriotic, but whether journalism as an impartial activity is congruent with such sentiments. That was the challenge, and that, for the journalists involved, was the problem.

The war was supposedly about the defence of liberal democratic principles, of which the freedom of the press remains a key commitment. The war was also against the 'Argies', and patriotism was defined as support for Britain in its campaign against the enemy. In such a situation, where does the responsibility of the journalist lie: to his profession or to his country? To the Government and the military these two elements were separate and one had to make a choice. To the journalists, however, the situation was not simple, the issues were not clear, the solution uncertain.

Values which serve an occupation well in peacetime or amid the pain of someone else's wars do not necessarily serve the individual journalist well in the midst of his war. The values of impartiality and objectivity when compared to other people's efforts look wrong or misplaced or even shabby. Away from the sounds of battle it is easier for producers and editors, 8000 miles away in England, to hold on to the central idea of objectivity even as their representatives in the field find the concept less easy to grasp. This was precisely the point Ian Bruce made in his own inimitable way to his editor after the fall of Port Stanley:

> I'd got to the stage where I was making subjective judgements. I was told on one occasion when I got a phone call through to the office, perhaps I could do 'a more reflective piece'. I'd been sending stuff constantly for three days; I 'sounded very bitter'. I said: 'That's because I am fucking bitter at this stage of the game. I want to come home. I'll hang on until everything's over but, [I'm] fairly shagged out. Bitter about people I know who are dead, and I think the whole thing's a waste of time in some ways. What have we done, we've liberated 700,000 sheep and 1800 sheep-shaggers. Terrific'.

John Martin, a soundman, described the special problem of covering the Falklands Conflict:

> We did an absolutely horrendous massacre in Uganda; we actually fell upon it just [after] it happened, hours before in the middle of nowhere, children mutilated and everything. [That's] no problem at all – it's not pleasant, but you do it with no feeling. And Beirut the same; it's not your problem. It becomes different when it's people you're involved with.

John Shirley agreed:

> I think the thing that really differentiates it from anything else, is that we weren't observers, we were participants in the damn thing. This really affected the copy we wrote . . . I was in Lebanon last year with the PLO for three weeks. OK, they show you around, they take you down to the front. You talk to people, but you go back to Beirut at the end of the day . . . to your hotel. You've got the opportunity of withdrawing. You've also got freedom to write what you want. You're an observer, and that's how you attempt to retain some objectivity – some distance from it. But on this thing (a) we were actually directly involved because we had been made captains; (b) we were absolutely dependent on the military – literally, for food, anything, company, survival – and there was nowhere else to go, you had no choice but to stay with them. You could get back to your cabin on *Canberra*, but you were still surrounded by these guys, and when we were on the Islands you were marching with them, you were cooking with them and eating with them, you were part of the unit. You were just as likely to get killed as they were. And your actions could affect their safety.

Asked if he suspended his 'journalistic critical ability', Shirley replied:

I don't think one suspended it totally, but it certainly changed. I started writing copy that said 'we'. That story I wrote about the weather, the sentence I used 'Only the weather now holds us back from Stanley', and I think I finished another story 'We are one step nearer Stanley'. I was with the troops, I mean emotionally I was with them. I wanted them to win . . . I think certainly the reporters I had most contact with, Kim Sabido, Bishop, Hastings, Bob Fox, Charlie Lawrence – they're my main friends, to some extent Les Dowd – were all aware that it was happening.

The correspondents, according to Shirley, discussed their growing sympathy with the troops:

In a jokey sort of way. Foxy kept on calling everybody 'troopie groupie'. He was right. We did actually become – I'm not necessarily proud of this, but I'm trying to answer your question honestly . . . – we did become 'troopie groupies'. That's not to say that we were going to go and write glowing copy singing the praises of the Paras all the time, but we were with them. I don't think the problem of withholding material really affected us on the Islands, because you couldn't have put over critical material anyway. Because of the censorship, there was no possibility of putting it over. So in a sense that helped. It's very interesting that the first piece I wrote after censorship finished, the week after we got to Stanley – big two and a half thousand word piece that the *Sunday Times* ran – a big double page spread, which I was very pleased with. And I was very critical of some elements of the campaign, I pointed out the mistakes that happened, I said where things had gone wrong and talked about the animosity between the Navy and the Commandos . . . But there was one bit I put in which said something about all the units here have distinguished themselves in the last three or four weeks – the Paras and the Commandos have done this and that and the other. And I thought I'd better be fair to 5 Brigade, too – the Guards, and I put in a paragraph which said something like 'And 5 Brigade, though very unprepared for the marching, fought a wonderful campaign'. I genuflected towards them in a favourable way without having any factual basis for that whatsoever. That was a very unjournalistic thing to think.

As John Martin has said, it is 'different when it's people you're involved with.' Although analytically impartiality and objectivity are not the same, for practical purposes then, given the power of the forces in question, to lose impartiality in those circumstances was journalistically to lose objectivity. Only by remaining completely impartial and unmoved by events would it have been possible to hold to a totally objective account. That was, however, far from the case; events did move the journalists and they were involved. For example, if Bruce was bitter at the end of the war about those soldiers whom he had known and who had been killed, he was also upset by one particular soldier's injury.

One guy, an Argyll, I'd done a story for the evenings on him, he'd been seconded to the Marines. I asked for him when I got to Stanley. 42 Commando were coming in, 'where the hell's my Argyll, he'll be a general when he gets home' . . . it turned out that he'd lost his right shin bone from a machine-gun round. And he's probably crippled now. Jesus, you know, a guy I'd drunk with most nights on Canberra, hadn't seen him for six weeks and he was hit two days before the end.

Bruce was so upset that he did not attempt to interview his Argyll.

Of all the journalists, the broadcasters most successfully retained their independence. This was partly because the principles of 'balance' and 'impartiality' are more firmly entrenched within that medium than in print journalism, and the journalists' role is correspondingly more clearly defined. Perhaps, too, the broadcasters were better able to weather pressure towards partiality because, compared to the press, they were more regularly in touch with their home offices. Hastings was a declared patriot. He insisted, however, that he constantly resisted filing copy that was obviously being fed by the Army:

> I think some people were extremely naive in what they filed, for instance, atrocity stories . . . They'd all come out with these terrible stories about [Argentinians] shooting British soldiers holding white flags. Frankly, this . . . happens in every war on every side, and I just never file that sort of thing at all. And the napalm found at Goose Green, they were very keen for us to file [that]. I said, 'I'm just not going to file it', and didn't because we were using white phosphorus, which is every bit as unpleasant. After there had been an air attack on 40 Commando's positions very close by San Carlos settlement, Dave Nichols [military public relations] said: 'You must all report disgraceful Argentinian behaviour, bombing so close . . . might kill civilians'. And I said: 'Come off it. You know, what's really criminal is that we're using the civilian settlements to house military installations and supplies'. He blahed on . . . It was done on a very simple level, there was no sort of Byzantine cunning, it was all pretty childish . . . Basically . . . operational commanders were not that interested in PR. The only case I know of where there was a slightly more sophisticated attempt to push propaganda was when [Jeremy Moore] asked the MoD and everybody to play up the scale of the disaster at Bluff Cove because he believed . . . the Argentinians thought that we were going to take another ten days to get our act together.

Hastings continued:

> There is a popular lay perception that in journalism you get [reporting] either right or wrong. Whereas you would know very well that in fact what you're actually trying to do is have a sort of stab at the truth, in which case if you're getting it right about half the time you're doing rather well. In war, that drops to about 30 percent and I think one of the reasons why I got more out of the war than most was because I set my sights a lot lower . . . In some ways I set them higher, in that I didn't expect to get anything done for me, but in another sense I set them lower because my expectations about what we would actually be able to transmit were pretty low and therefore I concentrated on the kind of material I thought it would be possible to transmit, rather than the rest. And that's not unique to this war, it's also true of most wars, and the only real difference . . . is that [whereas here] I was sending [material] through official channels, in Israel [let's say] you'd make your trip to Cyprus with the real thing in your shoes. In this case you neither could nor would do that sort of option.

In the Falklands a clear clash occurred between two competing sentiments. On the one hand the journalists carried the occupational ideology of impartiality and objectivity whilst the Bergen rucksacks on their backs symbolically carried more than the single source of their provision: in effect, where did their commitments lie – to traditions of journalistic practice or to those who could and did protect them, the military?

It is important to explain how the journalists were slowly moved into a partisan position. The fact that this was inevitable ought not to obscure the importance of understanding the process of its occurrence. It not only informed the coverage of the war in the Falklands but raises serious questions concerning the whole nature of war-reporting and the position of the war correspondent. For example, should war-reporting be seen as a separate branch of journalism where the accepted canons or occupational rules of procedure are inapplicable and as such inappropriate in judging performance?

By not having a clearly worked-out position based on informed understanding of what being a war correspondent in the context of the Falklands would mean, the options available for reporting and the emotional feelings they were likely to encounter, certain activities were thus unwittingly engaged in which, rather than ensuring journalistic objectivity, served to hasten its undermining: protective distance gave way to the affinity born of proximity.

For example, when we asked John Martin, the ITN soundman in *Canberra*, whether he was given any instruction by the military about what the crew could or could not film, he replied, 'No, it was just burble really; they were being helpful'. But he went on to describe what, in retrospect, was evidently a growing affinity with the troops:

> The various different commanders were very good at arranging us to have a day with the Paras. We did a PR thing on board, too, we did a film of the Commandos, with their chaps living in quarters, training, each one separately, and at the beginning the commander of each one introducing it and then finishing it off and then transferring . . . to their wives' clubs. It ended up as being very good PR. Also we were running out of things to film and, instead of just sitting there doing nothing, we could go out and make a half-hour programme. I think it helped cooperation because the chaps were getting bored as well. In the evenings when they were in the bar we would put a tape on and they could watch themselves training; it was quite good for their morale. We were doing lectures, showing them how ENG worked, and then filming them and then playing them back to them, lectures for up to seventy or eighty at a time. Just to give them a bit of light relief, tell them about how news works and everything else.

Such friendly cooperation undoubtedly helped the journalists to establish their credentials with the troops, but it also carried the danger of the journalists forgetting that though they were with the Task Force, they were not of it. Once ashore, according to Martin, the journalists gained if not outright respect, certainly bemused appreciation.

> They were actually quite amazed that we were living the same way as them. Not asking for anything more than them. Thought we were bonkers being there. Once we got rid of the minders we got more involved with soldiers, trying to get as far forward as we could all the time.

The journalists in this case had only a few weeks in which to resist 'going native' but conditions and circumstances were such that the process was accelerated. Robert Fox, for instance, told us about the evolution of his relationship with the Captain of *Canberra*, Chris Burne:

> We did establish a *modus vivendi*, . . . a very good rapport and he was taking me aside and mapping the way it should've been going on a basis of trust, saying, 'Look, you must believe me, it's not because of propaganda, but you mustn't mention that, because that ship is in considerable danger . . .' He didn't actually say that, but he implied very seriously . . . He told me a great deal about the Exocet attack on *Sheffield*, because he had been the first Captain of HMS *Coventry* and he was explaining what that kind of ship was like, how it was very vulnerable to this kind of attack, how this could have happened, and why he thought many more were going to happen. We had to be snug, not censored, with the Task Force, with the troops themselves. We were coloured towards them because that was *our community*, we had been in service for two or three months.

The reference to 'our community' is significant. Fox is far from military-minded. As he emphasized, 'I thought very hard about the adjectives I was using'. As an example, he talked about his thoughts after Colonel H Jones was killed: 'I can remember at four o'clock in the morning writing a despatch about Goose Green. Would I describe what H Jones did as heroic? Was that really going over the top a bit? . . . There was a hell of a lot of hype around'. When we asked Fox whether he excised references to 'we', he said:

> No, no, after a thing like Goose Green it was just 'we' all the way through. It was 'we, our group', you know, I mean it wasn't 'we, Britain'. I'm afraid, people back here might have thought it was 'we, Britain', but it was 'we, the soldiers', 'we, that group of people immediately in my earshot'.

Peter Archer said more about this. As a Press Association representative, he is obliged to take particular care to avoid seeming biased or partial. We asked him whether living so closely with the troops made this very difficult:

> It gave me more insights and I suppose the more insights you have the more sympathetic you tend to be. However, I was always trying to be impartial. It was never an us-and-them war. The BBC, for instance, never used the word 'enemy',

> 'enemy planes' or 'enemy ships'. I believe we did, but that was a conscious decision. On one occasion the sub-editor talked to me about it . . . but, you see, it was very difficult to remain impartial. It made no difference to me; it could have been another story. But it's difficult when you are being shot at by the other side not to refer to them as 'the other side'.

Pressed for more detail, Archer explained that he had used phrases like 'British ships attacked by enemy fighter bombers', but because, he emphasized, 'They were enemy fighter bombers to the British ships . . . but I wasn't referring to mine.'

One interesting and complex question concerns the extent to which the style of the journalists' copy was consciously chosen and, if so, why. The device of referring to the Argentine forces as 'the Argentinian troops' rather than 'the enemy', might, for example, have been no more than a rhetorical trick, a habit, in which journalists engaged because that was how correspondents, reporting from the front, customarily referred to 'the other side'. It might, on the other hand, equally well have been a sign of a journalist's deliberately trying to disengage his own emotions, exclude sympathy with the British troops, from his reporting. Like Fox, taking care with his adjectives, the correspondent who watched his prose might nonetheless have been won over by the subjects of his reports.

The actual arrangement of words and their implication for content are however examined in detail later in Chapter 11 – for the moment what is intriguing is the process of identification.

To the extent that they could, the journalists sought to protect themselves against too close an identification with the troops. Jeremy Hands, for example, admitted that he had become quite fond of the military. He went on to say:

> I was constantly aware that I was reporting for a nation of civilians and living in a very, very close-knit service environment; and, being welcomed by them, you tend, unless you're careful, to become slightly swamped by it. You start talking in initials, using their phraseology sometimes . . . You'd suddenly find yourself saying, 'I'm just going down to the bar for a razz and a bottle of Scotch'. And you'd think: Hang on a second. Come back to life, son, you're a civilian.

Recognizing that a process is at work does not necessarily enable one to resist its influence. The journalists' adoption of military jargon, however strenuously they sought to excise it from their vocabulary, indicates how efficiently they were being assimilated. Fox stressed the difficulty of their situation:

> It was much too close. You couldn't get out of it, you couldn't get away. I actually went and hid in my cabin and listened to music, after a time, just to get all the

military shit out of my head. You were completely overtaken by it. You began to think like them.

Though, like Hands, the journalists may have tried hard to remember they were civilians, the enormity of events entrapped them. Few people can stand aside in the face of anguish and suffering, especially when those who need help have been companions, hosts and mentors. Shirley was indeed deeply upset by the sight of the tangled bodies he helped unload. Nicholson and Hanrahan pulled ashore boats of shocked and wounded after the Bluff Cove disaster; Tom Smith and Les Dowd assisted the wounded at the Battle of Mount Longdon and, according to Ian Bruce, 'gained a great deal of respect from the Paras for doing so'.

We asked Cleaver of the Press Association whether he could 'take a sympathetic portrait of, say, a young Argentinian'. His answer was straightforward: 'I did it quite often. I did sympathetic portraits of young kids being disarmed and the rest of it, the dejection of it all, but *that's the photograph*. It didn't alter my viewpoint'.

'That's the photograph' is significant. Cleaver was reminding us of the way in which a picture can transcend national and political boundaries. Robert Capper's picture of the white-uniformed Republican soldier hit by a loyalist bullet, his back arched as he falls to his death, could have been making the same statement about any soldier of the Spanish Civil War. The awesome picture of the *Antelope* exploding, the most famous shot of the Falklands war, might be a photograph of any ship of that fleet, or any ship of any fleet. By and large therefore the photographer, if left alone free from overt direction, will not make just the 'routine' record of, say, Britain's military progress but attempt thematic shots about the human condition, or the human condition of war, such as misery, suffering, dejection or especially dramatic incidents, the quintessence of which may be caught in the shutter's movement portraying friend and foe alike. The delight is in the technical composition and the power of the statement, not in the non-artistic sentiment of patriotism. That may be there, but more than likely subsumed under a higher artistic category of feeling. In other words, photographic images can be as ideologically or culturally constructed as can print, but there is also the question of technical accomplishment to contend with, and to gain his images the photo-journalist tends to share the artist's pursuit of perfection as an ideal to be chased at almost any price. Ian Bruce described Cleaver's patience, as he waited to capture the moment when *Antelope* exploded:

Actually Cleaver almost got frostbite that night, he'd sat there so long before the fire reached the magazine; that's probably the best shot of the war. He sat there for something like five hours with no gloves on; it was something like −7, −10, he told me afterwards. When the magazine did go up, his fingers were so frozen he could hardly get the shutter closed to get the shot. That's dedication.

The journalists found it harder to demonstrate detachment. McIlroy believed that in this war it was altogether more difficult to resist assimilation:

I've been in campaigns where I've been up to two weeks with troops, longer sometimes in Third World countries where you just can't get out, but this was a sense of involvement; it was not easy to be totally detached about what was happening around you because you were acutely aware that this was an all-British operation, . . . you were seeing this incredible array of ships with Townsend Thoresen and British Rail Ferries. All of this was a tremendous reminder to people on the scene that it was a British operation. To see a British Rail ferry-boat in Port Stanley is just not possible by any stretch of the imagination, but there it was.

He asserted, however, that this had not affected his copy:

After a few years, you have an ability to split yourself into two. You never write anything or go anywhere without being involved; the degree of involvement will sometimes make it more difficult for you to be detached. For instance, you're seeing kiddies starving or the results of a massacre. It's very hard to . . . keep out of your copy something dreadful about who you know has done it, but you are able to confine your reporting to saying what you've seen and what people are saying . . . Sometimes, occasionally, I've been able to say to the readers of the *Daily Telegraph* who has done it without quoting anyone or [saying] this is the result of a particular regime. But 99 percent of the time you are just reporting what you see and what you're told and you have a formula for doing that and within that you get a balanced picture back, hopefully.

In effect, as with any other group whose work brings them into contact with the unfortunate and sad side of life, to function at all it is necessary not to become part of the suffering, but just as a doctor may nonetheless be harrowed by the agony of someone close, so the journalist may be knocked off balance when tragedy hits soldiers he has come to know. It is the relationship to others that either protects or hurts, consequently it was sometimes impossible for the journalist to divorce professional and personal feelings.

We alluded earlier to the possibility that, in their closeness to the troops, the journalists may have failed to notice or to recognize the significance of certain statements, behaviour or incidents. But did they on occasion deliberately overlook something that they might otherwise have reported? We asked McIlroy, who replied:

No, quite the contrary. I think you'll find a number of things I reported which were not the sort of things that British soldiers should do according to the Geneva Convention: having people walking around on their hands and knees picking up rubbish and Marines giving some of the Argentinians a hard time before they were repatriated. You could get away, especially in the *Telegraph,* with writing about these things. There was nothing that I think the British public wasn't told about what was happening . . . All the pop papers, as well, gave stories about how the Paras and the Marines weren't behaving themselves and looting. It's a basic maxim. If you're anywhere, you are the eyes and ears of people who have paid for your paper, so you're doing for them what they'd want to do for themselves.

The nature of the campaign was such that it would have been difficult for the military to hide or disguise their behaviour. In this case there was no 'hidden war', apart from the occasional rumour which went unexplained. Misdemeanours, including looting, were indeed reported, although it is fair to say that the incidents to which McIlroy referred occurred at the end of the war and were reported after censorship was lifted and correspondents were able to speak directly to their home offices.

In fact the hidden incidents of the Falklands war, even if true, do not dramatically affect the nature of the overall war as reported, although it is certainly questionable at what point an incident becomes important: the killing of one prisoner or fifty? We would argue that whether an incident is important or not depends on whether it is a standard feature of that particular war or simply something that ought not to but *can* happen in war. There is a big difference. That is, does it owe its presence to *war* where unfortunate practices do occur, or is it a product of the particular war within which it occurs? For example, the My-Lai massacre was not such an incident by our definition because it was a clear expression of the type of war Vietnam was, and how it was conducted and therefore could not be overlooked.

In the book they published on their return home, *Don't Cry for Me, Sergeant Major*, McGowan and Hands give an excellent account of something we would consider, by our definition, an incident. A Paratroop patrol had captured an Argentinian soldier and brought him in for questioning. He was wearing a sweater with 'Royal Marines Commando' on the shoulder flashes and it was believed he was one of those responsible for shooting down a British helicopter and firing on its crew as they struggled in the sea. The sergeant wanted to shoot him; instead he was interrogated. To quote from McGowan's and Hands's book:

'Said he was a private', said Intelligence Officer Captain Giles Orpen-Smellie. 'Anyway, after a little heart to heart, in which I will grant you the odd voice was raised, it turns out that he's now a sergeant . . . The chap was a bit reluctant to talk to us at first, but he was encouraged to see the error of his ways and now he's singing like a bird. All very useful stuff'. To those outside, 'seeing the error of his ways' was a phrase that would benefit from a modicum of elaboration. A sergeant came out of the interrogation shed and obliged. 'Gave the cunt a kicking,' he said. 'Don't have time to fuck about with the niceties'.

The little 'heart to heart' was clearly more than a fireside chat, but nevertheless is an incident because such things happen in all wars, and its public exposure will not stop such events. They are embedded in the very nature of things. They have therefore a lower claim for the reporter's attention, unless, that is, the reporter switches to the role discussed in the opening of the book, to that of the moralist intent on attacking war exactly because such incidents are typical of it. As Hastings reasoned to us in not reporting the showing of white flags and the shooting of British soldiers on moving forward to accept surrender, it was the type of occurrence obtaining to war: they are merely incidents of nastiness, the sum total of which is war. However, had the interrogation described by McGowan and Hands been put on a formalized basis of systematic and agreed torture rather than an individual sergeant showing initiative, then it would not have been an incident but a feature and therefore have a higher claim to being reported.

As we noted in Chapter 1, this was for many of the correspondents their first experience of war reporting. Some found themselves questioning their customary practice; they looked for new techniques and new ground rules. Ian Bruce was one:

> In the end I stopped doing hard news, except if something like the bombing of *Galahad* came up. I began to do pieces about how black masking tape was the actual war-winner in the Falklands; it kept the springs in rifle clips, it stopped your lips being scalded on the edge of mess tins, it bound up bandages on the wounded . . . [I did pieces about things] like quartermasters wondering after the whole thing had been solved, whatever way it went, [how] they were going to catch up with the red tape, and do their book-keeping and accounting. An endless story. There's a book by Steinbeck called *Once There Was a War*. When he had . . . tried to get away from what the other correspondents were doing, he'd go for the off-beat, and found his stories were passed by the censors because they [couldn't] really get onto his line of thought. It didn't quite work that way for me but I thought, if I'm going to get stories through, they've got to be more feature.

Max Hastings explained his method:

> One has to distinguish between what happened before the landing and what happened after. When you come on to the war, the basic decision that I made was that it was almost impossible to get quick accurate information on, for example, aircraft shot down, or details on casualties. And, anyway, there were likely to be a lot of problems arguing this stuff through censorship and therefore I made a very conscious decision at the begining to concentrate on writing feature material.

He compared his own approach to that of various colleagues:

I was seeing some other people's copy coming back; it sounds as if I'm rather knocking them, but one has to do it in order to explain why what happened did happen. [It] was heavily censored . . . I thought [they] were absolutely out of their minds because they tried to write stories, 'We are now ten miles from so and so, advancing towards Teal Inlet, we have lost twenty men with sore feet'. And nobody but an idiot could have imagined that they were going to be allowed to file that kind of thing. Before we landed, I said to Martin Helm, the senior MoD man: 'Look, you ought to be saying to everybody here: "These are the facts of life, this is the way it's going to work".' . . . And I do think that if you'd had somebody with some brawn and brains running the MoD operation who could have . . . explained the facts of life about war-reporting, they could all have saved themselves a lot of aggro later.

Hastings, who had already covered eleven wars, felt he had grasped those 'facts of life'. He was altogether better prepared and less equivocating. From the outset, he understood the ambiguities of the war reporter's role; and resolved the tension between observer and participant by openly deciding, at least on one occasion deliberately to assist the efforts of the Task Force by his writing.

Was there a moment of being actually knowingly deceitful about how things were going? I think there was a moment, yes. The night the *Atlantic Conveyor* and *Coventry* were sunk. Morale in the beach-head was low and everybody was bloody nervous; it suddenly seemed a very, very long way home. And I remember one young Marine saying, 'Well, if all else fails, we'll get the Yanks to come and bail us out'. And I said: 'Forget it, kid, there's only one lot that's going to get us out of here and that's ourselves'. And, yes, even at that time I continued to file stories about how well the build-up was going; and, yes, at that particular moment I was knowingly writing more optimistically about the spirit in the beach-head than one knew it to be.

We asked him whether, had he not written 'optimistically', his copy would have passed the censors. He agreed, but went on to say that, in any case, that was not the point.

. . . I remember one journalist, who shall remain anonymous, talking to me at one point about possible ways of breaking censorship and I said: 'Well, to be quite honest, I don't feel that that's the name of the game at the moment . . . For better or for worse . . . this is a Brit. war. We can all argue afterwards about whether it was actually a ridiculous war, but at this minute, especially when all our necks are on the line with everybody else's, I wouldn't want to file a despatch that is likely to give the Argentinians any hope or comfort'.

There was no self-delusion on Hastings's part about what this meant in terms of standard journalistic practice: 'We've thrown aside all the sort of "Insight" rules for how you set about being a journalist.' We then asked him whether he could have written a story sufficiently skilfully to indicate that things weren't going well, without otherwise circumventing the censors. His reply shows that he did not even wish to do so:

I might have been able to, but I didn't try to. I sought to convey the impression that the build-up was going splendidly and we were all getting on pretty well. The Argentinians, who had taken pretty severe losses themselves, were probably at that stage considering how much further they were willing to stick their necks out in order to press home their air attack. And obviously if they had received a secondhand despatch from somebody at the beach-head saying, 'We are in real trouble and things are not going well,' it might have made them feel that it was worth another crack. But I think that was the only moment of the war at which one was knowingly distorting the feeling as one knew it to be.

When set against the wider context of the war, Hastings's last point is very important. Although the argument has been, and is, that the journalists developed a growing respect and often fondness for the troops in terms of excessively sympathetic copy, exemplified by Hastings's single occasion of distorting 'the feeling as one knew it', this was never really tested to the full. There was no call to. The troops' own performance and behaviour took care of that. Triumph and victory need no defence. Only defeat and failure require apology or an explanation to turn, Dunkirk-like, loss into achievement. Thus, the journalists' sentiments were in harmony with the play of battle, moving and developing as the opposition was rolled back to cram them eventually into Port Stanley. There is no need to be sensitive about success.

The journalists observed the troops, and in large measure liked what they saw. They were impressed by their comradeship, fitness, dedication to their occupation and competence as a fighting force. Thus, particularly when ashore, the fact that the journalists were affectionately or sympathetically involved with the troops and consequently loath to criticize does not alter the fact that it was not just a question of patriotism, but also a product of objective conditions. The troops were good. they knew what they were doing. Like a foreign football team, well trained, victorious, they would have got respectful copy whatever their nationality.

Were there, even so, aspects of the war which, because of censorship went unreported? We asked Max Hastings:

It's certainly true they didn't get the story of the naval war. And we didn't understand, I didn't understand, what was happening at sea until I started interviewing people after I came back. It's arguable, whether [telling] everybody about what we were trying to do would have been in everybody's interests or not. On the land side, the 5 Brigade saga was the major cock-up of the war. Everything relating to it. It's really naive to imagine that you could file despatches from San Carlos saying '5 Brigade . . . – they're the most unsuitable troops that could have been sent to do this job; . . . and they're well on their way to inflicting a major disaster'. This is what it would have amounted to and yet you couldn't really expect to send this and also we didn't know at the beginning . . . I think, again, you've just got to be realistic and say, well, could you ever have expected that a story of that kind was going to come out while the war was being fought?

It is worth examining an instance of what 'totally open' war-reporting would involve. After the war, in their book, *Battle for the Falklands*, Max Hastings and Simon Jenkins did tell the story in full. It appears that Major-General Moore, overall land commander, was very disturbed by Wilson's (Commanding Officer, 5 Brigade) independent dash for Bluff Cove, throwing Moore and his staff into a state of alarm as attempts were made to bring up support. The Welsh Guards, however, part of 5 Brigade, had to get up with A and B Company, who having jumped forward by Chinook helicopters were dug in covering the approaches to Bluff Cove settlement. The shortage of transport meant that the Welsh Guards had to march to join them. They set off in the afternoon of 3 June to march to Goose Green. Lacking adequate tracked vehicles, overladen with equipment and fresh from public duties, unacclimatised and not especially fit, the exercise, much to the derision of 3 Commando to whom it was a modest 'yomp', had to be abandoned after twelve hours. They returned over Sussex Mountain to San Carlos where it was decided to sail them round to Bluff Cove to land at Fitzroy. It was a risk, and in a series of mistakes, misunderstandings and faults the Guards were left exposed and unprotected as they waited to disembark in broad daylight. Slightly after one o'clock in the afternoon of 8 June, two Skyhawks and two Mirages screamed on them. Thirty-three Guardsmen were killed and many more injured, some hideously burnt. It was a disaster in the sense of human error linked by a chain of mistakes to produce an almost inevitable conclusion. The survivors were badly shaken and taken back to San Carlos to recover from their nightmare experience.

In their book, Hastings and Jenkins are able to analyse and criticize that episode in detail. At the time, however, it was not only impossible for Hastings to discover very much about that complicated amphibious operation but, as he indicated, to report it. If published, the history of the exercise would have given incalculable comfort to the Argentines.

Hastings, being particularly confident, may have consciously 'distorted the feeling'. Others, too, certainly recognized the special difficulties of their situation. David Norris, for instance, told us that:

> I can honestly say that I don't think I wrote a single word that would have been against the British operation and I felt I had to do that. It was my country. I've got my own feelings about whether the whole thing was necessary or not, and I certainly think it could have been avoided . . . but, once it was happening, I think

you'd had no choice – and you'd have to suspend any impartiality because it's a life-and-death situation.

Jeremy Hands, however, strongly disagreed with the view that copy should even be 'softened':

> . . . I don't believe any of the decent journalists would have done that. The moment you start altering your copy just to make it easy for yourself, then you can chuck out all your professionalism and all your objectivity and credibility. You lose it by altering your copy to suit circumstances. You're not telling the truth, you're telling a version of the truth which you think might be got through more easily. I don't think anybody did that.

In summary, Hands believes that: 'Anyone who will say that he won't report something because it might reflect badly, as far as I'm concerned, is a traitor to his own profession'.

> I also did a story . . . which created another stink back here . . . Some friends of mine in the SAS said: 'You really ought to see some receipts we've found from the Falkland Islands Company showing that they'd been trading openly with the Argentinians'. And, again, I sent that story back, totally unhesitantly . . . I didn't say it was disgusting; I said the soldiers were very angry about it, which is true and . . . let people make their own minds up, I only reported the fact. Those were the facts, there had been trading going on, money had changed hands between the locals and the Argentinians. I reported it, and only later were excuses made. 'Well, it was either that or have your goods stolen.' And they were doing that for good relations. That was crap; the Falkland Islanders are a bunch of absolute arseholes, and they were doing it because they don't really care who they are trading with, to be honest. They don't really care if they're British or Argentinians, that's my opinion.

This insistence upon 'the neutrality of the facts' is particularly interesting. 'Only reporting the facts' fits Jeremy Hands's model of the objective and impartial reporter. Establishing the truth, or what the truth is at any point understood to be, is more complex; 'facts' alone are insufficient. In the example quoted above, Hands falls back on an argument about the character of the Falklanders to justify his interpretation of the evidence. He gave us another example of the 'use' of 'facts' in his account of an incident at Goose Green. First we give David Norris's version. He is describing how his paper, the *Mail,* splashed the story.

> They [the *Mail*] did something which I found out afterwards . . . which I didn't like at all. They would link my name with a piece by Jeremy Hands which found its way to the *Daily Mail* as a front-page leader, which was absolute nonsense. It was classic gung-ho stuff, about an incident which happened during Goose Green . . . they said 'The Argentinians had treacherously raised a white flag and as soon as the Paras went over to their trenches, they'd shot them'. And it didn't happen of course. I saw the incident and in fact I didn't even mention it. It was just complete confusion. Smoke and flames and white flags going up all over the place in the

Argentinian bunkers, and there were shots still being fired and a Paratrooper was hit by one. I would never have gone as far as that, to gild the lily to that extent. You asked me if I was on the side of the British. Yes, I was, but as far as invention went, no. It was wrong to do that because – apart from crapping in people's houses, things like that which are fairly minor things – I think they behaved perfectly properly. The few prisoners they took, like the Harrier pilots, were treated very well and they studiously avoided bombing civilian property.

Hands had been refused permission to film at Goose Green but he heard the story of the incident. According to Norris:

> . . . a lot of the Toms, the young private soldiers, had heard it secondhand. I'd seen it as far as I could see it; but they were talking about it afterwards and a couple of days afterwards saying 'Did you hear what the bloody spiks have done?' And the story was growing by that time and I think it had filtered back to Brigade Headquarters.

Hands explained how he came by the story and how he decided to use it:

> There is no question that an Argentinian white flag was raised. British soldiers went forward to accept that surrender and these soldiers were shot by Argentinians. That is fact. What has since been said, and I reported this as well, is that in the fog of war it might have been that the guys in the trench intended to surrender, somebody in another trench who hadn't surrendered had seen British soldiers advancing, and had shot them from a different angle. And there was confusion. But again, I didn't go on air and categorically say: 'I have seen white flags flying and I have seen British soldiers being shot by people waving white flags'. I said that British soldiers have told me. I did this interview and I can remember the quote: 'We saw the white flags, they fought hard, then they waved white flags and they fought on and that sickened us'. That was said outside the community hall in Goose Green when everybody was still covered in sweat and shit.

True, the Argentines, after raising flags of surrender, fired on the British. That is not in dispute. The question, and the only truth to establish, is what did it mean? The same can be asked of the trading receipts. Were they evidence of a forced exchange or free commercial transactions? Whatever the answer, it is of no matter here, of more importance are the methods adopted to establish truth.

Material, especially hard news, must be sourced, but the problem with sourcing is that it is a spurious way of establishing 'truth'. It is not in any systematic way geared to it. It operates instead as a method of protection and a way of strengthening a story. Providing the source itself is not fictitious, then admittedly it does protect against fabrication. The manner in which a story is strengthened is as often as not by the collecting of another statement in support of the original statement but from a different source. The eliciting of more supportive quotations does not demonstrate truth; rather, that other individuals believed something to be true. Given that the additional quotes, usually few in number, are often drawn from the same circle of participants as the original, they are quite often of little veridical merit.

Whilst journalists in general offer the primacy of facts as demonstration of truth, well illustrated by Hands's statement, really such faith is epistemologically better seen as no more than a talisman, a magical touchstone by which they hope to get the account right. Apart from the most simple situations such as the number of dead or whatever, when the fact is the report, facts can never provide the hoped-for protection: facts form the basis for judgement, and judgement itself influences whether or not something is given the status of a fact.

In the main, journalists operate like any social enquirer: from established procedures – and from past experiences, general knowledge about the world, and understanding of the type of event or topic under reportage. For this reason, then, in any other than the most elementary situations one set of facts given to one journalist will be taken to mean something different, no matter how slightly, to another. Two statements, one referring to Hastings and one by Hastings himself, will help clarify the point. In discussing the public relations side of the war, John Shirley observed that the Royal Marines, who had suffered particularly badly in defence expenditure, saw the campaign as a heaven-sent opportunity to demonstrate their worth and therefore the validity of spending some money on them. Shirley believes that Hastings, because of his military background, was the only journalist to be really sensitive to the issues.

> He picked up on cuts in the Navy, cuts on the ships and cuts in the Armed Forces generally. But I think that's because he recognized it more easily than we did. If we'd been with the police force – it's a very good analogy with me and the police force, because I used to do a lot of crime reporting and I know policemen fairly well – I think I would have had the same kind of sensitivity that Max had to the military. You just know the way the guys think and you know what obsesses them and what their particular little things are. And Max knew that about the military, but we didn't.

Facts therefore took on a different meaning for Hastings than they did for Shirley. But more than that – or, rather, expressed another way – Hastings's knowledge transformed information into 'facts' in a way not possible for Shirley. What was to most journalists background noise became a tune to the experienced ear of Hastings. Hastings himself talked about the way in which experience helps in applying judgement to the 'facts':

> When you've got very little hard information and you're attempting to cobble together a story that you can transmit it's an enormous advantage to have some

feeling for the way that military operations work. If you don't have that instinctive understanding, the whole thing is completely meaningless.

That 'instinctive understanding' was what, as we saw above, decided Hastings not to 'go with the napalm story'.

Sometimes the information the journalists were given was simply wrong. Ian Bruce, for instance, told us:

> There were briefings each evening (on the long march across the Islands) and we had to attend the groups with the officers to find out the general situation, but not having seen it I thought it was unfair to report it, because there were inaccuracies in the briefings. We were told at one stage that *Antrim* had been sunk and in fact it was *Ardent*.

Some correspondents did report such erroneous information; their doing so was, as Lieutenant David Tinker wrote in his letters home, an astonishing example of their 'readiness to lie'.

There is little a journalist can do where a briefing is wrong, especially when he depends on only one or two sources. The experienced Hesketh, for example, described the Commander of 5 Brigade as 'very, very helpful. But maybe some of that was disinformation, but nevertheless . . . you came away from a briefing from him thinking: Well, he's really keeping you well informed'. Jockell, the soundman, emphasized that 'we were very much in the hands of the information we were getting from the military', adding that 'If a naval person or an Army person says . . . something, then you assume that this is pretty well true. You always treat people as truthful until you find out that they are dishonest . . . There was no reason for us to assume that'.

John Shirley's opinion was:

> . . . what manipulation went on went on at this end (London). And I'm sure the same is true for Bluff Cove as well. As soon as the Bluff Cove thing happened, we knew it was a catastrophe; the casualty figures just kept on mounting and mounting. And it was going to change the whole of the plan, they couldn't really stop that, because there were reporters there. BBC crew was filming, Mick Seamark was in the landing-craft next to it. I don't think they tried to falsify things. Although McDonald told me last week in London [that] the Chiefs of Staff had been in favour of putting out misinformation. He said the Army were particularly keen in London to put out inaccurate information; he said: 'We resisted it. We did not put out false information'.

The journalists did have access to people and events and in that sense the war was openly recorded. Attacking the idea of cover-up and conspiracies, Hanrahan said:

> Nobody believes just how close you were to the military. Nobody believes how aware you were of what was going on and who was doing what. And buzzes and rumours came into your ears as fast as they did into anybody else's and we're not

used to that. In Northern Ireland, the military keep anything secret for ever, because you just don't get close enough to them. But here you couldn't. You were just on top of them the whole time. There were secrets, operational secrets. But things like human behaviour, that got round very fast.

For the most part the correspondents were not obstructed. Their problem was, rather, a logistical one. It was simply very difficult for them to find out, at any moment, who knew what. John Shirley gave us one example, the Argentine strike on *Atlantic Conveyor*:

> . . . when it was first hit, we asked, what the hell's on it? And you'd go and ask an engineer and he'd say: 'Well, I know there's a Harrier strip on there, because it's an engineering supply, and I know this and I know that . . .' But nobody actually knew everything. They would all tell you bits and pieces. And then people boarded *Conveyor* after it had been hit to try and salvage stuff and they were on for two days and then, I think, it sank. But, the commanders in the field didn't know what had been salvaged, because the information would probably all go back to London; it might come to one or two people on the Islands, but it wasn't a question of being given false information, it was a case of information genuinely not being available.

In the absence of any deliberate witholding of information, or the issuing of misinformation, the task was to decide what to send and how to write it. As Nicholson put it: 'You would have had to be absolutely thick, blind and deaf not to have sent back good copy. I could've sent back the menu of *Fearless* and they'd have gone wild for it because of the appetite here for anything'. Concerned that his copy might not be getting through and, like Nicholson, appreciating editors' insatiable appetite for news, Hastings's policy was to file and file again:

> Every day I just tried to file everything that one could lay hands on. If you happened to run into a Harrier pilot who had been shot down, you banged out 400 words and shoved it on the line. And you worked on the basis of, let's suppose it doesn't all get through, or suppose it's not all Tolstoyan, just keep chucking it out.

Some stories, even so, were not sent home. Tony Snow told us about one discovery he did not report:

> . . . I'd met quite a few nice people out in the sticks, but in Stanley it was quite amazing. The bloke at the Upland Goose Hotel put up the price of drink as soon as we landed. He'd never allowed the Marines into there because they would interfere with the Argentinian tourists who stayed there. He upped the price of the beds there; it was supposed to be $20 a room and he was charging $20 a bed and four beds in the room. Two on a bed and two on the floor, so he was doing marvellous business. And the people in Stanley – they were quite amazing. They said: 'When are we going to get rid of all these soldiers?' They weren't a bit grateful. They thought it was their due that they should have been baled out. And they were quite happily talking within the hearing of Paras and Marines who had seen their mates shot to pieces, who had lost legs, who had been blinded, and

these people were saying: 'When are we going to get rid of these soldiers? They're dirtying the place up. When are they going to go?' And I thought there would be some nasty scenes actually. A lot of the soldiers afterwards said that they didn't think a great deal of the people, they were so ungrateful and that it wasn't really worth fighting for.

But, as Snow recognized, that would have contradicted the *Sun*'s editorial line: 'Our paper wouldn't have stood for a story like that. They wouldn't have taken it'.

Other stories went unreported, not so much because correspondents believed their editors would think them irrelevant but because the journalists themselves questioned the propriety.

We asked Hanrahan about the stories of bayoneting. He told us:

I heard not a word about that. The interesting thing is that there hasn't been anything about that, nobody has produced it. I was assailed at one point, at one public meeting, by someone who said I had failed to tell the real story, the disgraceful behaviour of the troops. If someone can tell it to me, I'd be more than happy to put it out. I think what happened was that there were a lot of rumours flying about. I think the rumours in this country were rather greater than they were there. And I found no evidence of that sort of misbehaviour. I heard rumours about Goose Green, but when I looked at them quite early on there was nothing to substantiate any of them.

David Norris was more blunt. When we asked him about the stories circulating in the Upland Goose, he said:

Yes, there were bits of looting, pilfering. Most of the reporters who'd been with the Marines or the Paras said: 'We'd rather that somebody else did that; it's a valid story, but I'd much rather another reporter did it'.

The entire experience – not surprisingly – had brought the journalists to understand the nature and purpose of the campaign, the behaviour of the military, the conduct of the war, as participants rather than observers. When we asked Shirley whether he had consciously refrained from sending back stories of possible British misconduct, he replied:

I'm afraid that subconciously we probably didn't want to hear it. I'm not particularly proud of saying that. If one had come across something of My-Lai proportions, one would have done something about it. But lesser things one did turn a blind eye to . . .

Afterwards, things might be different, as Max Hastings assured us:

We have a completely different perception when the war is over. A lot of people who buy mine and Simon Jenkins's book bought it under false pretences. They will think that that will also be fairly jingoistic. In fact it's a much more critical and cynical look at the whole operation . . . But at the time I felt, for better or worse, we're in this war and we'd better try whatever contribution we can make towards winning it. I think a genuine dilemma would have come up if, supposing we had got bogged down on the mountains around Stanley, the war had gone on for another three months and somebody had been cocking it up. I honestly don't know what we would or could have ended up doing in that sort of situation. As it was at the time, the whole thing was being very efficiently conducted, so there wasn't a sense of there [being] a great scandal that I'm constantly suppressing, it wasn't like that. I mean most of it. Of course, 5 Brigade's operation was a cock-up, and the day the war ended I wrote a piece saying so.

But at the time, the journalists' ground rules inevitably changed. One way or another, they all sooner or later adapted to the situation in which they found themselves. Hastings may have known this from the start, but, as Shirley told us, even he had initial doubts:

Very early on, I think before we arrived on the Islands . . . [Max] wrote this piece about something like 'nobody can be neutral in this campaign'. He wrote a piece saying, 'When my father was a great war correspondent he used to tell me that you didn't have to report objectively what was going on. Your job was to put out stuff that cheered up the lads at home. I thought he was wrong. Now I believe he's right, and I intend to cover this war as a patriot and write good stuff about the British Army'. And he recognized the dilemma, he saw which way he was going and, to his credit, he said so. If you read anything after that, you know precisely the position it was coming from – there was no element of deceit about it at all. And I think that is a great credit to Max actually, intellectually. He acknowledged that pressure and he acknowledged that role and he said that that was how he was going to report it. My respect for him is considerable for that, actually.

The journalists had entered a different, closed world; their values shifted with them.

Lessons, reasons and results: an overview of identification

So far, the process of identification has been examined in terms of the specifics of the setting and of how the close involvement of the journalists with the troops, as they faced common danger, led to feelings of attachment. Yet the identification with the troops was not a product of just living together and appreciating their world at close quarters, but of experiencing it at first hand, and experiencing unique events incapable of incorporation into existing definitions of the world. A situation, new to both troops and journalists alike, involving forces that threatened individual existence itself, could be expected to produce shifts in understanding and it is this general shift, as part of the social construction of reality, that we now wish to examine theoretically and by way of example point to the implications for reporting. It is best approached through the question of 'atrocities'. John Shirley:

There were two or three things in Stanley which I think people turned a blind eye to. When [the soldiers] arrived in Stanley there was a bit of looting. [They] went into a number of houses and wrecked them and nicked stuff. I was told secondhand by somebody in Stanley, a fairly senior citizen, civil servant, a guy you'd tend to trust, that somebody had lost about £2000 worth of jewellery, that some . . . had nicked the jewellery. But could you ever prove that? Very difficult. But there were one or two stories which I think people tended to ignore. One didn't want to hear it, and in another situation I might have done. The actual whole business of gathering information is so difficult in a running story like that. There is now some controversy about whether or not [the soldiers] at Goose Green exaggerated the Argentinians' casualties . . . It has also been suggested that they bayoneted rather a lot of people on Mount Longdon – they acknowledge themselves that they did bayonet people on Longdon after the battle was over, but how many is uncertain.

Shirley was asked, when 'is a story a story?'

You were constantly having to make political judgements about the value of getting a story: (1) if you can stand it up, and (2) if you can get it out, will the impact of it at home be sufficiently strong to counterbalance the animosity that is going to greet you at the time? Is it a story that is better hung onto until you get home, when do you play it, how do you play it? The fact that we became so much participants in the thing affected it, too. I didn't see so much myself, but [one journalist] told me, that he had seen occasions on which people had shot unarmed men, unarmed Argentinians who were in the process of surrendering. He didn't report it because he said that, although he disapproved of it, he felt he could understand it. In the tension of battle and given what was going on it was an understandable action. That is not a very objective journalistic judgement. That is the judgement of a participant, and to that extent it's wrong. You see, I think that this is an absolutely central problem – this kind of crisis of identity. This problem of participant versus observer.

Yet it is not just a question of becoming a participant, of being with the troops; the question also enters of accommodating a world which shifts to include behaviour no 'decent' person would consider possible of himself outside the sanctions of that particular situation. Even so, it is not a straightforward matter of sanctioned behaviour; engagement also involves the psychological adjustment to and accommodation of gradation of acts. Without even considering questions of desensitization, then, the meaning that acts have, whether permissibly sanctioned or not, must shift in the changed conditions of combat. They cannot possess the same meaning as in civilian life. The horrors of war cannot, in effect, be understood from within civilian values, they can only be judged by them. The point is that to hold to a set of values is to exist in a social world where the plausibility structure supporting those values remains sufficiently intact. Thus, to be the witness to or author of macabre permutations of death is not to place other acts in perspective as if ontologically there was a correct perspective but, rather, to alter perspectives so that acts such as rape, looting or summary executions are no longer capable of possessing their original values and meanings. It is a problem of credibility.

There is something incongruous in holding on to civilian notions of the sanctity of human life in a situation where the whole point of the exercise is to destroy as much life as possible in order to defeat the enemy. Death becomes a technical question, the conclusion of which is a framework of statements about the ability to kill, not a fine concern for individual life. Thus, it is not just the scale of killing, which is a contributory factor in the journalists' glossing over of individual deaths, but the lack of a civilian reality by which to hinge the significance of death.

Hardly anyone with the Task Force had experienced the type of combat situation met with in the Falklands. It was a new experience for both the military and the journalists alike, and this 'newness' meant that it had to be made sense of. Meaning structures, however, are not built from nothing, they are negotiated in interaction with the elements already there – language, culture, beliefs – and with others in the shared community. It is by and large not an individual enterprise at all, therefore, and it is consequently hardly surprising that the journalists, in common with the troops, faced by new conditions, were presented with the necessity of constructing a new reality by which to make sense of their experiences, not just in terms of circumstances physically going on around them, but in order to give meaning to new emotions. In fact, the social construction of reality, the activity itself, is the process by which the emotions become known.

The fact that the journalist did not bother to report the killings because, according to Shirley, 'he felt he could understand it' ought to be viewed therefore in terms of the dismantlement of the plausibility structures within which violent death draws its usual meaning and the construction of a new world of realities. Indeed, it would be surprising if what was deemed acceptable behaviour, especially at the margins of the permissible, was not shared to some degree by soldier and journalist alike. To disapprove therefore but yet not report because 'one could understand it' takes on a somewhat different meaning when one understands the *context* within which the event occurred. Had, for example, the killings been of members of the IRA in Northern Ireland, then no matter what the sympathies of the journalists, such incidents if witnessed would no doubt have been reported for the reason that within the setting of Northern Ireland the plausibility structures supporting civilian values, and notions of appropriate behaviour, remain sufficiently intact for such killings to produce shock and thus register as news items. They are, in other words, out of place in reality as constructed in and about Northern Ireland.

It is not a question, however, of a reality, some ultimate base of being – or, at least, operationally it is not – but a variety of realities containing a variety of assembled meanings which jostle together producing tension and confusion. The soldier's fond letter from home for example, can disturb at the same time as comfort. The letter brings voices from a reality where violent death is not present, where behaviour and values prevail which are totally inappropriate to, and at odds with, the soldier's setting, and it is from within that context that one must understand how, for example, the correspondent did not choose to report what Shirley clearly considered ought to have been reported if one was acting as an 'objective' journalist. It is no good saying what journalistically ought to have occurred if that 'ought' excludes lack of appreciation of what was likely or possible within the particular context.

Attitudes to death are revealing, for the world of the civilian tends to be built around an assumption of its absence. Yet for the soldier death, or at least its possibility, is part of the nature of things.

The journalists went to war without the benefit of military symbolic support to sustain them in the face of acts they were to witness and, in the case of some, 'friends' they were to lose. How was reality to be constructed?

There was, right from the beginning, a general feeling amongst the journalists of something vaguely not quite right in the head about the whole affair, a kind of military Mad Hatter's Tea Party. That was so even for those who accepted the important principles involved, of sovereignty and right to self-determination, and accepted them to the point of considering the response of sending a Task Force the appropriate one. Thus, a favourable diplomatic settlement would without any doubt have been preferred by the journalists, and indeed by most of the troops as well. Something can be ludicrous, accepted as ludicrous, but nevertheless engaged in because there is no other way out. Yet as unrealistic as the atmosphere may have been on the voyage south, the military were better placed to cope with it than the journalists. For example, their refusing, as noted by Shirley, to ask questions about the wider political sense of the operation, reduces the area of strain by containing meaning within the activity itself, the rationality of which is structured into the raison d'etre of military life and collectively cemented by unstated appeal to those all around. As Hastings mentioned, the military never truly respects the civilian, the reason being that different worlds are at work. In fact, it makes sense to talk of 'military life' in a way that it does not for most other occupations. The more enclosed a particular world, the greater the applicability of such notions of totality. Thus, in the case of a war or other posting not only are men physically transferred, but all the established meanings of *their* world are also carried along. The journalists, however, had left their world behind.

We referred earlier to news as a social construction; that is, that news does not exist independently of someone defining events, happenings or processes as news, but news values, as collections of occupational understandings about what is of interest to specific publics, are basically the worked-through knowledge of civilian interpretation. For example, the visiting fireman to one of the world's troublespots retains within him the civilian's sensibilities and values capable of moral outrage at acts outside the norm of civil experience, and which by definition of the extraordinary gives them news value. It is possible therefore to talk of thresholds of morality as well as of cognition. In practice they are not unconnected. It may be, for example, that something which at first visually stands out because it is uncommon to the nature of the event examined, after repeated exposure becomes no longer noticeable as special and thus not reported, until, that is, within its own terms it becomes so extreme an example that it once again forces its attention on the journalist.

Thus, for the correspondent of the type operating alongside the action and living with the troops it could be expected that he would adjust to the routines of war so that sights and experiences once beyond imagination became not accepted in the sense of narcotized but, rather, expected and taken for granted: they were accepted as part of the nature of things, and it is this acceptance which helps explain the non-reporting of the killings. It is not, as suggested by Shirley, a question, as with other similar 'oversights', of professional torpor or poor practice, but a matter of the new construction of reality which allowed the entry of values that downgrade in significance acts which would normally have been reported, and it is from within that framework that the position of the war correspondent ought to be understood; not from the accepted understandings of Fleet Street. It could not be expected that the larger social values drawn from a different reality and upon which news values themselves are structured would not on entering a closed military world and military activity change, and in doing so change, or at least affect, news values.

It could not be expected that the journalists' construction of reality would differ dramatically in certain respects from that of the military; nevertheless, their occupational position was different, and they would claim that irrespective of wider interpretations of the world their methods of procedure, the reporting techniques they use, help protect objectivity. It is, however, a false claim. The methods journalists in general use cannot achieve such a position, and require, in light of the defence, some exploration.

Jeremy Hands of ITN mentioned that on one or two occasions he used 'we' in his reports when referring to the British, but deleted such references before sending his despatch: 'Those were the warning signs at the back of my head that I was beginning to get a little too close to them and too far away from reality'. Reality for Hands meant objective and impartial reporting. The entry of 'we' would not on its own question the objectivity of a report, but it would cast a shadow on the idea of impartiality. What, then, are the distinctions between objectivity and impartiality?

Hastings on his own admission was partial in his approach in that he made a conscious decision not to report anything detrimental to the war effort, but such partiality did not exclude him from being objective. This is easier to understand if we take objectivity not as a state, but as a procedure. To be objective does not mean to be accurate in some ultimate sense, but to follow the accepted procedures of the journalistic community. If, as most individuals do, one confuses objectivity with complete accuracy, then the problem of 'knowing' does not go away, the circle is merely squared: is something objective because it is accurate or accurate because it is objective? Most would hold, and the expressed views of journalists would tend to concur, the former to be the case when in fact it is more useful to accept the latter. It is not in any epistemological sense the case, but it more accurately passes for what is taken as knowing in a systematic procedural way. That is, having laid down the rules against which information must qualify to pass muster as evidence, it is possible at least independently to check that it does so. It would not make an enquiry accurate, most commonly referred to as reality, but it would enable it to be judged as accurate against some test for accuracy.

If journalists in general tend to misunderstand the status of the knowledge produced by their methods, and the protection such methods might afford, the danger is of presenting those procedures to themselves and to their public as appropriate for the task of deciding objectively based truth, especially the quote. Those in the Falklands were under no illusion about the tensions they faced and which might influence or rather compromise their copy.

John Shirley, for example, argued that when copy from the Falklands was printed in London it should have been noted that this

material was censored and that it was by somebody who was partici-
pating in the campaign. In fact Shirley, and to an even greater
extent Hastings, can be considered to have created a new and
reasonably well-defined role within British journalism – the participatory journalist. Given their self-awareness of the way in which
this role had evolved, and given their understanding about the ways
in which this served to compound the problems of censorship, the
journalists were thrown back onto strategies to circumvent such
difficulties. Hastings:

> When I was writing copy I kept trying to think of ways of saying things that would
> circumvent the minders. For example, I wanted to say: 'Many people down here
> think that Woodward is a cunt'. And in the end the form that I came up with, in a
> piece about attitudes, I said: 'It should come as no surprise to anyone, however
> great is the British public's appetite for heroes, to discover that there was no
> sensation here that a new Nelson had been born.' Now, that sounds a rather
> convoluted way of putting it, but everybody had got the message, everybody who
> read that said it was a great shot, they were staggered that I had been able to get
> that through censorship, because it was perfectly clear to everybody who read it
> that was what it was intended to signify. And actually you could get a lot of things
> like that, if you wrote generally upbeat pieces, and you slipped in the odd sentence
> about the problems, you'd get away with a lot.

Hanrahan mentioned his approach to the difficulties he faced:

> I changed it deliberately between radio and television. Radio was descriptive and
> television was much more analytical. I think that if you look at the scripts you'll
> find that . . . literally on radio I described what I'd seen in detail. In television I
> didn't describe what I'd seen, I talked about the consequences of certain decisions
> and what the effect was. And in the television despatches there was all the stuff
> about how it was a decision of the Argentinians to attack the warships rather than
> the store ships which saved the landing. I knew that (1) it would be going out
> sufficiently after the event for it not to be dangerous, by then the air defence
> would have been set up and (2) it seemed to me to be the sort of analytical
> information which was available at the time and could be written at the time which
> could fit into a television script. Radio, which is primarily concerned to know what
> the hell is happening, really didn't have time and censorship again would stop me
> . . . I can remember putting into the Bluff Cove, one message about why the hell
> there were no air defences and why the men hadn't been got off the ships earlier. I
> mean, all that was in a television despatch which came out three weeks later.
> Although it wasn't in the radio one at the time, it was in the first available
> television despatch. So although the radio one was restrained and didn't seek to be
> critical, the television piece certainly was . . . that saved my pride . . .

It is understandable that holding to the idea of the journalist as an
observer Hanrahan should be thankful that his professional pride
was saved by the delay in getting his television reports back. In
general the participant will be less ready to write critical copy than
the observer, but there is nothing determinate about this as

Hastings's account shows. Furthermore, in certain circumstances the participant is likely to be more critical than his erstwhile 'objective' colleague, the observer.

The worth of any story is judged in terms of news values, but those values do not come from nowhere. They are human judgements, accredited estimations about what is or is not news, and that judgement is one which is learnt over time in the process of going about being a journalist. It is an occupational, and hence shared, understanding of what will and will not make news. The occupational consensus means that the news values have an 'inherited' component and consequently they are not made and remade on the spot, or fashioned by the situation, but involve the journalist in examining events in terms of recognizable characteristics, and the more such characteristics there are the greater the likelihood of it 'officially' becoming news. Thus, for example, even though Ian Bruce changed his reporting tactics because as he said 'I thought if I'm going to get stories through they've got to be more featury', he did so by adopting as his model Steinbeck's book *Once There Was a War*, concentrating on the 'off-beat'. To beat the censors may have been his reason or uppermost motive, but Bruce knows as well as any other journalist that the odd or unusual is a sedementary characteristic of news values.

The reporter as observer works within this system of news values to place and judge events. It is the news values in an unstated way that guide him and provide a degree of predictability in selection. In that sense he is more secure and protected by the accredited acceptance of understandings than his counterpart, the participant, who, whilst not operating entirely outside such values – he must still 'make' the news – intercedes with his own individual personal judgement of events related to emotions unconnected to journalism itself. In other words, an extra dimension is added in the newsgathering process which in extreme cases leaves him vulnerable to challenge, on the basis that because his judgement is distinctly individual it would, when judged against all the other stories he might have filed, not be shared by his editorial staff. They are not with him at the reporting scene and cannot therefore share his emotions.

The responsibility for the story or story selection is for the participant therefore a greater individual act than for the observer, where it is dispersed amongst collective values. Thus, the participant having dismissed a story not on the grounds of newsworthiness, but from personal values means that the accepted story is his own *property* rather than an occupational *product*. Because of its exclusivity, the personalized decision, the direct emotional as opposed to occupational connectedness, the journalist cannot with-draw behind the blinds of news values and news expectations to defend his story, but confronts it as a moral or emotional commit-ment. By way of contrast, for example, Tony Snow in sponsoring the Sidewinder missile secured himself against criticism by appeal to professional values, not emotional necessity. Left to his volition Snow would have preferred not to have anything to do with such an enterprise. He found it distasteful, but went ahead, wrote the slogan 'Up yours, Galtieri', wrote his story and weathered the resulting attacks with remarkable ease. He could do so because in an analy-tical sense it had nothing to do with him, it was not personal, but the application of news values: he was representing the *Sun* not himself.

The participant is not as secure as the observer but, as stressed, the two categories are empirical and not ideal types. And thus in practice movement does occur within and between them.

The problem for what we have called the participant journalist, wedded to the events around him, is how to respond when events force him to choose between his professional commitment and his participatory loyalties.

Freed as prisoners of news values, the deliberate allowing of affection to influence operations, there is no reason to assume that the witnessing of disasters would have resulted in a linear move to the position of 'analytical observer'. The very affection which for-med the basis of sympathetic reporting could equally have formed the basis for outright critical onslaught at the slaughter of men with whom they identified. Thus, rather than move back into the tradi-tional camp the participant role may simply have been extended to include righteous wrath. The participant, governed by emotions of a different kind from those of the observer, is potentially the much more uncontrollable of the two types. Having already overturned accepted news judgement to pursue feelings of his own, the partici-pant is free to move his affections where he will. Thus, whilst the observer would not overlook a military setback, his reports would still be bound by the developed options of 'impartiality and objec-tivity' and constrained by efforts at fairness. Not so, however, the participant with his loosened attachment to such values. The very feelings that prohibited his copy reflecting badly on the troops could easily move to expose weakness, incompetence, or the mere fact that the war was unwinnable, all done in the name of the men whom he so fondly regards and with whom he feels affinity. From such feelings the crusader is made.

7

The minders

We have heard a great deal of the difficulties facing the journalists who accompanied the Task Force but little of the problems of their minders. Their life, far from easy, was made still harder by the behaviour of their charges. Ministry of Defence information officers are not unused to journalists. 'There is no worse sight,' to quote one of them, 'than being in the middle of a press pack determined to get what it wants.' They go with them on manoeuvres, work alongside them on courtesy visits, give what assistance they can. Such experiences, however, normally last for a few days at most. Spending months together in the South Atlantic was a completely different – and for the minders an appalling – experience.

It was not that relations were desperate all the time. Friendly drinks were often enjoyed in the bar, but as the journey progressed it became obvious that the minders, as much as the journalists, were working in unpredictable and unfamiliar territory. There was no straightforward set of procedures for them to follow, no framework within which to place specific issues. Authority was not clearly assigned; Whitehall had not briefed its servants or given them any plan. Squabbles erupted, petty incidents took on too much importance, attitudes hardened. By the time the Task Force reached the Falklands, at the moment when the journalists and their minders faced the biggest story most of them had ever seen, or could hope to see, relations had reached rock bottom. This was the point where, given the discomforts and difficulties of their situation, the maximum cooperation was required. Instead, the journalists, impatient and resentful, looked to their own individual talents for organization, and the minders, frustrated and bewildered, clung to what shreds of their authority remained. Each exacerbated the others' difficulties.

Let us take, as an example, the story of the deterioration of relations between one group of journalists and their minder. We return to the *Invincible* Five, hearing the account of their tribulations, this time through the eyes of their minder, Roger Goodwin. In order to appreciate thoroughly the strains and stresses and tedious, grinding difficulties of what it was like to be a minder, Goodwin's account is given considerable length. By doing this it will

131

hopefully take the reader into the world the minders inhabited which at times for them looked like a vision of hell. The Five, we recall, found their situation frustrating in the extreme as, marooned out at sea, they thought of the rich pickings awaiting their more fortunate colleagues on land. Furious and impotent, they turned on Goodwin, who was equally powerless. The more he sought to guide them to behave in a way which might help their cause, the more they resented it and him. Whatever he did was wrong and, by undermining him, his charges were making it even more impossible for him to help them.

The *Invincible* Five had, we remember, so angered Captain Black that he was determined to get them off his ship at the earliest opportunity. Much of his outrage had been caused by what he regarded as the reporters' irresponsibility in sending service messages to their editors in London. Goodwin's account begins with the incident that was, for Black, the last straw:

> There was only one service message that I know of, that was ever delayed. And it's a perfect example of the situation we had with the press. This was the day before the landings. The Captain went on the ship's closed circuit television and informed the ship's company that the landings would be tomorrow and that was it, big day. Half an hour later Mr McIlroy sent a service message to his office. It said: 'would you please close my New York bank account because there's only one dollar left in it'. And he would swear to you to this day that it was perfectly genuine – 'I only did have one dollar left.' I give you that as an example of their great cry, their great claim is: 'Why don't you trust us? Why don't you tell us these things?' The answer is because they're not trustworthy. They were told that the landing was going to be the following day and one of them wanted to send what I honestly believe to have been a coded message, to alert his office to the fact that the landings were due to take place the following morning.

We asked Goodwin whether he discussed the signal with Captain Black:

> As I remember it, it was the Captain's secretary who came to me and said 'Hey, have you seen this?' And I hadn't for some reason. He said: 'We are not going to allow this signal to be sent until after the landings'. I said: 'I quite agree with you.'

Goodwin, already despairing, now saw his difficulties becoming hourly more acute:

> They themselves assumed that they were going to cover the landings ... all the way down ... I never gave it a thought that they wouldn't. Because of the pressure on signals a system was established whereby I couldn't send a signal anyway, nor any other officer on board the ship, without the personal authority of the Captain. He was being very strict, I doubt whether he would have allowed me to have sent an administrative signal saying 'What are your plans for getting the press ashore?' I never even thought of sending such a signal because I never, in a million years, thought that my colleagues on *Canberra* wouldn't be working on

that basis. So about a week before, and I don't know what the date of the landings is going to be, but I know the amphibious group is approaching, I start making noises to Graham Hammond [minder] on *Hermes* and saying 'What's happening?' and 'I'll come back to you,' and he was going away and talking to the Admiral and all the rest. They were going to cover the landings. They went off and phoned their editors who said: 'You bet your bloody life we want you to cover the landings.' Mick Seamark came back from that and I've never seen a man with such a manic drive to do something as he was to get ashore. We were advised by the flagship *Hermes* that we should transfer to *Resource*, because *Resource*, which was a supply ship in the company of the carriers at this time, would be the first ship to move from the carriers to San Carlos. That was our best chance of getting ashore. I am not sure just how much I was being told by *Hermes*. I've got a feeling that *Hermes* already knew at that stage that there was a problem. Basically they were not telling me that they were not going ashore, they were simply telling me, 'The best thing you can do is get on *Resource* and get inshore.' In fact I got a signal, which I've still got somewhere, which said: 'You are to transfer to *Resource* which will enter the Area Of Action. Once you have entered the AOA you will be given instructions about landing the troops.' . . . I started working on McIlroy to try and persuade him to stay on the ships and cover the air war. I stopped doing so because it was conveyed to me that, whether they liked it or not, those guys were getting off.

According to Goodwin:

[Captain Black had] become increasingly fed up, and McIlroy and his signal which had been literally the night before – the general behaviour of the press. I mean . . . [naval officers are] a fairly traditional breed of stuffed-shirt type characters and they tend to look down on such behaviour from a great height . . . And that was happening increasingly, screaming and shouting in the ward room, demands to send a deputation to see the Captain. This is the Captain of *Invincible*, fighting an air war, sitting in his bloody comcen with headphones on. He's saying: 'I actually sat watching my radar screens, waiting for enemy aircraft to come in, with the headphones on, reading press copy.' And he used to do that. And the next thing he knew he'd got a message from one of his officers saying that there's a deputa-tion of pressmen outside and they want to see you. It would be a complaint about me, or it would be a demand to send a signal that they're not getting the assistance they think they're entitled to etc. All this is building up and the guy's had enough. And they're going to get off whether they want to or not. That was never conveyed to them at the time, it didn't need to be. They were going to be transferred to *Resource*. Now the fact that she was an ammunition ship – none of us, I suppose I knew it, I didn't give it any particular thought, I knew she was a supply ship and she'd probably be carrying ammunition, but it did not assume, believe me, the great factor that they have subsequently tried to maintain that it does. It's not reasonable for them to say they were shocked when they found out. They'd have got into a bloody rowing boat being towed behind the ship if they thought it was going to go into San Carlos. Frightened be damned. They weren't so frightened. They had reason to be frightened when they were in San Carlos on *Resource*. I mean they knew by then it was a bloody ammunition ship and you're lying flat on the deck and there's a machine gun going 'dagadagadaga' at a passing Mirage, . . . Anyway that's by the by. They were concerned. They found out the Marisat wasn't working. They had a minor bloody eruption about that. One of the things they were looking forward to in getting on board *Resource* was the fact that she had a Marisat. Communications problems were going to instantly disappear. Certainly things were going to be a lot easier. . . It's entirely possible that, yes, I think I remember that I left them in the officers' bar, went up and met the Captain, got briefed by him, and discovered that the Marisat was out. I may well have gone back and used a phrase like 'Sorry guys, bad news, the Marisat's out.' But that's just a form of address, and to say that I was not concerned is bullshit.

Goodwin despaired of the journalists' attitude:

I was sufficiently concerned to put pressure on the 60-year-old senior radio officer who was crippled with arthritis, to do everything he could to get that Marisat back in operation as quickly as he could, with the result that this 60-year-old man spent something like thirty-six hours in daylight in the bloody golf ball up above the bridge in bitterly cold, freezing conditions working like stink to get the damn thing back on, so these bastards could use it. I've not seen a single one of them give that man any credit for that work. He was an old man who shouldn't have been down there in the first place. He spent over a day up there in freezing conditions working to get that Marisat back on line for nobody other than them, because there was no military need for it. No credit for that whatsoever. None at all. And I'm sorry, that's one of the things I hold against them fairly heavily. To say that I was not concerned about it is total nonsense. In fact if anything I was annoyed, I was hacked off and annoyed myself on a personal basis because I knew damn well it was going to lead to more ructions with these characters, and it did. You know, I wasn't enjoying the situation at all, having rows with these guys, so I wasn't looking forward to it at all. So if you want a social explanation, it's quite the opposite. It's totally incorrect to say that I was pleased. Why the hell should I be pleased when it would only lead to more trouble? Anyway, on the *Resource*, next thing we find is that instead of going directly into San Carlos . . . the Master didn't even know. Masters of RFA don't know exactly where they're going or when. They go where they are told, when they're told. The naval officers on *Hermes* decide when. He had a vague idea that he was going in San Carlos some time, but he didn't need to know when. And he didn't want to know when. And his way of operation is to sit there and do what he's told. And until he's told 'Go to San Carlos' he doesn't go to San Carlos.

Goodwin continued:

So we got on board: 'I want to see the Captain. When are we getting into San Carlos?' 'I don't know, guys, I really don't know, they're not telling me anything.' The Master quite rightly said privately to me in advance: 'These guys *are your responsibility*, I will do everything within my power that I can to help, but *they're yours*, you look at their copy, you do whatever you have to do'. While we were alongside, charging up and down beside *Canberra*, I took the opportunity to go over and talk to Martin Helm [minder], it was the first time I'd seen him, to find out what was happening, and that was the first occasion that I knew that they were not going to be allowed ashore. He didn't tell me fully, he just said: 'Well, I think you're going to have trouble, because Brigadier feels he's got quite enough press ashore . . .' I transferred back onto *Resource*. I can't remember in all honesty how much of that particular conversation I told them, if any, you can understand I was not exactly leaping over myself to tell them that they weren't going to get ashore.

Anyway, we went in and we arrived on the morning of 19th, I think, 20th, 21st, when the hell was it? So we arrived there on the morning of the 21st before dawn and the first thing we could see was this bonfire at the front which was *Antelope* burning. We get there and we anchor, and I expect to get signals or messages, I think the phrase was something like: 'The Brigadier will accept the press ashore once *Resource* has entered the AOA and the situation ashore has stabilized.' So we got into the AOA and I sat there, and I immediately banged out a signal to the PR guys ashore saying: 'Right I'm here, what do you want me to do?' Silence – not a word, didn't hear anything all day. I'm being blasted so viciously, by Seamark in particular, at ten-minute intervals. I'm sorry, I don't have too much sympathy with the fact that they found themselves on an ammunition ship. Seamark in particular was the one who was paranoid about getting ashore, they were taking no more risks than anybody else in that Task Force, no more risks than anybody else on that ship. I mean are they something special that they're entitled to special treatment . . . that others in the Task Force aren't? This was at the stage when we were having screaming matches, or they were screaming at me and I was getting more and more uptight. I can remember Seamark being abusive, calling me names behind my back. I'm sorry, I'm not the kind of guy who normally takes situations like that without shooting back. I was firing signals ashore – nothing happening.

In desperation, Goodwin got a helicopter to *Fearless* to try and find either Alan Percival or Allan George. There were no minders on board. There was, however, as Goodwin informed us:

A naval lieutenant who was on the staff of the Commodore who'd been involved on the press side, and I said, this is the problem, I got my signal saying bring them in here, the Brigadier will accept them ashore and nobody's told me what's happening, what do I do, and all the rest of it. He said: 'Leave it with me, I will sort something out overnight.' I went back to *Resource*, told them this and they were literally climbing the walls by now, . . . to get off, not just because of fear, because of desperation to get ashore and get stuck in – they were missing out on the stories, their desperation was that their competitors or colleagues were getting it all and they were missing a lot. I was saying: 'I'm going to lose my job', and Mick Seamark was quite clearly afraid that he was going to lose his, the popular newspapers being what they are. I'd found out that Alan George was on board *Stromness* . . . and I sent him a message saying come over and talk. The next thing I know there's this helicopter. So I dive onto this helicopter, find he's on there and he says 'I'm doing various things with the TV boys, I didn't have time so I thought I'd pick you up and we'd talk'. It wasn't particularly convenient at that moment because he was heading for *Fearless*, so I got to *Fearless* and I got a message that Alan Percival and David Nichols [military Public Relations Officer] were awaiting me ashore. They wanted me to go ashore but not the press. And I got told on *Fearless* by this lieutenant . . . that they weren't going to accept the press on shore, the *Invincible* Five, because the Brigadier wouldn't have it. A situation with which, in all honesty, despite everything that had gone before, the problems I was having with these guys – I totally disagreed. I still disagree to this day. I went back to the ship and I said 'I'm going to put you ashore anyway'. This was a great big discussion between us. They knew at this stage the Army was refusing to take them ashore. And they knew what kit they had . . . I came to the decision that I was going to put them ashore anyway, and I think, I might even have it . . . my signal.

Goodwin did his best to obtain authority from the Ministry in London:

> . . . I'm quite prepared to take decisions which maybe should be left to people above my level, but I mean I'm not a total suicidal idiot. I actually signalled the MoD and said, 'Nobody will talk to me so I propose to do the following,' and I might even have the signal here. It's quite a classic and I've kept it safe all this time, because it was my lifeline, I was fully expecting when I did this to find a bloody party of Marines whistling me off to a painful interview with the Brigadier or something, but I'm quite unrepentant about doing it. I signalled the MoD saying, 'They won't talk to me, can't get any answer, so therefore I propose to put them ashore anyway'. And I got a message back from John Wright (MoD London) saying, 'I advise caution, hang on, I'm going to talk to Neville Taylor' . . . This is a teleprinter conversation that's going on by Marisat between him and me. Then I got Mike Peters (MoD London) coming up saying he's just gone whistling off upstairs to ask Neville Taylor . . . And the message came back that Neville Taylor thought it was a matter for local decision. However he agreed on the face that press should not be prevented from going ashore. And I sent back a message saying, 'Right, based on what I've already discussed and on what you tell me Neville Taylor's attitude is, I intend going ahead and putting them ashore'. As I say, I'm not totally suicidal, I wasn't going to do that without any authority and that's what happened. This is all with their total knowledge and agreement.

Goodwin claimed:

> At all times. I was showing them the signals, but they knew that the Army didn't want them ashore, they knew that I was proposing to put them ashore anyway. Believe you me, they were demanding to be put ashore, they would not stay on the ship, under whatever cirumstances. They realized the problem of kit, they were happy about the kit that they had, every bit of kit that I'd been able to scrounge for them on both *Invincible* and on *Resource* . . . I was supposed to go ashore and see Alan Percival and David Nichols. I wanted to avoid that because I felt that, if I did go ashore and see them, I would finish up by being ordered, not ordered   they couldn't order me – but in my situation if I were to be told that the Army won't accept them ashore I would be in a much more difficult position for putting them ashore. So I was trying to avoid a situation in which I personally could be told by the Marines ashore, 'We will not take your press'. The press understood this totally, completely, clearly, this was all clear between us, they wanted to go ashore, so on that basis, I put them in a helicopter and I flew them ashore, with the exception of McIlroy who felt that he wanted to stay on *Resource* and have access to communications and have access to that day's air battles and then go ashore later, as he subsequently did.
>
> Again, I tell you in all honesty that, when that helicopter lifted off towards the beach, I breathed a big sigh of relief, I thought 'thank God' for that, I was very glad to see the back of those bastards, I really was, not Mac because, despite all the problems, we were getting on well at that stage.

And Goodwin himself?

Nobody told me what I was going to do at this stage, so I decided to stay with *Resource*, because she had a Marisat, and thinking at that time that she was going out and coming back in again. So I would stay with *Resource*, I would stay out of the way of the Army, of the Marines, so that I couldn't be ordered to take them away again, I stayed with *Resource* and I sailed off on *Resource*. I sent out a signal saying, 'I'm on *Resource*, send me your films and all the rest of it and I will transmit it through my Marisat'. The first result of that was a signal from the bloody boat . . . half a mile away saying, 'Rog, Roger, we're . . .' and I can remember thinking, 'Oh God, I don't believe it, Jesus, it was by light'. They tried to transmit copy by light.

The minders, unlike the journalists, were 'organization men'. Goodwin, abandoned by his organization, told by Taylor to use his own discretion, had to act independently, much as his charges were used to doing. What the journalists operating on the basis of their own talent were confronted with were individuals acting as operatives of a system: organizational men of an organization which had abandoned them without a clear framework of performance. Within limitations, an organizational performer cannot be much better than his organizational set-up. However, to a highly individualistic group of competitive people such as the journalists, the failures in the system were personified and projected, in their minds, onto the individual qualities and personalities of the minders as people. It is also the case that in such a situation the minders' performance did indeed separate, to depend more on individual character traits than would normally be the case, in their role as information officers. Hence some minders came in for more attack than others. Each one was forced to make ad hoc decisions, each attracted not only the hostility the correspondents felt towards officialdom but personal abuse as well. Allan George told us about one incident:

> The Hastings thing was that he, about a fortnight after the landing in *Fearless*, asked Martin Helm to allow him to make a service call. And Martin refused, on the grounds that the press couldn't be trusted as far as security was concerned to make telephone calls, with the obvious exception of the broadcasters because they had to . . . [The] second reason was that, if you give it to one, all . . . will want it. It was damned difficult getting their copy through as it was; if we did this, they simply wouldn't have got their copy through. Hastings . . . wrote a most vitriolic piece . . . which you probably saw, added to which Martin Helm wrote a memo to the Chief of PR saying that this was done in a fit of pique, etc. etc. I took these pieces to the RFA . . . to be transmitted, and I added my own twopenny worth on the bottom, saying . . . to find out whether this is actionable because it was saying minders were sleeping in their beds whereas the hacks were on shore roughing it.

Once he had returned to Britain, Hastings' complaints about the minders grew milder but, as he told us: 'I supposed I shut up a bit because it would have seemed pretty ungracious . . .' McGowan and Hands remained severe, writing in *Don't Cry For Me, Sergeant Major*:

In *Fearless* the appalling 'minders' of the MoD were still living in comparative luxury, with the exception of Alan Percival, who was doing his utmost at Ajax Bay to get reporters' copy back to London when military traffic on the satellite permitted.

War-weary and exhausted journalists returning with their stories from the frozen trenches and sheep-sheds of the front line found little solace among the minders. The MoD men, still crisp and clean, were loath even to allow the journalists to sleep on the carpet of *Fearless*'s wardroom floor while they of course remained firm in their bunks.

In this book Allan George was singled out and made the focus of attack. Even aboard *Fearless*, his life was not easy. He told us how his transfer to *Fearless* took place and about the strenuous times that followed:

I think it was the Tuesday or the Wednesday we went to *Fearless* and I had Hanrahan and Nicholson and Martin Cleaver with me. Of course the press descended on us, I had all their copy . . . and I had to censor. They came on board and they wanted showers, clean shirts, meals and so on. The broadcasters wanted to broadcast, Hanrahan and Nicholson, and I had to monitor that, and then Fox and Sabido, so I spent a long time sitting opposite them monitoring their broadcasting. And I had to censor all the press material. I had to cut a telex tape of all the copy and I was two-finger typing all night. The last night . . . we had . . . an attack, so I didn't get any sleep at all. I cut something like a quarter of a mile of tape – an enormous amount of it – littered on the floor, every night, simply because if I hadn't, it wouldn't have gone. I was literally going to sleep over the machine. And all this having been bombed during the day, which was a new and very frightening experience . . . Then *Stromness* finished unloading the airfield and went back to sea and we transferred to *Fearless* which didn't have a Marisat. I was so glad it didn't have a Marisat because I was on my knees at that stage. It meant that I could actually sleep at night. Those are the sorts of things the press don't realize. Martin Helm was stuck on *Canberra* and the senior naval officer wouldn't let him off, Alan Percival was ashore with 3 Brigade, I was getting all the copy and the press. Then Alan Percival went to the military satellite communication centre when it was set up in Ajax Bay; I was sitting on the phone box. Alan then took some of that load but, I think there were something like 1000 military signals at any one time there waiting to go, so he had to slot press copy in as best he could. But at that stage he was ashore and was generally dealing with the press there. It was a sort of ad hoc 'catch as catch can' thing and one did one's best. At the same time we were having to censor material, but without knowing what the operational situation was. So we didn't know what was sensitive and you had to use your loaf. I'm sure we made mistakes but under those sorts of pressures I think anybody would.

There were certainly mistakes. In any case, at the end of a long, difficult day, even sensible decisions could look silly to the journalists. Relations quickly became acrimonious; tired officials looked incompetent to the journalists, while the journalists seemed ungracious and insensitive to the minders. The danger, however, is of personalizing failure by overlooking the structured failure to prepare properly for a reporting war. This is not to suggest the minders were indeed blameless for what went on, but that it is difficult to understand how, given their position, they could have appeared at times as anything but incompetent to the journalists. It is also to suggest that the Ministry in London has been well served to allow the fostering of personal culpability: that somehow the problems which arose rested with the minders in their individual capacity as information officers, rather than on the absence of an information policy for wartime.

Much of the minders' troubles stemmed from the ambiguity of their position. They were among the military but not of them; they found themselves despised by both the reporters and the Services. Unlike information officers in other government departments, those attached to the Ministry of Defence tend to stay in that department. They are psychologically very much a part of the Ministry of Defence, interested in military matters and, in the case of those we interviewed, affectionate towards their Service colleagues and aware of their own honorary military rank.

The lowest civil service grade of their profession is Assistant Information Officer, reporting upwards to Senior, then Principal, and, last, Chief Information Officer. In the Ministry of Defence the lowest grade is simply Information Officer. The press desk is manned by Senior Information Officers, the chief press officer is a Principal Information Officer. Deputy directors of public relations are Chief Information Officers and the chief of public relations has the title of Executive Director. This last, highest grade is roughly equivalent to that of an Assistant Secretary. In terms of military rank, an Information Officer would roughly equate to a Major, a Senior Information Officer to a Lieutenant Colonel, a Principal Information Officer to a full Colonel, a Chief Information Officer to a Brigadier and an Executive Director to at least a Major General, if not higher.

However, the highest 'rank' enjoyed by minders despatched with the Task Force was that of Senior Information Officer, in the case of Barrett, Helm and Hammond. This was not the original intention. The Ministry had intended to send the Fleet public relations officer, Laurie Phillips, a Principal Information Officer, but apparently he declined to go. His place was taken by one of his staff, Robin Barrett, an experienced man but, as he put it, 'an old man in a young man's war'. He was forty-nine years old and unfit, with a damaged nerve in his right shoulder. 'I just became increasingly tired,' he told us, 'the shoulder wasn't helping. We had a ladder that I went up I suppose twenty-five times a day, which we used to call Cardiac Hill. I was just totally physically flaked out.'

By Ascension, after a fortnight of strenuous work and thirty-six hours without sleep, he was 'almost deliriously tired', though not, as his office told his wife (according to Barrett), 'gaga and failing to wash'. Although Barrett believed that a short period of uninterrupted sleep would restore him, the Ministry demanded that he should be recalled. Hammond, who was already on Ascension, was flown out to catch up with the Task Force to take Barrett's place. Hammond and Helm were the two most senior minders. No real effort was made by the Ministry, however, to ensure that they, or their colleagues, were accorded the correct military recognition, and, accordingly, their authority was undermined. Instructions that should have been issued from Northwood were not sent. Like the journalists themselves, the minders were 'piggybacked' onto the military expedition. Unlike the reporters, they were unused to muddling through. Unlike their charges, they needed clearly delegated authority in order to work effectively.

Even so, as Hammond emphasized, their problems were in large part logistical. No amount of authority would have helped: 'The biggest problem that we faced was one of lack of assets, we couldn't snap our fingers and draw helicopters out of the air. If we'd have had a captain or an admiral looking after PR we still wouldn't have been able to magic helicopters or equipment.' Others probably felt the lack of authority more because as Hammond himself admitted:

> I was in a very fortunate position in that I'd been submarine flotilla PRO and the Navy's deputy PRO. The submarine flotilla is a very small club and I had a super time working for them, the first guy I met on *Hermes* was a submariner who was an old mate of mine. He then introduced me to another submariner, the Admiral was a submariner, and, although I had not met him, he knew me by reputation. I was recognized equally as a staff officer. There was no question that I was a civilian. The only thing that mattered was the level of my security clearance.

Hammond went on to explain the process of assimilation:

> If I'd gone on board with three stripes as a commander, then I would have been automatically accepted. The fact that I was a civilian, you find that every time you go to a new job you have to prove yourself to the military. And that's no difficulty if you're competent. If you lack it or if you're seen to fail then the military say, 'He's a civilian'.

Subtlety was needed as well. Hammond continued:

> I had a very good relationship with the Captain of HMS *Hermes*, I found that by going to him privately I could achieve a lot and that by going to the Admiral privately I could achieve a lot. You've got to know your way round a ship really, and I knew that I could find the Admiral on his own in the afternoons at such and such a time, when I could barge in and he would then talk. He would appreciate the opportunity of talking to an outsider, who nevertheless was on his side . . .

Alan Percival, who was to be promoted to Senior Information Officer on his return, also understood where he might most usefully gain advantage. He described his Falklands experience by reference to his time in Zimbabwe, monitoring the cease-fire:

> It would be bad organization to have a team to handle the press which didn't have a clearly defined and understood person in charge, be it civilian or military. I don't think it matters very much, frankly, whether the person in charge is civilian or military, as long as the team works as a team, so that the supposed professional advice of the civilian information officer can be given due consideration by the force commander. 'In that particular case in Rhodesia it was dead clear. [In Northern Ireland] it is dead clear at the moment because I am in charge and I have an Army major working for me and a civilian information officer, and I consider those two exactly equivalent.

We asked Percival to tell us more about the advantages which 'rank' conferred:

> I don't think it's a question of pulling rank, it's a question of the normal facilities that are available to that particular post. I think it would be fairly unwise for any civilian in the military organization to stand on some supposed rank or dignity and I don't think many do it. But it's necessary to have an understood position within the organization so that the military and ourselves quite know who does what.

Percival was asked whether the position had to be re-established for each new posting:

> No. It's understood. We have grades and the military invest in those grades a sort of equivalent status and that's the way of looking at it. In the Falklands my grade was information officer, which the military consider to be equivalent in status in headquarters or anywhere else to a lieutenant colonel. (sic) That doesn't mean that I can go and lead troops to an attack on the enemy . . . but it does mean that this headquarters considers my level of advice from my office in the same way as they would consider the level of advice of a lieutenant colonel on a military topic. In other words it gives a degree of clout to your advice. In the end it doesn't matter what the hell you're called if the GOC loses confidence in you. One is in this job, be it in the headquarters or on an operation, to advise the force commander on information matters. It is for the force commander to decide whether or not he wishes to accept that advice, in whole, in part, as a basis for discussion.

Asked what the procedure would be if advice were consistently disregarded, he replied:

> If the press officer feels that clearly the local commander is acting wrongly, and the effects are going to be seriously detrimental to the PR operation as a whole, or indeed to the operation as a whole, then he must consult his conscience and decide whether or not he should go to a higher military authority and say, 'Look, I really do think in this case we should do this, and I've told Fred Bloggs that I disagree entirely with him, and now I've come to make my disagreement to you'. If it then gets to the force commander and he says, 'Well I'm sorry, but I stand by Fred

Bloggs, I disagree with your advice', well that's that . . . I think the important thing on all of these operations, though, is to keep open the lines of communication with all concerned. You are part of the force on the operation, you're not the press's man, and you're not really a man somewhere in the middle ground between the press and the military. You're on the force commander's staff to make sensible arrangements to meet the press's needs, while not jeopardizing the operation. And you therefore, I think, need to have the attitude that you should operate within the military structure, while at the same time keeping completely informed your own organization back in London or in Fleet, or the strike command, or wherever it may be.

Percival's example was, as he emphasized, based on arrangements in Northern Ireland, where the question is as much politically as militarily sensitive. There the allocation of authority and responsibility is, as he stressed, well-established. In the Falklands case, on the other hand, the frailty of civilian authority was all too plain, as Barrett described when he first arrived aboard *Hermes*:

I'll take you back to the meeting I had with the Captain on board his flight deck, the morning we sailed. 'Who are you? What are these people doing on board my ship?' I don't think anyone actually told him officially in writing that we were there. So you had this unreal situation. Not having been told that he was going to have journalists or me on board his ship, and he didn't really want them on his ship because he'd got better things to do, so that sort of set the scene. I explained to him that I had been ordered down there by C in C Fleet, who as I understood it had got all of this from up above, possibly as far as Number 10, and if he wanted to argue the point, that was where he'd got to go. In the meantime, I was staying.

We asked him to tell us more about his exchange with Captain Middleton: 'It wasn't friendly, it was more frustration on his part at not having been informed beforehand that he was going to receive journalists'. On the Sunday evening before the fleet sailed, Barrett telephoned from the shore base, HMS *Nelson,* to Ian McDonald and DPR Navy, to enquire as to whether they had any instructions: 'They told me they hadn't, but that I would get them eventually.' Several sets of instructions then arrived:

The first . . . came from Fleet, they were strictly PR instructions; thou shalt do and thou shalt not do. They were probably two or three days sailing from the time we sailed. They would have come from the Fleet PRO, approved by a committee of Fleet, and then sent to me. And, of course, all the commanders within the task group will have had copies, so I had those and they more or less fell into line with the policy we'd adopted. And then, a couple of days later, we got the security instructions [from Fleet] which literally pulled the rug from under my feet. The initial stuff I got on the PR side was reasonably explicit, and – one would hardly say helpful, just workable. Then we got the security instructions, which more or less stated thou shalt not describe the weather, because it might give an indication of where you are, thou shalt not mention names, because if anyone gets captured it might give the other side information which could be useful, thou shalt not do quite a lot of things. That gave the Captain a great deal of power to say 'no'.

That's when I think the real frustrations began. Then a third signal came from the Commander of the 3 Commando Brigade, which virtually said thou shalt not talk to any of the civilian PROs or pressmen, thou shalt nominate your own PRO. Which again pulled the rug from under my feet and gave me less authority and less status. And this is one of the things I had asked for, that I should be given proper status to do my job, in other words, people on board should realize that I was the coordinator of PR.

Barrett sympathized with Captain Middleton's difficulties but he was aware that his own position had been completely undermined. (The strain of his role doubtless contributed to his exhaustion.) Moreover, these constraints also inhibited the information operation:

Security was paramount of course, and so the Captain took it upon himself to release all information, which meant that whenever any copy left that ship in the form of a signal . . . I used to have to stand in line with all the other heads of department, sometimes for forty minutes, just to get a few lines cleared.

In Barrett's opinion, he should have been given delegated authority to release material. Even so, while this would have eased congestion, it would not have removed Barrett's principal difficulty – his lack of status in negotiating with military personnel. He compared the Navy to 'a bit like being in a club':

The Navy tend to trust their own and protect their own, they don't have that much contact with civilians and therefore their frustration, I imagine, after seventeen years of working with them, when you meet them they always want to know what you are, what status you might have, and then when you tell them, they don't believe you because you're not wearing gold bars on your shoulder. I could only get my way on board that ship, and I must admit I didn't always win, by the sheer force of my personality. I had no backing. What would have helped me enormously would have been if [a signal had come] out from C in C Fleet. They wouldn't have accepted it from the Ministry of Defence, it would have had to come from their boss, C in C Fleet, establishing my status and my authority on that ship. I never received that, so, as far as I was concerned, I was just a bloody civilian.

Authority, formally established, would have made some appropriate difference to a situation which was inevitably uncomfortable for the minders. Resources were always scarce; military needs always took priority over reporters' 'demands'. However thoroughly the journalists sympathized, even identified, with the troops, they remained reporters. They wanted information, access, rapid communications. The minders were at the centre of the inescapable tension between the correspondents and the soldiers. As Barrett told Captain Middleton, when he left him at Ascension: 'It's been no fun in this bloody job. I've been the raspberry jam in the sandwich'.

The minders occupied a no-man's land. The press, as much as the military, refused to acknowledge that they understood their world, let alone that they had ever been a part of it. Roger Goodwin, for example, had been a reporter on the *Wolverhampton Express and Star*, one of the country's biggest provincial evening newspapers. Like his colleagues, he was charged by the journalists with failing to grasp the importance of deadlines. On the contrary, he told us:

> We were each and every one of us ex-journalists. Of course we understand deadlines. We may not have the great driving pressure behind us to meet them that they had, I would say frankly it's one of the excuses with which they have subsequently come up, to explain their lack of performance. If they produce a piece of copy – it was one of Witherow's tricks incidentally, to produce copy to me very very late indeed, then try and put pressure on me not to vet it because of the danger of him missing his deadline. He'd stand over me and say, 'Come on, come on, you haven't got time to read this . . .' Of course, all of which only made me more determined, to wonder what the hell it was he was trying to get past me.

Witherow was not Goodwin's favourite:

> I think there are one or two journalists on the Falklands war who, if I had anything to do with it whatsoever again, I would fight to prevent going, and I will name them for you. John Witherow is the first on my list. . . He does not consider himself in any way subject to the exigencies of the situation in which he finds himself, owes allegiance only to what he sees as his journalistic guidelines.

According to Goodwin, Witherow alone among the *Invincible* Five was reluctant to obey the code of instructions:

> We were all allocated action stations on HMS *Invincible*. During the practices we had on the way down, everybody rushed off to their action stations. On the very first occasion when we had an action stations for real, which was the day *Sheffield* was hit, my action station was on the bridge – now that was deliberate, theirs couldn't be because the bridge was too damn small to accommodate them all, and anyway there was a lot going on on the bridge that the Navy didn't want them to overhear. There's a lot of slanging backwards and forwards, you know, swear words, bandying, which doesn't really mean anything, it's just people letting off steam . . . They were on an empty bridge below the admiral's bridge where they could (a) hear some of the stuff that was going over the Tannoy, they could (b) see out, they were fairly close to me, I was on the bridge, I could hear everything that was going on, I could go down and brief them. Before we got to that situation, *Sheffield* was hit and I was on the bridge. John Witherow's action station with several of the others was down on the main deck I think. What you do at action stations, you report to the head of the section who ticks you off on a list, because obviously in an action station situation the ship might have been hit and you want a roll call. John Witherow . . . turned up on the bridge, so we had a face to face. I said, 'What are you doing here? You shouldn't be here', and, we weren't friends at that stage, far from it, anything but . . . I'm a fairly short-fused character, as probably several people have told you, but in fact I deliberately didn't try to couch that in aggressive terms. I suddenly found myself being poked in the chest by a guy saying, 'You don't seem to realize that I work for *The Times*. Not any

other bloody newspaper, but *The Times*. You don't talk to me like that.' . . . The result of that is one very worried chief petty officer, five decks below, who doesn't know where this man is. He considered himself not subject to even that sort of authority, to be totally free to do anything that he chose at any stage during the war.

Personal and professional animosities were no doubt intertwined. The relationship between Goodwin and Witherow is interesting here, however, because it illustrates the difficulties of the minders' position. There was, for instance, the episode of Witherow's alleged telephone call to his girlfriend: a practice expressly forbidden by the Navy and which the journalists were on trust to honour. Although Witherow was supposedly talking to his editor this is how Goodwin saw the issue:

> He put a call through and it was quite plain he was speaking to his girlfriend. And I had to fight hard in a fairly explosive interview, I wasn't being explosive, but the Master was. I had to fight bloody hard to prevent the whole of the *Invincible* Five, not just Witherow, but all five of them, being banned from that machine for the rest of the duration.

There was more. Goodwin continued:

> After the surrender when *Fearless* had moved round to Stanley and Menendez was being held prisoner in a cabin, I happened to be flat on my back with a bug in a bunk on *Fearless*, when the door was flung open by an irate Navy commander, who said, '*Two of your people*', meaning the press, 'had the audacity to try and interview Menendez'. I staggered out of my bunk thinking, 'Oh Christ'. A few seconds later, I was confronted by Witherow and Bishop, they had flown onto *Fearless* by helicopter and they were all dressed in combat kit, bits of military equipment, they'd used their knowledge of the ship to make their way to the cabin where Menendez was being held, they bamboozled and talked their way past the young 18-year old Royal Marine guard who was on the door, got into the cabin and started firing questions at Menendez. They had no feeling, no consideration whatsoever for what they'd done. They couldn't give two hoots that that 18-year old Marine found himself in very deep water indeed. He got into serious trouble for having allowed it to happen. Their only excuse was that it was 'journalistic initiative' to try something like that.

Clearly, Goodwin believed that Witherow had actually telephoned his girlfriend and was displeased by his appearance on the bridge during action stations, but it is interesting that, in reference to his attempt to interview Menendez, with Bishop, he should say, 'I'm not saying they were necessarily right or wrong'. The phone call could be classed as an infringement of privilege in that it was not essential to the journalist's reporting task, but Witherow's appearance on the bridge is not so clear cut. Although not fitting with naval instruction, journalistically it must have been a more advantageous place than some muster point away from the centre of activity and therefore, on those terms, it is perhaps defensible. The attempted interview with Menendez, however, was his journalistic duty. Any editor would not be pleased by a failure to respond to such an opportunity. It was the young Marine's job to keep the journalists away from Menendez and the journalists' duty to get at him.

Goodwin's examples demonstrate the ambiguities of the minders' role. They were despised as non-journalists; worse, they were despised as ex-journalists who had moved to public relations. As Goodwin put it, 'Having crossed the great divide, you become a non-person in their eyes'. At the same time, the Navy considered the minders as the journalists' associates; Bishop and Witherow were 'two of your boys'. This was understandable. The minders, after all, were there only because the journalists were there. They came in a package together.

The minders could please no one. Their job was to assist the journalists, while protecting the interests of the military. Because the journalists' work often interfered with that of the military, the minders dissatisfied their charges, and appeared ineffective in the soldiers' eyes. At sea and on land, the Navy and the Army were used to people and things being under control. The minders, however, refused to accept the role of controllers. Their job was that of escorts, not wardens. Much against their will, the role of supervisors, was thrust upon them. The journalists were seen as the minders' responsibility – and that, disastrously, included responsibility for censoring their copy.

An information officer can work effectively only if he has both the respect of those who have given him authority and the confidence of the journalists with whom he works. Nothing was more likely to upset that balance than the decision that the minders should also be censors. They were caught between the military and the journalists, bound to antagonize both. Vetting copy was absolutely necessary and was a nuisance for all concerned. The Services were anxious about leaks of intelligence, the journalists furious at such an infringement of normal reporting rights, while the minders did not know what to do for the best. As censors, they would lose their cordial relationship with the journalists; if they shunned the role, they risked reducing their fragile authority still further. They also feared that, if the journalists' copy were entrusted to the military, it would be badly mangled. Goodwin described their dilemma:

> There's a strong professional belief that you should never be involved in matters which are going to bring [into question] your credibility in the eyes of the press man, such as psychological operations, psychological warfare, for instance. Censorship is one of those things. Censorship is something in which no PR man, particularly an ex-press man, would wish to get involved in, certainly I wouldn't,

and as I understand it there was a discussion back in the MoD, it was after Neville Taylor arrived so that would give you a rough idea of the date, when it became known to them that the minders were actually doing the vetting . . . they were thinking in terms that the minders can't maintain their usual role of being friend and adviser and general sort of father-figure. By then it was far too late, of course, and it was wrong thinking in the first place because the alternative would have been far worse in my view. It was a personal decision by me to do the vetting on board *Invincible* . . . and other people chose to do the same.

The Ministry signalled an instruction that the minders should not be involved in vetting, and that, if they already were, they should cease. The minders, however, had by then decided that, as Goodwin put it, 'the alternative would have been far worse'. The journalists, as we discovered, despaired. Ian Bruce told us:

I don't think I can remember a single serious disagreement with a military censor. They excercised common sense, and they excercised purely military judgements on the copy – what would be secure and what wouldn't be, what would endanger life and what wouldn't. And with that we had no argument, no possible argument. The MoD tended to bring their own personal fears, their own insecurities, misinterpretation of signals and political overtones.

By and large, the journalists enjoyed a better relationship with the military censors than with the minders. Their confidence was, nonetheless, not wholly justified. As Allan George explained:

Thank God it was us, because at least we had been journalists, we would not dream of altering style. I know of an instance of a military officer who was involved in censorship, who was actually putting in descriptive words and descriptive phrases in people's copy. Luckily that subsequently passed through Alan Percival's hands or my hands and we took his work out. And we knew it was his because it was quite easy to identify and it was signed. I mean you can imagine the row there would have been over that.

Roger Goodwin was equally horrified at such interference, and not simply because the military censors altered style. He described one incident after the San Carlos landings:

A lieutenant colonel in so-called PR in 5 Brigade, an Army lieutenant colonel, was seeing copy that was coming back from guys and he was saying, 'You can't say that about my Brigadier. No, you can't say that kind of thing about Major Bloggins, he's a friend of mine. We hunt together. Take it out.' The information officer involved was quietly letting him do it and, as soon as he left, would reinstate it. Now no matter how much the press go on about how well they got on with the military, and how much they would like to see military people doing the minder's type job the next time around, that is the situation that they would find. That's why I didn't want the Navy doing it on *Invincible*, and that's why I chose to do it.

Goodwin suspected that the Captain, Jeremy Black, 'felt at some stages I wasn't doing enough'. Furthermore, Black had his own view of what the minders' role should be. Goodwin told us of this exchange, after a second signal had come from the Ministry, again forbidding the minders to take part in censorship:

> I was still doing a vetting job on *Invincible* because of the arrangement that we had, in fact, it was getting vetted three times. We were seeing the copy first and the Captain said, 'you look at it for political content'. Well, frankly, I wasn't going to vet for political content anyway. I couldn't – don't forget I'm being given no advice or guidance on this, but, I suppose, looking over my shoulder towards MoD, I suppose I'm doing that more than your average naval office is, more than the press is. I was going through the copy and maybe talking to the guys and saying, 'Here guys, you can't say this, you can't say that'. I was in practice also deleting military stuff that I thought should be taken out. I was then taking it along to the Captain's secretary and whenever possible I was standing over his shoulder to make sure that he didn't overstep what I considered to be the normal guidelines anywhere. I do not accept that what went on down there was censorship. In my view the word censorship means total control of everything that is said. And to the best of my knowledge at no stage was that ever practised.

In general the minders preferred the term 'vetting' to 'censoring'. In either case, what they were doing represented a departure from the normal practices of news gathering and dissemination. Again, their position was unclear. The first signal from the Ministry, received shortly after sailing, was a broad-brush instruction, but its very looseness meant that the minders could use their own initiative as they saw fit. Some, however, perceived it as the classic political ploy of shielding the central authority from blame should things go wrong: the fault would rest with the minders, not Northwood or the MoD. And things did go wrong. The journalists complained to their offices, via service messages, demanding that restrictions should be eased. It was at this point that a second signal was sent, not countermanding the first, but 'clarifying' it. The minders, now forbidden to do any censoring at all, did not know where to turn. We asked Roger Goodwin about his reaction to the second signal. Had he ignored it?

> No, I wasn't allowed to ignore it. In fact it drove a coach and horses through my authority, and I was bloody annoyed about it, and it allowed the Navy to maybe turn round and say, 'You are not to be involved in vetting and you're going to have to sit back'. When the signal arrived, it removed that authority from me and made life a lot more difficult all round.

As it turned out, the minders continued to take part in the vetting process. It was unavoidable, especially once the journalists went ashore. None of the minders had any previous experience of vetting. In Alan Percival's opinion, 'That in itself is not particularly important, because one already had by virtue of one's background, an appreciation of what was genuinely of some threat to security'.

The journalists disagreed, giving us many examples of allegedly foolish decisions on the part of the minders. We cannot judge whether the reporters' complaints were justified, and to what degree. We can, however, emphasize that the minders were in a position in which they simply could not win. They had no friends.

For one thing, the minders were sometimes as much in the dark as the journalists themselves. Brian Barton explained:

> The attitude of some of the journalists, seemed to suggest that we were as thick as thieves with the military establishment, that we knew what was going on, but we were not telling, that we knew far more than we actually did. In fact we were in many cases struggling for our place in the sun as much as they were, which I don't think was appreciated.

The military public relations officers tended to be better informed, as the journalists suspected. Roger Goodwin described the advantage the military officers enjoyed over their civilian counterparts:

> The military will always go to the military. That's one of the problems that we've got to learn to live with and learn to overcome. The Royal Marines in particular are a very small, very introspective, very elite unit, who grow up together, live their lives together. There's only 800 officers I think in the entire corps. There is a natural tendency therefore for the Marines to go to David Nichols. And the Colonel would listen to David Nichols, and the General would listen to David Nichols, and David Nichols would go to them, and they would do things for David Nichols that they would possibly resist doing for a civilian PRO.

This was the position that, on paper, Martin Helm should have enjoyed. Goodwin continued:

> In practice of course, the military were able to get the minders to communicate to the press all the unpopular decisions, which meant that they were sitting back quite happily not involved in the ructions that resulted from those unpopular decisions. So when the press went to them and said, 'Can I do this, can I do that?', they were able to adopt the role of Captain Bountiful and say, 'Yes of course, old boy, no problem at all. Let's do it this way, that way and the other way'.

Damaging though this was, Goodwin accepted it as part of a minder's job:

> I think it's right and proper, that's what we were there for, I accepted that role, certainly, and I felt it was my duty to impart that kind of information. It's just that, in practice of course, the way it turned out, we were the guys saying 'no' and the military were always the guys who were being friendly, and nice and helpful and doing what they could.

Philosophical though Goodwin and his colleagues might be, it was, nonetheless, difficult to convey unpalatable decisions, as Brian Barton recalled, when he described how he had to give Bernard Hesketh an order from General Moore, forbidding Hesketh to go forward to Port Stanley to film the surrender. Hesketh, according to Barton, was 'crying, swearing and cursing that he was to be denied such an important moment after all he had been through . . .' Conveying such bitter news was hard enough. Even worse was the fact that the minders were often unable to give the journalists the reason for such decisions. The military might decide, or change a decision, but the journalists held the minders responsible. The journalists held the minders in ever-diminishing esteem; what is more, they believed that they were conspiring with the military.

Pat Bishop, along with his colleagues, believed the minders to have deliberately misled some journalists at the end of the conflict, in recommending that they embark on *Resource* as the quickest way to get home, as a last parting shot and 'final triumph'. When *Resource* was found to be heading first to South Georgia, then, after a change of plan, to resupply ships in San Carlos, the journalists disembarked, to the amusement of their other colleagues who had remained and to the minders' dismay. As Allan George told us, however:

> What we did was in good faith, and it all went sour on us. And then they came back and said, 'You bastards, you stitched us up' and they would never believe it was done in good faith. You can't imagine what we felt when the buggers came back, knowing full well they would never believe us.

Relations between the minders and the journalists were by that time at their lowest ebb. Some journalists even refused to talk to the minders. Roger Goodwin was one of the victims. It was Goodwin, described by McGowan and Hands as 'the imperious Ministry of Defence minder', who told those lunching in the Upland Goose that *Resource* was about to sail. It is interesting to compare his account of the episode with that of the reporters' beliefs.

> It is total bullshit. There was no conscious desire, . . . there was no friendliness whatsoever between us . . . the last triumph be damned. Yes, we wanted to get them off the island, we wanted to see the back of them purely on personal grounds, not professional grounds, we'd had enough of the bastards anyway. In all seriousness I was told there was no chance of getting them a flight out by Hercules for a very long time. But I can remember that we were told, '*Resource* sails 12 o'clock, you've been allocated, whatever it was, thirteen spaces, there is a boat leaving the jetty in forty-five minutes or whatever'. So again, you're not stopping to work things out carefully, I went belting down to the hotel, charged in. I'm said to have said it imperiously, it's very possible, I was feeling imperious towards these bastards at that particular stage, there is a ship leaving, the boat leaves the jetty in an hour and a half, if you want to go, move. To suggest that that was a conscious trick of the minders to put one over on the press, rubbish.

By this time the strain had begun to tell on everyone, journalists, troops and minders alike. Tempers were at their worst. The journalists' story was over; they clamoured to get home. The minders, whose authority had crumbled, wanted to be rid of their difficult charges as soon as possible. For once at least, journalists and minders shared the same objective. As so often before, however, the minders could not deliver. It was for the military to decide who stayed and who went, and in what order. It may have seemed, as it so often had, that the decision was open to appeal, but the military would, as always, grant such requests only when it suited them. What was conducive to them one moment was not the next, and as fitting their training, orders given appropriate to one situation were countermanded the next. It is not, furthermore, a principle of military life always to explain the reasoning behind decisions to those who are affected by them. Goodwin emphasized the weakness of his position:

> This is one of the final instances that finally confirmed to the press everything they'd ever thought about the minders. After the war, after it was all over, there was an intense passion to get out and get home, hardly surprising. We were going to the brigade staff, the headquarters staff, the movement staff, and saying, 'Hey, these guys want to get out, you've got to get them home'. And we were being told in no uncertain terms by the military, 'There is no way those fucking bastards are jumping the queue to get out of this bloody dump – don't you know . . . we've got wounded guys, compassionate cases and guys whose mothers have died and all the rest of it, and SAS have been in these islands for six weeks, those bastards can take their place in the bloody queue.' And we were going back and saying, 'We're sorry, fellas, there really isn't that much chance', toning it down a little. But then the General turned round, quite rightly, and said, 'Things are calming down, we've got all these national journalists here, if they are left to sit around Stanley with time on their hands they're going to start firing back nasty stories which I don't want, get 'em the hell out of here as quick as you can, Mr Movements Officer.'

Back the minders went to the journalists:

> The movements officer allocated five seats per flight per day for the first few days, and they (the journalists) turned round and said, 'There you are, everything we always said about the minders, they're ineffective, they can't hack it, they can't do anything, they tell us one thing and . . .' They thought that it was their pressure on the General – there's the famous story of Max Hastings for instance going to the General and saying, 'General, I've been thinking, I'm going to recommend to Express Newspapers . . . that there should be a massive great Lord Matthews Wingding for the entire Task Force, which the *Express* would be happy to pay for . . . Now what's the chance of me getting on the next aeroplane?'

The minders had been on a losing wicket all along. By the time they reached Port Stanley, nothing they told the journalists would have been believed.

Although the minders were dismissed by the journalists as incompetent having, according to Hastings, 'a bottomless capacity for cocking things up', the journalists were in turn viewed by the minders as difficult to deal with. Some understanding is therefore required of journalism as an activity which made the correspondents both difficult to handle and quick to be infuriated by those sent to 'mind' them.

To begin with, journalists have a tendency to view proceedings conspiratorially, and secondly to show a lack of appreciation for the needs of others around them, or at the more general level, the requirements of anything other than needs of the system they serve. Such traits, however, while making them difficult to control also provide the making of a good journalist, as conventionally understood.

Why journalists would have a heightened feel for the conspiratorial is that the world they deal with often moves on the basis of conspiracy, not just in the sense that the events they wish to cover are the product of conspiracies, but that conspiracies exist to keep information from them. When it was put to Hammond for example that the minders did not appear to understand the needs of the journalists, he said:

> We had two diametrically opposed positions – the Task Force commander wanted total secrecy for his objective, the journalists wanted total access and total freedom to report. And we had to try and steer a line between the two and negotiate between the two sides. There was no question that I was a member of the staff of the Admiral, there wasn't any loyalty towards the press other than one's basic feelings towards the need for a free press within a democracy. That sounds a bit trite . . . but if the Admiral said no, then it was my job to enforce his decision.

When information is kept from the journalist, he will ask why. Hammond's ' . . . while we didn't tell them the whole truth, we never lied to them' cuts no ice at all. To the journalist, lying by omission is enough to suggest a conspiracy. Furthermore, the way a journalist works, by asking one person or the other for their reaction to what has happened, to what is happening now, encourages them to see the world, and to present it, as a scheming place, where people are manipulated. The journalists' picture is given through the eyes of individuals; they, not social processes, are the focus. This, too, displays events as the outcome, not of larger, accidental forces, or of circumstances, but as the result of the machinations of individuals. It is difficult to convince journalists that things are not as they suspect; 'they *must* be'. They believe it is always possible that they are being lied to, that some conspiracy is afoot, and that their colleagues are in the know. This world view was what the minders were up against. Reflecting the *Invincible* Five's belief that they had been 'stitched up by the journalists on *Canberra*', Roger Goodwin said:

One thing that I was forcibly reminded of . . . down in the Falklands was the way in which the press as a breed grasped what appeared to be particularly Machiavellian tricks and immediately invested them with total belief. If the MoD had been so clever and so subtle as we have subsequently been accused of being, we'd be only too pleased. All this superbly thought-out reasoning behind why the Ministry of Defence refused to allow foreign journalists to accompany the Force and all the other things – it would be all very nice if we had thought it out like that, but it's just not true.

Individuals who believe that a conspiracy is at work are difficult to pacify by evidence which rests outside the logic of the conspiracy, but by their nature, conspiracies are not easily open to evidential examination. In fact, as a source of 'understanding' or making sense of proceedings that is their strength: something is going on, the detail of which is not quite understood, but everything occurring seemingly fits, in terms of its consequence, into some kind of deliberate design. The most extreme example of this thinking among the journalists in the Falklands came at the very end of their stay. Port Stanley had fallen to the Task Force; the journalists had written their copy and given it to Max Hastings to deliver. Hastings described how he became the first journalist into Port Stanley:

I've come round to the theory now – I used to think it was a conspiracy, now as usual I've come round to the cock-up theory more . . . What happened to me was perfectly simple; I was with 2 Para and they got to the racecourse and they were told to stop and I just thought when I looked up the road and I couldn't see anything much going on ahead and there was only a little bit of shooting going on a mile or two over the hill. And I just thought very consciously, as you often think, 'If you can get away with this one, you've got a marvellous scoop'. So I just walked in and gassed them for a bit and then came back to the British lines on the racecourse and I went to Julian Thompson and I told him what I'd done and Julian very decently called down a helicopter and the chopper took me out to *Fearless* and I grabbed one of the minders and said, 'Come on take me off . . . and we'll file this.' And by this time it was about 8.00 p.m. London time and I was still thinking, you can make all the morning papers, . . . and I was virtually hysterical and anyway of course they just said, 'There's a complete blackout'. I was carrying the pool despatch . . . which I did send, in the presence of Kim Sabido . . . and that's why I was so livid with McGowan having the cheek to suggest that I buggered his copy because Sabido was there and told McGowan that he'd seen me give it to him. Furthermore, if I'd been destroying their copy – David Norris's copy got through – well it's hardly very plausible that if I was going to start destroying their copy that I would chuck away McGowan's and not chuck away Norris's as well. They were all getting hysterical. Kim actually said, 'Well, for Chrissakes, I saw him say, "Get it out as soon as his own stuff's gone"'. But then Derek Hudson of the *Yorkshire Post* changed his line of attack and said, 'Well, even if you did give it to him, you should have let him file the pool despatch before you filed your own copy'. To which I just said, 'Well, fuck you'.

The scene moves to the Upland Goose. Hastings continued:

> I got into Stanley and it was hell. One can laugh about it now, but there we all were in the Upland Goose and all these papers turned up with a lot of my stuff in it, and everybody started getting pissed every night and I thought, 'What's your most frightening moment of the war? Being in a bar full of thoroughly pissed journalists when they see their papers come in.'

As McGowan put it to us: 'There was a great suspicion among all the journalists that Max might not have been the best representative to send back with all that copy'. Ian Bruce then confronted Hastings, 'I asked him outright, 'Have you been sending my copy back?', and he said, 'Um'. Hastings invariably tends to insert 'um' into his speech; Ian Bruce did not wait for a full answer but attacked him with a bayonet. His action was, he asserted, conscious and deliberate.

> For a start, I wasn't drunk. We'd discovered that a lot of the copy that we'd sent back with Max wasn't getting through. Bob McGowan of the *Express* made a call to his office and, instead of receiving a verbal hero-gram, was given a bollocking and at that stage he came back . . . 'Call your own offices and find out how much is getting back'. When we tried that, we discovered that a fair amount had gone missing, and all of it had been entrusted to Max Hastings. He then said that wasn't down to him, that it was down to the MoD, or the Navy or whatever, but his copy got through. Anyway, enraged that night by the fact that I'd spent the last four nights in hellish conditions and seen some friends die – not drunk – I must confess I tried to bayonet him. Soberly and quite rationally. Now it seems crazy, but in the circumstances . . . I tried to explain that when I got back here but there is no rational explanation for it.

Bruce believed that Pat Bishop of the *Observer* pulled him back. Were his colleagues laughing?

> Derek Hudson, I think, was going to take a swing at him, and McQueen gave him verbal lashing, then McGowan said he was going upstairs for his gun, everyone had one by that time, Smithy had two. The biggest threat to life and limb actually was being shot by a drunken [reporter] when the conflict was over.

What actually happened? Hastings had arrived, by helicopter, on the deck of *Fearless*. Not surprisingly, he was very excited, 'the first man into Stanley'. He had brought the copy entrusted to him by his colleagues. Meanwhile, on the RFA tanker *Olna*, Allan George and Kim Sabido were clearing Sabido's copy and filing it by Marisat. As they did so, however, Sabido and George heard the news that white flags had gone up in Port Stanley. Sabido asked George whether he could use this information; George sent a radio request to *Fearless*. He spoke to the Chief of Staff, General Jeremy Moore, who imposed a news blackout. The Captain of the *Olna* was also instructed by *Fearless* to prevent any broadcast of the news of the cease-fire. George then came over to *Fearless*. As soon as the news blackout was lifted, George, on Helm's instructions, returned to *Olna* with Hastings, in the same helicopter in which Hastings had come from Port Stanley. Helm and General Moore then left *Fearless* by Sea King helicopter for Port Stanley, to arrange and accept General Menendez's surrender.

The important point is that the instruction for a blackout came from the General, not from the Ministry of Defence nor, as some of the journalists suspected, from the Prime Minister, anxious to be first with the news to the House. It was a military, not a political, decision, taken to ensure that nothing would interfere with proceedings towards the acceptance of formal surrender. The Argentinians in Port Stanley were still heavily armed, with a considerable number of civilians at their mercy. These, it was feared, could have been used as a bargaining counter. They were certainly still at risk.

The news blackout, therefore, could not be ignored. Allan George described himself as being 'in a desperate position', since his superior at the Ministry in London, Neville Taylor, had asked him to confirm the news of a cease-fire. George refused to do so, hoping that Taylor 'could read between the lines'. At midnight or thereabouts, those journalists and minders who were on hand, including Allan George, dined with the Captain. The blackout was lifted in the early hours of the morning and the journalists began to file. According to George, who was present as copy was transmitted, 'To the best of my knowledge the pool was sent. I might even have typed it myself', he said, but he was unsure: 'There was a lot of material'. He could not say whether every journalist's story was there but he was certain that all the copy Hastings produced was transmitted. He agreed that 'Hastings cleared his stuff first', but considered 'that was only right'. In fact, George was mystified by the assumption that Hastings, or, for that matter any other journalist, would not clear his own material before that of a pool. For his part, Hastings was adamant that: 'It would be the ultimate crime in journalism not to hand over other people's copy'.

Nevertheless, many of Hastings' colleagues believed that he failed to deliver their copy. The fact that he did hand it over is immaterial; what is instructive here is the firmness of their disbelief. To some extent it derived from their view of Hastings. They saw him as capable of such an act. That, however, is not the whole story, only part of a wider occupational play. Nicholson, too, it will be remembered, found his colleagues reluctant to entrust their copy to him for delivery. It may be that Nicholson was also seen to have many of the same characteristics as Hastings, but how many characters are to be held at fault in what after all entailed the breaking of a strongly held professional norm, before the attention is removed from the individual and suspicion seen as the social property of an occupational group: change the players and the parts would have been the same.

For example, Bruce's reaction was not, as he viewed it, beyond 'rational explanation'. The stark violence may seem an excessive response, but even that is not out of character with the setting. It is not often that a journalist would have a bayonet to hand, but what is more typical is the ready seizure by the journalists on the idea that someone had deliberately interfered with their ambitions. That something had gone wrong was not seen as an accident or product of circumstances, or a fateful calamity, but evidence of purposeful intent to restrict their efforts. It is not that their estimations of the way the world is organized are wrong, but rather that emphasis is accorded to the conspiratorial side of it. Emphasis is given to the engineered and engineering aspects of human conduct and unfolding of events, to the detriment of processes over which individuals do not have the imagined precise control or influence they are credited with.

Most individuals probably view the world this way, but journalists operate with it as part of their professional practice. What shows as understanding becomes a performance of suspicion, making all unfavourable explanations which do not conform to the practices of a conspiracy difficult to accept. It not only fits their knowledge of the world, it also fits their own self-image of the journalist as 'fixer'. Because the gathering of news requires the development of persuasive skills – the setting up of difficult interviews, the establishment of trust with sources, the pressuring for facilities not readily forthcoming, the detection of more information than that revealed – the occupational value developed is that of the good journalist as being one who skilfully and tenaciously gets his own way. Thus the professional jealousy towards Hastings was also tinged with respect for his ability to summon up helicopters, even though it was seen as a product of having curried favour with senior officers. It was all part of the same game of manipulation and presentation of self that prompted Hanrahan, for example, to consciously promote his association with the BBC, in the hope that to do so would facilitate cooperation from those whose assistance he needed.

This professional value, the ability to manipulate the environment so that hindrances to performance are removed or lessened, based as it is on a very individually developed talent, accounts in part for the unprintable nature of the vehemence of the journalists towards the minders, even long after the source of the annoyance had gone. Some of the journalists went so far as to feature the minders' physical characteristics in their tirades. There was no relation, however, between how well individual journalists performed and the depth of their dislike. Hastings, for all his recognized success, delivered one of the most personalized criticisms to us of the minders. It was full of abject abuse. Had he not performed well, and had he held the minders responsible for his failure, such outrage would have been more understandable. As with the rest of the journalists, what was at work in his anger was the frustration of the professional value of being able to manipulate the environment. It is a value journalists hold dear. The ability to manipulate is a mark of their journalistic self-esteem. Yet whichever way they attempted to operationalize that skill, by bullying and threatening or by being pleasant and seemingly cooperative, it had no effect on the minders. They were defeated and in that defeat furious. The defeat irked because they failed to make the environment respond to their demands.

The journalists realized that those with the authority to alter the situation, the military, could be practised on to deliver what they wanted. The military public relations people consequently appeared by comparison more competent than the minders. This view did not necessarily stem from any objective perception of competence, but from their embodiment of the principles of movement which the journalists understood. Having more authority they could more easily accede and respond to the journalists' manipulations. Nevertheless, because of the military's strong ethos of correct procedures, their response was not as effective as the crude bribe to the telex operator in Lagos in producing movement, but there was sufficient possibility of accommodation to satisfy the minimum of the professional value: to get on would assist in getting by.

As much as the working of this professional value helps in part to explain the bitter abuse of the minders, and the retention of that abuse over time, it is also in part responsible for the development of the conspiratorial mind itself.

It is not argued that conspiracies do not exist, they indeed do, or there would be no basis in reality for the conspiratorial mind which journalists demonstrate. What is suggested is that the high level of suspicion that journalists harbour means that, when conspiracies do occur they act to over-determine the view of a conspiratorial world, so that when events possess even the weakest clue of a conspiracy, a conspiracy is registered. The attack on Hastings is a perfect example of this. The action of Bruce in the bar of the Upland Goose was not therefore, as he presented it, beyond 'rational explanation', but was the product of a collectively suspicious mind, operating on an incident which possessed certain features sufficient for them readily to invest it with planned interference. Given that they believed

Hastings to be the agent of the interference, he was fortunate, given the atmosphere and recent experiences of the journalists, to escape with his life. Within that framework of thinking and understanding of their colleagues' propensity to scheme, it would have been surprising had they arrived at a different conclusion. It does however make for a type of personality that is not easily satisfied with explanations which run counter to their interests, which instead sees explanations as part of a conspiratorial attempt at limitation. Although functional for journalism, such refusal is awkward for those who wish to control them. Descriptions of the journalists as unruly, or as incapable of doing what they were told – frequent complaints to us by the minders – whilst accurate from one perspective, from another, describe no more than journalists going about their business in a manner that their personality traits well equip them for.

Yet this general element of the journalists' make-up has, as previously mentioned, a second part to it. That is, they have difficulty in recognizing the needs of any system other than that for which they work. For example, the fact that some of the journalists, somewhat amazingly, did not realize that the Marisat was an insecure system of communication is not some cerebral weakness but a product of viewing the world from one obsessive perspective. The observation made earlier, 'Give a journalist a typewriter and he's happy,' is a fair reflection of this concentration of perspective, but offer him the possibility of filing copy, and he is ecstatic: 'in business', as Cleaver described his delight upon receiving his picture transmitter. Access to communication facilities meant the journalist's basic logistical problem of his trade had been solved. The Marisat was the magical link to the journalists' offices and audience. The perception, therefore, was one of narrow professional sight, disallowing the intake of other information which was of concern to minders and military.

Hammond gave us an example:

> On the *Hermes*, even when you arranged for helicopters and you said, 'Right, helicopters will be ready at 6 o'clock', and the helicopter would then be on the deck 6 o'clock, burning and turning, ready to go, and the guy would turn up and you'd say, 'You're not dressed. Where's your survival suit?' 'Oh Christ, I've left it in my room'. So he'd be ten minutes late getting onto the helicopter. Meanwhile, the pilot was sitting there waiting for the bloody journalist to turn up. And it was little things like that which showed, not a disregard, but an insensitiveness to the needs of the rest of the ship.

The minders gave us innumerable examples of incidents of this kind. It was not a staightforward disregard, but rather the social working of a job encasing the journalists so tightly in its grip that everything is seen to be for their use. The result is the taking over, like cuckoos, of the domains of others. Given its vital importance to the journalists, the radio room of the ship is a good instance of this at work. Did the minders find this behaviour amusing? Allan George:

> . . . it wasn't amusing because it was a bloody problem. Sooner or later somebody was going to have to pick up the pieces and that somebody was us. Somebody was going to have to find a new kit for Bob Fox when he lost it, as he always did. Somebody was going to have to soothe the radio officers, who were offended at the lies that certain reporters were telling, and win their confidence back for the following day, when they all wanted to come in and send more copy. Somebody had to cool the radio officers down when they had six journalists arguing in the radio room about who was going to go next. You know, that sort of behaviour. In some ways it was funny but it wasn't funny if you had to sort it out. And everybody looked at us and said, 'It's your responsibility'. One evening after the war, I think on the Friday or Saturday after the surrender, there were half a dozen journalists in *Sir Belvedere* . . . and they were arguing like fury about who was going to go on the Marisat first. And they all had deadlines and so on. And the radio officer was going to have them chucked off the ship, I could see it happening. At one stage Bob Fox was virtually banned from *Stromness*'s radio room because of his behaviour . . . He wouldn't get out when he was finished and so on. And the radio officer would have had him thrown off the ship. Consequently we were in the business of having to go back to these people and say . . . 'Can we come on board and transmit. It is desperately important'.

Of all the minders, George, the victim of so much hostility, was the least likely to be well disposed to the journalists' behaviour. It is also true that the minders' own position meant they were keenly aware of the needs of the military and therefore perhaps over-reactive. Nevertheless, George's remarks are instructive. The squabbling over radio facilities stemmed from the occupational individualism that forces the journalists to put self first, but what it really expresses is the engaged nature of their work making them oblivious to other features of their setting. Hammond again:

> In trying to transmit Michael Nicholson's copy on one occasion, we gave a tape which he had produced to a helicopter pilot, and said, 'Deliver that to the RFA *Resource*', where they had a facility to transmit the tape. A chap took off, it was foggy, the first thing he saw of *Resource* was the mast as it went past his cockpit and he said, 'Bugger this,' and came back. Now he was able to land on *Hermes* because *Hermes* had a super set of navigation aids. *Resource* was a different kettle of fish, it didn't have the same navigation aids, it was a smaller deck, the ship pitched more. And getting back to Nicholson and explaining was very difficult, to put across to him that actually we had tried very hard to get his stuff across and we weren't being deliberately obstructive.

Given the atrocious conditions, it is not surprising the pilot did not wish to risk his life as a courier for ITN, but Nicholson's unwillingness to accept obvious constraints – in this case, fog – baffled Hammond. Reflecting on the whole experience, he said:

> The thing that stands out in my mind about the Falkland campaign is the fog, not the rough seas, but fog so thick that you couldn't see the end of the deck. Fog so thick that sailors stood on the stern of the *Hermes* throwing flares at the water for a makeshift flare path so aircraft could be recovered.

At one point, exasperated by Nicholson's demands, Hammond said, 'Look out of the window, Michael, you can't see the end of the deck. There isn't a helicopter flying'. As Hammond said, 'You began to despair about what explanations you had to give some of these guys before they'd accept it'.

If it was difficult for the minders to register such a basic meteorological fact as fog to explain the problems they were facing, when it came to something such as the transmission and relay of service messages, not only did the journalists refuse to accept the necessity of interference, but imbued it with a calculation deliberately planned to make their life more difficult.

The minders could not understand the journalists' inability to survive without praise from their offices. As Alan Percival put it: 'Whether all the hero-grams got to all of the heroes I don't know . . . Possibly some of them didn't, if somewhere along the line it was felt that they didn't contain actually any instruction or message for the journalists'.

Roger Goodwin's attitude was:

> All right, so they lived by it and they're used to living by it. Given these communications problems, why on earth should they be given a special facility which nobody else has got, which they don't actually need, in order to be able to complete their work properly. The fact that they live on a diet of false praise from their bloody editors, because that's what these service messages are: you're doing a grand job, keep it up, keep the copy flowing, this that and the other, that's all
> . . .

According to Hammond, 'Hero-grams were held in some contempt by the military, who felt that our communications were busy enough without taking long laudatory messages for journalists'. Ian Bruce, however, saw matters in a different light, as he and his colleagues were bound to do: 'My office sent twenty-four messages of congratulations in the course of the Falklands Conflict, of which I received three'.

Goodwin had a less charitable view:

> I can remember getting a signal for Ian Bruce from his newspaper in Scotland which went into detail about how many pints of beer they were going to buy him when he got back and certain favours that the buxom barmaid in the local pub had promised to confer. There's a mass of it like this, about half a page, I can

remember it covering about half a foolscap page of stuff, there was no way that Captain Chris Burne would allow me to send that signal on from the ship, because what would happen – it was coming in by commercial Marisat – there was only one way of transmitting it ashore to these lads, and that was by sending a Navy or military signal throughout the military net. It was coming in, and I was saving it until I could get it ashore and then sending it ashore by hand. If a message arrived that actually contained work instructions – 'We require this from you, or we want that from you, we need 700 words on such and such by Sunday', I'd take that out, put it into a military signal and send it off. And I make no apology for that, there were 27,000 other guys who weren't getting hero-grams down there either. Why the hell should these guys get the special treatment?

The pressure on the signal system was the minders' chief professional concern; they were, however, candid about their own attitude. As Goodwin said, 'Hero-grams, and that's exactly what they were. As you know I spent ten days on *Canberra* and the stuff was coming in there by the ton: "You're doing a marvellous job, we back here are filled with admiration at your bravery and courage".' Allan George was even more scathing:

> From time to time they were allowed to talk to their offices. But actually they didn't want to talk about anything, other than have their egos massaged. That sounds a bit cruel and critical . . . Well, I managed to work without having my ego massaged, why can't they? I didn't need to ring up the MoD every ten minutes to be told that I was doing a great job. In fact I would have been bloody worried if the MoD had been ringing me up to tell me that. There was something very wrong, but they needed it and I find that is a very sad comment on journalism.

Genuine service messages, as opposed to hero-grams, giving direct instructions, are vital for a working journalist abroad. Nonetheless, and the minders clearly did not appreciate this, journalists need encouragement and flattery, just like actors or other public performers. Even so, the journalists' failure to acknowledge the special difficulties of the circumstances in which they, and the Task Force, found themselves goes to the heart of the inability to see beyond the bounds of their own operations. As Alan Percival said, 'We had enough problems getting the stories from the front to the back, without trying to get more paper from the back to the front'. Their editors, too, were unable to consider the wider perspective. Percival continued:

> I don't think, despite the efforts of the journalists, that their own offices really had too much grasp of what the hacks were having to put up with . . . You know, in listening sometimes to the service calls, as one was required to do, there seemed a frustration on the part of some of the journalists to actually explain to their offices what the genuine problems were, without trying to give an impression that they were somehow making excuses.

One typical incident occurred early in the campaign:

> David Norris, who was then wallowing along, as I recall, on *Stromness*, received a
> service message from his office, asking him to go to South Georgia and interview
> Cindy Buxton, and David was at that time somewhere north of Ascension Island.
> But someone or other presumably assumed that he should go and browbeat some
> military man to put him in some helicopter and fly 4000 miles or something.

Such an example is not uncharacteristic. A journalist's organization,
like the journalist himself, is obsessed with what is perceived as *a
good story*. Circumstances and contradictions are irrelevant. To
anything other than the story and the fact that it might appear in a
rival newspaper, the organization is *blind*. Furthermore, foreign
correspondents often hide their difficulties from the foreign desk in
order not to lose their editor's confidence. A journalist who gets
into too many difficulties is viewed with suspicion by his office. He
has to negotiate his own way, as the *Invincible* Five tried to do, and
this restricts his perception of the demands of the system around
him.

Alan Percival summed things up:

> I think sometimes the military have a fond impression of the ideal journalist, who
> is little more than an army officer in style, in breeding, who would pass entirely
> unremarked in the hottest officers' mess. They fondly imagine that really some-
> where in the world there must be journalists who are really not journalists, in the
> sense that they report for their newspapers, but are a channel through which the
> military says what it wants in newspapers. I don't think that sort of journalist
> really exists. I think a group of correspondents entirely compatible with the
> military is, you know, just a fond hope.

8

Getting the story back

In this chapter we will examine another aspect of this complex story: the method by which reports of the conflict eventually reached listeners, viewers and readers. The chain stretched from the Falklands to the UK; its links included the Task Force, the journalists, officials in Ascension and at the Ministry of Defence in London, the BBC, ITN and Number 10 Downing Street. We will inspect the connections each had with the others for these are crucial to two central questions: to what extent was there censorship and what form did it take?

We will begin by looking at a technical issue: the manner in which television was able to cover the war. This needs to be investigated in detail, since the absence of television pictures from the South Atlantic has provoked suspicion that here, in particular, there was political interference. Whenever journalists have been given access, television has taken pictures and sent them home. The lack of film from the South Atlantic suggested to some that the Government – here represented by the Ministry of Defence – believed that visual evidence of death and injury might fuel opposition to Britain's prosecution of her aims, and that they had accordingly ensured that no such sights should be seen. Certainly the official view was that the conduct of the war might be impeded if too much was shared with the public. Simon Jenkins, then political editor of *The Economist*, gave us his impression of the Navy's view:

> What is the point of having the journalists there . . . as historian?, collator? We have not got room for historians. You want pictures? Pictures of ships being blown up? Well, there is not any country in the world that can sustain ships being blown up. They can see soldiers being shot, they can take funerals in Northern Ireland, but ships being blown up and sailors screaming in agony with flesh hanging off their faces, on television each night? And you want people to continue supporting this war? You are out of your minds, just leave it to us. We will send back the victory pictures.

Both the BBC and ITN complained vigorously and persistently about the lack of television pictures from the South Atlantic. The House of Commons Defence Committee observed that, 'Such frustration was only to be expected in a television age' but, in his evidence to the Defence Committee, David Nicholas, ITN's editor, said, 'It is our conclusion that the will was not there to pursue this'. Alan Protheroe, Assistant Director-General of the BBC, agreed. Asked whether he thought it would have been possible to get pictures back, he told us:

> Yes I do. When you look at what was achieved by highly intelligent people sitting round a table . . . in air-to-air refuelling, for example, in converting bulk carriers to carrying Harriers and things like that . . . when you think of all the technology that was changed and developed in the space of weeks, that would have taken years to go through the normal Ministry of Defence staging processes and papers, moving back and forwards up the chain, I have no doubt at all that if the Government had said, 'Call in the best brains in the British electronic industry,' and locked them up in a hotel for a weekend and said, 'Now . . . let's hack this problem,' they would have found a solution. I still believe it was possible. The problem was that it was too low a priority.

Was it inertia, or lack of enthusiasm, or deliberate discouragement? The Commons Defence Committee failed to resolve the question. Its report stated that, from the evidence it had heard on technical and operational difficulties, and on the decision not to seek American assistance, it was unable to reach any clear conclusion. The Ministry of Defence had certainly declared its belief that more extensive television coverage would have added to its difficulties; those journalists who had given evidence believed that the Ministry's view explained their own lack of success in transmitting film. Nevertheless, as the Defence Committee pointed out, it is a fallacy to assume that dishonesty has been practised simply because a motive for dishonesty existed.

There were three ways in which pictures might have been sent from the South Atlantic. The first was to transmit them, via the British military satellite, SKYNET, from terminals in the aircraft carriers and larger Navy ships. The difficulty here, however, was that such terminals (known as SCOT) were designed to carry communications signals – encrypted voice or teleprinter messages. Television pictures need far more bandwidth. The naval system could carry many such communications simultaneously, between the ships themselves, and between the ships and the Fleet Command Centre at Northwood in Britain. The total bandwidth of the system was nonetheless inadequate for filmed colour television signals.

It was, on the other hand, just sufficient for a black and white picture, as Peter Heaps, the ITN engineer on *Hermes*, had ascertained. He therefore decided to try to send back black and white pictures only; there was no room for sound as well. After three days on board, he sent a signal to ITN, asking for a modulator, of the sort which ITN uses for radio links in London, to convert the video signal into one which could be transmitted by microwave. He hoped to produce a standard intermediate frequency, which he could plug into the Navy's radio link. The modulator, however, failed to reach him. Without it, he could only hope to conduct limited experiments to see whether a wideband television signal could be transmitted; these, it turned out, were forbidden. Bernard Hesketh, who was also on board *Hermes*, described the efforts he and Heaps made to persuade the Ministry of Defence to allow them to try a test run with the satellite and the SCOT terminal on *Hermes*:

> We tried desperately hard to persuade the Ministry of Defence to make these facilities available to us and a number of officers aboard . . . the engineers were most helpful . . . because they desperately wanted to try it . . . just as a technical exercise . . . to see if the thing would work . . . but . . . they were not allowed to do so. The reason they gave in our case was that *Hermes* was the flagship and the command ship and that it would be quite impossible to take SCOT satellite, which was carrying most of the communications, out of commission . . . it would be a long process . . . it would take an hour at the minimum (I would have thought) to do an initial test . . . the problems were quite enormous really . . . and you'd have to send the sound sequentially . . ., if you had a ten-minute piece it was going to be twenty minutes with sound. So, whatever form the test took, it was going to take a long time and they were not prepared to give us that time.

When *Hermes* reached Ascension, ITN called Heaps home (to coordinate the technical planning of the Pope's visit to Britain).

At this point, while the Task Force was still en route, there were some technical discussions between the broadcasters and the Ministry in London, though these got off to a slow start. There was one early meeting to consider the transmission of material from ships, attended by Mick Neustan of ITN and Ken Oxley of the BBC, who asked to be put in touch with a technical expert in the Ministry of Defence with whom they could discuss which methods were, and were not, worth pursuing. Between four and six weeks later, there was another meeting with the Ministry of Defence, at which Neustan and Oxley complained that they had not yet been given a 'technical' contact. A Ministry of Defence official had by now rung up Oxley, but he appeared to believe that television pictures could be sent down a telephone line. Their complaint produced some results, for, shortly after, on 12 or 13 May, a more technically sophisticated official was produced and things began to move more quickly. By now, moreover, the politicians were asking why there were no television pictures. More meetings were held and on 19 May the BBC and ITN were allowed to make tests from RSRE *Defford*. These simulated the power provided by a ship's terminal, using real satellites and a modulator. They showed that black and white pictures of acceptable quality could be relayed via SKYNET, but, as Oxley told us:

We managed to demonstrate fairly conclusively that as a technical problem, it was feasible to get black and white pictures back from the ships, . . . *not* ships that were on station near the Falklands. They would have to be detached several hundred miles nearer the UK due to the position of the satellite. It's to be within range of SKYNET's footprint.

Furthermore, transmission of black and white pictures alone would require the satellite's entire bandwidth, and this would have obliged the broadcasters to commandeer every available channel. All twenty to thirty links from the fleet to Northwood would have been needed but these were the Navy's only secure channels of communication. For outbound communications, from Northwood to the fleet, high-frequency radio could be used, as a less secure alternative, but the Task Force could not use this means to communicate with Northwood, since this would have enabled the Argentinians to chart the fleet's position as ships tracked south. Radio silence was therefore maintained during the whole journey. The SKYNET link, on the other hand, was relatively secure, it being impossible to 'Direct Find' the origin of the signal without highly sophisticated technology (at that time possessed only by America and the Soviet Union). There were, of course, times when the Navy was not using the satellite link but, even then, it was impracticable for the television companies to exploit it. All terminals throughout the Task Force would have had to shut down completely and, in an emergency, they could be reactivated only when each ship had received a high-frequency broadcast signal – easily intercepted – telling commanders that the system was operational again. The fact that the system was being used not for commercial or experimental purposes but in war, when an emergency might arise at any time, also precluded any arrangement to set aside specified periods for broadcasting only.

What is more, SKYNET was useful only as far as South Georgia. To use SKYNET after the Task Force had passed South Georgia would have required a ship to be stationed within the reach of the satellite's footprint, and keeping a vessel there permanently, with the necessary escort ships to shield it from attack, would have diverted scarce resources from the main purpose of the expedition. Once the Task Force had moved on, communications could be sent only via the American DISCUS satellite, which in its given position could not be used for transmitting television pictures. By tilting the satellite, it could be made to do so; even so, pictures would need to be sent from land-based rather than ships' terminals since it utilized a signal incompatible with the relay system of the Task Force. These technical problems were explored. Engineers from the Ministry of Defence, the BBC and ITN were able to demonstrate that pictures and sound might be sent from the Army's mobile earth terminal and, prompted by the BBC and ITN, the three American networks approached the Pentagon to discuss whether DISCUS might be tilted to the appropriate position. The Ministry of Defence also made its own approaches. As Commander P. H. Longhurst, of the Directorate of Naval Operational Requirements, told the Defence Committee: 'We made an informal approach [to the Americans] at desk level, to see what their reaction would be. The reaction was, as one might expect, very negative. But there was no formal approach made.' Neville Taylor, Chief Public Relations Officer at the Ministry of Defence, confirmed this account to the Defence Committee:

> I had a discussion with a very senior officer in the Department to consider whether we would pursue talks with the Americans at a more senior level. Because of the advice that I was given, which I totally accepted, I did not pursue any further approaches to the Americans. It is obvious to me that the answer that we had got was not because it had been at a desk level and therefore might be slightly different if we put it at a ministerial level; there was a very, very sound operational and security reason for not risking further use of the satellite, so we did not pursue it.[1]

These remarks were, perhaps deliberately, obscure but it is hardly surprising that the Americans were reluctant to alter the footprint and polarization of their satellite to suit the convenience of the television companies, particularly since DISCUS' sphere of operation included Central America, with which the USA was having problems of its own. As for British military requirements, once the Task Force had reached the Falklands and the Argentinians were well aware of its position, high-frequency radio could again be used. The only other method by which pictures could be relayed was via the international satellite system INTELSAT. To do so, however, would need large high-power terminals: the terminals used by the military are inadequate. The mobile terminals used by the BBC and ITN operate on the wrong frequency for that area and, while such apparatus can be obtained from the USA, it is very expensive and very bulky. Each mobile terminal costs more than £1m. Furthermore, they can only rarely be used other than on land. (One was placed on an aircraft carrier to transmit pictures of the *Apollo* splashdown.) It was highly unlikely that the Navy would have allowed space on its carriers to accommodate a 40-foot dish, and thus interfere with the landings and lift-offs of the much valued Harrier jump-jets. Once the Task Force had landed, a terminal of the appropriate size could have been set up on the Islands, but the expense and difficulty of doing so made such a project impracticable, not least because it was not clear who – the television companies or the Government – would be liable for the cost, and to what extent. There remained, then, only the military's mobile ground station, suitable for speech and teleprinter communications only and subject to the same constraints as SCOT.

It is clear that, even without obstruction from the Ministry of Defence, there were sufficient obstacles of a technical kind to prevent the transmission of pictures of the war. Nonetheless, it is equally true that the Ministry and the military were far from helpful. For example, at an early stage in the conflict, the BBC arranged that Cable and Wireless PLC should improve their satellite transmission arrangements on Ascension Island so that pictures could be carried. This took a couple of weeks; when things were ready, the BBC flew their engineer, Mark Singleton, to Ascension, with the necessary equipment to feed signals to the BBC and ITN. Little use was made of the system, however, since it was difficult to send film from the South Atlantic to Ascension. Film that did reach Ascension took an inordinately long time to arrive in London, not because of technical difficulties, since by that stage transmission should have taken, at the maximum, only one more day to get back. The problem was, rather, that of authority. Sometimes Singleton was given access to tapes as they came in from the South Atlantic; more often, he was told that they should go first to the Ministry of Defence for scrutiny. In one case, where film was sent from a ship sailing south, Singleton was instructed to delay outward transmission for twenty-four hours, to give the vessel time to move on. The naval commander on Ascension then took the film from Singleton and sent it himself to the Ministry in London, ordering Singleton to hand over any more film he might receive to the Commander of British Forces on Ascension. Singleton remained there for some four weeks, until all telex telephone links to Ascension were cut off for operational reasons, and the use of the satellite prohibited. He returned to London for instructions and, on being told that lines of communication would soon be restored, returned to Ascension. As Table 8.1 shows, however, no further transmissions came through to London of news material that was less than eight to ten days old.

In the absence of satellite transmission, film was sent back to Britain by ship, although the first batch, from *Hermes*, was brought by helicopter, since at that stage the ship was only twenty-four hours out at sea. For the next week or so, Hesketh saved his film, dropping some off at Ascension and, during the last part of the voyage, entrusting it to the supply ships which accompanied the fleet and returned periodically to Ascension for fresh stores. They carried Hesketh's film back to Ascension and from there it was flown back to London. This was the route Hesketh used until the Argentines surrendered at Port Stanley. Although there was no deliberate

Table 8.1   *Timetable of delays*

Contents of story	Date of filming	Date of trans-mission	Delay (days)
South Georgia: still pictures of British Forces' repossession	25 April	18 May	23
First pictures in South Atlantic	28 April	13 May	15
Harriers/*Sheffield*/Capt. Salt interview	1–8 May	26 May	18
Sheffield pictures	7 May	28 May	21
Pebble Island	15 May	7 June	23
Ardent	21 May	10 June	20
San Carlos/*Canberra*/Bomb Alley	21 May	8 June	18
Goose Green/casualties/medical team/children	28 May	14 June	16
Sir Galahad/*Sir Tristran*	8 June	24 June	16
Shelling of Stanley (from Argentine sources)	13 June	22 June	9
Shelling of Stanley (BBC/ITN pool)	13 June	25 June	12
Surrender	14 June	25 June	11

Source: ITN memorandum to Defence Committee

conspiracy to prevent television pictures from appearing on screens at home, both the military and the Ministry of Defence were acutely anxious about the possible effect that any pictures might have on the morale of both the troops and their families. The general view among the military was that it was the nightly showing of television pictures from South-East Asia which undermined popular support in America for the Vietnam war. This was the firm and unanimous opinion of those Task Force commanders, Major-General Moore, for example, who gave evidence to the Defence Committee. Ministers and civil servants were seriously concerned about the influence of any television pictures on morale. The evidence given to the Defence Committee by Sir Frank Cooper, then Permanent Under Secretary at the Ministry of Defence, is a good illustration:

> To be quite frank about it, one of the problems is that, if we had had transmission of television throughout, the problem of what could or could not be released would have been very severe indeed. We have been criticized in many quarters and we will no doubt go on being criticized in many quarters, but the criticism we have had is a small drop in the ocean compared to the problems we would have had in dealing with the television coverage.[2]

The debate about the lack of pictures was confused at the time, as well as afterwards. The military, particularly the Navy, were, as we have seen, opposed to television crews accompanying the Task Force, demonstrating their antagonism by sometimes failing to

provide the necessary facilities, by preventing the filming of particular incidents and refusing interviews with military personnel. At
home, the Ministry was slow to cooperate with the BBC and ITN in
discussing technical difficulties. When these had been surmounted,
and political pressure had been applied, 'operational reasons' were
cited as the obstacle to bringing pictures back. Had the conflict
lasted for more than twelve weeks, the Government might have
been obliged to answer criticisms of the absence of normal
coverage. As it was, the war was so short that any complaints were
quickly drowned by the cheers at Britain's victory.

Afterwards, however, ministers and civil servants spoke more
frankly of their worries over the televising of conflicts and admitted
that any embarrassment that the lack of pictures may have caused
was outweighed by the idea of their being shown at all. In his
evidence to the Defence Committee, John Nott, Minister of
Defence when the crisis began, stated:

> I must say I personally rather shared the view of some of the military people who
> came to this Committee. I do not think television would have made our operations
> any easier to conduct and, after all, we were trying to win a war. I am not quite
> clear how television would have helped us to win the war. I would not go as far as
> to say: 'It would have led to us losing it or extended the conflict'. We intended that
> television should go and there were technical obstacles we could not overcome.[3]

When we spoke to Bernard Ingham, he denied that ministers were
relieved at the absence of television pictures:

> I fully accept that there would have been a problem if indeed you would have had
> immediate transmission of television pictures, but what is absolutely and funda-
> mentally wrong is that there was a deliberate plot to prevent them from coming
> back. It was not possible, notwithstanding what people say . . . they just didn't get
> it technically feasible as far as I can see. Heaven knows, I spent enough time in
> this room throughout that entire crisis wondering about this point.

Television broadcasters were, however, not the only ones to meet
technical and human obstruction. Radio communication turned out
to be almost as complicated. Voice reports were transmitted from
ships fitted with links to the commercial maritime satellite system,
INMARSAT. As we have seen in earlier chapters, only radio and
television journalists, not the newspapermen, were allowed to use
this equipment. Some of the merchant ships and Royal Fleet Auxiliary ships with the Task Force had a Marisat system but many
vessels including the warships, did not. Journalists had to transfer to
those ships with the equipment whenever they wished to send
despatches. Nicholson and Hanrahan, for example, were obliged to
leave *Hermes* and move to another ship when the need arose.
Hanrahan described their difficulties to us:

We always had to go to another ship to a Marisat system . . . and the RFAs, for much of the time, were pushed out of the way. Once the fighting started, nobody wanted any of those hanging about if they weren't needed. They were either terribly close being protected or a long way away trying to get lost. *Hermes* . . . did not have a commercial telephone system except high-frequency, which was susceptible to direction-finding. So they weren't prepared to use it. What we wanted was a voice circuit. Now, although the Navy does have voice circuit, it was very reluctant to (1) concede it and (2) do anything about giving it to us.

Robert Fox, Jeremy Hands and Kim Sabido had an easier time, since a Marisat system had been fitted in *Canberra* just before it sailed. Their problems began once they went ashore. Then, like Nicholson and Hanrahan, they too had to look for lifts to a Marisat ship. All the radio journalists had the same dilemma: whether to stay with a ship from which they could communicate or to go with the troops to the action or, at least, to a place where information could be acquired. Hanrahan, aboard *Fearless*, explained:

You could not radio from *Fearless*; we just thought it was better to stay there than go off to a ship that had a telephone because what is the point of having a telephone but no information? When the ship we *had* been on went off, there was no point going back with it; we could have rung up every day, we could have told them that we were bouncing about at sea, but we couldn't have told them what was happening . . . And that was what we were there for, so better to stay there without communication than to have communication and no information.

On occasions, rather than transferring from ship to ship, the journalists would tape their despatches and give them to a Ministry official to take to the Marisat vessel. Rather than relying on the military or the minders, the broadcasters nonetheless preferred (unlike their colleagues from the press) to take their pieces back themselves. Hanrahan, for instance, often left his camera crew:

I was going back to the ships to get radio out and leaving them in the forward position. I would only be away for a day or so . . . [when] . . . something . . . had happened and I wanted to go back and do a despatch on it. But there was no point in them uprooting themselves to come back with me . . . It was just convenient, I could jump into a helicopter and get there and back quicker than I could if all three of us packed everything and went.

At times it was necessary to depend on helicopter pilots as couriers. Hanrahan again:

. . . for example, we had another week in Goose Green, . . . and I was writing stories fairly regularly about burials of prisoners, and a couple of other incidents that happened round about that time, and I could see no point in going back because every time . . . I lost a day going and a day coming back. Whereas I could spend a day getting a story and writing it and doing other things, so at that stage when there wasn't a lot going on I was recording cassettes and sending them back in the hope that somebody would play them over the Marisat.

According to Nicholson, without the Marisat the war would have gone unreported:

> The Royal Fleet Auxiliary crews were marvellous and gave us unstinted coopera-
> tion. There was constant physical risk in getting from *Hermes* to RFA Marisat
> ships, often winching down in exceptionally rough seas. Eventually, and only
> because of the cooperation of David Cameron of RFA *Olmeda,* we began to send
> cassette tapes which were dropped on deck in a bag. We asked if we couldn't
> transmit over the ship-to-ship radio, which would have meant we could have sent
> our reports directly from *Hermes* to the Marisat ship for onward transmission via
> the satellite home. This was refused by Captain Middleton of *Hermes* on the
> grounds that the transmission would give away our position. Yet twice he gave us
> information this way because he wanted good news to get to London quickly. One
> instance of this was his telling us of the sinking of the *General Belgrano*.

The Marisat communications system is not, however, secure. It is simply an international maritime telephone system which, unlike the Navy's own communication channels, can be bugged, as signals are bounced up to the satellite and relayed down to the ground station on land. This makes a nonsense of the Ministry of Defence's insistence on monitoring and censoring all broadcasts as they came into Broadcasting House in London. The Ministry's reasoning was that, if the Argentinians were not listening to the Marisat – and the Ministry could not tell – they should not be given information by the BBC or ITN. A senior Ministry of Defence official elaborated to us:

> I think we've all accepted that, if you allow a transmission by Marisat, you can
> possibly prejudice security. But the fact was that we were unable to say whether or
> not the Argentines were able to. But we don't think they were able to eavesdrop
> on Marisat. Although it is insecure it is very difficult. That thing in my office is
> totally secure, that telephone enables me to communicate via military satellites
> and that is a secure telephone. For instance, I was able to talk in total security to
> Sir Rex Hunt on the Falklands, a week before the Prime Minister went . . .
> knowing that that can't be intercepted. We haven't got the same guarantee with
> Marisat . . . There was a dilemma. Either the broadcasters couldn't broadcast at
> all because the speech quality on that thing is totally unacceptable for broad-
> casting. Even when you've got the best of conditions, it is still very difficult to
> converse on that thing. And had we insisted on secure communications only, then
> broadcasters would only have been able to transmit written copy, which would
> have come up on telex this end over a secure link and then be read out in the
> studio or [to have made] tape recordings that they would have to send by ship –
> ten or twelve days to Ascension, and then flown back. Or we [had to take] the risk
> that some material could possibly be compromised because it had been inter-
> cepted, but nevertheless we would maintain a check on it at this end.

Some Ministry of Defence officials suspected some broadcasters of circumventing the monitoring procedure. One civil servant told us:

> I think it was accepted that . . . we could possibly have compromised communi-
> cations. The chances were, however, that we didn't, but it was the compromise we

reached, against, I may say, very, very strong pressure not to allow the broad-casters to broadcast, for the very reason that, when they were in the process of broadcasting, it may have been too late to shut the stable door. We had to persuade the military and the Secretary of State that there was a sufficient safeguard that stuff wouldn't get out publicly and generally until we'd agreed it. I have some suspicion, but no evidence, that there may have been other material which we never heard at this end. I suspect that the reporters, in talking to their own technicians, their own studios before we were plugged in, possibly gave them additional detail . . . it was just occasionally that stuff got out which can only, I think have come from that voice link . . . it wasn't on our tape.

The Ministry was particularly worried about the broadcasters talk-ing over the Marisat to their editors back home. As one official said: 'What we were concerned about was when a correspondent would fly to a ship and broadcast and would be asked questions and answers by somebody at the studio. That was where stuff was being given away.'

Kim Sabido, the IRN man on board *Canberra*, gave us an example of the Ministry's nervousness. He described how Allan George, one of the minders, viewed some of the responses Sabido sent back to his newsroom:

One time he said he considered me to be the most dangerous journalist on board because I was able to do these two-way interviews with my office. They would ask me questions and he would listen in to them. They went through the MoD and they'd be listened to by them. But he still found that he thought I could say something that I shouldn't say, without being censored.

The Ministry was also concerned by the fact that journalists were sometimes unchaperoned. A senior official told us:

There were instances [when] they did not have a censor beside them, although they complained a lot about censors; sometimes Mike Nicholson particularly would say 'Oh, bugger it . . .,' and go off and broadcast without checking. We had to have a check on that in case operational information was being given out, and to be fair to everyone, except for one or two occasions when we had to read the Riot Act. Certainly the BBC and ITN fought us like hell and made life bloody difficult for us, wanting to get stuff out . . . but we resisted this if we hadn't checked it, and if we weren't certain we got an operational man to do it; the trouble was that very often the stuff would be coming in just before or during a news broadcast and so we would find ourselves in a very difficult position of having to say, 'No, you may not use it, not because we think it necessary, but we've got to check'. Because there may have been operational nuances which we didn't know.

Though the Argentinians might not have been eavesdropping on Marisat communications, they might obtain information from World Service broadcasts. The Ministry was particularly worried about the consequences for the troops, especially those who were vulnerable to surprise attack. The Ministry of Defence official went on:

> Think of the soldiers, our own soldiers, their anger if they were told that they were
> sitting without aircraft cover in their ships in Bluff Cove and suddenly an aircraft
> comes in and bombs them. What are they going to say about us letting the BBC
> World Service broadcast that?

It seems that, for the most part, operational reasons account for the delay in the BBC's or ITN's broadcasting material from correspondents. Some of the delay was, however, caused deliberately by the Ministry. As a senior military offical told us:

> It was all a fudge, frankly, but it was an attempt, and I think by and large it
> worked. If the Argentinians did get all the stuff, they didn't appear to use it. And I
> think it is difficult to explain, thinking back to it now . . . but this [was] a system
> . . . we were determined to control it, [by] assuming that the Argentinians hadn't
> got it, and anything that had anything about future intentions or overall plans we
> removed, quite deliberately.

By and large, the system worked. Hanrahan confirmed this:

> The only time it backfired was this huge row about Goose Green. When people
> said they'd heard on the World Service something about Goose Green, very few
> people [actually had]. Somebody obviously heard something, and to this day I still
> don't know what it was . . . They said it was news, the BBC said it wasn't,
> obviously the word got round very quickly that the BBC had broadcast the news
> about Goose Green because rumour spreads, and I got particularly hostile com-
> ments from people when I turned up. They said, 'You're the man', and I said,
> 'No, I'm not the man'. In fact I got angry about it and had a big set-to with
> somebody or other . . . But that was the only time there was any kind of comeback
> and I just got the backlash of somebody else . . . For all I know, they were all
> going around saying, 'For Christ's sake, keep it away from Hanrahan; he always
> gets it wrong', and nobody ever told me.

If the World Service did carry sensitive news of that kind, it could equally well have come from Government offices in London.

During the Conflict there were, from time to time, other ways in which journalists would try to transmit information. One was in the satellite communication link established at Ajax Bay, after the landings at San Carlos. Copy could be sent by telex from this system and Michael Nicholson attempted to use it to get a voice link to Britain. He was told, however, that the line was too busy, that it was out of order, and that there was too much interference for successful voice communication. The other method was inspired by Fleet Headquarters, which after the conflict persuaded the BBC to estab-lish a line between RAF Oakhanger and Broadcasting House. This promised to give direct voice communication to a satellite-based land-link on the Falkland Islands but according to the BBC, use of the connection was eventually vetoed by the Ministry of Defence.

It is helpful to know something about the technical and procedural arrangements by which radio and television correspondents' copy reached the listener and viewer. To some extent these followed the normal pattern. For example, a BBC foreign correspondent can use any sort of telephone system; he or she will telephone the 'traffic department', which is manned twenty-four hours a day. Calls are accepted by a traffic manager, who finds out who is on line, with what material, for which programme or bulletin. This information is then announced on a Tannoy system serving BBC newsrooms, Broadcasting House and Bush House. Broadcasting House, Television News and Bush House are all linked into a conference system so that news editors, foreign editors and home news editors can not only hear but also talk to the correspondent in question. Radio correspondents deal mostly with editors in Broadcasting House, but the television editors may sometimes join in to ask whether something can be done for their departments. Radio correspondents also file for Bush House, as a matter of course.

As all three services can speak to the correspondent simultaneously, a four-way conference can occur, though this is rare. At Broadcasting House, editors of current affairs programmes may also join in such conversations. If, for example, *The World at One* or the *PM* programme wants to interview a correspondent, he or she can be switched to the necessary studio, before being re-routed elsewhere. During the Falklands war a piece from Robert Fox would produce, for instance, material for six or seven different outlets. Moreover, Fox, a radio man, was extensively used by television, while Hanrahan, a television man, produced far more for radio than would usually be the case, not least because, since the Broadcasting House traffic unit was the central receiving unit, all Hanrahan's television news material came via Broadcasting House.

Hanrahan himself described how these arrangements differed from those he was used to:

> We've got a single foreign news circuit which comes into the BBC. I'd come up on that and I'd have the despatch ready, which might mean a minute, it might be five, it might be ten, depending on how much had been going on. Or it might be three or four pieces which had been written over several days. And the first thing I would do was quite simply say 'I'm up' and I would bang off all these pieces. And you would normally find that there would be one radio and one television interviewer waiting to talk to you. I made it clear that there wasn't going to be time for everybody in a line . . . because there was pressure on me to give the phone to other people. So we did the television and radio interviewers, normally someone from television news and then whichever was the next current affairs programme that was on the air. If there were any queries, you'd sort those out and you'd go back to the mainstream line and then you'd occasionally get people like

the World Service [who'd] say 'Could you redo this in such a way that it would take account of the fact that we'll be running it after midnight?' And also you'd find that people like the *Today* programme would sometimes say: 'Look, we'd like to do a talk with you not about news but about feelings and atmosphere or food . . . medicines or anything else. Do you think that would be possible?' And you'd normally say, 'Well, I'll come back to you later,' and give the phone to somebody else. We did it by agreement . . .

The broadcasters were fortunate in that they could receive immediate feedback from their editors. As Hanrahan described it:

> It is very useful to send . . . back . . . your choice of what is interesting and to check it with somebody else's choice of what they think is interesting . . . I was tailoring despatches in such a way that they had segments in them for different people, and if the World Service came up with a bit that I had tailored for domestic consumption and left out the bit that I'd tailored for World Service consumption, you began to feel that perhaps you'd got it wrong . . . We weren't particularly trying to write radio pieces, I was trying to write information. I was writing the kind of thing *The Times* would print, because that was the only way the information was getting back. So almost every despatch started with an account of what was going on and that's exactly the style of the stuff that the World Service uses and they don't want fancy writing, they simply want to know what happened.

The principal change in this system during the Falklands war was, obviously, the introduction of arrangements for Ministry of Defence guidance on matters of operational security. Once the principle had been accepted, the Ministry and the broadcasters had to decide how it would be realized. The broadcasters were anxious that their deadlines should be met; a system of, say, recording incoming material at Broadcasting House, the tapes then being vetted by the Ministry, would have been intolerable, especially to news editors. They needed the quickest possible clearance. ITN had some experience of the sort of problems that could arise. In the early stages of the conflict, correspondents' material, recorded on cassette tapes, had been carried by hand to the Ministry, where they were played and studied before clearance was given by telephone to ITN.

The moment at which the deficiencies of this scheme became most obvious was on the night the Task Force landed at San Carlos. Mike Nicholson sent back a graphic description, some eleven minutes long, about half an hour before the *News at Ten* was to go on the air. The cassette was rushed to the Ministry; clearance came at about ten minutes past ten. There was just enough time to send the report out in the second half of *News at Ten*. It was then decided that all correspondents should send their material to the Broadcasting House traffic department. On being told to use the BBC link, Nicholson, Hands and Sabido were, not surprisingly, cautious, particularly since there had already been confusion about 'pooling' arrangements. They were eventually reassured that the scheme was merely procedural and had the blessing of the ITN and IRN. Editors from those organizations were also brought into the system, so that they – as well as their BBC counterparts – could talk directly to their correspondents. The Ministry of Defence was also brought into the conference circuit. To allow editors to talk privately to reporters, without being heard by the Ministry, arrangements were made to switch the Ministry into the system only when the broadcasters wished. When a despatch was expected, the BBC would alert the Ministry, despatches would then be recorded by the Ministry on machines provided by the BBC. A logging system was also devised. Despatches were numbered, to minimize delay and confusion in discussion.

The BBC emphasized that monitoring should be instantaneous and that an officer of sufficient authority should be on hand either to give immediate clearance or to indicate which bits of the material were thought sensitive. According to Bob Kearsley, news editor of BBC radio news, things did not always go smoothly. He told us: '[The Ministry] either couldn't get the right people in the right place at the right time or something was thought sufficiently important to have to go to some kind of clearing committee upstairs, or they had to bring in extra technical sources or whatever . . . We did become extremely frustrated with the delays.'

The officers the Ministry appointed to clear copy were of relatively senior rank. Material was, indeed, often given immediate clearance with specified exceptions, for example: 'Piece X cleared with the exception of the naming of SAS unit.' At other times, there was a five or ten minute delay and on such occasions the BBC would set aside two telephone lines for a Ministry of Defence call. Any request from the Ministry would then be relayed, via the central traffic point at Broadcasting House, to all others on the circuit. According to Bob Kearsley, the longest delay was one of forty-eight hours, on Mike Nicholson's ITN despatch on Bluff Cove.

On one or two occasions editors refused to delay the piece any further, arguing that, where they believed a story to be perfectly safe and the Ministry could not say what, if anything, was wrong with it, there could be no justification for holding back. Certainly the Ministry was not always helpful. As Bob Kearsley said:

They would simply say 'It's not cleared yet'. It depended how high up the chain of command you could get in your own phone call . . . If every senior officer was in the clearing process and you could not reach them behind some kind of locked door it was a very unsatisfactory situation where a very friendly and helpful technician was only able to tell you that he was not able to tell you anything.

Which became maddening when the editors were watching the ten o'clock
deadline coming up and knowing that they had a bloody good despatch.

Though radio and television editors could talk to their correspondents, this luxury was, as we have seen, denied to their colleagues in
the press. Messages between newspaper correspondents and their
editors were, however, occasionally passed on via the BBC traffic
system. *The Daily Mail*, for example, was at one point worried
about David Norris, from whom they had not heard for several
days, and, asked the BBC for help. 'We asked Foxy. He said, "Yes,
he's OK, he's up on the road". And we passed that back. It was
simply an informal colleague-to-colleague kind of relationship',
Kearsley said.

From the broadcasting correspondents' view it was a tremendous
asset to be in touch with their office. Print journalists certainly
suffered a severe disadvantage.

What sort of arrangements were made for the despatch of pictures?

Of the two press photographers who were sent with the Task Force,
Martin Cleaver from the Press Association was on *Hermes* and Tom
Smith of the *Daily Express* was first put on board RFA *Sir Lancelot*
and then transferred to *Canberra*. Many photographers, from
Britain and abroad, hoped to sail with the Task Force, including the
experienced war photographer, Don McCullen. As we saw in Chapter 1, the Ministry had been accused of refusing a place to McCullen, because of his reputation for controversial work. The Ministry
replied that its choice was dictated by circumstances. As a senior
civil servant told us:

It was not really a question of our not wishing to have them there, there was no
way in which we could get them there in time. In my view we had enough
photographers to cover the war and I think, indeed, the coverage showed that
later – but they were not experienced war photographers. The *Daily Express* too
had a photographer there; we did not say whom they could send, nor did we tell
the Press Association, and there was nothing to stop the *Express* or the Press
Association [picking] somebody who was experienced in war photography.

Official war photographers, and an artist, Linda Kitson, were sent
by the Ministry and assigned to individual units. Pictorial coverage
of the war was nevertheless skimpy. As Martin Cleaver said:

The Ministry seemed to think that two was plenty to look after and fill in the gaps
with their own blokes running around with cameras, which is not quite the same
thing. I think another couple or even three photographers would have covered the
whole thing better.

As well as Cleaver and Smith, there were several photographers from the Services. They and the press photographers together transmitted, according to the Ministry of Defence, some 202 pictures. The number was so small for an operation of this size because, the Ministry explained, of the lack of facilities and the technical difficulties.

Means for transmitting still pictures were certainly scarce. There were four Muirhead facsimile transmission machines, which worked in conjunction with the Marisat. These travelled with *Canberra* and were only later transferred to other ships equipped with Marisat. Cleaver and Smith took rolls and rolls of film, most of which had to go back to London by ship, delaying the publication of their material by two or three weeks. Cleaver described the process:

> You wrapped them up in the caption, stuffed them in an envelope and you waited . . . Initially, for the first four or five days, helicopters were going back to the UK because we were still in range. After that it was the first ship going north. A ship went every five or ten days.

The Press Association itself supplied Cleaver's Muirhead transmitter but, since it travelled on *Canberra*, days behind *Hermes*, Cleaver obtained it only two days before the landing. Even then, he could not operate it himself; according to an agreement between the Press Association and the National Graphical Association (NGA), photographers are not allowed to use the machine. On this occasion the Press Association got special permission from the NGA to circumvent the regulations. As Cleaver said: 'That's how we got round the problem. I mean, I know how it works, I know how to wire it up. But Service personnel used it.' The transmitter, which weighed about 28lb, worked on a voltage-drop principle. The picture, the print, is put on a drum and the communications line connected. One sensor produces pinpoints of light, another reads them. As the drum revolves, the second sensor scans the picture (which resembles a television picture); the voltage alters according to the lightness or darkness of the picture. To transmit colour, three printers are needed to make colour separations. Having converted a picture to an electrical signal, the transmitter can convey it, in this case via satellite, at a cost of $11 a minute. The downlink was to a receiving station in Scandinavia. From there the signal was sent by landline to Electra House, the telecommunications centre run by Cable and Wireless, and then to the Ministry of Defence. The Ministry's receiver, a K5–50, could produce a facsimile of a photograph, on poor paper and of unimpressive quality, but sufficiently clear to give an idea of the original picture. On this basis, the Ministry could clear a photograph and the Press Assocation was then free to collect the original, and a copy of the negative, from Electra House.

The Permanent Secretary, Sir Frank Cooper, admitted that facilities had been poor:

> We are at fault in that we should have taken much more care to have more facilities available in terms of being able to transmit still photographs, but again – and I do not think this has been fully appreciated – we did not have operational plans. The operational plans were worked out as the Task Force was sailing . . . It was decided when the Task Force was sailing that we would go to South Georgia first and what kind of operations were going to take place in the Falkland Islands was being worked out by the staffs at Northwood in the Ministry of Defence as the Task Force was sailing down there, so this meant people were not on the right ships, the necessary equipment was not on the right ships, a lot of the equipment had to be flown out and put on ships and then re-ordered and re-sorted in terms of the operational need.[4]

Since there were so few photographers, several important events were not covered. There is, for example, no pictorial record of the battle at Goose Green. Martin Cleaver was prevented from going:

> The famous excuse was that there was not any transport going that way; there were no helicopters. You know, eventually, you were just bashing your head against a brick wall, you just gave up. If they did not want you to go somewhere, you were not going to go since you had to rely on them totally for transport.

On other occasions and at other times, however, Cleaver and Smith were given more latitude than the journalists, not least because it was known that their film usually took a fortnight or so to reach London. Cleaver described one incident on *Hermes*:

> The mentioning of names of ships was a very touchy point . . . *Broadsword* . . . was *Hermes*' minder, and there were terrific ructions about the fact that it had slipped out. One of the TV boys, Hanrahan or Nicholson, said this. And Peter Archer said it – he had phoned over a story. There was hell to pay. I'd taken pictures of *Broadsword* leaping around and put on my caption 'HMS *Broadsword* in close company with *Hermes*' and they looked at the captions and said: 'No problem. Stick them on the film and away they go.' Because they know there's a built-in delay of two weeks. So they're not worried about it. I could get away with it, but the reporters couldn't.

On the voyage south, Cleaver, on *Hermes*, and Smith, on the *Sir Lancelot*, were obliged to send their pictures back to London by ship, the Muirheads being on *Canberra*. For Smith who moved ships, matters eventually improved: 'Once on *Canberra* it was superb. I could start working then. There was a good darkroom and a terrific-quality wiring machine for a satellite. There was a Navy photographer on the *Canberra* just processing prints for me'.

After they came ashore, Cleaver and Smith devised arrangements for sending their film to *Canberra* for transmission. Cleaver gave an example:

> The *Galahad* getting hit at Bluff Cove – I was there when they actually hit – I got my two rolls of film, put them in an envelope, gave them to a helicopter pilot who was going back to *Fearless* darkroom, picked out about four pictures and got them printed, captioned them, sent them to *Canberra* for wiring. So two days later they appear in London.

Some pictures reached London sooner than others. The Commons Defence Committee enquired, for instance, why Smith's photographs of the villagers of San Carlos offering a Marine a cup of tea preceded, by such a long interval, that of Cleaver's picture of *Antelope* exploding. (On his return to London, Smith was surprised to learn of the reaction to that photograph. 'The reception I got here was, "That was a great cup of tea picture". You know, I thought, "What the fuck about all the rest, I've just covered a war," and everybody was patting me on the back saying that was a good cup of tea picture . . . and I couldn't believe it.')

Smith told the photographer on *Canberra* to print at least six pictures from every roll of film and to move some five pictures a day. They were indeed transmitted; it was in London that trouble began, for the publication of certain pictures was deliberately delayed by the Ministry. As Bob Hutchinson, defence correspondent of the Press Association, told us:

> There was an occasion when some photographs came to the Ministry from the South Atlantic, one of which was a photograph of the *Antelope* blowing up, taken by our man there, Martin Cleaver. Several other photographs came in at the same time and they were not released for quite some time afterwards. I might be wrong on this but, if my memory serves me right, they were not released until three weeks after this because we were told Number 10 felt that enough bad news pictures had come out.

The photographers themselves were unaware of this. Smith, for instance, believed that most of his pictures were getting through. From the Falklands he had no contact with his office and he believed he was having a 'pretty good war':

> You had no feedback at all, you see. Being with 3 Para, there were no telephones and you never got anything back from the office, so you were coming back here thinking you were going to get the hero treatment and the office are pretty cool about everything.

Smith firmly believes that the Ministry blocked most of his work:

> And then when I got back and showed them the negatives, they couldn't believe it. I couldn't believe it, because I knew that my stuff was physically wired. As a photographer once it goes on the drum and you hear from the other end that it's

good quality, you go to the pub, you know. But they were all blocked at this end. Do you know, there was not one single picture of a dead body released by MoD.

The fault does not only lie with the Ministry. Some pictures were held back but many did get through to the Press Association, which issued a great many over the wire to newspapers. As Cleaver said:

> Mine got through. They were not published but they did get through. There are pictures of dead bodies, gore and red meat in the PA library, which were released by the Ministry, but people obviously did not want to see it . . . I suspect that the PA edited some of the blood and gore out. I know for a fact that they did issue some of it, but what they did issue did not get published, which did not surprise me.

Newspaper editors themselves exercised some censorship. In contrast, *Paris Match* carried many pages of Cleaver's work, as did some of the Argentinian and American magazines.

At one stage, while his colleague was at home, Cleaver himself processed Smith's pictures for him. Cleaver had the use of a darkroom and could process, print and wire the films. This gave Cleaver some insight into reasons why much of Smith's film was not getting back:

> I think the problem with Tom Smith's stuff was it was going through too many people and along the line it was getting edited out all the time. Editing is a pretty skilled job. You take pot luck. Fortunately, I only sent films back on about three occasions. Sometimes I took them back myself. When I did send they managed to pick something that was reasonable. Of course, you can also pick them for them by shooting only two frames of something and telling them to pick one of them. Don't press the shutter until you're absolutely certain. You can pre-empt – that's what I say at PA sometimes – and when you know that guy is on you can do the editing for him, by only going back with ten frames, any one of which will do. Whereas, if you've got somebody who's switched on and knows what they're doing, you can file bursts of things and shoot a lot more than you would and it will be edited out. Overshoot. But if you know you're shooting for the lowest common denominator, then that's what you do – you pre-edit it. And also you make sure everything's framed properly so they don't have to start trying to frame by pulling things up and selecting enlargement. Just print the whole thing and it's right.

Smith had to rely on a chain of other people to process, edit and send his film, whereas Cleaver had a direct link to a darkroom in *Fearless* or *Canberra*; only one person saw his work before it was despatched. He also made off-the-record arrangements for getting stuff back. They worked; the material emerged in London. Cleaver told us how he managed to set up the darkroom on *Fearless*:

> You've got a bloke there who the Navy told to be there but he didn't really want to know, and he did his job and that was it. With a little bit of pushing and a little bit of bribing with cans of beer, he pulled his finger out and pushed the films through and he could pick pictures. So if the minder wasn't very sure, he would just print

three for him . . . Dunk, it was done, and the minder would look and say 'Great', and away it went while other people were arguing about it.

The Ministry of Defence has denied that pictures were blocked once they reached London. One senior military spokesman said to us there was 'no censorship at all – absolutely none'. However, he did give an example of partial censorship:

> . . . the only thing there was was control at this end of operational things. Now, I quote a classic example. We asked for a photograph of *Rapier,* and when it came not very long afterward, because of the directness of the thing, there it was sitting on top of the hill, a ridge running down to a jetty with houses below it. Now quite obviously that was San Carlos settlement. We were not prepared to release the whole photograph because, again, the Argentinians could have picked it up and seen where it was, and put an air attack on it. So we cut the thing, let *Rapier* go without the jetty on it.

As for Smith's claims that pictures of dead bodies were blocked or delayed, the Ministry spokesman denied to us that a great many had been received:

> They came into the Old Admiralty Building, I think; there was somebody permanently on duty there, and then they were rushed straight through, checked for security, and then sent to the PA and the PA then issued them. What we were actually looking at . . . three weeks, five battalion attacks, four of which always took place at night. You're not going to get many dead-body pictures actually in that, and when you look at the number of dead bodies, there weren't all that many anyway, and there weren't all that many cameramen. There were lots of amateur people with cameras in their pockets, but this is where I say, right from the beginning, that we did not make adequate coverage for professional war photographers. Look at Martin Cleaver, he was not at Goose Green until the next day, nobody was actually on the ground on the day of the advance to Goose Green, so you didn't have a picture of H's gully. Tumbledown, you had pictures, you've seen dead Argentinians crumbling in the rocks there. We've had British Paratroopers being carried in screaming after being wounded, but, you see, the thing was the casevac . . . the . . . bodies were picked up and rushed straight back to Ajax Bay, and that's where the casualties were . . . but of course the correspondents didn't want to be at Ajax Bay, they wanted to be up at the front end. If a chap was killed at night and you then whip him away by helicopter as soon as you can, there's not many photographs.

We have seen how the ships' military communications system was, of necessity, used for the transmission of written despatches and 'service messages'. On board *Hermes* and *Invincible* journalists used the Navy's signal channels to send their copy back, while on *Canberra* they used Marisat. As the Task Force moved south and the amount of copy increased, problems inevitably arose over the use of facilities, particularly on *Invincible*. On *Hermes* there was only one PA journalist, with television journalists and a photographer who had other communications arrangements. On *Canberra* the journalists were using a commercial system. *Invincible*, on the other hand, had five press journalists, all needing to use the Navy's own facilities. At times their difficulties were acute; on occasion a backlog of a thousand signals awaited transmission.

All press material from *Invincible* was given 'priority' classification, as set out in a signal sent to *Invincible* from Northwood. This is the middle level of precedence for a Royal Navy signal; 'routine' is the lowest; 'priority' that at which 90 per cent of signals are rated; 'immediate' and 'flash' the most urgent. Roger Goodwin, the Ministry of Defence official on board *Invincible*, left it to the journalists themselves to decide the order in which their material should be transmitted, he told us:

> They agreed between them that the order would be *Sun* and the *Star* first, because they had earlier deadlines than the others, then *The Times, Telegraph* and *Guardian*, whichever order they came in, but . . . within those two groupings, it was first come first served. They would then, [have] been seen by the three of us, and it's entirely possible that, when they'd produced their copy, the Captain was in the middle of his meal, or was even asleep. I make no apologies for saying there was no way I was going to wake him up, for the sake of a twenty-minute delay or something, given that it was going to take a long time to get out of the ship. You've got to appreciate the overall size of the problem as far as communications is concerned. At one stage there were something like 22,000 signals backed up here in the Ministry of Defence waiting to be transmitted to the fleet. They instituted a system under which you were required at both ends to put on your signal priority a time after which your signal had no further value . . . It didn't matter what priority or the precedence of it was, if it had not been transmitted by that time, it just got thrown away. And that's part of the explanation why there were an awful lot of signals that were sent by editors, that were sent by pressmen, that were sent by my people, that were sent by me, never got to the other end, just disappeared into the system.

Press copy accounted for up to 25 to 30 percent of the workload of *Invincible*'s signal system in any 24-hour period. Goodwin explained the problem:

> When the Navy writes a signal, you're trained in the Services to write it in signalese; it's done in paragraphs, it very seldom stretches – you know the signals pad has got an address block and the signature block . . . and the actual text part . . . and 90 percent of all signals will be fitted inside there. So when you get McIlroy coming along and churning out 1000 words, it tends to put a spanner in the works, to be honest, because the system is not used to dealing with massive great chunks of toilet paper like that.

Gareth Parry of the *Guardian*, also on board *Invincible*, described the filing problems in the Falklands Conflict as being 'completely unique'. Though, as we have noted, the five journalists in *Invincible* – Snow, Seamark, Parry, McIlroy and Witherow – worked together, and although on any particular day only one story would usually stand out, each would write it in his own and his paper's style. Mick Seamark:

> There was no real rivalry. There were three separate stories, if you like. There was the *Sun* and the *Star* at one end, there was *The Times* and the *Telegraph* at the other, both doing the same stories, obviously written in slightly different ways and picking out the different angles, but basically the same markets, and there was Gareth Parry of the *Guardian* somewhere in between.

To file copy on board *Invincible* and *Hermes* someone in the communications centre would sit at a video console and type the signal, making any necessary corrections on the screen. The signal would then be transmitted by the Navy's own military communication satellite to the Ministry of Defence. It was at this point that problems first arose. On board ship was a dish aerial, with a direct line of sight to the satellite. When the ship changed direction and a funnel broke the line of sight, transmission was interrupted. The line of sight returned, transmission could resume but a signal had to be begun again. Roger Goodwin gave this account:

> You're in the middle of a massive 1000-word article from McIlroy and you get two-thirds of the way through it, and bang the bloody ship suddenly swings through it and you break the transmission; you've got to go all the way back and start again. So material that was taking half an hour for them to type up and put on tape was often taking one and a half hours to actually subsequently transmit, and get a successful transmission through the MoD.

Matters became even worse the further south the Task Force sailed. Transmission is most reliable when the satellite is directly above the dish. Eight thousand miles south, however, the line of sight from aerial to satellite being fairly flat, was more vulnerable to interruption by, for instance, a funnel. (The technical phrase for this is 'wooding'.) Furthermore, aboard ship it could take two or three hours to learn that a message had not got through. It might be apparent that there had been a break in transmission, but the communications chain was so long – from a satellite to a land station to a Whitehall communications centre – that until the Ministry replied, hours later, it was impossible to tell what had, or had not, been received.

It is therefore understandable that Captain Black did not wholly sympathize with some of the journalists' complaints. Yet his objection to the communications system being blocked up with non-military information appears also to have been fuelled by what he saw as trivial copy. He singled out the *Sun* in his evidence to the Defence Committee: 'I will just read, if I may, part of one man's copy: "The Page 3 girls are going to war. Fifty outsize pin-up pictures, each one 2 foot by 6 inches, were airlifted to the Task

Force and are now on their way to the Falkland Islands".' Clearly Black did not like the kind of journalism that some of the correspondents engaged in. Moving on later into the same article:

> Skinhead Ian Walter Mitty would put the frighteners on anyone. With his close shaved head, tattoo covered body, and heavy bovver boots, he looks every inch what he is – a hard man. But Walter, 20, from Richmond, Yorkshire, was near to tears yesterday when he learnt that his dearest wish to get at the Argies with his bare hands, had been denied.[5]

A naval captain, as Roger Goodwin emphasized:

> . . . may be forced to accept but he will never understand why a story like that is required to take precedence over him trying to get a signal out about the latest list of modifications to his Sidewinders. I must tell you, as an ex-journalist, especially one whose neck was at stake at the time, I have some sympathy with his view. You know, if it was a more important story, the 'Up yours, Galtieri' one is a real case in point.

Goodwin told us that eventually he decided to limit the journalists to 700 words a day:

> They would not discipline themselves, despite appeals over periods of weeks. I was getting blamed by the telecoms officer, who was a lieutenant-commander, and I finally felt I had to impose a word limit. We got this arrangement where they would send material overnight; the system was a little bit slacker then anyway, and it was easier to transmit that kind of material. But of course it's far too late for the following morning's deadline. So I tried very often to get them to write their stuff sufficiently far in advance for two days later. That was total anathema to them, too; they couldn't somehow grasp the concept. Most of the material they were writing on the way down, which is the period we're talking about, was in fact colour material. I tried to explain to them that it didn't matter whether it was published Thursday or Friday, quite frankly, so there was no real reason why they couldn't write up how they'd spent a day in the engine room, or last night they were drinking with the chef's mess or whatever, or the dentist is renovating an organ that came from the original *Invincible* . . . they had to insist on trying to live by their normal Fleet Street stimuli of 'must get the news in for tomorrow', etc, etc. And then we had a period where . . . McIlroy produced three 1500-word articles in one 24-hour period. And the coms officer more or less snapped; I said: 'Sorry, guys, 700 words a day.' Now 700 words was carefully calculated. The *Sun* and the *Star* being the *Sun* and the *Star* can say everything they want to say in about four or five hundred words anyway; 700 words was about the kind of figure that the *Guardian* and *The Times* were normally writing anyway, and it was only aimed at McIlroy, but it was taken as a great *cause célèbre*.

Journalists on the other ships had a much less difficult time, although the vetting procedures on *Canberra*, and the animosity that accumulated among correspondents and minders, brought other sorts of friction. David Norris, who spent the first part of the journey in the *Stromness*, had a more or less trouble-free time:

I was very happy because in the two or three weeks up to Ascension Island, I got to know 45 Commando quite well and I didn't have any problems in sending copy from the ship. It was vetted by a Royal Marines Office Lieutenant and if he was worried about it he would take it to the CO, and the Captain of the *Stromness* also had a look at it and I didn't have any problems at all. I had sole use of the Marisat, which they installed as we were sailing, but I had to use the ordinary Marconi radio for the first few days. And then we got this beautiful Marisat system – and I was the sole user of it and I thought my ship had come home. Then they switched me to *Canberra* and it all went a bit sour, really.

Another journalist who sailed part of the way down on his own was Bob McGowan in *Sir Lancelot*. This had no Marisat facility, so McGowan had to rely on helicopters to transfer his copy to RFA ships. After the landings, his colleagues had to do the same. Once the journalists had gone ashore, the problem of getting copy back became severe. Some correspondents achieved more success than others. Their first need was to transport their copy to a ship and this was, to a large extent, a matter of luck in finding a helicopter or a pilot who could take it. Copy had often to pass through many hands before it was eventually transmitted to London.

Max Hastings, the most successful in getting his copy back, himself went to a ship whenever he could. On the few occasions when he was obliged to entrust his copy to a helicopter pilot, it was, he said, never seen again. Some journalists eventually realized that their copy might not be reaching the ships, and therefore delegated one of their number to act as courier, Gareth Parry, for instance:

> . . . If you run to a helicopter it's down on the ground for a couple of seconds, you run to that and give him this and it's dark and he can't bloody hear what you're saying. You've got to reckon what is the likelihood of his taking the trouble to look at it . . . 'Ah, press,' you know, urgent despatch. It's much more urgent for him to fly below the artillery gun-fire. So I had this terrible feeling that stuff wasn't going back that way. So we decided to split up again and try and file. I'd go back to *Fearless* – and don't forget it was only a trip in a raft of about thirty or forty miles, but you could take all day.

A communications centre manned by one of the minders, Alan Percival, was also set up at Ajax Bay and an additional line of communication established in RFA *Stromness* in San Carlos Water, manned for the vetting and transmission of pictures and stories prepared at the time of the landings. Most copy produced by the journalists ashore first went to *Fearless*, for vetting by a minder, and then to another ship or to Ajax Bay for transmission. Patrick Bishop described the process:

> It was a very lengthy business. If you were anywhere, once we moved the bridgehead, the beach-head moved forward . . . you had to get a helicopter back to either . . . actually it was San Carlos they were at for a while, or on to *Fearless*

and have your stuff vetted by the Ministry of Defence man there and then go from
Fearless either to Ajax Bay or to one of the ships.

At sea the operation had been run by the Navy, and vetting was
mainly the responsibility of the minders and the captains of the
various ships. After the landings, the Army took charge of operations, including the vetting of copy. Army press officers became
more closely involved. Mick Seamark described the procedure:

> I was with the Welsh Guards, 1st Battalion Welsh Guards, but I didn't join them
> until about three or four days after getting on land. I was with 5 Brigade
> Headquarters Staff. Then it was a question of writing copy, handing it in to an
> army press officer, who would vet the copy, who would then put it on a helicopter
> to be whisked back to San Carlos where the Ministry of Defence had their tent and
> their satellite communication.

It was only at the very end of the fighting that Tony Snow realized
his copy was being vetted by Army public relations officers.

> There was a satellite communication centre up at Ajax Bay, and the idea was to
> send stuff back there on a helicopter and there was supposed to be a Ministry
> man there to have a look through it and then send it out. But when we were fairly
> well towards Stanley I was told by an Army PR major to send the stuff back by
> helicopters going back there, and he had a telex there and he would telex it back,
> straight to the communications centre at Ajax which would be much quicker,
> rather than get a helicopter back to Ajax. That turned out to be a lie; he didn't
> have a telex there, he just wanted to see all the stuff we were writing about the
> Army before it went back to the Ministry man at Ajax Bay. We found this out,
> because on the last day we were trying to get a story out and we went back to
> Fitzroy and he wasn't there, and I went to the Brigade HQ and said, 'Look, can
> you send this story on your telex to the communications centre at Ajax Bay?' and
> they said, 'We haven't got a telex; there is no telex. Who told you that? That's a
> load of old nails.' It was just so . . . the Army PR people could look at it before it
> got to the Ministry to see that there wasn't anything in it adverse to the Army.

This story sums up the journalists' predicament: their means of
sending pictures and stories home were cumbersome and scarce;
some material never even left the Islands; reports and photographs
that did reach London had to have Ministry of Defence approval,
secured through yet another awkward and overloaded procedure.

Having examined the difficulties and restrictions faced by the
Task Force journalists, the next two chapters look at the release of
information in London and the resulting controversy.

Notes

1. House of Commons, First Report from the Defence Committee Session 1982–83,
   HMSO, Dec. 1982. Q 1041, Vol. 2, p. 270.
2. Op. cit. Q 71, Vol. 2, p. 28.   4. Op. cit. Q 64, Vol. 2, p. 26.
3. Op. cit. Q 1860, Vol. 2, p. 440.   5. Op. cit. Q 1179, Vol. 2, p. 294

9

Censorship and information policy

The two themes of censorship and information policy attracted more debate and more complaint than any other aspect of the coverage of the Falklands campaign. The public's right to know must be weighed against the Government's responsibility for the handling of a military conflict. In the words of the House of Commons Defence Committee, 'the fundamental issues will need to be addressed seriously when contingency plans for military operations in the future are drawn up'.[1]

The Falklands campaign was unusual and unexpected. Many of the Government's critics in the news organizations have compared the episode to their experience in the Middle East and Vietnam and found that the facilities they were given and the procedures they were expected to follow were in the Falklands severely wanting. The British Government – the British public, too – had, however, been involved in no such major conflict for many years. The Army had devised ways of handling information in Northern Ireland, but this took several years to develop. The Navy now had little time to do so. It was not easy to get the Whitehall information machine on the road.

It appears to be commonly agreed that a government may legitimately withhold information on the grounds that its release might endanger its nationals' lives or jeopardize the security of an operation. The grey area, however, is in defining the scope of these categories. In the Falklands case, that of the first category was fairly clear although we should note the Defence Committee's observation that 'there was no threat to the security of the nation itself as there had been in the Second World War, which might have limited the public's basic right to be informed about all actions taken in their name.'[2]

The second category, on the other hand, is very wide and accordingly, the greatest controversy has centred on this. The Ministry of Defence has been accused of making 'operational security' all-embracing, using it as an excuse for delaying and censoring information and disseminating misinformation. The Government has been criticized for using the category as a cover for poor organization, lack of planning and the absence of any agreed procedure or criteria, exacerbating friction within the Ministry, among commanders with the Task Force and between the Services. There was simply no policy; that is the key. There was no centralized system of control, no coordination between departments.

At the time of the Falklands Conflict, the most recent document on information policy was a report prepared by officials in 1977 which for six years had been gathering dust; its existence was unknown to the Ministry public relations staff. According to the Ministry's evidence to the Defence Committee, this document had been circulated only within the Army. It had not been circulated within the Ministry; nor had it been cleared to do so. From time to time, one defence correspondent alleged to us that officals would telephone him to discover the customary procedures. In the Defence Committee's words: 'the direct harm caused by the non-availability of this document during the Falklands Conflict may have been negligible, but the system's failure it reveals extends far beyond a deficiency in the Ministry's filing system. It represents a major lapse on the part of the PR department.'[3]

The Falklands Conflict raised important questions about relations between government, the media and the public, particularly those relations concerning the disclosure of information, the use of propaganda and misinformation, and, especially, the propriety of a government seeking to employ the media for its own purposes.

The Ministry's view of its information policy during the Falklands crisis is outlined in the memorandum it submitted to the House of Commons Defence Committee:

> Our general policy is based on the assumption that the public has both an interest in and a right to know about defence. But we do not regard these rights as unlimited. Thus, while we maintain the fullest possible flow of information about the Services, their activities and the policies of the Ministry of Defence as a whole, this must be compatible with the overriding dictates of national and operational security and the protection of the lives of our servicemen and servicewomen. We also have a duty to protect their privacy. During the military operations to recover the Falklands Islands, our policy was to tell the truth as quickly and accurately as we could, consistent with the safety and security of our forces. At the same time we had to minimize distress to the families of the servicemen, merchant seamen or civilians who were killed or injured in the action. Of course, we do not work in a vacuum. There was an enormous amount of speculation, disinformation and propaganda from Buenos Aires and elsewhere. With the speed of modern communications, the publishing and broadcasting of all this created additional pressures and difficulties. Sometimes we were obliged to release information about the operation sooner than security or family considerations would otherwise have dictated. But at all times we were concerned to establish the truth. At no time were Government Information Services involved in psychological operations of 'disinformation'.[4]

As a statement of principle, this is clear. In practice, however, the decisions the Ministry actually took were inconsistent with this outline and at times in flat contradiction to it. Officials, for instance, differed from the military as to what was and was not appropriate to release, not least because officials, being closer to their political masters, are inevitably influenced by the judgements of Ministers as to what is politically the correct course.

Brigadier Ramsbotham put it like this to us:

> I do not believe that there is an absolute right to know in war. On the other hand, I do not believe there is an absolute right to suppress, either. But on this particular issue I believe that the operational imperatives were overriding.

Brigadier Ramsbotham himself based many of his decisions on his experience, in particular, his own record as operational commander of a brigade in Belfast. Control of censorship, he believed, should be based on operational needs, not public relations. 'I was taking decisions about whether information should be adjusted, or questions raised about things, based on my operational knowledge, speaking as an operational man who happened to be in PR rather than a public relations man.'

Ministry of Defence officials with the Task Force had no operational knowledge. It was therefore all the more difficult for them to make consistent decisions. It was noticeable that the journalists with the Task Force dealt far more happily with military public relations officials than with their civilian counterparts. Ramsbotham continued:

> I think the whole Army feels that it was a great pity that our expertise in Northern Ireland and in Germany working with the press was not used. When we got ashore and therefore did have the right, as it were, to deal with things in our way, I think it's true to say that things went rather better.
>
> Journalists were there and we spoke to them and looked after them . . . we were in business in the way we are. But before we got on land, the view was, 'Well, they've got nothing to teach us'. I personally believe the biggest lesson of all . . . that the Task Force Commander [should] have had a military public relations officer, in whose confidence he was, so that he could explain the Commander's policy and also he should have had an information officer working with him who was able to translate the journalists' wishes, and between them they should have served the Task Force Commander.

Even allowing for traditional inter-Service rivalry, there is much in what Brigadier Ramsbotham suggests about the Navy's inexperience. The First Sea Lord Admiral Sir Henry Leach and Commander In Chief of Fleet Admiral Sir John Fieldhouse, acknowledged the Navy's lack of experience 'as far as carrying the press in ships was concerned'.[5] As for the relations among the media, the Task Force and the Ministry of Defence, Admiral Sir Henry Leach, a past Chief of Defence Staff, had this to say:

I think that we were gaining experience, all of us, we in the Navy, we in Whitehall, and – I suggest – the media, but the fact was that at the outset of the campaign none of us had any practical experience of a modern war with today's media technology and this led to a learning curve which frankly continued till well on almost to completion of the campaign.[6]

The sole precedent available to the Navy was the cod war of 1976. Robert Fox, who took part in both campaigns, told us that, over censorship, 'they were jolly difficult for reasons I still find hard to appreciate'.

Bob Hutchinson, who had covered the cod war from London, when asked about his experiences, recalled:

The Icelandic embassy here were very smart and they used to have a communications network. When any incident happened, they used to be on to me like a dose of salts and give their version of it. The MoD would plod in five hours later with its version of events. I am a firm believer that that is one of the reasons we lost out in the cod war, because the Icelanders always got their version in first.

The British Navy refused to take television crews on its ships during the cod war or even to arrange for film to be sent back. British television crews were obliged to go to Iceland and board Icelandic gunboats, to film random, or in some cases, deliberate incidents. Derek Hudson of the *Yorkshire Post* remembered one such episode:

The Icelandic gunboat skipper . . . was very cunning. I was actually on the bridge of the HMS *Leander* where there was, I think, an ITN crew on the Icelandic ship, an icecutter, and it reversed into the frigate. But the film looks as though the frigate is ramming this old gunboat. This was ridiculous because the skin of a frigate is not meant as a battering ram, but it looked as though it was and of course there was a hole ripped in the frigate. The Navy didn't seem to learn anything at all from the lessons of the cod war in terms of public relations and getting your version in first by fast communications.

Civilian public relations officers suffered, as we have seen, as much as journalists. Being, while abroad, under the Navy's command, they were unable except on very rare occasions to communicate with the Ministry in London. This increased their isolation and strained their relations with the journalists and the military still further.

Meanwhile, in London, civilian officials at the Ministry were ordered to work via the military hierarchy. To communicate with the minders, for instance, they had to report to the Task Force commanders, and work down through the various levels of command. Their own lack of focus on what was and was not important in operational matters led to a lack of coordination in communications among the relevant Whitehall departments and divisions, and to strained relations with their normal clients, the defence correspondents, who suddenly found themselves cut off from their usual flow of information.

The information side at the Ministry of Defence has as its head the Chief of Public Relations, a member of the Government Information Service, who runs the Defence Press Office and four sections dealing with promotions and facilities for the three Services and the civilian aspects of the Ministry's work. All sections report to the Chief of Public Relations through a civilian deputy and three military deputies – the three Service Directors of Public Relations.

The Chief of Public Relations had recently retired. Ian McDonald, the Deputy, had put his name forward for the post but was not selected. He had also, however, recommended that whoever did become Chief should assume all the management functions of the present Deputy Chief. His recommendation was accepted, and on Neville Taylor's appointment as Chief of Public Relations, McDonald's job thus lapsed.

McDonald was waiting to be moved when the Falklands crisis erupted. At that point Taylor, who had last served at the Ministry of Defence twelve years before, was still at his old post in the Department of Health and Social Security. It was therefore agreed, largely at John Nott's instigation, that for an unspecified time McDonald should remain in charge of information policy, until Taylor had not only been transferred but had had time to settle in. Nott subsequently gave his view of this decision: 'In retrospect, it is a pity that at the very moment that the Falklands came there was this six months' interregnum before Mr Taylor was appointed.'[7]

The date of Taylor's arrival was in fact brought forward, from mid-June to mid-April. McDonald, who found himself in a delicate position, insisted that he would continue after Taylor's arrival only on condition that the whole of the Falklands issue was kept quite separate from the division's other concerns. 'There was no place for two people at the top,' one senior defence spokesman commented to us.

McDonald was not by profession a public relations officer. Like his predecessor, he had been brought into the division to stand at the Secretary of State's side to help him deal with the press and with the troops. When McDonald was offered the post he took it on condition that he would be the Secretary of State's professional public relations person, looking after nuclear arms and NATO issues and tri-Service matters but leaving the Chief of Public Relations to look after the organization as a whole. John Nott declared, 'Mr McDonald was, as it were, my man'.[8] Since McDonald, rather than the then Chief, had been responsible for dealing with the press during Nott's difficulties with successive Defence Reviews and since, indeed, McDonald had a policy-making background, the Secretary of State was happy to have him in place as the Falklands crisis unfolded.

McDonald therefore remained in charge, as acting Chief, until 18 May, when Taylor assumed control. McDonald then became the 'spokesman', helping to draft statements and reading them himself, but without being involved in the preparation of 'information policy'.

These office politics certainly did not help the climate within the Department. The Defence Committee's comments were harsh: '. . .the lack of an experienced public relations officer at the head of the Ministry of Defence PR organization was widely felt in the Ministry's response to the need to make arrangements for press coverage of the Falklands campaign'.[9] McDonald himself has been criticized severely in some quarters for some decisions. Bernard Ingham, the Prime Minister's Press Secretary, was particularly unhappy with McDonald, and had pressed for Neville Taylor's appointment to the Ministry to be expedited and for the new Chief to be given immediate overall responsibility. Ingham was annoyed at having to deal with irate editors, telephoning him first to ensure that their reporters sailed with the Task Force and then to complain at lack of off-the-record briefings, he told the Defence Committee and later confirmed to us: 'I found I was getting an enormous amount of flak which ought to be directed to the Ministry of Defence'.[10]

The Service Directors of Public Relations also had their reservations about McDonald. They were particularly unhappy at having been omitted from general information policy-making. Ramsbotham offers an insight into the jealousies which were evidently at work:

> I think it is always better to have a professional head of an organization at a time when its professional abilities are required more than ever. The problem was that by not having a Chief we did not have a Deputy . . . and poor Ian McDonald had a tremendous amount on his plate, quite apart from being made the spokesman as well when that happened. And we, the single Service Directors, were not used by him in a way which had been done previously.

The existence of these tensions within the Ministry was apparent to the media and added to the frustrations already felt over the lack of information. As David Nicholas, the editor of ITN, explained: 'It seemed that there were three tiers there – the information machinery, the directors of public relations and military branch, and the upper echelons of the career civil service. There were times when it seemed to us that one side did not know what the other side was doing'.[11]

Another difficulty was that the DPR Navy, Captain Sutherland, had taken over the post on the second day of the Conflict. According to the defence correspondents, he was helpful, in spite of being appallingly overworked. As one said to us:

> He was trying to feel his way in, I am sure the poor guy did not have a list of phone numbers in his book of where he could contact us. He did not know anybody and he was as helpful as he was able. But, again, he probably suffered a cultural shock; it was the first time he had come across the press.

In the memorandum the Ministry of Defence submitted after the campaign to the House of Commons' Defence Committee, it explained that its information effort was coordinated from day to day by the Number 10 Press Office. The Ministry itself took the main role in briefing the world press on the military operation, the Foreign and Commonwealth Office took the lead in briefing on the diplomatic aspects of the crisis.

Since the conflict ended, there has been some difference of opinion as to who was actually coordinating these activities. Sir Frank Cooper, John Nott, Neville Taylor and Bernard Ingham, for instance, all see the matter in a different light.

Sir Frank Cooper has, for example, disagreed with his own Ministry:

> I think it was a slightly odd statement, quite frankly. I think what that is shorthand for is that there was a daily meeting in Number 10 under the Chief Press Officer, Bernard Ingham, of all the departments that were in any way remotely connected with what was going on. I would put that in our jargon as a touching hands exercise rather than a coordination exercise.[12]

Sir Frank has also said that he did not in any case think a high degree of coordination was needed. The main links were between the Foreign Office and the Ministry of Defence, who work very closely together at all times, and these in his view were sufficient.

Neville Taylor's view was that Number 10, in the person of Bernard Ingham, coordinated the dissemination of information among departments, primarily the Foreign Office, Number 10, the Cabinet Office and the Ministry of Defence. Sir Frank and John Nott emphasized that matters were principally decided at the Ministry of Defence itself and that, although Ingham acted as chairman, Number 10's influence was small. Our informant, a senior official, said the purpose of Ingham's briefing meetings was to find out what was likely to happen, what the Ministry would be saying about it, and to scoop up any problems there had been from the last incident or statement. It was also to ensure that the Foreign Office was fully in the picture so it could brief people overseas, to tie the information effort in with what the Cabinet Office was doing to rebut Argentine propagandist exercises and so on. Such briefing was done at Number 10, according to this official, but:

> . . . it started from the assumption that the Secretary of State was the Minister responsible for the conduct of the operations and therefore was in the driving seat of the PR aspect as much as any other. The Prime Minister herself did get involved in some aspects of presentation, but where she did it was outside Bernard Ingham's special group . . . it would be a group of Ministers who decided that a particular statement was to be made, for instance in Parliament rather than to the press in the first instance. That decision had to be taken by Ministers.

Ingham has stated that:

> The position is that day in and day out Number 10 tries to coordinate as between departments to find out the line each department is taking and to inform ourselves of that line. During the campaign I held 53 meetings, in the morning, between 8 April and 25 June and those meetings were attended by the Ministry of Defence, the FCO and others. At each of those meetings each of the participants made their contribution, and, may I say, fairly quickly because we met for only 30–35 minutes. They made their contributions and we looked at the events of the past twenty-four hours and the events coming up insofar as it was possible to anticipate them, and towards the end it was not possible to anticipate a great deal. Where we were concerned about the presentation, where we thought something ought to be done, the Ministry of Defence played a full part in the meetings, just as the Foreign Office did; they were the two lead departments in this because they were responsible for the two major elements of policy.[13]

John Nott was emphatic:

> Of course Number 10 did not coordinate. Number 10 had an overriding responsibility for the presentation of the Government's broader policies. Number 10 were kept informed, and we made our announcements as we went along.[14]

The lack of clarity as to who was accountable for what, allied to the friction within the Ministry of Defence and between the Ministry of Defence and journalists and broadcasters, was altogether disastrous. It is hardly surprising that there was such a barrage of complaints about the handling of information policy. The Defence Committee described the situation as 'extremely disturbing'.[15]

An additional complication was, as the Committee called it, the 'somewhat mysterious role' of Cecil Parkinson, then Chancellor of the Duchy of Lancaster. Parkinson, with Mrs Thatcher, Nott, Pym and Whitelaw, was a member of the War Cabinet. According to Bernard Ingham, on 12 May, Parkinson took over the job of inter-ministerial coordination.[16]

Normally the responsibility for such a job would rest with the

Lord President. At that time the post was occupied by John Biffen, who was not, however, a member of the War Cabinet.

John Nott, like Sir Frank Cooper, differs from Bernard Ingham in his view of Parkinson's role, or indeed, its necessity. Nott made his position very clear:

> I am saying that, when you are fighting a war, information about the progress of that war is much the best handled by those who are closest to it and the most responsible . . . in this case [that] is the Ministry of Defence. To put a Minister who is a non-Ministry of Defence Minister – he is not the Secretary of State for Defence – in charge of coordinating the issue of releases which are concerned about matters of operations, would be an absurdity. That is my personal view.[17]

The Ministry of Defence and Number 10 had entirely opposite views as to the necessary ministerial demarcation. Nott went on:

> He [Parkinson] played a very valuable and important role in presenting the Government's case on television and before the press, but he was not specifically, as far as I recall, given a ministerial coordinating function.[18]

Sir Frank Cooper had this to say of Parkinson: 'I think he did have a group role for a period, in that he was there just to see what was going on and happening'.[19]

The evidence from Nott and Cooper implies that their Ministry was running the show and that anyone who assumed anything else was deceiving himself. As the Defence Committee put it: 'If the main achievement of a Minister who is detailed to provide coordination is to demonstrate the lack of it, then something is very wrong'.[20] There were, moreover, other points on which the Ministry of Defence and Number 10 took conflicting views. Two cases stand out: the decision to stop off-the-record briefings at the beginning of the conflict and that to announce the casualties at Bluff Cove.

First, however, we should examine the Ministry's response as the Falklands Conflict grew more difficult and complex. In the early days, the practice was to put together statements based on all the signals at the information centre. McDonald himself would do this. Approval would then be sought from three different quarters: from the civilian side, on policy aspects; from the military side, on North-wood's reactions; and from the Secretary of State for Defence. McDonald would then tell the Foreign Office and Number 10 what was to be announced. On 18 May a News Release Group came into being to tighten up this process. There were three people on this committee: Neville Taylor, Moray Stewart (Assistant Under-Secretary at the Ministry, the Group's chairman and secretary) and Admiral Whetstone (Assistant Chief of the Naval Staff, Operations). When Moray Stewart could not attend, Ian McDonald or one of the Service Directors took his place.

Whetstone and Taylor slept in their offices so as to be always available, and Stewart lived near enough to be able to reach the office quickly. According to a senior official of the Ministry of Defence, some matters were referred to others for checking:

> If it was a piece of background, then obviously one would go to the Service Directors of Public Relations. For example, how to describe a particular unit because of some aspect of sensitivity about how many people were in a company. A referral would then be made to the DPR Army [Brigadier Ramsbotham]. On the other hand, if it was something to do specifically with an operational matter, then the relevant Army duty colonel or brigadier would attend the meeting since they were at the receiving end of the signals.

However, these lines of communication and delineation were not strictly adhered to because Brigadier Ramsbotham had close links with Northwood, not least because the deputy to the military commander at Northwood was from the same regiment as Ramsbotham. The Brigadier could therefore acquire information far more quickly than the News Release Group could via official networks.

Organizational arrangements were, as always, bedevilled by personal idiosyncracies. One of the most significant of these, it has been said, was McDonald's attitude to press briefings. According to Christopher Wain, the BBC's defence correspondent, McDonald believed that if you were a spokesman for a Minister you refrained from giving deep background briefings. The Secretary of State himself was vague. Wain recalled that Nott had said at one meeting of correspondents, months before the Falklands crisis: 'This is all on-the-record or off-the-record or background or whatever you call it.'

In the year preceding the Falklands Conflict relations between correspondents and McDonald and Nott had grown steadily worse. Christopher Wain told us: 'McDonald had lost credibility and protests against him were going to be made.' The Navy, which was particularly anxious to publish its argument over proposed cuts in expenditure, began wining and dining defence correspondents, and stories began to seep into the press. Nott, who disliked the press at the best of times, was annoyed; when pressed, he referred all questions to McDonald.

Up to the taking of South Georgia, on-the-record briefings were held at noon every day. They included a certain amount of manipulation, in the sense that each day the Ministry tried to provide a major story, to deflect the journalists' questions from more sensitive matters. As it became apparent that there would be no negotiated solution to the crisis, the Ministry, anxious to minimize the release of information as to the size and disposition of British forces, maintained that the less said the better. McDonald proposed to the Secretary of State and the Chief of Staff that they restrict themselves to a daily on-the-record, question-and-answer session. This was agreed. McDonald's reasoning was understandable. As a senior colleague of McDonald put it to us:

> At the time not only did the MoD not know, but Northwood didn't know, the Commander of the Task Force didn't know, what his plans were. It was all being worked out. That was one problem. The second was [that] in the public perception and very much in the political perception in some areas, the Task Force was still seen as an adjunct to diplomacy. The Foreign Office were continuing to have at a more feverish pace normal unattributable briefings and the Task Force's presence was part of that. In so far as the Task Force might be called on to take an operation, it was very important that we did not tell people where the Task Force was, whether it was splitting up in different formations, how long it was staying on Ascension Island, which parts of it were going on and which parts were remaining. As a result, we had to abstain from unattributable or off-the-record briefings with the press.

McDonald's decision did not come as a total surprise to the experienced defence correspondents. What astonished them, however, was the cessation of all accreditation to the Ministry of Defence. In the months preceding the conflict, the Permanent Under Secretary, worried at the deteriorating relationship between defence correspondents and his Ministry, had started once-a-month 'deep background' briefings with the provision that all information should be embargoed for three days. Passes were issued and correspondents became used to the new arrangements. Suddenly, six months later, it all stopped. Sir Frank, who was liked and respected by defence correspondents, announced that now he was too preoccupied to see them.

Bernard Ingham, himself a former journalist, correctly foresaw the damage that these decisions would do to relations with the media. 'I certainly took the view,' Ingham stated, 'that when you are in a crisis of this kind, the last thing you do is withdraw your service to the media. I think one of the objects of the Government Information Service is to try to build a bridge with the media and to keep it in good repair, not a bridge to be trampled on.'[21] In discussing this point with us Simon Jenkins said:

> It's crazy to spend years and years building up a close working relationship with journalists, the purpose of which being that when you really need them you can cash in these chips, these credits, these little secret deals you made with those guys and if you are in the MoD the one time you are going to need to cash them in is when you have got a war, and as soon as the war came along they stopped the whole thing.

McDonald was backed by Nott. Only on-the-record meetings were held. Furthermore, the statements were made by one spokesman only, McDonald himself, to camera, on the grounds that this would minimize any opportunity for journalists in general and television journalists in particular to introduce nuances or to insert their own commentary. For this reason, too, the briefings went out live.

Though it is quite common in the USA, it is rare that a Government spokesman, especially a Ministry of Defence spokesman, delivers statements live on television. The only comparable precedent was the briefing given by the Foreign and Commonwealth Office at the time of the Lancaster House Conference on the future of Southern Rhodesia. The then head of the Foreign Office News Department gave on-the-record press conferences and made statements to camera, without, however, becoming the notable figure that McDonald became.

Neville Taylor, who took over from McDonald on 18 May, was also opposed to ending off-the-record briefings; had he been in charge from the outset, they would probably have continued uninterrupted. Sir Frank Cooper agreed: 'I think again with hindsight that was probably an unwise decision – that we should have gone on with them or restarted them rather more quickly than we did.'[22]

From 11 May defence correspondents were once more given unattributable briefings, and in the last month of the Conflict there were more than a dozen. Separate briefings followed for regional and specialist correspondents, and unattributable briefings were also given to London-based American correspondents, to the exclusion of other foreign correspondents, in the light of the military and political support the United States Government was giving to Britain. Particularly important actions like those at Goose Green and San Carlos were the subject of separate briefings after the main statements had been given. That was another sore point. Having stopped giving background briefings to the specialist defence correspondents, Sir Frank nonetheless held unattributable meetings with the editors of the broadcasting organizations and major newspapers. According to the Ministry of Defence, between 7 April and 14 June seven such meetings were held. It was here that editors complained about the provision of pictures and facilities and the vetting of copy. Sir Frank was able to use these occasions to put over the Ministry's position; the defence correspondents, however, felt their position had been usurped. Insult was added to injury in that the political correspondents were still being given unattributable briefings by Number 10.

For experienced defence correspondents the situation was intolerable. The Ministry seemed to believe that if the press and television were told nothing, nothing would be published. It failed to perceive, throughout, one of the main tenets of journalism that when a vacuum arises, it has to be filled. Speculation and rumour flourished.

Bob Hutchinson, the Press Association defence correspondent and one of the most experienced, told us how, before the Falklands Conflict began, a correspondent could ring up the Ministry of Defence and ask for an unattributable meeting. Then:

> Overnight we found the Services, the Navy particularly, unhelpful. Whereas before they were terribly keen to put their case in the press in the great battle against the Treasury, as soon as the bullets started flying the great shutters came down and they were telling you to take a run and jump, which we found cynical to the extreme.

Peter Snow of BBC Television's *Newsnight*, described the relations between the journalists and the Ministry as being absolutely dreadful:

> We were getting a lot of stuff out of Argentina and . . . virtually nothing out of the Ministry of Defence . . . what actually happened in the end was that so rife was speculation getting and so full were the columns of the newspapers, and indeed television programmes, with speculation . . . Argentine-based information and arms experts from the [Institute of Strategic Studies] or whatever, sort of waffling away, that in the end of course they actually went off the record, and what happened was that after a couple of weeks of this ridiculous charade of sitting round the table and asking these on-the-record questions . . . We all the time had been saying, 'Look, for God's sake, let's get off the record . . . let's go more senior, let's get Frank Cooper or someone to talk to us who can give us more background information, all right, not on the record if you must, but at least he can start countering some of these stories we're getting and help us to give a more balanced view.' And this of course happened, but very nearly too late . . . you tend to get suspicious about everything you're told . . . And I think that what happened at the end was that we all got really so furious with them after about two or three weeks of the Task Force sailing that they realized that it would be very counter-productive if they didn't produce Frank Cooper. And they did . . . in the end and that helped a lot, although the problem was initially we didn't feel they were trusting us with anything at all. Well, they weren't, and so they didn't get much coverage, full stop. The second stage was: 'Well, if they won't trust us, why bother to go along, and why bother to badger anyway? We're busy guys, we'll just take our information from where we can get it and just write the stuff.' And there was a growing, rather irrational sort of anti-Ministry of Defence feeling which was quite nonsensical . . . that's no good because they have the information . . . therefore you must go on badgering them. And there was a sort of barrier building up between the press and the Ministry of Defence which was really hurting both sides . . . and it was getting very very serious and then suddenly they produced the Cooper briefings which were extremely valuable and, on the whole, one believed they were accurate . . . they were no doubt leaving out a lot of information, of course they were, but a lot of the stuff was very sensible from their point of view and useful from our point of view. In so far as those briefings occasionally were slightly slanted, or in so far as those briefings occasionally told us things and then

said, 'Please don't use that' . . . for reasons that we occasionally thought were slightly unsatisfactory.

As the campaign proceeded, newspapers which had lacked defence correspondents began to appoint them. The noon briefings became overcrowded and, after the taking of South Georgia, the Ministry of Defence decided to set up a press centre, asking defence correspondents for their advice. The centre was opened on Sunday, 2 May on the ground floor of the Ministry, and remained opened every day until Friday, 18 June. All accredited journalists, British and foreign, could use it. It was there that McDonald gave his official statements; the BBC and ITN, who had installed cameras, would broadcast any statement live. Undoubtedly, relations between the press and the Ministry were helped by the establishment of the centre, as much as by the decision to resume off-the-record briefings. However, lack of information and the variability of its quality were still bones of contention.

One complaint was that although Army and Marine representatives attended the briefings, no one came from Northwood. According to the defence correspondents, there were only two Navy representatives present: Captain Sutherland (the DPR) and the Director of Naval Warfare, (a former captain of *Invincible*) who between them knew a number of the specialist journalists. Bob Hutchinson described him as being ' . . . absolutely first class – he would give official unattributable briefings and he tended to lean over backwards to tell us as much as he possibly could'.

Generally speaking, however, there was a clear distinction between the Services: the Army gave information, the Navy did not. The lack of coordination among the Services and within the Government was highlighted by the episode of the Bluff Cove tragedy. It also illustrated differing ideas of what constitutes misinformation. As the Ministry saw it, the sequence of events was as follows:

8 June. Ministry press release announces attack on HMS *Plymouth* involving five casualties. 'The logistic landing-ships *Sir Tristram* and *Sir Galahad* while unloading stores were also attacked and suffered some damage. We have no reports on casualties.'

9 June. Ministry press statement confirms that there were no deaths in *Plymouth.* 'It is, however, feared that casualties from the attacks on *Sir Tristram* and *Sir Galahad* were much heavier; early reports indicate a number of killed and injured.'

10 June. [0329Z]Reuters in Buenos Aires carry report of military experts in Argentina saying that the Argentine air attacks are likely to cause serious delays to the expected British attack on Port Stanley.

10 June. [1455Z]Reuters reports quote Argentine military sources as saying that 500–900 troops were killed or wounded in the attack. Later (evening of 10 June) reports from 'Noticias Argentinas' state that 350–400 Marines were estimated to have been killed in attacks on Fitzroy.

10 June. [c1600A]Secretary of State makes statement to House in which he says: 'Having consulted the military authorities, I am not prepared at this stage to give the total numbers of our casualties, and to do so could be of assistance to the enemy and put our men at greater risk. Meanwhile next-of-kin are being informed and I shall give further information as soon as is reasonably possible.'

10 June. In Bonn the Prime Minister says that information is not yet available on numbers of casualties but figures of about 43 killed and 120 wounded are said to have been provided at lobby briefing at Number 10. Secretary of State and Ministry of Defence refuse to comment on these figures.

12 June. The *Guardian* and other papers carry reports of radio hams picking up reports from Falklands Island farmer who was an eye-witness of the Fitzroy attack and estimated the casualties to be 200 dead and 400 wounded.

12 June. [1930A]The Deputy Chief of Public Relations announces that next-of-kin of *Sir Tristram* and *Sir Galahad* dead have now all been informed.

13 June. [1930A]Secretary of State announces that British forces now hold Mount Longdon, Two Sisters and Mount Harriet. He also gives casualty figures for the Fitzroy attack: 43 men killed and 46 wounded, with 7 officers and crew of the LSLs killed and 9 injured. In announcing these he explains:

> It was important for success of the land operation that the Argentinians were not able to assess exactly when, how or in what strength we would attack. It is clear that the Argentinians greatly overestimated the extent of the casualties and damage resulting from their air attack . . . We wished them to remain uncertain about our strength on the ground and our capability to mount an early attack.[23]

The Defence Committee stated in its report that: 'It remains the case that at a time when the Ministry of Defence was seeking to prevent disclosure of the order of magnitude of casualties and the size of the setback to the Task Force, accurate figures were leaked in London'.[24]

John Nott blamed the lack of coordination between the Ministry of Defence and Number 10 on the Prime Minister's absence in Bonn: 'If she had been in Number 10 I think that misunderstanding which did arise would not have occurred'.[25]

How Mrs Thatcher's presence would have changed the situation is unclear. When we asked a senior Ministry of Defence official, whether the Prime Minister was fully aware of the situation, he replied:

> There was intense pressure to come out with the figures and we kept on refusing to come out with the figures. Now, that pressure came initially as well from Number 10, because they had not been taken in. When I say 'they', the Prime Minister knew, but the Press Officer did not know, that we were deliberately implying that if Thatcher had been around she would have told Ingham not to say anything.

At the time two explanations were given for the Ministry of Defence's failure to release figures for the number of casualties: that the Ministry did not wish to lower the public's morale; and that exaggerated rumours of the incident would lessen its eventual impact.

The Ministry has stated that there was no question of its seeking to play down the scale of the losses until military progress could be reported. Their explanation is that the decision to delay the announcement was taken on purely operational grounds and on advice from senior military staff.

However, one defence correspondent who covered the campaign from London was Jim Meacham of *The Economist*; he cited the Bluff Cove incident as a case of disinformation:

> . . . The casualty figures were the issues of the disinformation here. Somehow, once the Bluff Cove operation had fallen to pieces and they had attacked the two ships, the figure of 750 got into the press. The Ministry of Defence then thought that it would be a good thing, according to discussions I have had since that time, if the Argentinians believed that 750 casualties had been sustained in these attacks, and therefore refused to give the accurate casualty figures. We had a figure in *The Economist* that we were given by a source at the Ministry of Defence of about 200 casualties for the whole day . . . Several days later the Secretary of State himself met with us and we questioned him on these figures and he said: 'I am not going to give you these figures. After the war is over you will know why I do this but I am not going to give them to you'. Some of us pointed out that the figure of 50 dead had come from 10 Downing Street and asked if he could confirm or deny that. He said: 'I do not know what has come from 10 Downing Street but I am not going to tell you anything about casualty figures.' The reason for this,

according to MoD now, is that they hoped the Argentinians would take on board the 750 and change their dispositions and their preparation for battle.[26]

The Ministry of Defence has stated that there was no question of disinformation, citing instead the difficulty of getting accurate information from the battle zone.[27]

From this and other information it is clear that the wish to remain silent was initially that of the operational commanders with the Task Force. Jeremy Moore, Commander of Land Forces, has stated that he spoke to Fleet Headquarters himself in order to prevent knowledge of the number of casualties sustained by the Welsh Guards:

> . . . my initial reaction was to prevent him – the enemy – drawing comfort from that and being able to deduce actual facts and the actual effect it would have on my ability to conduct operations against him.[28]

According to one senior source within the Ministry of Defence, it was not Moore's instruction but doubt about the accuracy of the first figure that led to the Ministry's hesitation. Casualties were being dispersed, some being transported by field-ambulance to hospital, some picked up by helicopter and some taken by ship and sent to other ships. As soon as an Argentine agency release was issued, claiming several hundred dead, the Ministry of Defence decided to allow the Argentines (and the British public) to continue to believe that casualties were much higher than they were. Next of kin were to be informed but there was to be no public confirmation of the figures.

The Defence Committee did not see Nott's refusal, and that of his colleagues, to deny the rumours as misinformation in any sinister sense. They agreed that to have done so would have explicitly undermined the considered military view of the situation. An alternative policy, however, might have been to brief defence correspondents on the situation, with a request not to publish. Altogether, the incident reveals a striking lack of coordination and cooperation between the Ministry of Defence and Number 10.

As a senior official at the Ministry has said to us:

> We had not alerted Bernard, and it was just one of those things that nobody thought of doing at the time, to ensure that Bernard knew that at the same time when we were seeing defence correspondents we were going to be saying nothing about casualty figures. There was just a failure, a huge failure of communications. None of us, because we thought somebody else was doing it, actually walked across the road or rang the secure telephone number and said 'If you are asked about these figures, we are still not going to give any details, don't give any details at all'.

When asked about this Ingham informed us that, after he had given the briefing, he rapidly became aware that there were things to which the Ministry did not want him to refer. 'But this merely illustrates one of the extremely difficult problems in trying to coordinate across a substantial number of departments an exercise which is going on 8000 miles away.' The fact that the correct casualty figure was fed out first through the political lobby appears, then, to have been by accident.

Such lack of coordination, as we have emphasized earlier, was prevalent throughout the conflict. In its own memorandum to the Defence Committee, the *Scotsman* went so far as to suggest that

> Political journalists were being fed a line for reasons of political expediency rather than factual accuracy. The recapture of the Islands in 'days not weeks' was out very early on, flying in the face of everything being said by MoD officials and Task Force officers and the 'final battle for Stanley' was being started through the political lobby.[29]

Three other lessons may be drawn from the Bluff Cove incident. The first relates to the Ministry's use of misinformation; the second to the Ministry's handling of the release of information relating to casualties and the loss of significant military assets, and its tendency to exaggerate successes; and the third to the confidential embrace extended to the defence journalists and editors.

First, misinformation. Three further cases arising from the Falklands Conflict have provoked argument as to the merits and wisdom of using the press and television as channels of misinformation. The Government, in a situation such as this, has to weigh up the advantages which in the short term may assist the military but in the long term may shed doubt on the credibility of the Government when the true facts emerge or are discovered. After all, if a Government is prepared to lie in a crisis, and that is characterized as being in the 'national interest', it is only a short step to extending this to other areas.

The Defence Committee's report gave the green light to the Government's actions in this matter:

> We accept that there can be sound military reasons for withholding the whole truth from the public domain and equally sound military reasons for believing that particular rumours will rebound to one's own side's advantage. We have no quarrel with the Government for having quelled such rumours during the Conflict, and believe that such and more emphatic acts of misinformation can generally be justified if their net contribution to the prosecution of a war is a positive one and if they are calculated to protect operations of major importance.[30]

The three main instances of 'misinformation' were: the landing on the Falklands at San Carlos, the use of the nuclear-powered submarine, *Superb*, and the landings on South Georgia.

The misleading information on the landings at San Carlos was given by Sir Frank Cooper, the Permanent Under-Secretary at the

Ministry of Defence, at an off-the-record briefing. This is exactly the kind of meeting at which journalists expect to be taken into an official's confidence; its use on this occasion provoked considerable animosity between the correspondents and the Ministry of Defence.

Sir Frank Cooper, however, was delighted at the press speculation and admits that it was very helpful as he put it: 'We did not tell a lie – but we did not tell the whole truth.'[31]

The Defence Committee believed Sir Frank's conduct to be fully justified, given the crucial importance of the landings and the limited scope for surprising the enemy.[32] The Committee's last comment on the affair was the suggestion that only if journalists took an unreasonably severe view of the incident would the credibility of the Ministry's off-the-record briefings have suffered any lasting damage.

Sir Frank decided that the briefing should proceed in a two-hour meeting at his Ministry. The final decision was his; a senior official present at the meeting told us that the matter was not discussed with the Secretary of State:

> He [Sir Frank] misled the press as he did because he appreciated the vulnerability of the landing in a way not everyone did outside the very close circles. And he made these decisions himself. I remember sitting through about two hours before [he] went into that conference room when he decided to do this and I was arguing against it and he said: 'Well, I hear all you say, of course you are right, but I am going to do it because I am right. We are so vulnerable. Anything I can do to persuade the Argentinians that we are not going to make this kind of landing is worth any dent it makes in my reputation.'

The majority of journalists, broadcasters and editors did in fact understand something of the military need for the ruse.

In discussing the point with us Christopher Wain, Defence Correspondent for BBC Television News, thought that Cooper had been wrong to mislead on an unattributable basis: 'He should have gone on-the-record. That way it would not have looked as though the journalists themselves were part of the conspiracy.' Wain added: '[It] can be acceptable but it destroys credibility for ever.'

The journalists were not alone in questioning the wisdom of such procedure. For example, Sir Geoffrey Johnson Smith, Conservative MP and former minister, stated his position to us:

> I think if disinformation of this kind is to be given out I would think, don't use your straight man. Your Permanent Under-Secretary should never be used.

Would the situation have been different if the editors and correspondents had been taken into the Permanent Secretary's confidence? Every editor to whom we spoke told us that there was no attempt to bring them into the conspiracy. All emphasized that only in the rarest circumstances would they participate in any overt misinformation.

We asked David Nicholas, editor of Independent Television News, when such support might be conceivable:

> I think there must be a 99.9 percent presumption that you just do not do that. . . . I wonder what one's position would be in law. After all, we weren't operating under an Act of Parliament. But I think the huge presumption must be that you don't under any circumstances, and I think you've got to start from there. But if you're in a total war . . . – say all editors got called to Number 10 or something . . . supposing they actually said: 'Look, there are absolutely no defences from Dover to Portsmouth because everyone's got bubonic plague but I want you to say that two divisions are playing football down there . . . because otherwise they're going to be across the water in the next hour.' You can't actually say 'Never' . . . under no circumstances would you do it. But I cannot possibly conceive of any circumstances that would obtain . . . short of a national war of survival where you'd accede to any such request.

The most important issue, however, is that of the credibility of the Ministry of Defence and the Government. As the BBC succinctly pointed out in its evidence to the Defence Committee: 'The line between "tactical untruths" and "disinformation" can often be dangerously fine.'[33]

There was, in fact, one major instance where journalists were taken into the Government's confidence; that concerned the story of the bombs that failed to explode. Like the Goose Green incident, this was a case where the early release of information could have had adverse military consequences. The Ministry refrained from mentioning unexploded bombs and briefed defence correspondents on this; an example, cited by journalists and their editors of their being taken into confidence and, in their opinion, acting responsibly. We asked Peter Snow about this:

> Occasionally they actually trusted us with information they needn't have given us. They actually said occasionally: 'A bomb dropped on HMS *Glasgow* and it didn't go off'. Now, they needn't have told us that but they did, and they said, 'Please don't use that because it will tell the Argentines that their fuses are not being properly screwed up,' so we didn't use it. We accepted that if we had used it it would have told the Argentines. So one did in a sense twist one's professional journalistic ethic. We simply said: 'All right, our job is to get the information out. But in this case we will not put the information out because we actually believe that we shouldn't because it could jeopardize men's lives on our side.'

The editor of the *Daily Star* also pointed out the uniqueness of the episode: 'One of the rare occasions where we were taken into the MoD's full confidence was over the unexploded bombs . . . Not one correspondent breached that trust'.[34]

The second case of misinformation concerned the allegation that the Ministry of Defence allowed the press to gain, and remain under, the impression that the nuclear-powered submarine HMS *Superb* was in the South Atlantic from early April 1982. It was widely assumed by the press and broadcasting organizations that the submarine had sailed from Gibraltar to the Falklands, though later it was found that the submarine had sailed back from the South Atlantic.

Several correspondents believe that the Ministry should have denied the story. John Connell, defence correspondent of the *Sunday Times*, thought that, again, long-term damage could be done to the Ministry's credibility:

> I know the Ministry of Defence argument is that it was a good idea to encourage the Argentinians to believe there were as many submarines down there as they could. However, . . . what was clearly a lie was allowed to continue and it was damaging for one thing to us as defence correspondents . . . We were eventually tripped up and the truth did come out and therefore we looked pretty silly in our own newspapers because obviously our sources were not good. For a small gain (it was known that submarines were going down there anyway and all we were arguing about was the name) that myth was allowed to continue and it should not have been.[35]

The Ministry's line was simply that 'it would have been contrary to MoD's established practice to disclose the location of submarines on patrol'.[36]

Throughout the campaign Ian McDonald made it clear to the press that he worked to two guidelines: that he would never knowingly tell lies; and that he would never say anything that would threaten the success of the operation. In this context, according to senior officials within the Ministry, there were no regrets about the nuclear submarine incident. In keeping with standard practice, no public relations official had said that Britain was sending submarines.

There were, however, doubts over the landings on South Georgia. The main charge against the Ministry was its denial that the Task Force had landed when reconnaissance forces were already ashore. That night the atmosphere at the Ministry was highly charged. A senior official who was present told us that news came through that two helicopters had been wrecked on South Georgia. This was the first real action of the conflict and it looked as though it had all gone wrong. Distorted signals were coming through. McDonald was worried about what he should say at the next on-the-record briefing. At that briefing one journalist asked if forces had landed on South Georgia. This was the actual exchange:

> Q. Can you reassure us that there is no action going on in the South Atlantic at the moment?

> A. I do not want to be drawn into a question of this sort. However, the main Task Force is not involved in any landing action. There are many rumours going

around but to put them at rest I have heard that the Task Force has not landed anywhere.[37]

When we discussed this with a senior Ministry officer he explained that, in McDonald's view, he could say nothing else. He might have said that what had landed was not the Task Force but a reconnaissance party; he might have said 'No comment'. In that case the headlines next day would have been enormous.

We come now to the second lesson, the handling and release of information. It was here that the Ministry probably scored its best own goals. As an example of the Ministry's exaggeration of news of a less than totally successful operation, the announcement of bombing raids on Port Stanley airfield is a case in point. The Defence Committee has dismissed any suggestion of a deliberate intent to mislead in that case. It nevertheless highlights the Ministry's incompetence in assessing operational matters or in coordinating information policy, or both:

> This human error need not incur any criticism, although it may be that the Ministry incorporated a certain amount of wishful thinking into their announcements of the results of the bombing raids on the airfield, and certainly did not share with the public subsequently their own increasing doubts about how far the airfield had been put out of use. This is scarcely a matter of scandal, although an interesting feature of the case is that the motive of deceiving the *enemy* could not have been adduced in support of the policy of concealing the whole truth – unless, that is, the Ministry of Defence had wanted the Argentines to think that the British Government knew less than it actually did.[38]

The South Georgia landings and the Bluff Cove disaster were incidents which concerned the management of casualties and the loss of military equipment. There were, however, other incidents in which the handling and release of information leaves open questions about Ministry policy and about disagreements between the military and the Ministry of Defence. We should look in particular at the reports of loss of Harrier aircraft and the sinking of the destroyers *Sheffield* and *Coventry*.

The Ministry version of the Harrier incident was that at 1450 hours on 6 May they received a signal advising that contact had been lost with two Harriers from *Invincible*. Search and rescue operations continued until sunset. Military staff argued that the Ministry should not announce this significant reduction in British air power, as the accident had not involved Argentine forces and they could therefore be presumed to be unaware of it. On the other hand, civilian staff were anxious that the story should be released.

At 2100 hours the same day the Deputy Chief of Public Relations announced that, at about noon London time, contact had been lost with the two Harriers: 'In view of the time that has now elapsed the aircraft must be announced missing. Search and rescue operations are in progress. The next of kin are being informed.'

David Nicholas was at an editors' briefing with Sir Frank Cooper on the night the two Harriers collided:

> . . . that was a classic case of cock-up really. We had been given a tip about four o'clock . . . that an announcement was coming and it was put to us . . . 'It's an important announcement, but not as bad as *Sheffield*' . . . so we stood by for a flash and got everybody in the studio and . . . We did a conventional early bulletin news and it still hadn't come on and at about five or ten past six McDonald came on and . . . I can't remember exactly what he said but it was absolutely banal . . . and I thought 'This can't be it' . . . And then I went to the editors' meeting and then . . . they announced that . . . at eight or ten to eight . . . we flashed a PA defence cover story saying that two Harriers were missing, believed crashed. By this time we were getting vibes from New York . . . it was a common talking-point there that two Harriers had crashed. The MoD were quite embarrassed about the whole shambles and I later learnt that what happened was that these members of the Chiefs of Staff had urged very strongly that it should be kept quiet, not announced at all . . . I could see the logic . . . nineteen aircraft down there and one had been shot down in Goose Green and now two had gone and that's a significant reduction. And because of the way it happened, there was a good chance that the Argentinians wouldn't know . . . I think that while this was being considered, the normal practice of sending a senior officer out to tell the families was got under way . . . So they tried to get hold of these guys to stop them going to break the news and then the argument went, 'You can't do this sort of thing, it's bound to get out . . . So they said 'Get hold of these two blokes, send them out again to break the news'.

The episode of the Harrier collision also revealed how a confusing environment can cause a defence correspondent to make mistakes. Bob Hutchinson, who practically lived at the Ministry of Defence during the conflict, told us the story:

> The difficulty was actually to find somebody who actually knew what was going on or actually to find them physically because they were all running around like blue-arsed flies all over the place and they were under pressure just like we were. But it was very difficult to get guidance, which you could have done in the halcyon days of peace, during the Falklands. So we tended to pull back from releasing misinformation. Occasionally we did – once, I think wrongly, which was the release of the Sea Harrier collision which we broke.

Hutchinson would not talk about his sources, but continued:

> Basically the scenario for that particular night was the MoD were going to announce something at six o'clock and we were told it was bad news . . . and there was a rumour going around that it was postponed because it was a local election that day and it would be postponed till the polling-booths had closed. Again, you're being hyped up into this sort of confrontation mood and there was a rumour going around that it was Prince Andrew who had been shot down in his Sea King . . . again, a sociological thing . . . rumours in this thing were unbelievable . . . and there were lines of communication between the House and that press centre . . . we were told

by lots of different sources what the score was and . . . that the next of kin had been informed and that this was what the Ministry was going to announce. So we ran it. In fact the next of kin hadn't been told because they were so panic-stricken about the loss of these two Sea Harriers they put an embargo on even telling the next of kin. And I should have realized with my experience that you were handing critical information to the Argentines and it was a stupid thing to do. But that was the one occasion when I let my emotions get ahead of me and I should have been mature about it and said, 'Let's think about this for a minute'. I had to talk my editor-in-chief into it. But, again, they confirmed it at nine o'clock, which they didn't have to do . . . but that was a mistake on my part . . . I'm the first one to admit it.

The release in London of the news of the Harrier loss and the subsequent announcement on television, radio and the World Service occurred before journalists with the Task Force were able to send details of the story. This provoked great bitterness among the correspondents.

Orders not to release information would come from Northwood. Roger Goodwin, the Ministry official in *Invincible*, found it hard at times to appreciate the reasons for a request to delay. In the case of the two Harriers, he did see why:

The Navy, quite understandably in my view, said to me Harrier numbers at this stage are vital, they are absolutely critical, we see no reason why we should tell the Argentinians, who were patently not involved in the loss of these two aircraft, that we've got two less Harriers than they think we've got. Even the basic layman can see that point. And indeed I then went to McIlroy and said, 'Mac, we don't want you to put this story out because we see no reason why we should tell the Argentinians, etc,' and he got very huffy. Well, of course you don't, what a stupid thing to say, I'm not going to write a story like that? And that was generally the attitude of all five of them. They agreed they wouldn't write the story, they wouldn't file it. Nevertheless, the information was known back in the MoD, it somehow got to the ears of the Press Association and it broke in the British press, picked up by the World Service, transmitted out, heard on the radio of the ship, and of course the guys were furious, quite understandably. This is where I as an ex-journalist can perfectly well understand their feeling; they'd agreed not to do it, we'd not allowed the release of the information and bang it's on the World Service and they're going up the wall. Particularly Tony Snow and Mick Seamark. And they reverted to pop-type foot-in-the-door, selling-Grandmother-for-a-story-type journalists. All hell broke loose. There was a hell of a row, they demanded to see the Captain, and I can remember the following morning they indulged in the good old Fleet Street practice of doorstepping the squadron commander, and they literally camped outside his cabin till he came out in the morning, then started firing questions at him, trying to get quotes about what a marvellous couple of guys these were and all the rest of it. Now, naval officers' mentality comes into this again; they don't appreciate things like that, they don't want to comment on a situation like that, they can't comment because there's a board of enquiry. And, frankly, practices like doorstepping are not designed to make their practitioners particularly popular with the people that they're practising it on.

It was not only the journalists who were bitter about the release of that information but the whole of the ship's company. *Invincible*, like any other ship that loses an aircraft, must send a casualty information signal back to base. This is then distributed to the policy and operational branches of the Ministry of Defence. In this instance the news was leaked to a defence correspondent by a staff officer within the Ministry. This happened on several occasions and, according to various sources, was leaked primarily by military as opposed to civilian personnel within the Ministry. Once a story had been leaked the Ministry was obliged to confirm it.

The journalists with the Task Force became increasingly unhappy that stories were being broadcast over the World Service before they were allowed to file them. As well as the Harrier story, correspondents were forbidden to report on the sinking of the *General Belgrano* and the attack on *Sheffield*. The Defence Committee concluded:

> This can be regarded as nothing more than a source of frustration for individual journalists, but it does have the extra dimension that apparent differences of perception between the Task Force commanders and the Service chiefs in London about what news was sensitive might have undermined their joint authority on matters of operational security.[39]

The Committee discussed suggestions that censorship should have been fully coordinated in London, rather than being imposed in two centres 8000 miles apart:

> This suggestion has obvious attractions but, apart from technical difficulty – communications from correspondents with the Task Force were not a secure line – [in fact only the journalists using Marisat did not have secure lines – those on *Invincible* were using the Navy's secure communications] – it ignores the fact that there were local security concerns which had to be taken into account in addition to those affecting the military operations in their totality, and that censors in London could not necessarily have been aware of all these factors.[40]

However, on one or two occasions it was from Northwood that signals were sent instructing those on board not to release certain information, while on other occasions information was released early in London through leaks emanating from the Ministry of Defence. To some of the journalists with the Task Force it seemed that it was the Navy or Ministry officials on board who were preventing them from sending copy. Most of the time, in fact, it was London. On one occasion Captain Jeremy Black of *Invincible* sent urgent messages to the Ministry requesting that correspondents' stories should be sent embargoed to the Ministry for simultaneous release with Ministry anouncements. The Ministry failed to reply for at least two weeks and further delays resulted.

The announcement over the sinking of *Coventry* illustrates the various conflicting pressures. It was felt that no information should be released until next of kin had been informed or at least until the Ministry was in a position to inform them. It was also felt that information on the loss of a ship should be given as soon as it was assumed that the news of the attack would be announced in Argentina. The military, meanwhile, were preoccupied with the operational judgement that no information about losses should be given which might allow the Argentines to deduce that major elements of the Task Force had been lost.

It was such warring pressures that in effect prevented the journalists with the Task Force from sending copy, only to hear a Ministry of Defence announcement on the World Service. As a senior Ministry official put it to us:

> Very often things were held up, quite rightly, [so] that we came under pressure because the Argentinians were putting out things [and] we had to decide to release it then. Very often the pronouncements we made were against screaming protests from the Services saying, 'We haven't finished letting the next of kin know' and we were saying, 'We know that, but the Argentinians are broadcasting this and we have got to tell the truth and put it in perspective'.

The main charge against the Ministry of Defence over its handling of the loss of *Coventry* was that unnecessary anxiety was caused to thousands of families by announcing serious damage to an unnamed ship in the Task Force. All the pressures we have indicated were encompassed in this episode.[41] When we discussed this with a senior Ministry officer who was present that evening he described that night as 'terrifying':

> It was about eight o'clock when signals started to come in. I was up in Private Office and the signal came through that . . . a ship had been hit and hit badly. And then about fifteen to twenty minutes later it had capsized . . . We did not have any information about casualties . . . but the professional advice we had was that, if it has capsized as quickly as that perhaps the whole crew has gone. Now, the Secretary of State was doing an interview, I think it was with New Zealand radio, . . . and we said to him that we really did not know what was involved at all. And so he did the interview. However, he did have in his diary an obligation to talk to ITV and there were already the first rumblings coming out from Argentina, they were announcing a ship being hit.

The 'rumblings' were Press Association tapes coming out over the wire, and as a result there was an urgent discussion. The official continued:

> We had a meeting with [Nott] against [the background of] the very little information we had, which was that the *Coventry* had been hit, that within a short while it had capsized, no word of casualties and the implication being perhaps that the whole thing had gone down. A very, very major setback . . . we knew he was going

to be asked on commercial television, had the ship been hit that evening. He could not say, 'No' and he could not say, 'I don't know', so what could he say? . . . the dilemma was present . . . What could he say? . . . we had about ten minutes to make up our minds before . . . the programme, waiting every minute anxiously to see if new information would come in. It was a hellish night. The Chief of Defence Staff and the Commander-in-Chief of Fleet said: 'We believe it is absolutely wrong to name this ship at this stage . . . because you will cause untold agonies to wives and mothers.' We argued, the civil servant and the Under-Secretary, very strongly the other way. The Secretary of State said: 'Well, I cannot accept in this situation military advice I have been given.' As Nott walked down the corridor to his car, he was told that he could not just announce it on ITN, it would have to be done nationally as well. So walking down the corridor three sentences were scribbled out which, at the same time he used on ITN, McDonald would use on BBC.

Admiral Sir Henry Leach, the First Sea Lord, Admiral Sir John Fieldhouse, the Commander-in-Chief of Fleet, and Sir Terence Lewin, Admiral of the Fleet and Chief of Defence Staff at the time, have all admitted they made the wrong decision. As Leach said: 'In retrospect I think that was wrong. I think we should have announced it and I think the tactical consideration was not an overriding one then. I think the humanitarian one was. We got it wrong'.[42]

The next day, 26 May, a press statement was issued from the Ministry of Defence, naming *Coventry* and saying that she had been lost. The attack on *Atlantic Conveyor* was also announced. That afternoon Nott made a statement in the House of Commons on the loss of the two ships, giving initial numbers of casualties. Nott went on to outline the dilemma of the previous night – whether to decide to give the ship's name straightaway, when only very limited information was available or whether to hold back any announcement until there was more news. He admitted that 'we should probably have released the name of the *Coventry* the previous night'.

The press carried critical stories of the Ministry's handling of the announcement. There were also complaints that when relatives began to ring up the information centres, following the announcement at 2220 hours on 25 May, they were told nothing was known about the incident.

On realizing that every family with a relative on a ship had spent all night worrying, the Ministry of Defence changed its policy from that moment. One senior Ministry officer has told us:

Whatever the military staff said, we named ships so that it minimized the distress of people. The confusion as to what the press were being told that end and what we did at this end was really accounted for by the fact that this two-tier system of vetting, or censorship, inevitably led different people to come to use different judgements. The political element was one which didn't exist at the other end.

When the Secretary of State was given a piece of operational news, he had to decide whether that was something that he had got to announce straightaway, whether it was something he had got to tell Parliament about first, or something he would keep totally quiet about. Those were all political judgements he made. There was no one at the other end who was in a position to reflect what the Secretary of State's thoughts were going to be, so a correspondent would file a story, only to have it sat upon. On other occasions, they at the other end will have decided to advise a correspondent, 'No, you can't say anything about this', only to find out that it came out on the World Service because we had announced it. Inevitably, I think, given the 8000-mile gap. If we had always been able to pick up the telephone or flash off a signal . . . to say 'Following being announced in thirty minutes' time' . . . the correspondents could just have filled in all the detail . . . but we weren't able to do that, communications weren't good enough . . . the speed with which things were having to be announced at this end meant that there just wasn't time to get through, even when we could get through, and the pressures on signal traffic, on telephone communication and so on, just made consultation impossible.

Another incident which reflected on the Ministry's competence concerned the release of information on the attack on the Argentine fishing vessel *Narwal* on 9 May. The BBC has argued that the Ministry's version of the events was both tardy and inaccurate. Alan Protheroe, Assistant Director-General of the BBC, has said that 'the incident raises a question – perhaps quite wrongly – about the honesty of the Ministry of Defence'. According to Protheroe:

At 1800 hours London time on 9 May the claim by the Argentines was that an innocent ship had been bombed and that the crew had been strafed in the water. At 2100 hours there was a carefully worded statement, a carefully constructed statement, by the Ministry of Defence, which said that the ship had been taken, that a bomb had been dropped nearby, that the crew had abandoned ship and had been recovered by helicopters. In the interim the Argentines were still pumping out propaganda, pumping out claims that members of the crew of this so-called innocent fishing vessel had been strafed while they were in the water. At 2300 hours the Ministry of Defence announced that fourteen Argentines had been injured, and that one of them was dead. There is no question that those men *were* strafed in the water. That does not arise. They were *not* strafed, and I reject that absolutely. My point is, very simply, that when you have delays like that, first of all the Argentine claim has echoed around the world, and because there appears to be some confusion between the statement issued at nine o'clock which says that there are no injuries, and the statement issued at eleven o'clock that there *were* injuries, then it is possible for others to interpret that as a valid and proper Argentine claim which would enhance the credibility of further claims.[43]

The Ministry of Defence has said that it was well aware of and deeply concerned by the fact that the delay and confusion over the announcements of the *Narwal* incident tended to enhance the credibility of Argentine propaganda.[44] It has said that the problem – as on other occasions – was the lack of immediate and detailed information from the Task Force. The Ministry declared that, to minimize the risk of inaccuracy, it was consistently concerned to release information only confirmed by signal from the Task Force. However, it says, there were occasions when the pressure for an early release of news was such that this procedure was circumvented and information was sought and obtained by word of mouth.

According to the Ministry, the 2100 hours announcement was therefore made on the basis of telephone conversations from the Task Force to C in C Fleet, who in turn reported them by telephone to Ministry operational staff:

> We learnt by this experience (experience that was to be reinforced by our premature announcement of the capture of Goose Green): that it was essential to await signal report of an incident before making an announcement in view of the clear risk that those reporting events by telephone might (unbeknown to themselves) not be in possession of all the facts.[45]

The confusion concerning the announcements about *Narwal* prompted urgent reconsideration within the Ministry of its procedures for reporting incidents. Again, as with so many aspects of the Falklands Conflict, procedures evolved as the campaign proceeded.

The Ministry of Defence learnt another lesson from such incidents. As one senior official put it:

> We learnt very early on to say, 'We want confirmation', so, although the press were with their feet in the door saying, 'Give us the copy', we had to say, 'Wait, we have got to confirm the facts'. On two occasions we did not and we fell flat on our faces. One was the *Narwal* and the other was Goose Green.

Throughout the Conflict there was a continuing struggle within the Ministry of Defence. From the Services came pressure not to give gratuitously to the Argentines information about British losses, at least not until all next of kin were informed. The civilian officers thought that, in principle, this was right but that, if the Argentines had already released information for propaganda purposes, Britain should say clearly what the true facts were and put any occurrence into perspective.

It was these delays that led to accusations that Britain was losing the information war. As a Ministry official said to us:

> There was a point when I told the Chief of Staff formally that we were losing the information war. Information wasn't coming in quickly enough by signals and [we could] not rely on telephone information because we had fallen down desperately on two occasions when we had ... The Argentines at the latter end started to become much better at the information game than they were at the start. They were giving accurate information and they were giving it quickly. We were giving accurate information, but we were giving it slowly.

Claims that the information war was being lost did not come solely from journalists and civilian Ministry officers. Sir Geoffrey Johnson-Smith informed us that he had expressed his own concern to the Ministry at a meeting with Sir Frank Cooper, Richard Luce, the Minister for the Army, Peter Blaker, a former junior minister at the Foreign Office and Anthony Buck, a former Navy minister and the then current Chairman of the Conservative Defence Committee.

What annoyed Johnson Smith was that insufficient thought had been given to problems that would undoubtedly arise. He was offered a number of excuses and given some assurances.

> First, and this was where the phrase was coined, I think it was the first time I had heard it . . . 'They are in the charge of the Royal Navy and they are not called the Silent Service for nothing'. Secondly, it was all done at great speed. Thirdly, we hadn't had a director of publicity, there was not one there, and we then had to draft someone in. And, fourthly, we are pretty sure some pictures will be coming back this weekend. I said: 'Well, at least we ought to see a picture of South Georgia.' So I went away reasonably happy.

The biggest rift between the media and the Ministry of Defence was caused by the lack of a flow of information. Journalists are fed a diet of information. When it dries up, starvation sets in. Those who curtail the flow are then the target for objections and criticisms. Bob Hutchinson described to us his colleagues' reactions:

> Some of the stories the press were sending out to fill the vacuum [were] not mere speculation, [they were] total invention. We kept well away from that, but you could see some of these guys sitting down there pounding away on their typewriters, and they would come up and say, 'Is this plausible?' and you would say, 'That's a load of crap,' and they would say, 'Is it plausible, never mind if it is right or not', because they had to fill up space in the paper.

Part of the difficulty was caused by the machinery with which the Government chose to manage the war. Things were run only by the War Cabinet, Northwood, the Ministry of Defence and Downing Street. Parliament, the Treasury, and other departments became superfluous. We asked Simon Jenkins about this:

> All these other elements in the constitutional equation are completely *hors de combat*. You used to be able to learn everything you wanted to know about how Britain was run by having lunch with the political adviser to the Chancellor of the Exchequer – that poor guy was no better informed than you or I. So you have to find new sources. Now, the War Cabinet were just too busy . . . You might meet them occasionally at a party or something, but basically you got nothing out of them. Cabinet Ministers were certainly quite open, or as open as they normally would have been, but they did not know anything, because the Cabinet was kept in the dark. Where they were occasionally told things, they were very tight about them, except when they had been told not to be. Like there was a moment just

after the *Belgrano* sinking, when they were all terribly keen on peace. So you would meet a Cabinet Minister and he would say: 'This is serious, we are going to have to come to some terms to prove the initiative . . . it has to be the right one.' But you knew they had been told to say that.

The suspension of off-the-record briefings marked the closing of the tap. Journalists looked desperately for other oases. The previous trust between correspondents and the Ministry of Defence was then damaged further; information now came from other sources: the crashing of the two helicopters on South Georgia, for example, known only when a serviceman wrote home about it. As the BBC has remarked in its evidence to the Defence Committee:

> Shortcomings would not have damaged media confidence in the MoD as much as they did if correspondents had been able to resort to other channels of communication to discover what was actually happening.[46]

The resumption of briefings by military personnel and senior officials restored a certain amount of trust between the media and the Ministry, with the media being at least better informed even though on many occasions forbidden to publish. With the start of hostilities, however, came the use of disinformation, this soured the atmosphere still more. This brings us to the third lesson of the campaign, the dangers of the 'confidential embrace'.

Disinformation takes one of two forms: either the Government or the Ministry of Defence tells the media a lie, or it asks them to tell a lie. All the journalists and editors to whom we spoke said they would prefer to be told a lie and then to evaluate information for themselves. One journalist said to us:

> I think if you sat in a room every week with guys for a year and you developed some sort of trusting relationship with them and you suddenly discover that they are telling you lies, then you are bound to get upset. It is quite difficult to accept that the man who was previously telling you the truth is now telling you less than the truth.

Some defence correspondents have suggested that even Sir Frank Cooper was not fully informed of what was happening and that this added to their confusion. Bob Hutchinson described one incident:

> . . . there was one particular occasion when I went bananas at Nott. Frank Cooper said to one of his sidekicks, 'Don't let him out of the room before he's had a drink,' and I said: 'I don't want your filthy liquor.' And they gave me a gin and soda water and I said: 'You can't even get that fucking right.' Anyway, just after the fall of Stanley, Frank Cooper took me aside and we had a long chat and he was maintaining that the Ministry of Defence was not told very much at all of what was going on. And I said: 'I can't believe that.' And he said: 'No, it's actually a policy that was laid down after Suez.' And I said, 'What do you mean?' and he said, 'Well, when Eden was Prime Minister, during Suez, he used to keep sending

signals to the Task Force Commander saying, 'When I was a platoon commander
in Egypt there was a super place for a machine-gun . . . just on the corner of . . .'
And the Task Force got so pissed off with that they then decided as a matter of
policy (there were three Ministries in those days: the War Ministry, the Air
Ministry and the Admiralty) . . . they would never tell the politicians what was
going on, that detailed operational information would never come back.' And so
Cooper was maintaining that the Ministry of Defence was operating that system
here, that all they would get was requisitions for 228 white tropical shorts and
wouldn't be told exactly what was going on. I have doubts about that, but the story
about Suez sounds quite true.

Other journalists who were operating from London have told similar stories. David Fairhall, defence correspondent of the *Guardian*,
has said how surprised he was at the paucity of detailed and specific
information which filtered back even to the highest levels of
Government while operations were actually under way: 'Much of
what suspicious journalists regarded as news management could
probably be explained as a mixture of ignorance, wishful thinking,
and a natural desire to put the best light on things when seen from a
particular point of view.'[47]

There are, of course, laws and conventions upon which the
Government may draw to prevent the publication of information.
These include, notoriously, the system known as 'D-notices', of
which a new version, a consolidated list of updated notices, had
been issued on 30 March 1982, three days before the Argentine
invasion. No D-notices were issued during the conflict. Instead, as
ITN described it, an ad hoc system of censorship grew up under the
umbrella of the Ministry of Defence.[48]

The Ministry thought about using D-notices throughout and there
were occasions when the Secretary of the D-Notice Committee had
discussions with various parts of the media on points on which he
was concerned and consulted informally with the media. Sir Frank
Cooper has said that there was a considerable increase in the
number of enquiries to the Secretary of the D-Notice Committee.
Attention was drawn to the particular D-notices which gave editors
the kind of background guidance and indicated the areas about
which the Ministry of Defence was most sensitive.[49]

According to the BBC, it received, under the aegis of the D-
notice system, a request that there should be no speculation in its
programmes about the possible use of Chilean bases by British
forces. No new and specific D-notice was issued since the request
was within the embrace of the existing D-notice No. 1. The request
was made by the Secretary of the D-Notice Committee to the then
Assistant Director-General of the BBC, Alan Protheroe. He then
communicated it to departmental heads and senior editors of news

and current affairs programmes, who referred to him on any possible use of items on relations with Chile. The guidance was not formally withdrawn, but it became redundant after the revelation that a British helicopter had crash-landed in Chile; thereafter the possible use of Chilean bases was openly discussed.[50]

No editor or journalist particularly likes the D-notice structure; they prefer the ad hoc method that evolved during the conflict. There were, nonetheless, times of such frustration that they longed for the wider use of the D-notice system.

On several occasions the media complied with requests not to use information. This was done for both officially and unofficially released information. As far as film was concerned, the difficulties did not apply, since most of it arrived days, sometimes weeks, later. Had the pictures been immediate, Ministry interest would undoubtedly have been more intense.

According to Peter Woon, editor of BBC Television News, an official would come down from the Ministry to view film when it came in via satellite from Ascension. Woon would say to the official: 'Is there anything in that? You do understand, don't you, you are looking for security reasons and all you can do is ask?'

This process happened on several occasions. Woon told us:

> The only things they ever asked to be taken out [were] 'Oh, that picture shows a shot of a particular mechanism on a missile which we would prefer not to be seen'. And since, frankly, as far as we were concerned, or the viewers were concerned, it did not matter a damn, we would never be able to identify what the bloody thing was anyway . . . I think literally that in the whole of the war I would guess that no more than about ten seconds were removed.

The broadcasting organizations also operated their own system of self-censorship, without Ministry prompting. The BBC has given a number of examples. For instance, it became known by those producing one programme that 5 Brigade had landed at San Carlos. Bi-weekly briefings with the Ministers, and increased communication, meant that it was difficult for the makers of the programme not to seek advice. On being advised that premature publication could cost lives, publication was withheld. In its evidence to the Defence Committee, the BBC stated:

> On other occasions the BBC was asked to exercise restraint not to save lives, but to 'keep the Argentines guessing', part of the operational strategy. The BBC naturally complied.[51]

The BBC outlined part of its strategy:

> Speculation about future operations was avoided except in the broadest terms of describing British options. Studio analysis tended to confine itself to comment on

the day's press statement, coupled with whatever could be gleaned from Argentine communiqués. Less information was broadcast than was available from foreign sources. For example, Washington revealed (and the US networks broadcast) that the Task Force would first take South Georgia, several days before it was broadcast by the BBC.[52]

There has been little criticism of the media's self-censorship in operational matters. The argument has mainly centred on the question of taste. Would the pictures of wounded servicemen or interviews with their wives have affected the attitude of the viewing public towards the campaign? Should broadcasters have different standards for British troops and for foreign troops? David Nicholas told the Ministry of Defence that matters of taste were the broadcaster's responsibility. While ITN accepted the Ministry's rulings where security was concerned, taste and tone were purely editorial considerations. A notorious example occurred in a filmed interview with a Harrier pilot, who was asked about his reaction when going in on a strafing run over Stanley airstrip in the face of heavy flak. 'I was scared fartless,' he said. The Ministry of Defence in London argued forcefully that ITN should not transmit that.

More important decisions had to be made when pictures such as those from Bluff Cove started to come in. There was one particularly nasty shot of a soldier being carried on a stretcher with his leg blown off. The BBC showed the clip. ITN did not. Peter Woon, described it as the 'most provocative shot we ran'. He recognized the dangers of 'lingering', but stated 'we wanted to show the horror of it'. We asked David Nicholas for his reasons for not showing it:

> Perhaps we were wrong. I do not blame the BBC for showing it. It is a purely subjective thing. When you see something you might actually throw up at . . . I can fill the screen with that every night – a road accident or a Belfast bombing. The only other rule we applied to that coverage was that we should not show anybody that was recognizable. We had one or two shots we kept in of morphine being given to a very badly burnt guy and a couple of others, but I thought it was not right that if you were sitting at home you could see your son writhing in agony. The general rule put out to film and ENG editors was, 'Don't show a recognizable casualty'.

Both ITN and the BBC were criticized during the campaign for conducting interviews with wives of men serving with the Task Force, for 'dwelling on private grief'. David Nicholas described ITN's policy:

> We passed the word to the regions as well. We must not crash in and do it. We did interview the wives, but we always sounded out a third party, the local padré or somebody else. We were not to go snatching off the mantelpiece and that sort of thing.

The issue was also discussed at BBC news and current affairs meetings. On 1 June 1982, for instance, Alan Protheroe announced a ruling by the Board of Management that there should be no such interviews under any circumstances. This direction had, however, been lifted the previous day for an item on the issue of whether the bodies of those killed should be returned for burial in Britain; in the event no one could be found to give an interview. Protheroe said that any further cases where editors believed there was good cause for an interview with a bereaved relative should be referred to him. There was some dissent from this ruling. John Wilson, editor of BBC news, agreed that there had been some inept interviews with the bereaved, but that an important purpose could be served by those that succeeded: Radio Medway, for example, had been approached by the widow of a chief petty officer in the Royal Navy, killed in *Atlantic Conveyor*, who had wanted to make a contribution because she felt that she had something helpful to say to other Falklands widows. Because of the Board's ruling, her offer was refused. John Wilson was still more concerned that contributions by Field-Marshal Lord Carver on the repatriation of bodies were not being counterbalanced by the views of dead servicemen's relatives. This, said Wilson, had the effect of making the BBC appear to be on the side of the authorities.

These discussions continued at the next meeting on 8 June. Alan Protheroe pointed out that memorial services were public occasions and there could be no objection to sensitive coverage, while Richard Horobin said that his staff had carried out two interviews with bereaved relatives, one with the mother of a chef on the *Sheffield,* who had been informed that her son was missing. Apparently she had been keen to give an interview. The second had involved the mother of a Paratrooper who wanted her son's body brought home. Horobin was disappointed that he had been unable to use either of these contributions. The editor of *Nationwide,* Roger Bolton, whilst agreeing that the BBC should not intrude upon the bereaved and that all such interviews should be carefully arranged and scrupulously executed, thought there was also a strong case for making them subject to referral. Surely, he asked, there was a place for these interviews, especially since some of the deaths had occurred three weeks previously and the bereaved relatives had reached some kind of perspective? Protheroe was firm, warning strongly against 'knee-jerk' journalism, and threatening to dismiss any reporter who asked dead men's relations, 'How did you feel?' He rejected the idea that by broadcasting an emotional interview the BBC would be charged with undermining national will. He did not see it in these terms. The issue was, he said, one of intrusion into private grief, compounded by mindless questions. He stressed the need for editors to control the style of interviewing and for stringent editorial assessment.

Later, the Director-General, Sir Ian Trethowan, ruled that the general prohibition on interviews with the bereaved would remain in force, but editors who wished to make a case for the use of such interviews could refer to the Assistant Director-General for permission. He would then consider and advise on the suitability of the inclusion of such interviews.

The Bluff Cove pictures did not appear until a few weeks after the event; by that time the campaign was over. We asked Peter Woon whether his criteria would have been different, had he received live pictures, or pictures only marginally delayed:

> I don't know, I really don't know . . . I would hope not . . . this was a major difference in that if we had had satellite on board ship and stuff had been banging back every day straight away, then one would have had to have considered family or relatives who perhaps till the moment you put it on the screen didn't even know that anything had happened. In this case, every time we showed the pictures, the public was already aware of the horror that had brought that picture. So that in many ways it wasn't as horrific . . . If Bluff Cove had come through that night and no one had ever heard of Bluff Cove and the first they're going to hear about it is when these pictures are going to hit the screen . . . I'm reasonably certain that what we would have done would be still to run them in exactly the same way . . . exactly the same length, cut them in the same way, but one would have had to put a heavy order on it saying, 'During this programme pictures . . .' and I think we would have to repeat that warning about the pictures . . . The question which I have asked myself is, would one have done the story of Bluff Cove without the pictures and then do the pictures in a later programme? . . . but I think not, . . . in that sense the public would have been aware, saying, 'This is going to be a war like Vietnam', where pictures just came banging back . . . and people very quickly adjusted to that.

Both ITN and the BBC have shown explicitly unpleasant shots from other parts of the world. At the time of the Falklands Conflict, for instance, dreadful pictures from the Lebanon were appearing on screen nightly. Both editors have identified a difference in that with foreign pictures they are less worried about casualties being recognized. Woon said to us:

> We edit for exactly the same reasons of taste and not lingering, but you do not have to consider in Beirut the impact on relatives and friends and all that: it is not their sons and daughters in Beirut.

And David Nicholas explained to us:

> I just don't know what effect that sort of thing would have, I don't. You could argue that it would fortify the thing . . . I think, rightly or wrongly, I certainly had very, very uppermost in my mind, the whole time throughout the war . . . after all,

even unlike Ireland really, there were 25,000 Service people involved in the operation, that's a sizeable number of concerned people. And as one welfare-type officer or padré said to me on one occasion, when we announce some bad news on the screen, in every naval depot in the country the wives clean the house from top to bottom that night. It's a very good expression: they couldn't sleep, so they just cleaned the house. So one had very much in mind the cause of distress to the people and I think the most distressing episode I've had in my entire experience of journalism was when we ran Nicholson's voice description of Bluff Cove in that early evening news. It came in at five o'clock and that was the first intimation of what had happened and I went down to listen to it . . . and he gave this account which lasted for six minutes . . . it was horrendous, and the Ministry of Defence cleared it like that . . . I couldn't believe it. I said: 'Are you sure?' Because we had suffered a huge loss of life and what we try to do, even in Ireland, if a soldier's been killed, the next of kin have been informed, if we have that information then at least you've lessened the distress. However, if you actually say 'A soldier has been killed in Northern Ireland . . .'. Well, there's 15,000 soldiers, that's 15,000 sets of distress you've caused. If you're able to say a soldier of the 3rd Cheshire in South Armagh, at least you've narrowed down the category. But I don't think you can be oblivious to that. I think it's more sensitive in broadcasting, we are going into people's homes. The art of newscasting, in my view, developed greatly during the Falklands, because these people were going into their homes . . . I think that was one of the reasons we came through reasonably well . . . I do believe that the way the newscasters, all of them, gave . . . I don't mean simply because they're journalists and they dealt with the thing and wrote a lot of it themselves, I think there was a sort of concern in the presentation of it, or a sympathy perhaps is the right word, which delivered the bad news in a kind of acceptable way.

In this chapter we have looked mainly at the functional arrangements between the Government and the press and broadcasters. In the next chapter we look at the political relationships and in particular that between the Government and the BBC.

Notes

1. House of Commons First Report from the Defence Committee, Session 1982–83. HMSO Dec. 1982 Vol. 1, p. xi, para. 20 – *see also* p. lix, para. 138 (ix).
2. Op. cit. Vol. 1, p. xi, para. 21.
3. Op. cit. Vol. 1, p. xxxv, para. 82.
4. Op. cit. Vol. 2, p. i, para. 2.
5. Op. cit. Vol. 2, Q. 1377, p. 339.
6. Op. cit. Vol. 2, Q. 1378, p. 340.
7. Op. cit. Vol. 2, Q. 1847, p.438.
8. Op. cit. Vol. 2, Q. 1852, p.439.
9. Op. cit. Vol. 1, p.xxii, para. 46.
10. Op. cit. Vol. 2, Q. 1721, p. 393.
11. Op. cit. Vol. 2, Q. 258, p. 82.
12. Op. cit. Vol. 2, Q. 48, p. 24.
13. Op. cit. Vol. 2, Q. 1665, p. 387.
14. Op. cit. Vol. 2, Q. 1868, p. 442.

15. Op. cit. Vol. 1, p. xlvi, para. 105.
16. Op. cit. Vol. 2, Q. 1667, p. 387.
17. Op. cit. Vol. 2, Q. 1871, p. 443.
18. Op. cit. Vol. 2, Q. 1874, p. 443.
19. Op. cit. Vol. 2, Q. 1874, p. 443.
20. Vol. 1, p. xlvi, para. 105.
21. Op. cit. Vol. 2, Q. 1729, p. 394.
22. Op. cit. Vol. 2, Q. 86, p. 32.
23. Op. cit. Vol. 2, p. 418 – for the sequence of events as seen by the Ministry, *see* Defence Committee.
24. Op. cit. Vol. 1, p. xxxi, para. 69.
25. Op. cit. Vol. 2, Q. 1843, p. 437.
26. Op. cit. Vol. 2, Q. 732, p. 228.
27. Op. cit. Vol. 2, p. 419.
28. Op. cit. Vol. 2, Q. 116, p. 291.
29. Op. cit. Vol. 2, p. 118, para. 5.
30. Op. cit. Vol. 1, p. xiv, para. 27.
31. Op. cit. Vol. 2, Q. 40, p. 22.
32. Op. cit. Vol. 2, p. 432, Cooper's briefing was tape recorded – for a full account *see* Defence Committee.
33. Op. cit. Vol. 2, p. 459, para. 3.3–3.4.
34. Op. cit. Vol. 2, p. 113.
35. Op. cit. Vol. 2, Q. 780, p. 235.
36. Op. cit. Vol. 2, p. 417, para. 3.
37. Op. cit. Vol. 2, p. 417, para. 4.
38. Op. cit. Vol. 1, p. xliv, para. 100.
39. Op. cit. Vol. 1, p. xl, para. 91.
40. Op. cit. Vol. 1, p. xl, para. 91.
41. Op. cit. Vol. 2, p. 430. For the facts as set out by the MoD *see* Defence Committee.
42. Op. cit. Vol. 2, Q. 1419, p. 348.
43. Op. cit. Vol. 2, Q. 226, p. 62.
44. Op. cit. Vol. 2, p. 428, para. 2.
45. Op. cit. Vol. 2, p. 429, para. 5.
46. Op. cit. Vol. 2, p. 46, para. 3.2(c).
47. Op. cit. Vol. 2, p. 107.
48. Op. cit. Vol. 2, p. 71, quest. D.
49. Op. cit. Vol. 1, p. xxix, para. 66.
50. Op. cit. Vol. 2, p. 46, para. 4.1.
51. Op. cit. Vol. 2, p. 46, para. 3.4.
52. Op. cit. Vol. 2, p. 46, para. 3.5.

10

The BBC, the IBA, the Government and the Conservative Party

In times of national crisis the press and broadcasting organizations are used to being criticized for their coverage. The BBC, in particular, is accustomed to attack: its news bulletins for example, had been criticized by politicians only the year before the Falklands campaign, at the time of the 1981 riots in Brixton and elsewhere. More serious, and engraved forever on the BBC's heart, were the attacks on its impartiality at the time of the Suez crisis in 1956. Memorable criticism had come, for instance, from Peter Rawlinson, Conservative MP for Epsom (who was to become a law officer in later Conservative governments). He complained in Parliament about both domestic and overseas broadcasts, especially 'on the time given to one . . . upon matters of emphasis, of selection, of nuance, use of adjective and the use of tone'. These, he maintained, added up to 'a slant on the news'. He was particularly troubled by the current affairs programme, *Panorama*. 'Who,' he inquired, 'selected these "men in the street"?' As for the World Service, he argued, 'The overseas broadcasters should speak in the name of the government of the day and present their foreign policy . . .' Indeed, 'there should be a ministry of information, so that this country could have a proper propaganda voice to go out all over the world'.[1]

Such attacks were to be repeated, almost word for word, in the spring and summer of 1982. The BBC had anticipated trouble. At a routine meeting of news and current affairs editors on 6 April, four days after the Argentinian invasion, Ian Trethowan, Director-General, warned that there might be 'pressure' from the Government. He outlined general guidelines for the coverage of its footwork right through the twists and turns that lay ahead. The Director-General was wary of drawing parallels with Suez; he nonetheless reminded his editors that the BBC was likely to find, as in 1956, that it was expected to conform to 'the national interest'. The Corporation should not, he observed, act in a way that might imperil military operations or diplomatic negotiations but it should report accurately and faithfully the arguments being voiced among all levels of British society. Even Trethowan did not foresee the extent to which the BBC would come under fire.

The main onslaught began on 3 May, when John Page, Conservative MP for Harrow West and former secretary of the party's
backbench Broadcasting Committee, complained about the previous evening's edition of BBC 2's programme of news and comment, *Newsnight*. According to Page, the programme was
'unacceptably even-handed'. He was particularly critical of remarks
made by the journalist Peter Snow, who had said:

> There is a stage in the coverage of any conflict where you can begin to discern the
> level of accuracy of the claims and counter-claims of either side. Tonight, after
> two days, we cannot demonstrate that the British have lied to us so far. But the
> Argentines clearly have. At 6.30 our time tonight the Argentines claimed that the
> *Hermes* had been disabled and three hours later we had the BBC reporter on
> board the carrier reporting there had been no attack and no damage to the ship.
> Now, there was already deep scepticism, to put it mildly, about the Argentine
> claim to have downed eleven aircraft. They have produced no further evidence to
> refute British denials on this. Besides, our reporter said he counted all the Harrier
> pilots from *Hermes* flying off and flying back. So, again, an Argentine claim that
> appears to have no foundation. Until the British are demonstrated either to be
> deceiving us or to be concealing losses, we can only tend to give a lot more
> credence to the British version of events.[2]

Snow's observations provoked fury among Conservative backbenchers and ministers. At midnight, after the programme, John
Page had telephoned the Press Association, so say that Snow's
comments verged on treason. From that moment, Page said to us, 'I
became an active critic'; his comments were reported in every
newspaper on 4 May.

Although this was the first time Page had aired his criticism in
public, he had been angered by earlier incidents. An item on Radio
4, for instance, had appeared to him to be grossly biased. As the
Task Force had sailed from Plymouth, a woman reporter had said,
according to Page: 'Now we shall go back to Plymouth and consider
the plight of the naval families left behind'. The Member was aghast
– and told us:

> 'Plight' is a word you use about the victims of the earthquake in Nicaragua, that's
> what plight is. As a matter of fact, the families of the naval people on the Task
> Force were in extremely good form with a high morale, nervous, of course, of the
> future, well and carefully looked after by the Navy. And to use the word 'plight', I
> thought, was absolutely disgraceful because it gave the impression that there were
> sort of pathetic wives left on the quayside with half-dressed children and nowhere
> to live.

The *Newsnight* programme was, in Pages's eyes, even more serious.
He was not appeased by Peter Snow's explanation that, after assessing and analysing the situation, the programme was simply telling its
audience that, when the Argentines said one thing and the British

another, *Newsnight* tended on the evidence of what they had heard so far to believe the British. As Snow observed, 'What one was doing was the very reverse of what Page accused us of'.

John Page continued his attack on *Newsnight* in particular and the BBC in general. At Question Time on 7 May he asked the Prime Minister to 'find a few moments to listen to the radio and watch television and judge for herself if she feels that the British case on the Falklands is being presented in a way likely to inspire confidence to our friends overseas and support and encourage our servicemen and their devoted families'.

Mrs Thatcher's reply did nothing to dampen the mounting controversy:

> Judging by many of the comments I have heard from people who watch and listen more than I do, many people are very, very concerned indeed that the case for our British forces is not being put over fully and effectively. I understand there are times when it would seem that we and the Argentines are almost being treated as equal and almost on a neutral basis. I understand there are occasions when some commentators will say that the Argentines did something and then 'the British' did something. I can only say that, if this is so, it gives offence and causes great emotion among many people.

This prompted a fierce attack on the BBC. On 7 May the *Sun* produced an editorial of particular severity under the headline, 'Dare Call It Treason' and the sub-headline, 'There are traitors in our midst'. Peter Snow came in for the main hammering: 'What is it but treason to talk on TV as Peter Snow talked, questioning whether the Government's version of the sea battles was to be believed?' The *Sun* also attacked the *Guardian* for printing a cartoon which showed a British seaman clinging to a raft, with the caption, 'The price of sovereignty has been increased – official?' It saved its most venomous criticism, however, for its biggest rival, the *Daily Mirror*. 'What is it but treason,' the *Sun*'s editorial asked, 'for this timorous whining publication to plead day after day for appeasing the Argentine dictators because they do not believe the British people have the stomach for a fight, and are instead prepared to trade peace for honour?'

The BBC felt bound to reply to these allegations of lack of patriotism. Statements were issued to the press and on the evening of 6 May, in a speech to the Chartered Building Societies Institute, the Chairman of the Board of Governors of the BBC, George Howard, took up the Prime Minister's remarks. Howard declared that, while the BBC had to make 'hard editorial decisions' in considering how to report Argentine views, the Corporation was not and could not be ' . . . neutral as between our own country and an aggressor'. He alluded to the BBC's difficulties:

It is a very serious state of affairs when we can interview on television admirals on the active list who command the marine forces of a country with which we are, to all intents and purposes, at war. But that, almost more than anything else, is the difference between our ability to report contemporary hostilities and the ability we had to report past conflicts. We now do have the opportunity not only to work in the aggressor's country, but the ability to report closely on his attitudes.

The Chairman emphasized that BBC journalists were aware that they might be used as propagandists. He believed, however, that they could recognize propaganda when they saw it:

We apply stringent editorial tests to everything we hear or see – and to what we say. The primary, the most fundamental of those tests, is whether what we are about to report actually adds to the understanding of the situation by our huge audiences. And coupled with that is our determination that in war truth shall not be the first casualty ... Our reports are believed around the world precisely because of our reputation for telling the truth.

Howard's words did little to soothe the critics. The next complaint concerned an early evening news bulletin on BBC 2 which had reported the funeral of Argentine seamen killed in British attacks. The BBC switchboard received many calls from the public criticizing the 'undue reverence' of the report. Robert Adley, Conservative MP for Christchurch and Lymington, described the BBC as becoming 'Galtieri's fifth column . . .', and spoke of 'a propaganda film of the funerals of Argentine sailors, some more propaganda in a film of the Argentine–Bulgarian football match, with a great show of national fervour'. He had formally protested, he said, to the Director-General and told him that the BBC's 'one sidedness' would lose it popular respect. Other national newspapers now joined the *Sun* – the *Daily Express*, for example, which on 10 May carried an article by its television editor, with the headline, 'Has TV strayed too far into the enemy camp?' Criticism also came from the left. Tony Benn, at that time out of Parliament, claimed that the BBC and ITV news were the mouthpieces of the Ministry of Defence.

By mid-May, however, criticism ranged more widely. It was said that the Government was orchestrating media coverage via the Ministry of Defence. Stories of censorship were coming in from journalists; in London the Ministry of Defence's off-the-record briefings ceased. There was concern at the use of retired military officials and admirals as television pundits and the early rumblings of a row over the absence of television pictures from the South Atlantic. The BBC itself drew attention to these issues, not unexpectedly, since to some extent they served to deflect criticism from its own coverage. In Government circles, too, there was increasing disquiet. Ministers and their advisers believed that Britain was losing the information war, that Argentine propaganda was being inadequately countered. Ministers wanted the British case to be presented with more urgency, with television film and still photographs from the war zone.

This underlay one of the chief complaints against the BBC, that official Argentinian film was being shown. Ministers seemed to agree, however, that since no British official film and photographs had been made available, even after five weeks of conflict, they were in a poor position to criticize. On 10 May, the newly appointed Foreign Secretary, Francis Pym, referred to BBC coverage at a meeting of the House of Commons Foreign Affairs Committee, in reply to a point made by Peter Mills, Conservative MP for Devon West, whose constituents were, he said, 'very concerned'. 'I think,' Pym told him, 'all of us are aware of the criticism of the present-ation, particularly by the BBC. The Government is very concerned about it indeed. The most effective thing to do would be for all those constituents to write to the BBC'. The Foreign Secretary acknowledged that there had been few pictures from the Task Force, explaining that, while ships were at sea, little could be done. That, he observed, nonetheless failed to excuse the impression the news was giving. 'It is not for me,' he said, 'to express a view about it, even if I have one. I think the evidence is that millions of people feel that it is not fairly done and that is much more important'.

On the evening of the Foreign Secretary's meeting with back-benchers, *Panorama* broadcast the programme that provoked the mightiest storm. In retrospect, the programme seems fairly inof-fensive. At the time, it was more than some could stomach. As soon as *Panorama* ended, outraged comments poured in from the public and from Conservative MPs. Geoffrey Rippon, a former Conserva-tive minister, called it ' . . . one of the most despicable programmes it has ever been my misfortune to witness'. Kenneth Warren, Con-servative MP for Hastings, declared that, 'It is time the BBC came back to earth and remembered its responsibilities'. Three of his colleagues, Eldon Griffiths (MP for Bury St Edmunds), Anthony Grant (Harrow Central), and Peter Mills (Avon West), put down a Commons motion in the following terms:

> This House, having provided the BBC shall enjoy all the benefits of broadcasting on the basis of a compulsory levy on the public and in the context of a democratic society whose freedoms require to be defended if they are to endure, records its dismay that some BBC programmes on the Falklands gave the impression of being pro-Argentine and anti-Britain, while others appear to suggest that the invasion of these British islands is a matter in which the BBC is entitled to remain loftily

neutral: and calls on the Corporation, if it cannot speak up for Britain, at least not to speak against it.

The attacks continued on the next day, 11 May. A letter in *The Times* from John Page asserted that: 'It is the superior tone of superneutrality which so many of us find to be objectionable and unacceptable when our forces are in action – we expected the BBC to be on our side!' At Question Time Mrs Sally Oppenheim, former Minister of Consumer Affairs, told the Prime Minister that the *Panorama* programme was an 'odious, subversive travesty' in which Michael Cockerell and other BBC reporters had 'dishonoured the right of freedom of speech'. Sir Bernard Braine, Conservative MP for South-East Essex, spoke of a rising tide of anger at 'the media's presentation of enemy propaganda and the defeatist views of an unrepresentative minority'.

In reply, the Prime Minister said that she shared 'the deep concern which has been expressed on many sides, particularly about the content of the *Panorama* programme'. She went on: 'I know how strongly many people feel that the cause of our country is not being put with sufficient vigour on certain of the programmes – I do not say all – of the BBC'. Referring to the Chairman's assurance that the Corporation was not neutral, she said: 'I hope his words will be heeded by the many who have responsibility for standing up for our Task Force, our boys, for our people, and the cause of democracy'.

Some Opposition MPs called for the intimidation of the BBC to cease. David Winnick, Labour MP for Walsall North, reminded the House that one of the virtues of political democracy was that radio and television were independent of Government interference. To this Mrs Thatcher replied that, while the freedom of the media was something in which to take pride, 'We are asking them, when the lives of some of our people may be at stake, when they have information which could be of use to the enemy, or discussion which could be of use to them, to take that into account'. Michael Foot, Leader of the Opposition, then asked the Prime Minister: 'Before you pursue further your strictures, would you take some steps to reprove the attitudes of some of the newspapers that support you, the hysterical bloodlust of the *Sun* and the *Daily Mail*, papers which bring such disgrace to journalism in this country?' Mrs Thatcher replied: 'Of course they are totally free to discuss and publish what they wish. Equally, as you have just demonstrated, we are free to say what we think about it'.

Later that evening the Social Democrats and Liberals sought to come to the BBC's defence, in a motion tabled by William Rogers and David Steel, regretting the 'intemperate attacks' of the Prime

Minister and her colleagues. They were, the proposers declared, 'deeply distasteful' to many MPs who had given the Government steady support during the crisis; furthermore, they could inflict permanent and unjustified damage on the reputation of the BBC at home and abroad. 'Free speech and honest reporting,' said the motion, 'should not become the victims of Government intolerance'.

Why did the *Panorama* programme so upset the Government and its backbenchers? At the time few critics publicly specified their objections but some have subsequently spoken more fully. Of these, several MPs thought that the programme was, simply, a journalistic failure. Their view is shared by some political commentators.

Simon Jenkins, political editor of *The Economist*, for instance, told us that he thought it 'an awful programme', which gave far too much time to irrelevant interviews with Members of Parliament, particularly Conservatives. 'There was not much Tory disagreement with the war, and what disagreement there was was over tactics. They thought that the Navy wasn't going to win and therefore it shouldn't have been sent, and that didn't come across in the programme. It's like doing a programme about the future of journalism and getting three journalists from the *Daily Star* as your main material'.

Alan Clark, Conservative MP for Plymouth, echoed this opinion. Indeed, like his backbench colleagues, he objected less to the fact that *Panorama* examined the opposition to the war than to those the producer had chosen for interview. As Clark put it to us:

> During the Falklands crisis dissent in the Conservative Party was confined to about three cranks . . . usually the Tory party is in a state of sulky ferment on any given issue, divided approximately anything from 70:30 to 50:50, but in this case there were just about two or three egomaniacs or bankeradoes who were shown as being quite serious elements within the party. If they had concentrated on the divisions in the Cabinet between those who felt that they really should be tackling this thing on a negotiated basis because of our commercial interest in Argentina and the pressure on the banks and those who didn't, if they had really sought out the seats of anxiety about the Falklands Conflict, they could have produced a very formidable presentation . . . that would have been very interesting and constructive. Instead, they simply, just out of laziness or what, . . . tackled it wrong and gave a distorted impression.

Others, however, denounced the style and tone of the programme – Mrs Whitehouse, of the National Viewers' and Listeners' Association, for example, who declared that: '*Panorama* was arrogant and disloyal. It prostituted the power their profession gives broadcasters. To spread alarm and despondency was a treasonable offence in the last war. One wonders what succour this sort of broadcasting gives the people in Argentina'.

The Army was also unhappy about the programme. Brigadier Ramsbotham himself spoke to its editor; he was satisfied, however, that *Panorama* had sought to question not the military conduct of the war but that of the Government.

The editor of *Panorama,* George Carey, told us: 'I think that when the history books are written it will actually be seen to be rather an important thing to have done'. He reminded critics that an earlier edition of the programme, that of 26 April, had devoted its entire length to an interview with the Prime Minister. In putting together the offending edition of 10 May the programme makers had been circumspect. In examining the views of opponents of the conflict they had deliberately avoided interviews with predictable critics of the Government, seeking instead people who were not really public figures of great standing. In the introduction to the programme and throughout, the four politicians interviewed were described as representing a minority view but one reflecting genuine uncertainty both inside and outside the House. According to Carey, *Panorama* had talked to between thirty and fifty Members whom they believed to have doubts about the progress of events. 'These,' Carey maintained, 'were saying one of two things: either "I am against this show", or "I'm very worried about this show but you are not going to get me on film saying so" or "My chums are worried about it, everybody's worried, but obviously we have got to back Maggie now".' *Panorama* had several times plainly stated that it was examining a minority view and, to balance it, Carey emphasized, 'we not only included parts of the fifty-minute interview with Mrs Thatcher shown in the previous edition but also an interview with the Party Chairman, Mr Parkinson. He had ample opportunity to put the majority view across'.

Sir Geoffrey Johnson Smith, Chairman of the Conservative Media Group, suggested to us that *Panorama* had not made matters clear:

> If you look at the script very carefully – and I did . . . I had it sent to me and I saw the programme . . . you could be pardoned for not understanding what the real intent was . . . it started off with the very long interview. Actually, if they had hit . . . this point very hard, that we are going to talk to those people in the Conservative Party who for various reasons are more concerned or worried about the escalation of this war, they represent a minority view, we shall be talking to them later and then outline why they wanted to talk to the Argentinians, I think then possibly people would have understood that this wasn't meant to be a programme in which the BBC was taking a side or even trying to convince people that what they were saying was a true reflection of the Conservative view. Now somewhere I think that is all stated, but certainly journalistically, from a written

point of view, let alone photography and the style of interview – that got lost. And I think from time to time these things get lost because so often people think the picture will tell you a story and they forget the importance of words and making sure. With your introductions you set up the scene. And because there's that long interview between your first setting-the-scene paragraph which you're doing verbally and the pictorial charts of this Argentinian along with this rather smooth interview – those coming in a third of the way down the programme – I think again it needed a restatement. I know it is a very detailed thing, but in fact that created a great deal of acrimony.

At the end of the week in which the programme appeared *Panorama* conducted an opinion poll, in its own name, on viewers' opinions of the way in which the programme was covering events in the Falklands. Sixty-nine percent of respondents approved. Furthermore, as the Foreign Secretary had asked, viewers and listeners were writing in large numbers to the BBC. According to Carey, of those who wrote, the numbers in favour of and displeased with the BBC's coverage were almost equal.

Panorama's troubles were increased by an unexpected defection. Robert Kee, the presenter of the series, wrote a letter to *The Times*, published on 14 May: 'I am,' he said, 'grateful to the Chairman and Director-General of the BBC for loyally defending me among other colleagues against criticism of the film section in the programme, but wish to release them from the obligation in my own case since I must disassociate myself from the defence. It is absurd to receive justification for something which, in one's own mind, cannot be justified.' According to Kee, when he was first shown a rough cut of the film the night before transmission, he 'criticized it severely for identifying in a confusing way *Panorama's* own view of the Falklands crisis with that of the minority view it was claiming to look at objectively'. He acknowledged that it was 'wholly appropriate to examine that minority view', arguing, however, that it should either have occupied a shorter part of the programme or that there should have been other voices to question it.

Kee's colleagues, already feeling beleaguered, not unnaturally resented his remarks. In the circumstances, they were, the team thought, 'a bit hypocritical'. Certainly, on first seeing the programme on the day before transmission, Kee had told George Carey and Christopher Capron, the Head of Current Affairs, that he disliked it. Changes were made which at least mollified Kee but, on the morning of the day of transmission, he and Carey had argued vehemently about the script with which Carey proposed to introduce and accompany the filmed interviews. As editor of the programme, Carey's decision was final.

The *Panorama* incident was a major skirmish in the war of words which continued, unabated, between the BBC, the Government and the Conservative Party. Richard Francis, Managing Director of BBC Radio, stated (in a discussion at the annual conference of the International Press Institute in Madrid on 11 May) that the BBC did not derive its reputation from 'being tied to the British Government's apron strings, nor from banging a jingoistic drum for the British Task Force'. To those who had complained at the tone of the BBC's coverage of an Argentine seaman's funeral, he replied firmly and memorably: 'The widow of Portsmouth is no different from the widow of Buenos Aires. The BBC needs no lesson in patriotism'. These last remarks stirred Conservative backbenchers to further fury. 'At least,' said one, 'the widow of Portsmouth pays a licence fee', a view echoed in the leader columns of the *Daily Express*. Alan Clark thought Francis's point curious in the circumstances: 'It indicates a very high level of detachment from the populist identity of interest with yourself and your own country . . . which was rampant during the War'.

Many newspapers revived the well-worn accusation that the BBC was managed by lightweight liberal intellectuals who were insufficiently patriotic. On 12 May, for example, the *Daily Mail* carried an article by Anthony Lejeune entitled, 'Whatever happened to the BBC Voice of Britain?'. In the *Daily Express* a piece by Geoffrey Levy had the headline, 'No wonder Galtieri is laughing!' Some defended the Corporation – the *Guardian*, the *Mirror* and the *Financial Times*, for instance, which all published leaders attacking the Government's criticism of the Corporation.

The climax came at a private meeting of the backbench Conservative Party Media Group on the evening of 12 May. The BBC's Chairman, George Howard, and Trethowan's successor, Alasdair Milne (the Director-General designate), attended the meeting to face more than a hundred Conservative Members. Howard and Milne were subjected to a battery of intense and angry criticism. The Group's chairman, Sir Geoffrey Johnson Smith (himself a former television journalist) had organized the session to air the growing feeling of anger he discerned among his colleagues at what they regarded as the BBC's 'leaning over backwards in their objectivity to such an extent that they almost appeared to be nothing to do with this country'.

The meeting was acrimonious. 'Everyone is roasting them alive,' reported Members as they emerged. 'They are going for their throats and there is blood and entrails all over the place.' One senior Member described it as the roughest meeting he had attended in all his years as an MP. Others described the performance of the two top BBC officials as 'shocking, disgraceful and appalling'. The *Panorama* programme was the focus of the row but, as the BBC's Chairman said when the encounter ended, while he acknowledged the strength of Members' feelings, he was not prepared to apologise for the programme. Sir Geoffrey Johnson Smith has since observed to us that 'some of the chaps went over the top . . . It was an almost ritualistic blood-letting on the part of the MPs and they behaved quite disgracefully'.

Alan Clark, who was present, had mixed reactions; he said to us:

> We got a kick in, we roughed them up and they were sweating a bit; and, although I don't think it had any particular effect, it is good for people in those sorts of positions to be roughed up. We have to go through it. It's quite funny, you know, those sort of self-satisfied creeps on big salaries and fixed contracts, when they have a nasty time. As an abstract spectacle that is always quite enjoyable.

The general view amongst Conservative Members was that the affair had probably diminished, rather than enhanced, popular respect for the Conservative Party and that on the whole it was likely to do more harm than good in the medium term. To some extent, it defused criticism, although complaints against the BBC continued, to a lesser degree, in articles to the press. On 14 May there was another hostile editorial in the *Sun*. Other voices now came to the BBC's defence. At the meeting of news and current affairs editors on 18 May, the Director-General's Chief Assistant, David Holmes, remarked that the gathering convened by Johnson Smith had served as a safety-valve, concentrating the issue into an argument between the BBC and backbench Tories and easing relations between the BBC and Ministers. It was known that the violence of the meeting had embarrassed other sections of the Conservative Party and when John Nott, then the former Minister of Defence, agreed to contribute to BBC Radio's lunchtime programme, *The World This Weekend*, it seemed that tension between the BBC and Ministers had lessened. Any remaining friction was firmly soothed on the evening of 18 May when Ian Trethowan met the all-party media group of MPs and Peers. The meeting, which lasted two hours, was in complete contrast to what had gone before. The Director-General spoke for about fifteen minutes outlining the problems of reporting the crisis and military operations, and the difficulties of reporting dissent in Britain and of deciding how much to report from Argentina. He described the care the BBC was taking not to endanger the lives of the Task Force. Members questioned him; after the meeting many said they believed the dispute with the BBC was over. Among them was one of those who had most strongly criticized the Corporation, the leading right-winger Nicholas Winterton, MP for Macclesfield, who said: 'I do not think you will hear much further criticism in this place unless there is another example of blatant distortion'.

The BBC had received the heaviest bombardment but it was not alone in attracting criticism. The Independent Broadcasting Authority was also subjected to pressure from the Government, most forcefully after Thames Television's *TV Eye* ran an interview with General Galtieri on 13 May. The two most senior officials, Sir Brian Young, the IBA's Director-General and David Glencross, the Deputy Director, personally vetted the interview before its transmission, after they had been told of the Cabinet's 'deep concern'. After the Cabinet had met on 13 May and had been told of the proposed programme, the Home Secretary, William Whitelaw, conveyed the Prime Minister's views to Sir Brian by telephone. Programme chiefs at Thames were called to the IBA's headquarters for discussions and were told that, after the criticism expressed by Conservative backbenchers with regard to *Panorama*, Ministers were now nervous. The IBA then watched the interview, transmitted by satellite, and approved most of it for transmission.

Arguments over *Panorama, Newsnight* and *TV Eye* are specific examples of the broadcasters' difficulties in reconciling free enquiry with 'patriotism'. Underlying these particular episodes, however, was a general feeling of unhappiness on the part of the broadcasters' critics. It centred on three issues: the use of Argentine film, the employment of retired military officers as pundits, and language.

Both the BBC and ITN were criticized for using too much Argentinian film. When we interviewed them, we found that Conservative critics of the news coverage did not distinguish between Argentine-made film from Argentina or British-made film from Argentina; any film from Argentina was judged inappropriate. It is interesting that the press were not criticized on those grounds, even those jingoistic journalists who reported from Argentina. The irritant was, specifically, film either by or from within the enemy camp.

From a professional point of view, the broadcasting organizations saw such coverage as an important and integral part of their story. In their eyes and, as our survey returns suggest, in those of the public, it would have been a dereliction of journalists' duty to fail to report the situation in Buenos Aires. To have wholly relied on Government information and official film, would have produced news bulletins that were no more than five minutes long. Bulletins can always be 'stretched', but the quality of information would have been damaged and the independence of the broadcasting organizations undermined. Without reports from Argentina the account of the conflict would have been one-dimensional; equally important, it would have neglected all diplomatic moves undertaken in the

Argentine capital, since for its part, the British Government was reluctant to release such information. A ban on reporting from or about Argentina would have been a massive gap in public information.

Working conditions in Argentina were far from easy for British journalists. In some cases they were downright dangerous. As tension mounted, the broadcasters came under increasing pressure from their organizations in London, for two reasons: first, the domestic condition of the broadcasting organizations and second, Argentina's own apparent success in the information war. The Argentinians certainly broadcast their communiqués much faster than the British did and, though their announcements were at first highly exaggerated, as the war went on they were for the most part accurate.

Though the Government initially claimed that Britain was failing in 'the Communications War', their allegations fuelled antagonism to the broadcasters. Their editors at home were impelled to look at their procedures and operations, and, as a BBC correspondent told us, the journalists and crews in Argentina felt vulnerable:

> Things became difficult with the office back home in London. We were all very well aware of the situation in Britain so we were careful in sourcing material as we always do. There were so many communiqués coming out from Argentina with many claims – for example, that *Hermes* had been sunk - that the London office wanted us to clearly identify the sources of any statements in our despatches. They often requested two confirmations about any communiqués. At one stage we were asked to supply the communiqués and announcements beforehand to London before we incorporated and sent the statement in our pieces. London would then say which we should use. We resisted this.

It is hardly surprising that they objected, for such requests were seen as insulting to the professional integrity of the correspondent on the spot. At one stage there was a meeting of all BBC staff in Buenos Aires, some twenty people, to discuss the deterioration in relations with the home desk. As another correspondent told us: 'There was considerable pressure from London and at times we felt isolated from the London office, as though we were exiles'.

It was pressure in London that led to editors' attempts to control their correspondents abroad but it is difficult to say whether the strain they were under affected the news itself. There are clues in the fact that the BBC did alter part of its general schedule, concerning, for example, the planned live broadcast of the first match of the World Cup, Belgium versus Argentina, relegating it to news reports and highlights.

Some broadcasters maintained that since very little film was being sent from the Task Force their only source was Argentina. News and current affairs editors themselves, however, disagree. Peter

Woon, for example, the editor of BBC news, told us that, had more film been available, news bulletins would have been not different but longer: 'We would still have carried the stuff from Argentina and the United Nations – because it was all part of the story'.

Three types of Argentine film appeared on British television during the conflict: Argentine film from the Falklands; British film shot in Argentina; and American network film from Argentina. David Lloyd, editor of BBC2's *Newsnight,* while agreeing with Woon, told us that, given a wide choice of film, he would have discarded material of poor quality: 'Where you can just about see a Harrier on the end of a lens, from the Falklands. I'd rather have Hanrahan tell me that Port Stanley runway appears to be rather undamaged than I would an Argentinian saying there isn't a pock-mark on it'. Nonetheless, he emphasized that film of mainland Argentina itself would not have been jettisoned.

Newsnight, which used models, rubber dinghies, artists' impressions and maps to illustrate aspects of the war, did so not as a substitute for film but to enhance the explanation and analysis of events. Peter Snow outlined the position to us:

> Satellite pictures can only give you a microcosm. If you are lucky you can get some fighting on that day's events. Normally you would be lucky to have that. You would probably get chaps having tea at San Carlos or an interview with some fellow who was in yesterday's engagement. Today's engangement is about something that happened the other side of the island and the pictures are still on their way back, or the cameraman who was there didn't get the key thing, which was the left flanking movement. You have still got to report that. And this is television; you have still got to illustrate that, and the fact that x planes were shot down and when . . . There probably wasn't a camera pointing at them – you have still got to illustrate and explain that.

Military comment from retired air vice-marshals, generals and admirals attracted criticism from several quarters, including 10 Downing Street. Even in 'normal' times news and current affairs programmes rely heavily on expert commentators; special operations, the World Cup as much as the Falklands war, impose an even greater demand. In this case retired military officials were particularly useful, since they may comment on both military and politically sensitive matters in circumstances where serving officers would have to exercise restraint. The demand for well-informed speculation may have been healthy and normal, as the Defence Committee acknowledged. Nevertheless, that body observed, it deserved to be resisted 'as firmly as the sometimes morbid preoccupation with casualties past, present and future'.[3]

During the crisis, criticism centred on the broadcasting of speculative questions about the British forces' next move. At Question

Time in the Commons, before the fourth emergency debate on the Falklands, Mrs Thatcher expressed her concern that the Task Force's tactics were being discussed in the media and in the House. 'If that concern is expressed here, some of the media may take notice,' she said. 'Everything they say may put someone's life in jeopardy. We all have a responsibility to those on Her Majesty's Fleet.' The Prime Minister was replying to a question from William Benyon, Conservative MP for Buckingham, who had urged her to persuade those 'in the media and in the House' who were discussing Britain's tactical options to 'just shut up'. We asked Bernard Ingham, the Prime Minister's Press Officer, to expand on this:

> Well, if you have a military expert there, maybe only latterly retired from active service (or whatever the peacetime equivalent of active service is), then he will be speculating from a background of knowledge of military tactics and strategy, and very often in these circumstances there is only a limited number of options and, if he rehearses them, then quite clearly he is going to hit upon one that would be chosen from the options, and that was the point of concern, I think.

Ingham's remarks echo those of Admiral Sir Henry Leach, the First Sea Lord:

> If you say to the media 'Now, they could land to the north, or to the east, or to the south, or to the west,' then you have really covered all the options and one of them was almost certain to be the right one. The trouble is you come back to security and endangering your forces. If you allow widespread speculation like that by people who are intelligent and more or less informed on the broad circumstances that confront you, it is inevitable that they will hit on a fairly accurate bit of speculation. It is then a matter of debate as to whether you judge the enemy has thought that through a similar vein or not, but it is open to him to obtain that information because it will emerge in, say, the next day's press and just in case he had not thought it out he then undoubtedly would, and that sort of thing, I believe, is potentially, if not actually, highly prejudicial to the success of the operation, and it certainly occurred over this one.[4]

Although the broadcasters were most vigorously criticized for speculating about battle plans and weaponry, the newspapers did so too. On 3 May, for example, the *Daily Star* had a two-page spread by its defence correspondent, giving probable sites for the troops' assault. On 7 April the *Sun* had an article on 'How Britain can win great battle of the sea' in which the Admiral of Fleet, Lord Hill-Norton, described how he would take back the Falkland Islands. On 30 April the *Daily Mail* had a piece on 'How a Harrier can master a Mirage,' and on 6 May *The Times* had, 'Battle plan when Marines storm ashore', by Vice-Admiral Sir Ian McGeoch. The *Sunday Times* of 11 April had an article discussing where to invade with submarines and the *Observer* examined Britain's battle options. On 2 May the *Mail on Sunday* explained 'This is how we should liberate the Falklands, by a brigadier', and on 4 May the *Sun* carried, 'Inside our killer sub'.

In no case has it been proved that such speculation helped the Argentines; it would be difficult to do so. Captain Middleton of *Hermes* did, however, give one example which particularly concerned him:

> There was a film on television which I would describe as an instructional film in air combat on how to shoot down a Sea Harrier with a Mirage, where the press interviewed a retired officer who had actually been in mock combat with a French Mirage and he was able to give tips on television as to where the Mirage had the edge and where the Sea Harrier had the edge. That is the sort of thing with which we in the ships got most distressed.[5]

Broadcasters from the BBC and ITN have dismissed as nonsense the idea that military pundits could have assisted the Argentines. In the first place, they maintain that any information imparted by such retired officers was in any case publicly available, in *Jane's Fighting Ships*, for example. Second, they point out that before the invasion Britain had been supplying arms to the Argentines and assisting in training. As David Lloyd, editor of *Newsnight,* said to us:

> They were top-drawer pundits – but basically they were there simply to fill out and to help the audience through these fairly difficult terms and strategies. But as for imparting information or great material to the enemy ... the idea that old Menendez wouldn't have known to stay tight in Port Stanley until some former general had said so is absolute nonsense.

David Nicholas, editor of ITN, mentioned that professional jealousies may have ignited some of the criticisms: 'I know that, not as a result of any formal complaint or anything but pure conversation, there was still resentment in certain areas of the military to see a whole new sort of industry of retired senior and military people formed'. Nicholas, who himself wanted to do a story on how much material was already published, certainly 'never felt that anything was actually blown'.

The third ground of complaint was that the language used in broadcast programmes was 'loaded'. In an interview with the London *Standard* on 12 May, Alasdair Milne, Director-General of the BBC said:

> When the crisis began we looked up the BBC-style book which had been used during the Second World War and again during the Suez Crisis. We always spoke of 'the British' then; one reason is that if you start talking about 'our troops' and 'our ships' then it is natural to speak of 'our policy' when you mean the present Government's policy, and then our objectivity would no longer be credible. There would be a risk of our credibility collapsing in our external overseas broadcasting. Credibility is a very tender thing. So 'us' is out.

Bernard Ingham has denied that he suggested a change in the language used by the broadcasters or that this was also the Government's view. He had continued to treat the media, he added, as he had always done in the preceding two-and-a-half years. 'I can assure you,' he said, 'that I was not, to the best of my knowledge, transmitting requests at all to them. I just accepted that we were into a situation which was absolutely abnormal in the sense that we were at war but that the basic relationships had not changed at all'.

The BBC World Service never uses 'we' or 'our' but always 'British'. World Service editors were to some extent amused by the allegations that their domestic colleagues were too even-handed. According to Ken Brazier, the editor of External Services News, being even-handed is the World Service's natural mode of operation. If Hanrahan or Fox, for example, used 'us' or 'we' in voice reports, the World Service left it in. The reporters were clearly with and identifying with the Forces, and to do otherwise would, according to Brazier, make the despatch sound stilted. Such despatches were in any case used only in newsreel programmes, *Twenty Four Hours* or *The World Today*. News bulletins are all rewritten.

Our account of the Government's criticism, and what provoked it, raises a number of questions. It is, for instance, interesting that the BBC was criticized so much more forcefully than ITN was and that in times of crisis the BBC is, it seems, expected to behave otherwise than in 'normal' times. The explanation that the BBC's coverage of the war gave the Tory right-wingers an excuse to indulge in bashing the BBC is too superficial, as is the view that the general disorganization of the Ministry of Defence's information policy provoked over-reaction or an hysterical response to what coverage there was. There may be something in these explanations; the timing of the attacks on the Corporation, and of their subsequent withdrawal, suggests something more.

The Government was, clearly, worried about its own position. The trouble began when Peter Snow suggested on *Newsnight* that perhaps the Ministry of Defence was not always telling the truth. The *Panorama* film caused an even bigger row; here two Conservative MPs appeared – but only appeared – to question the Government's policy. The subsequent criticism of the BBC indicated that Ministers appreciated that there could be no questioning of its policy on the Falklands issue. All news could, too easily, become bad news. Even victories would bring casualties. The Government knew that the campaign might go badly – they hoped that, even though soldiers' bodies might pile up on the beaches, the country would stand solid, unwavering, accepting the cost as the price of a policy that was politically legitimate. The hint of criticism sparked off a panic.

The offending *Newsnight* programme went out on 2 May. John Page then complained to the Press Association and Fleet Street picked up the story. On 6 May Mrs Thatcher attacked newsmen for their 'unpatriotic' coverage. The 10 May brought the *Panorama* programme, a Commons motion attacking the BBC and on the following day further remarks by Mrs Thatcher in answer to questions. The furore reached a climax on 12 May, when Alasdair Milne and George Howard attended the Conservative Backbench Media Committee. The attacks had significantly lessened by 18 May.

It is important to note that, until the end of April, the campaign was still going well. Though the American Secretary of State, Alexander Haig, continued his peace-seeking 'shuttle diplomacy', his mission was faltering. The Task Force had been successfully assembled, the two-hundred mile Total Exclusion Zone established. On 25 April the Royal Marines had retaken South Georgia and the Task Force Commander, Admiral Woodward, had declared his belief that the battle was going to be a walkover. On 30 April the USA formally announced its support for Britain. Britain had by then persuaded its fellow European Community members to boycott Argentina; the United Nations resolution, Number 502, condemning Argentina's invasion, had been passed at the beginning of the month.

By the end of April, then, the Government had reason to feel optimistic, if not over-confident. At the beginning of May matters changed; the mood was more one of nervous expectation. The worst disasters had not yet occurred – the operation at Bluff Cove was to take place on 8 June – but Ministers and the public knew that the campaign was neither easy nor the outcome predictable. On 1 May Harriers and a Vulcan attacked Port Stanley; three Harriers were lost but the runway was not destroyed. On 2 May the Argentine ship, *General Belgrano*, was sunk and more than 300 sailors killed. On the evening of 2 May the *Newsnight* programme was broadcast. On 4 May the first British vessel, the *Sheffield*, was hit by an Exocet missile and sank. The conduct and the development of the campaign were now being increasingly questioned. On 6 May more Harriers were lost; on 10 May the *Panorama* programme was broadcast.

The Government and its supporters were nervous but sure that the conflict must be sustained to the end; criticism of the BBC was forced, unripe, to the surface. If current affairs programmes led the public to believe that policy was awry, the news – any news – might be misinterpreted. It was, indeed, current affairs programming, not news, which attracted the complaints. Bernard Ingham confirmed this view to us:

I think that there were two concerns, as I recall them. The first one was that, apparently, British veracity was equated with Argentinian veracity, the same kind, as doubt was placed upon it. British assertions and statements were being viewed in exactly the same light as Argentinian, that is the first point. I think that was the *Newsnight* point predominantly. And I think, so far as the *Panorama* programme was concerned, my recollection is that this programme was constructed in such a way that virtually every dissident was given an opportunity to have his say, and this was presumably balanced by having Cecil Parkinson for ten minutes at the end.

The BBC's standing, history and reputation, including its reputation abroad, made it more vulnerable to attack than ITN. John Page, for example, admitted that, though he had asserted that ITN was less 'biased' than the BBC, he rarely watched ITN anyway. 'On the whole I get made less angry . . . by ITN than BBC though to be fair I am a very big listener to Radio 4. I listen to BBC radio whilst getting up, in the car, at lunchtime and going home at night. I get bored by the advertisements on independent radio and television.' According to Page, the fact that the independent service relies on advertising to finance it makes it less ready to ignore public opinion than the BBC. Alan Clark, on the other hand, believed that both the BBC and ITN should behave differently at times of crises. Months later, when asked how the BBC should behave, he said:

I think it's objectionable, when Servicemen are being killed in a conflict with another power, to cast doubts on the rightness of the conflict by innuendo. I am not saying why it is wrong or why the Continental Shelf attaches the Falklands to us, or whether the civilising influence of the police and educational system of Argentina is in the long run in the interest of the Falkland Islands, however grotesque that is. But you cannot say these things, so the BBC had to just peck away at it by being snide in the commentary, or by tending to be anti-nationalist rather than pro-enemy, because to be pro-enemy was so ludicrous that it would not have washed. But if you ask me how you control it, I could not make the suggestion even, because it has to be a matter for the good taste and internal regulations of the corporations concerned.

Bernard Ingham, after the Falklands had ended, took a middle line:

The *Panorama* one is the familiar question of balance in a programme. I think the *Newsnight* programme was the manifestation of a concern at that time that we were being bracketed, apparently, with the Argentines, whose reliability had been demonstrated for all to see. Indeed, speaking from recollection, if you read the Prime Minister's answers, I don't think anybody was suggesting that people suspend normal journalistic practices.

From a military perspective, the ideal relationship between television and government is one of continuous dialogue, so that when a crisis arises both sides are prepared. Brigadier Ramsbotham:

> I think that provided that television realizes it has got a responsibility to the public of its own nation and that they should look at what they are doing in view of that, then I am perfectly happy and I think that if we are going to live in a democracy, we must live with that.

Ramsbotham, however, would not countenance attacks on the military:

> I think it would go too far if they started mounting a campaign against the military forces and the military forces' competence . . . then I would take exception. But the Government decision, especially when there is a vociferous opposition on the other side, I think that up until the moment that hostilities are joined that people should have the right to question it.

Once hostilities are joined, however, Ramsbotham believes:

> . . . ground rules change . . . Then I believe that as a television company you have got to think through your programmes very much more carefully.

Even this 'basic relationship', as Ingham calls it, is seen by some broadcasters and journalists as unsatisfactory. In recent years, there has been growing opposition to the lobby system and routine 'off-the-record' briefings. It is increasingly believed that in Britain the media are too malleable, compared to their American counterparts, and that as a result the Government believes it can, if necessary, lean on the press and broadcasters.

In the words of Alan Protheroe, Assistant Director-General of the BBC:

> If the White House or the Pentagon says to the networks in the USA, 'This is what we want to do,' they get a very short sharp Anglo-Saxon-type answer. They get the same thing from us. But whereas the Americans in the White House or Pentagon sit back and say: 'OK, sure,' and leave it there, somehow in this country Government has a feeling of outrage: 'How dare you', etc.

The point is one of the utmost generality. It is a description of attitude, rather than a recital of fact, but we believe it to be valuable. It explains, for instance, not just the Government's behaviour towards the BBC's domestic broadcasting service but also its treatment, perhaps more curious still, of the External Services, to which we will now turn.

The BBC's External Services are financed directly by the Government, by an annual grant-in-aid on the Foreign and Commonwealth Office vote. In 1982 its cost was approximately £63 million; each year the BBC battles with the Government, always looking for economies, over the size of the External Services grant. The Service broadcasts in 37 languages, reaching some 75 million listeners, who receive a mixture of local services and round the clock broadcasting in English. Seventeen news bulletins are broadcast on the World Service in every twenty-four hour period.

In 1981 the Government had cut the External Services budget by some £2 million, a sum originally intended to be much higher, but which was reduced after considerable public and parliamentary pressure. Even so, the Services had been obliged to make extensive economies, reducing broadcasts in some languages and deleting others altogether. The attitude of the Foreign Office to the Services during the Falklands war was therefore particularly interesting.

External Services programmes can be received in both Argentina and the Falklands. Indeed, for more than thirty years the BBC had broadcast on Sunday evenings a regular 35-minute record request programme to the Islands, *Calling the Falklands*. On 4 April, when the crisis broke this was replaced by a news and current affairs programme. The BBC also proposed that local services to the Falklands be increased – the Foreign Office approves the allocation of time to each country and in each language – and, accordingly, two extra broadcasts were added, on Tuesdays and Thursdays.

The Foreign Office was to make full use of the External Services during the crisis. From 5 April, the day the Task Force sailed, each news bulletin included a special message to British citizens in Argentina. The first advised Britons to return home: 'British citizens who have no pressing need to remain in Argentina are advised to consider leaving the country by normal commercial means. Further information from the British interests section of the Swiss embassy in Buenos Aires.' The Red Cross, the Foreign Secretary and the Archbishop of Canterbury also broadcast messages and the Governor of the Falklands, Rex Hunt, used the Service to announce that he would return to the Islands as soon as he was permitted to do so.

The BBC's Spanish language services, together with the Italian and Maltese, had suffered the most severe reductions in the previous year's cost-cutting exercise. Now the Foreign Office gave its blessing to a significant addition to the BBC's transmissions in Spanish to South American countries. These were increased from four to five hours each night, the extra hour featuring interviews with correspondents in Britain and Latin America, reviews of the British and foreign press and telephone interviews with journalists at Argentine radio stations.

On 26 April the BBC replaced its thrice weekly broadcast to the Falklands with a daily transmission on short wave. Each programme, lasting forty minutes, included brief surveys of world news and the local and international press, with special messages for the Islanders. According to the BBC, people living in remote areas on the Islands recorded these programmes, to pass them to neighbours who were out of range. Every evening *Calling the Falklands* broadcast the voice of an Islander who had left the Falklands after the invasion.

Transmissions were boosted; instead of sending them direct from London, the BBC used its relay station on Ascension Island. From this station, too, the World Service and the British Forces Broadcasting Service together broadcast, three times a week, a request programme for those with the Task Force. This was apparently greatly appreciated, not just by the troops but also by their families at home.

By the end of April the Argentine government had become increasingly worried about the effects of broadcasts from foreign stations in general and the World Service in particular. They were infuriated when the BBC, which was believed to have a quarter of a million listeners in Argentina alone, was mentioned in a cartoon in *La Prensa,* showing a shady-looking character murmuring to another: 'Pst! Pst! What's the BBC saying?'

On 3 May Argentina jammed World Service broadcasts in Spanish to Latin America by interrupting three of the six frequencies carrying the Spanish service with a fast and continuous dialling tone. Douglas Muggeridge, the Managing Director of the External Services at the BBC, described this as clearly indicating that 'our objective and impartial coverage of the crisis is reaching a larger audience in Argentina than the Argentinian authorities would like'. The jamming began five hours after the cruiser *General Belgrano* was torpedoed but before the news was transmitted. As Argentine interference did not affect World Service broadcasts in English, the British Government continued to use *Calling the Falklands* to announce losses and successes. In reply to the jamming, however, the Government authorized a further half-hour increase in the Spanish language broadcasts from 7 May. The BBC also increased the number of frequencies used by the Spanish service from six to ten. On 8 May Rex Hunt broadcast a message from the Queen to the Falklanders themselves.

On 9 May the Ministry of Defence made an unexpected and, to many, disturbing move. The BBC was instructed to release Transmitter 302, one of four on Ascension Island, for use between 0815–0945 and 2300–0200 GMT, until further notice. The Government christened its new station Radio Atlantico del Sur (RADS); it was to be used for direct broadcasts in Spanish to Argentine troops in the Falklands. To establish the station, the Government invoked article 19 of the Licence and Agreement of 2 April 1981, which during times of crisis or emergency empowers the Government to use BBC facilities, including any or all of its transmitters, as it considers necessary in the public interest. RADS began broadcasting on the night of 9 May; it continued until 16 June.

According to the Ministry of Defence, its intention was to counter

Argentine propaganda, by making Argentine forces in the Falklands aware of events in the South Atlantic and of world news and opinion on the issue. The programmes consisted of news broadcasts, interspersed with popular music. Reminded that other stations broadcast to the Falklands, the Ministry of Defence asserted that there was 'a gap to be filled', since those broadcasts were of a general nature only and aimed at a wide audience rather than a specific target. The Defence Secretary, John Nott, was responsible to Parliament for the running of the station. The Government and, indeed, the BBC itself claimed that no BBC staff were involved, although we can assume that BBC technicians continued to operate the transmitters. Nor did the Ministry of Defence use a recognized BBC waveband, so that listeners tuning to the World Service would not accidentally find themselves listening to British Government announcements in Spanish.

The BBC gave no open, official evidence of its attitude to this operation. Reaction was left to the broadcasting unions, whose members were outraged. Representatives of the Association of Broadcasting Staffs and the National Union of Journalists protested vigorously to the Prime Minister. They wished, they said, to object in the strongest terms to the 'unacceptable requisition' of the BBC transmitter. 'Such action without a formal state of war existing is a gross interference in the independence and editorial freedom of the BBC which is respected throughout the world.'

The situation was certainly unusual. It was the first time in the BBC's history that the Government had felt the need to invoke such powers. The only precedent – and that was hardly comparable – had occurred at the time of Suez, when the Government had taken over a commercial radio station based in Cyprus, Radio Sharq al-Adna, which it operated for seven months in an attempt to counter propaganda from Radio Cairo.

According to Alan Protheroe, Assistant Director-General of the BBC, the Corporation made it quite clear that it wished to dissociate itself from the Government's action, which might gravely damage the credibility of the BBC's own services. In Protheroe's words: 'A society that stands up and says, "We have taken over these transmitters," is in effect saying "We are going to run a propaganda station," and you are immediately identifying that and therefore diminishing its effectiveness.' In evidence to the Defence Committee, Sir Frank Cooper himself cast doubt on the usefulness of the Ministry of Defence's operation:

We set up Radio Atlantico del Sur in a very short period of time with a single aim, which was to try and reduce the will of the Argentinian forces in the Falkland

Islands. That was its sole purpose and it was set up very quickly. It began operating very quickly. I think that our normal news media in relation to South America as a whole were very much more effective than anything we could have done. The BBC overseas radio news has an enormous reputation. There is no doubt about that, and I think without any shadow of doubt it was that which carried conviction in South America to a degree which I just do not believe anything we tried to set up to indulge in a psychological war in South America could possibly have done, and it was very much accepted. One of the lessons I would certainly take away with me is what a very powerful instrument it is, much more powerful than I think any of us ever supposed.[6]

From what we have heard and the transcripts we have seen, it appears that the Government's station carried a mixture of factual reporting, pop music and items intended to demoralize Argentine troops. The first programme began with a jingle and the introduction of three presenters, 'Francisco', 'Jose Miquel', and 'Marianne Flores'. (It was said by experts that they 'spoke the wrong sort of Spanish'.) After a selection of news, sporting news, gossip and music, an 'expert' gave a 'military review', with the latest Argentine casualty figures and a quotation from General Galtieri, who had said on Mexican television: 'If necessary, there will be 40,000 casualties.' There were such items as the activities of the SAS, whose 'clandestine attacks were noted for their fierceness'. The news included announcements of, for instance, the birthday of the Pope and the pregnancy of the Princess of Wales, followed by record requests, including one from a mother in Buenos Aires for her son, Ernesto, and another for the World Cup anthem from the 'Perez brothers'. The Ministry of Defence did not explain how these requests had reached its producers in Ascension. Argentina replied to the Ministry of Defence's efforts, rather, by jamming the BBC's service in English as well as in Spanish. By the end of May, *Calling the Falklands* was jammed; the BBC's response was to increase from two to four the number of frequencies carrying the programme.

Relations between the Ministry of Defence and the External Services became, understandably, less than harmonious as the campaign lasted. Not only had the Ministry commandeered an entire transmitter for what most who heard it agreed was an absurd propaganda programme, but there was also friction over the effects of the Ministry's domestic 'information policy'. It came to a head in late May.

Both the Argentine and the British forces could pick up the World Service broadcasts. This was important to the British, not simply to sustain morale but also to keep abreast of political developments at home and even, from time to time, of military manoeuvres in other areas of the conflict. The journalists with the Task Force also listened to such broadcasts and their frustration was increased on hearing reports of incidents which they themselves were prevented from sending home.

On several occasions Ministry of Defence officials and Royal Naval officers delayed or censored reports, of which full details were to be given only hours later by BBC World Service correspondents briefed by the Ministry of Defence or via statements from Whitehall. McIlroy, who was particularly incensed, gave us three examples. First, the sinking of the *General Belgrano*. Although correspondents on the *Invincible* had full details of the incident, they were forbidden to send despatches. Two and a half hours later, a report was broadcast on the World Service. Second, on the day *Sheffield* was hit by an Exocet missile, correspondents were told that Northwood had ordered a complete news blackout. An hour later they heard the BBC account of a press conference, held at the Ministry of Defence, to discuss the attack. Third, the loss of the two Sea Harriers in an accident on sorties from *Invincible* was known to correspondents as soon as the planes failed to return. They were told not to refer to these losses in their despatches, since the Navy did not want the enemy to know that the number of Harriers in the war zone had been reduced. That same evening the BBC World Service not only carried an account of the losses but also references to the exact number of Harriers remaining with the Task Force and to the reinforcements that were expected. It appeared that, when doubtful, naval commanders would await the broadcast of reports on the World Service before the corespondents were even permitted to send their reports to London for clearance.

The journalists' bitterness reached its apex on 30 May, over what became known as 'the Goose Green incident'. On that day the Sunday newspapers published a pooled despatch, over Max Hastings' name, attacking the BBC and in particular, its defence correspondent, Andrew Walker, who had correctly predicted that Goose Green was about to be hit by the Parachute Regiment. According to Hastings, there was intense bitterness all over the San Carlos beachhead at what he described as 'the extraordinary indiscretions by the Ministry of Defence and the World Service'. He quoted one soldier as saying, 'How many enemies are we supposed to be fighting? If the Paras lose a lot of people, you know who told them what we were going to do.'

A week later, on 6 June, in a pooled despatch in the *Sunday Times*, John Shirley, furious at the BBC's report of the imminent attack on Goose Green, reported that Lieutenant Colonel H. Jones, had told correspondents before he was killed that when he got home he would sue the BBC for manslaughter. It was clear, Shirley said, that after the BBC report, considerable Argentinian reinforcements were sent to Goose Green from Fitzroy, near Port Stanley. The BBC's announcement, which had angered all the British forces, caused a change of plan. They had originally intended to knock out the airstrips at Goose Green and Darwin and then withdraw. Now, since the Argentines had increased their forces, a major assault would be mounted.

Robert Fox, himself from the BBC, and other journalists with the Paratroopers at Goose Green, stated then and have since reaffirmed that the remark made by Colonel Jones was not wholly serious. In a report from the Falklands, Fox said that: 'At no time did Colonel Jones, a man I came to regard as a close friend, utter in my presence any kind of threat to take action against the BBC.' The remark, according to Fox, was ironic. What the Colonel had said was: 'I want to sue Nott, the Ministry, the PM if anyone is killed.' The mistake Fox made, by his own admission, was to tell the story to John Shirley, when he arrived in Goose Green two days later. In the light of Hastings' and Shirley's attack, the BBC itself issued a statement about the affair:

> The time scale alleged by the report is inconsistent with the facts. We also know that there had been a degree of reinforcement by the Argentines from the moment it became clear that we were going to constitute a beach-head at Port San Carlos. Two London newspapers, in fact, reported the taking of Goose Green two days before the assault began. The BBC has broadcast no information which has not been readily available to other broadcasters and other journalistic organizations from official sources in London, including the MoD. Naturally, too, the BBC is acutely aware of the dangers of speculation.

Furthermore, the Ministry of Defence has since admitted that officials announced on 28 May that Goose Green had fallen, the day after the alleged report on the World Service but also the day before the actual capture of the place.

The Defence Committee was unable to establish the source of the BBC's report. Ken Brazier, the editor of BBC External Services News, refused to disclose it. Moreover, he has indicated to us that there was no doubt that the story should be broadcast:

> [The British forces] had landed at San Carlos Bay . . . they had hung around there for some days. There had been a fair amount of speculation that they would go to Stanley either via Goose Green or across the mountains or both . . . there was little else that they could do, a bloody child could work that out . . . it was on the same day that Mrs Thatcher finally announced it in the House that they had set off for Goose Green, San Carlos Bay, that we canned a report that there had been a clash between . . . we actually did mention 2 Para, I think . . . and Argentinian troops five miles from Goose Green or Darwin. And it was that report, which we

picked up from a very reliable but unattributable source in London in common with our domestic colleagues and a number of other media organizations as well, we used, after it had been broadcast domestically. And since we reckoned that, if the Argentines had actually been involved in this clash, they could hardly not know about it, therefore we could hardly be telling them something that was news to them or of any value to them. That's all it was.

The report of the Defence Committee broadly supports this account, 'Set in the context of a general expectation of a move on Darwin and Goose Green, the broadcast of the story could have been no more than final confirmation of an already expected attack.'[7] For its part, the Ministry of Defence has subsequently conceded that the move on Goose Green and Darwin was most likely to be the next objective, one obvious to any armchair expert. Indeed, Neville Taylor himself has pointed out that for several days before the broadcast newspaper articles and television programmes had discussed the likelihood of a move on Goose Green.

The only suggestions that the broadcast might have influenced the outcome appeared in Major General Sir Jeremy Moore's evidence to the Committee:

> Some of the Argentinian prisoners did say, and whether the cause was what we might fear or not I do not know, but they did say that they had been reinforced in Darwin/Goose Green after that announcement. I do not know and I have no evidence to support a contention that the one was the result of the other but the timing was such that certainly many of my people thought it was.[8]

Did Major General Moore believe the broadcasts had been damaging to the British effort?

> I do not know. They could have been. I do not know whether that was the result of the broadcast or not. I just know that in timing it certainly took place very close to the time that 2 Para's assault on Darwin/Goose Green took place and it was said by the Argentinians to be after they had heard the broadcast.[9]

In its own written evidence to the Defence Committee, the BBC observed that:

> The report was true, but perhaps premature in the sense that it alarmed troops in a highly sensitive situation, although it was not operationally damaging. The incident underlines the need for very close coordination between those in charge of operations in the field, and public relations staff in London.[10]

It is still unclear as to why the Ministry of Defence announced the fall of Goose Green before it took place. The Defence Committee explained it in a useful phrase: the fog of war. It is, however, helpful to look more closely at the sequence of events.

On Monday 24 May, the Ministry of Defence announced that the bridgehead had been firmly established and that British forces were consolidating their position and patrolling the surrounding area. On the same day, newspapers carried speculative reports on the move to Goose Green. According to the *Daily Mail*: 'There were reports last night that Goose Green had been taken.' The *Daily Telegraph* had a short article on unconfirmed reports that the place had been taken. Their headline was: 'Goose Green Seized'. On 26 May John Nott told the Commons that 'Our forces on the ground are now poised to begin their thrust on Port Stanley', and on the same day there was further speculation in the press that Goose Green and Darwin were to be taken.[11]

In Question Time on 27 May, the Prime Minister said that: 'The House would not expect me to go into details about the operations in progress, but our forces on the ground are now moving from the bridge-head.' The Ministry of Defence issued an announcement referring to the Prime Minister's statement and, in answer to a question about land action, a spokesman said: 'All I can say is that they are not hanging around.' The newspapers carried yet more speculation, the *Guardian* and the *Daily Mail* citing 'unofficial sources' which had spoken of advances on Goose Green. The *Daily Express* had the headline 'Goose Green is taken'.[12]

On the same day, 27 May, the BBC's midday programme, *The World at One* quoted sources as saying that the 2nd Parachute Regiment had moved south towards the Darwin area. It was this report that was later repeated on the World Service.

At 1.30 on the afternoon of the following day, the Ministry of Defence issued a press statement: 'The first thing I would say to you is that offensive land operations are at this moment in progress in the Falkland Islands. You will understand that I cannot at this stage go further . . .' At 21.45, the Ministry announced that the 2nd Parachute Regiment had taken Darwin and Goose Green.[13] The statement read as follows:

> We have just learnt that the Second Battalion of the Parachute Regiment has taken Darwin and Goose Green. The Argentine forces suffered casualties and a number of prisoners have been taken. Inital reports are that British casualties are light and the next of kin are being informed. No additional information is yet available, either in Whitehall or in the Service Information Centre. Please do not ring them. As soon as we have any information, a further announcement will be made.

It was not until 29 May, however, that first Darwin and then Goose Green were taken.

The episode remains extraordinary but it is to some extent explicable in the light of the pressure for information that had accumulated over the preceding days. The Goose Green manoeuvre, like that at Bluff Cove, took place in an atmosphere of intense speculation at home. It was seen as a key moment; the Ministry was concerned. Ian McDonald, Ministry of Defence Deputy Chief of Public Relations at that time, has since said of the Goose Green affair:

> There was tremendous public interest; there was enormous speculation. There were many people saying, 'Unless you say something you will only encourage speculation.' At that time, I can well remember, in a question-and-answer session I was asked, would the men be advancing from the Bay, and the answer I gave was that they would not be hanging around, which struck me as good military sense without giving anything away and I think was very much in line, I am pleased to say, with what the PM said later that day in the House.[14]

McDonald continued:

> We had to reassure people that something was happening without being able to tell them precisely what. But if I could go on to the second point. The speculation was so intense, particularly on Goose Green, that for once we relied on a telephone conversation between Northwood and the Task Force to tell the world that Goose Green had been taken. We discovered subsequently – and this was purely a mistake in the communications from the Task Force to Northwood – that Goose Green had been surrounded but not taken and it was under the kind of pressure to get news that we deviated from the normal practice of waiting – and that was the hardest part of the job – to ensure that you got confirmation. We departed from that this time in order to get the news out quickly, and I am afraid we got it out too quickly. I say that just to emphasize the importance of getting written confirmation before we were able to make statements.[15]

Christopher Wain, the defence correspondent for BBC television, believes that McDonald had other reasons for issuing the statement that Goose Green had been captured. On 28 May Wain himself heard from sources in the Ministry of Defence that something had gone wrong at Goose Green. (He discovered only later that this was the death of Colonel Jones.) Wain telephoned McDonald for more information. McDonald refused to provide it, or to deny the rumours, to which Wain then referred in the BBC's 9 o'clock news bulletin. The Ministry's announcement at 9.45, in time for the *News at Ten*, was, Wain believes, McDonald's attempt to refute the suggestion that there had been trouble. Better to announce the taking of Goose Green.

A fortnight later the conflict was over. On the night of 14 June, after the surrender at Port Stanley, Argentina ceased to jam Spanish-language broadcasts to South America and BBC World Service Broadcasts in English. Two days later the Ministry of Defence closed down Radio Atlantico del Sur and returned the transmitter to the BBC.

Despite the intermittent friction between the Government and the External Services, in particular over the establishment of RADS and the Goose Green episode, on the whole their relationship improved during the Falklands crisis. The BBC's overseas service had demonstrated its special usefulness; as the *Daily Telegraph* put it in a leader published on 29 April:

> Is there not . . . a clear moral from the Falklands crisis for the BBC's Foreign Office budget controllers? It is that no one can predict where trouble will spring up, and no one can predict when the BBC will be most needed. Once closed down, a service is not rapidly reopened. Nor is a reputation for dependability made overnight. The trust which the BBC now receives in an enemy country is based on years of political independence and speaking the uncomfortable truth. With its prim, old-fashioned clarity, with its splendid marches, 'Imperial Echoes' and 'The Voice of London', it may seem a relic of greater days, a service needing to be trimmed down to size. It should be left alone.

The honeymoon lasted a little time. It was given added length by a report in the *Yorkshire Post*, published on 6 July, from a correspondent in Buenos Aires, Harold Emert. His source was the Argentine Military Chaplain, Padre Salvador Santore, who had described how General Menendez had defied his government's orders not to surrender, after hearing reports from Uruguay, Chile – and the BBC. The fact that Argentine troops preferred to listen to the BBC, because their own programmes were so suspect, and that their government found it necessary to jam British broadcasts, all reminded the British Government of the reputation for accuracy and impartiality which the External Services enjoyed. At such times, too, it found itself in even deeper waters than normal. This, however, was not new. As Mr Alport (the Assistant Postmaster General, with responsibility for broadcasting, and Conservative MP for Colchester) had put it to the House of Commons at the time of Suez: 'The BBC were doomed to sail eternally between what must appear to them to be the Scylla and Charybdis of Government and Opposition and, in stormy weather, the difficulties of setting their course were greatly increased'.[16]

For some months less was heard of future economies. Members of Parliament pressed for sufficient restoration of the External Services' budget to allow the resumption of broadcasting in Italian and Spanish. It seemed that, as with the Navy, the BBC's performance in the Falklands war had subdued the Treasury's appetite.

But some lessons go unlearnt forever. Only two years later, the Foreign Office was reiterating its view that one of the primary duties of the External Services was to secure British objectives abroad and, once more, the Services suffered cuts in their budget. For a time it had seemed that during the Falklands crisis the External Services, unlike their domestic counterpart, had found some friends

– but only temporarily. Broadcasters, journalists, politicians, officials and officers may, from time to time, recognize that they share the same purpose but, understandably, too many of their assumptions are irreconcilable.

Notes

1. *The Times*, November 15 1956, p. 4.
2. BBC TV *Newsnight*, 2 May 1982.
3. House of Commons First Report from the Defence Committee, Session 1982–3. HMSO Dec 1982, Vol. 1, p. xlix, para. III.
4. Op. cit. Vol. 2, Q. 1425, p. 349.
5. Op. cit. Vol. 2, Q. 1178, p. 294.
6. Op. cit. Vol. 2, Q. 116, p. 294.
7. Op. cit. Vol. 2, p. xxxiv, para. 77.
8. Op. cit. Vol. 2, Q. 1184, p. 296.
9. Op. cit. Vol. 2, Q. 1187, p. 296.
10. Op. cit. Vol. 2, p. 43.
11. Op. cit. Vol. 2, p. 426.
12. Op. cit. Vol. 2, p. 427, para 4.
13. Op. cit. Vol. 2, p. 427
14. Op. cit. vol. 2, Q. 1802, p. 403.
15. Op. cit. vol. 2, Q. 1803, p. 403.
16. *The Times*, November 15 1956, p. 4.

11

Content analysis

In previous sections we examined the way in which the journalists gathered the news, the arrangements for its transmission and the constraints on the release of information. This chapter focuses upon the news that was actually televised during the war and analyses the images on offer: the outcome of the whole production process.

The period analysed was from Friday 2 April 1982, the day of the Argentine invasion of the Falklands, to 15 June, the day the Argentine forces surrendered (14 June being the day the ceasefire was agreed). Some film material from the Falklands arrived in Britain after the surrender. This was shown in the weeks after 15 June, but was omitted from our analysis. We did so on the grounds that material arriving after the surrender was perhaps viewed differently by the public than film seen whilst the war was in progress.

The programmes analysed were the flagship weekday news bulletins of the *Nine O'clock News* of the BBC and the *News at Ten* of ITN. For the weekends when there was no BBC *Nine O'clock News* or ITN *News at Ten*, the main late evening bulletins were used. On the few occasions when we were unable to obtain the relevant bulletins, earlier evening bulletins were analysed instead. In total 146 news bulletins were analysed, 74 from the BBC and 72 from ITN. (On two days, Saturday 1 May and Sunday 2 May, it proved impossible to obtain the ITN bulletins.) A total of 74.5 hours of news bulletins were examined. Each bulletin, not surprisingly given the importance of the conflict, included material on the Falklands. The two and half months of the conflict were divided into five periods (Table 11.1).

Table 11.1   *Number and average length of bulletins within specific periods*

Period	Number*	Average length (mins) BBC	Average length (mins) ITN	Average length (mins) Total
2 April – 4 April	6	15.68	26.31	20.99
5 April – 24 April	40	24.26	29.01	26.64
25 April – 30 April	12	27.06	41.34	34.23
1 May – 20 May	38	25.29	37.88	31.42
21 May – 15 June	50	30.71	35.76	33.19
Total	146	26.80	34.65	30.67

*Both channels

The first period, 2–4 April, included the Argentinian invasion, the debate in the House of Commons and the preparation of the Task Force. The second period, 5–24 April, included the sailing of the Task Force, the Haig shuttle attempting a peace settlement and the UN and EEC resolutions in favour of Britain. It ended just before the capture of South Georgia. The third period, 25–30 April, included the recapture of South Georgia and ended with the US openly siding with Britain. The fourth period, 1–20 May, began with the bombing of Port Stanley runway (the first real action on the Falklands themselves) and included the sinking of the *Belgrano* and the shooting down of Argentinian planes. It ended with the collapse of any hopes for a peaceful settlement. The fifth and last period, 21 May–15 June, began with the landings at San Carlos and included the destruction of HMS *Ardent, Antelope* and other ships, the capture of Goose Green, the advance of the British troops, the Bluff Cove 'disaster', the ceasefire and the surrender of the Argentinian forces, (a more detailed chronological list of events is given in Appendix II).

In Chapter 8 we looked at the technical reasons for the lack of immediate pictures from the Falklands. But what effect did the lack of pictures have on the composition of the news bulletins?

Perhaps the most controversial aspect of the news was the absence of violent film 'action'. Less than 6 percent of the two and a half months analysed was of film from the Task Force after it left Britain and even then not all of it was violent action. The visual expectations set by the detailed coverage of the war in Vietnam meant that pictures of war in the Falklands were bound to lead to disappointment. Television in this case did not show us 'how it was' nor were we able to 'see for ourselves' the combat and clash of war. One consequence was that greater attention than might have been expected was given to the verbal text of reports and comment on reports. The attacks made by the Government on the broadcasters were over words not pictures. The pictures which were memorable – those from Bluff Cove – were shown only after the ceasefire and surrender: during the war it was the voice report of Brian Hanrahan that struck the public mind most forcibly, when in describing a Harrier raid he said, 'I counted them all out and I counted them all back'. Although basically a radio war and not a television one, nevertheless some pictures were transmitted during the course of the campaign.

The exact composition of the news programmes can be seen from Table 11.2. What is clear is that the greatest amount of time was given to studio-based reports. Nearly a quarter of the total coverage however consisted of interviews with politicians, parliamentary reports, statements and filmed reports from Britain. Included in this category is home news from abroad, such as the visits of British politicians to the EEC. Next in rank, taking up almost 16 percent of all coverage, was, first, British film from Argentina (9 percent) and then, diplomatic film including Alexander Haig's shuttle and reports of EEC reaction (7 percent). Whilst Table 11.2 shows that the audience was by no means starved of visual images, nevertheless the nature of the pictures with their absence of dramatic action was not the type that on past coverage of war the public had come to expect. After all the Falklands was the biggest military operation under-taken by Britain since Suez and the largest naval operation since the Second World War. What the audience was treated to were mun-dane everyday pictures of the type associated with 'normal' news – reports of parliamentary statements or pictures of the Foreign Secretary's visit to Brussels. Interesting but hardly the stuff of history. Nothing could have seemed more of an anticlimax, especially following the dramatic pictures of the battle fleet's departure.

If the public expected to be carried to war through the lenses of BBC and ITN they were to be sadly disappointed. What was missing from the Falklands was a sense of seeing things as they happen which the simultaneity of film and voice facilitates. This absence in the Falklands meant that we were all too clearly not there.

The shock to the professional expectations of the broadcasters led to a creativity of presentation – drawings, sketches and models were used to accompany the text to overcome the visual problem caused by the lack of pictures. At times a picture of a reporter was the only illustration to what was, in effect, a radio report. This latter tech-nique is not that unusual, especially on a breaking story, but it is less usual on a long running one.

Despite the fact that pictures help to give a sense of immediacy and create the feeling of being there, they do not necessarily pro-vide evidence of what is said in the text. Usually the pictures are complementary to the verbal text, adding a visual variation on the story. The absence of such variation in the coverage of the Falk-lands meant that the words themselves came in for greater scrutiny than might otherwise have been expected. Whilst it is always pos-sible that politicians are skilled semioticians it is easier for them to dispute the meanings of words than pictures. Without pictures the text can more easily lose its authority. Pictures help provide the news with a seemingly objective quality by appearing to offer con-firmation of the spoken word. For the viewer the film or picture comes to act as a neutral record of reality. What is overlooked, however, is that the pictures have been taken by a human eye: the

Table 11.2 *Percentage distribution of items by location of report in order of relative frequency*

Location & report type	Total (%)	BBC (%)	ITN (%)	No of bulletins in which location occurred		
				Total (146 possible)	BBC (74 possible)	ITN (72 possible)
Studio, e.g. newsreader, expert witness, studio discussion, drawings, graphs, maps, photographs and models	38.67	37.24	39.94	146	74	72
Home film – interviews with politicians, wives, parliamentary reports, statements, vox pop, home film abroad	21.27	18.98	23.31	123	61	62
British film from Argentina – interviews with Argentinians and British, parades, funerals, general film	8.61	11.48	6.06	110	62	48
Diplomatic film, i.e. Haig shuttle, EEC reports, UN etc.	7.40	8.57	6.23	76	42	34
Task Force film on board ships and on Falklands – radio report with or without still picture	6.67	5.82	7.46	58	28	30

Table 11.2 (continued)

Location & report type	Total (%)	BBC (%)	ITN (%)	No of bulletins in which location occurred		
				Total (146 possible)	BBC (74 possible)	ITN (72 possible)
Task Force film on board ships and on Falklands – commentary plus film – all ITN and BBC film	5.46	5.53	5.39	46	21	25
British film from South America excluding Falklands and Argentina	2.74	2.82	2.67	38	19	19
Pre-sailing Task Force film, i.e. embarkation, training preparation	2.29	2.15	2.41	23	8	15
Home film – official war statements only – i.e. Ian McDonald and John Nott or anyone making official war statements, but not at Parliament	2.14	1.92	2.34	24	10	14
Argentinian film – invasion film plus entry into Stanley and all Falklands film	1.41	1.73	1.13	16	9	7
Other film, i.e. NBC from rest of the world	0.77	0.56	0.96	10	4	6

Argentine film from Argentina	0.75	1.00	0.51	8	4	4
MoD and COI film, i.e. simulated, training and official Falklands film (historical film of Falklands Kelpers) Only if stated as caption or announcement	0.65	0.94	0.39	9	7	2
BBC, ITN film – i.e. simulated training and official Falklands film (historical film of Falklands Kelpers)	0.59	0.92	0.29	6	5	1
Other film, i.e. NBC from Argentina	0.27	0.33	0.22	4	1	3
Argentinian film – official Government information film, propaganda film	0.26	0.39	0.14	3	2	1
Other film, i.e. NBC from South America	0.10	0.11	0.08	2	1	1

images are not neutral either in the selection made or in the perspective adopted. Reality is edited, or more accurately, humanly constructed out of actual happenings. What disturbs and alarms, particularly those with political investment in the events portrayed, is that pictures have a rawness of narrative which the spoken word alone rarely conveys. It would take a master of description to capture the horror of the napalmed Vietnamese girl, scorched and stripped of her clothes, running down the street, but more than that it is the aura of objectivity and impartiality of television news created by the pictures that strengthens the credibility and legitimacy of broadcasting institutions.

It is the ability of television to combine pictures with words creating the impression of objectivity that helps satisfy the political demand for impartiality. If objectivity aids the sense of impartiality it also assists in instilling trust amongst the audience that what is seen and heard corresponds to what occurred.

It is ironic that while the absence of pictures led the Government to express doubts about the coverage and attack the broadcasters in a way that may not have been so easy had pictures been allowed to tell the story, it induced other critics to suggest that the Government had something to hide and by extension to see the heavy hand of political control resting on the broadcasters. If ever there was a case of broadcasting politically crippled by its own technology, this was it.

If we now return to Table 11.2, what is apparent is that the total amount of time spent on reports from the Task Force represented just over 12 percent of all Falklands coverage, but as we have already pointed out less than 6 percent of this was film. Of the 146 bulletins analysed, 46 had commentary plus film reports from the Task Force. However, matters are not quite as they may seem. Half of these were shown prior to 30 April, before any hostilities or military action. Up to the end of April just over 42 percent of news bulletins analysed gave filmed reports from the Task Force. Of the 90 news bulletins analysed between 1 May and 15 June, the day of the ceasefire, approximately a quarter included filmed reports from the Task Force. Once battle was joined, however, and the number of ships and lives lost began to grow – the real drama and centre play of war – the number of reports from the front, although there had never been many, dropped. It was only too apparent even at the time that the Falklands war was not going to be brought into the living rooms of the British as Vietnam was for the Americans.

In discussing the absence of pictures with Peter Woon (the editor of BBC News) and David Nicholas (editor of ITN) both agreed that had more film been available it would not have meant less verbal text. Their position was that more pictures would simply have meant longer bulletins. However, as it was a major and developing story more pictures would have affected the mix of verbal text to film and thus the visual images would perhaps have assumed prominence over the verbal text. They certainly might have detracted from the lexical scrutiny that took place, especially following the sinking of the *Belgrano* and the *Sheffield*. Even so the film that did appear did not entirely escape questioning. A major source of complaint by Conservative Members of Parliament was the use of Argentinian film.

It is difficult to establish whether the voices raised against the use of Argentinian film objected to film shot by Argentinians or to British-shot film sent from Argentina. In the angry heat of exchange, fuelled by sections of the popular press, the political charges levied by the critics at the broadcasters lacked analytical precision. Their general complaint was that British television was unpatriotic in allowing Argentina to make propaganda in Britain. One particular film which provoked a storm of protest, that of the funeral of an Argentinian seaman, held to have been reported with 'undue reverence' (May 8), was not Argentinian film but British film. Of course it can still be held that this supposed reverential portrayal amounted to propaganda – for Argentina – but it is difficult to sustain the charge that broadcasters were a conduit for Argentinian propaganda.

In answer to this type of charge it is important to distinguish between the different sources of film – who originated the material. This we did by creating five categories of 'Argentine film': British film from Argentina; Argentine film from the Falklands; Argentine film from Argentina; foreign companies' film from Argentina; and official Argentine Government film. Table 11.2 shows that the total amount of time devoted to Argentine-made film, that is: Argentine film from the Falklands; Argentine film from Argentina and official Argentine Government film, was just over 2.4 percent of all Falklands coverage. Furthermore, the amount of official Argentine Government information film or 'propaganda film' represented a mere 0.27 percent of total Falklands news coverage. British-made film from Argentina amounted to just under 9 percent of all Falklands material. Much of the film criticized therefore was more than likely that of British origin.

Given the amount of Argentine-based film, either British produced or of Argentinian heritage it can hardly be said that television operated as Galtieri's fifth column. Yet the charge was made. Quantity, however, does not necessarily bear any relationship to the ferocity of criticism, and the type of formal content analysis presented here can easily overlook the effectiveness of single items in creating imagery or implanting ideas. Propaganda, however, usually entails the notion of a sustained systematic transmission of messages and to be effective probably needs to be persistent. Furthermore, propaganda is usually associated with the intention of having a position accepted to the exclusion of countervailing positions, ideas or opinions. This can be achieved by a variety of techniques, but as Table 11.2 shows, the amount of 'Argentine film' is not good evidence for substantiating the charge that broadcasters acted as propogandists for Argentina. But the fact that charges were made was strong evidence that broadcasters were to be allowed very little leeway in exercising editorial independence of judgement in covering a war in which Britain was involved. Difficulties therefore were bound to follow any coverage, whether emanating from the Argentine or not.

Before analysing the specific content, such as the language used to describe the events and participants of the war and the themes which emerged, some comments on the sheer extent of coverage are necessary.

In the relatively short history of television other stories have at times dominated the news but not in the same sustained manner as the Falklands Conflict. Table 11.3 shows the length of the Falklands items within the news. Both the BBC and ITN extended some of their news programmes during the crisis and, although the total average figures for BBC and ITN (Table 11.1) are only a little longer than 'normal' weekday bulletins, they include the shorter weekend bulletins. Table 11.3 also gives the true feel for the importance which both companies attached to the story and shows the extent to which it dominated the news during the two and a half months of the conflict. Items about the Falklands on the BBC's *Nine O'clock News* took up 73 percent of the time of the news bulletins taken as a whole; on ITN's *News at Ten* the proportion was only slightly less – 65 percent.

Throughout the whole two and a half months of the war the Falklands story never became old or tired, requiring some new twist or event to justify coverage. Editorial interest was insatiable, although on seven occasions (three on BBC's *Nine O'clock News* and four on ITN's *News at Ten*) the Lebanon as a story pushed the Falklands into the second item, at the very time when the British troops were making their way to victory at Port Stanley. (As an addendum then, strictly speaking, in some bulletins the Falklands could be said to have been the third item, the first place been taken by news of the shooting of the Israeli ambassador in London.) Nevertheless, throughout the Falklands Conflict news was the lead

Table 11.3a   *Average length of Falklands item within news bulletins*

Period	BBC (mins)	ITN (mins)	Average combined BBC/ITN (mins)
2 – 4 April	12.23	19.35	15.79
5 – 24 April	17.83	20.50	19.17
25 – 30 April	22.51	29.37	25.94
1 – 20 May	20.16	26.63	23.31
21 May – 15 June	20.40	20.08	20.24
Average total throughout period	19.59	22.68	21.11

Table 11.3b   *Proportion of item to whole bulletin*

Period	BBC (%)	ITN (%)	Total BBC/ITN (%)
2 – 4 April	78.0	73.58	75.23
5 – 24 April	73.5	70.67	71.96
25 – 30 April	83.19	70.95	75.78
1 – 20 May	79.74	70.29	74.19
21 May – 15 June	66.42	56.14	60.98
Average total throughout period	73.10	65.45	68.83

story in 139 bulletins out of the 146 analysed.

The war in the Lebanon provided one of those twists of irony which litter the history of journalism: unable to get pictures for the main story, editors found there was no absence of material from what, in terms of British interest, was of secondary importance. The Lebanon, moreover, served only too painfully to remind editors of the type of images they longed for from the Falklands. Lebanon was full of live picture action rather than the painted verbal canvas of the Falklands, and it showed in the prominence given to both stories. Take 8 June, the day on which the British suffered heavy losses at Bluff Cove, both the BBC and the ITN news used a report from the Lebanon as their lead items. The previous day, 7 June, Nicholson sent a report of fighting around Port Stanley. It was placed after an item on the Lebanon. Although working for television, Nicholson was able to send a voice only report, which was then illustrated by an artist's impression. The Lebanon story on the other hand had the advantage of being accompanied by vivid pictures from the battle front, and hence took precedence over Nicholson's piece.

The lack of pictures from the Falklands was an editor's nightmare, but even radio reports caused some anxiety because of their delay. The description of the disaster at Bluff Cove with the attack on the *Sir Galahad* was not broadcast until 9 June – a voice report by ITN's Michael Nicholson, which the BBC also broadcast.

A delay of one day may not seem much but it is in the frenzied world of news editors. With respect to pictures, however, it was not so much a case of carrying yesterday's news as of transmitting history. The landings at San Carlos for example and the establishing of a bridgehead were not shown until the 8 June – 17 days after the event. The delay meant they did not make the 'top of the news', and were instead relegated to a position after reports from the Lebanon. It was three days before the BBC placed the Falklands back on the number one spot and four days before ITN followed suit.

The clambering back into the top position by the Falklands story was perhaps to be expected given its obvious importance to Britain, but it is questionable whether it would ever have been displaced had all reports been accompanied by the type of dramatic action pictures generated from the Lebanon. With or without pictures though the Falklands was never going to be far from the main item of the day, and never at any point did interest flag. News organizations are hungry institutions requiring constant feeding and the Falklands offered an enticing diet of sustainable morsels sufficient to feed the appetite of any editor. The logistical problem of getting the news from the South Atlantic however meant that when news did arrive it was exploited to the full and put alongside more immediate stories. One consequence of this was that the same correspondent would appear more than once in a single bulletin. For example there were times when a voice only report from aboard ship was broadcast the same day as it was sent and then, later in the bulletin, a filmed report by the same correspondent, sometimes days or even weeks old, was included in the bulletin. This occurred on five occasions with reports from Brian Hanrahan, on nine occasions with reports from Mike Nicholson and once with reports from Jeremy Hands. On two occasions three reports of Hanrahan's appeared on one bulletin, and on one occasion this happened to the reports of Nicholson.

Although no one may have objected to the amount of time devoted to events in the South Atlantic, criticism was of course made of the manner in which the war was portrayed. We have already mentioned for example the lack of pictures and the use of Argentinian film, but a further and more strident complaint was about certain linguistic expression used.

Throughout the conflict the broadcasters insisted on adhering to the principle of neutrality of language. The proposition that any language is neutral is of course untenable. All that it really means is that broadcasters will not adopt an expressive form that manifestly favours one side rather than another. The insistence on the principle is all part of the broadcasters' attempt at achieving objectivity. Their mistake however is in believing that objectivity is attained by balance, and not the adoption of procedures used to establish the independence of truth from those making claims. It was this attempt at balance, in a situation of clear-cut antagonisms between opposing forces involving not one section of British society against another, but the whole country against another country, that was seen by some critics as a totally inappropriate application of standard broadcasting principles.

Trouble was bound to follow from such insistence on neutrality and it did. The BBC had an advantage over ITN in that it could rest its case in history: it claimed that the style adhered to was no different from that which it adopted during the Second World War and more recently the Suez crisis. Whether that was in fact the case is difficult to say, but the point is the BBC felt it right to adopt such a position. Its appeal to history had more than a tinge of righteousness to it; a fact that did not escape the notice of some sections of the Conservative Party and helped to fuel their basic antagonism towards the Corporation. How far then did the broadcasters stick to the principle of neutrality?

We have discussed in previous chapters the way in which the Task Force journalists identified with the troops, and in the content analysis looked specifically for evidence of such identification surfacing in the language used in their reports. However, before proceeding to give the results, a brief methodological note about our procedure will help clarify this particular section.

The reason for focusing on military equipment to illustrate the presence or absence of patriotic language (Tables 11.4 and 11.5) is a methodological one only in that as a category of reference it possessed the benefit of producing more data than, for example, descriptions of government and country and could thus form a better basis for judgement. The coding of the language used was the most difficult and lengthy part of the content exercise; not least because it involved the analysis of the phrases and terms used by everyone who spoke in the course of the news bulletins, not just the journalists. All the figures in Tables 11.4 and 11.5 include direct quotes only. To have included indirect quotes would have distorted the results and made for difficulties in allocating ownership and responsibility for the words used. In examining for the language used the areas selected for Britain and Argentina were description of military equipment, description of government, description of country and description of the Task Force. In the case of Britain we divided the terms of each of these categories into British (as in British planes), our/possessive (as in our troops), the/neutral and Royal Navy. In the case of Argentina we divided the terms into Argentine, their/possessive, the/neutral, enemy and Junta. Over 200 people were identified as having used a description for one of our categories, some individuals such as news presenters and reporters did so repeatedly. For ease of analysis, individuals were put into groups.

In examining the results of content analysis studies what is often overlooked is that the findings only represent the news as measured against the categories employed, and that alternative ones would provide a different image. A question to be asked of any content analysis schedule therefore must be whether the categories themselves make good sense.

Table 11.4 shows that when describing military equipment, for example, the Task Force journalists used the possessive terms 'our' or 'their' on just over 13 percent of occasions, while other BBC and ITN journalists either in London or elsewhere hardly ever invoked such 'patriotic' references. It is important to add however that on some occasions those with the Task Force were referring to events in which they themselves had been involved and thus the collective pronoun 'we' was not only understandable but arguably legitimate. Table 11.5 also shows this process of identification at work in that journalists in the Falklands were twice as likely to use the term 'enemy' of the Argentinians' military equipment as were other correspondents. However, the frequency of use was not very high.

In any absolute sense the BBC's claim that its staff in practice

Table 11.4   *Use of language in description of British military equipment. Percentage of each description according to main groups*

Group	British %	Our/possessive %	The/neutral %	Royal Navy %	Total
BBC reporters, correspondents, presenters; ITN reporters, etc.	38.80	3.05	44.33	14.09	688
Journalists with Task Force	23.24	13.38	54.23	9.15	142
Military officers	6.25	31.25	59.38	3.12	32
UK Government incl. ambassadors	19.51	48.78	21.95	9.76	41
Backbench Conservatives	—	—	100.00	—	2
Labour MPs	—	33.33	66.66	—	6
Ian McDonald	20.00	25.00	45.00	10.00	20
Falklanders	33.33	—	50.00	16.66	6

Table 11.5 *Use of language in description of Argentine military equipment. Percentage of each description according to main groups*

Group	Argentine (%)	Their (%)	The/neutral (%)	Enemy (%)	Total
BBC reporters, correspondents, presenters; ITN reporters, etc.	58.18	11.24	28.79	2.16	507
Journalists with Task Force	53.61	9.28	31.96	5.15	97
Military officers	25.00	20.00	40.00	15.00	20
UK Government incl. ambassadors	46.43	28.57	17.86	7.14	28
Backbench Conservatives	33.33	33.33	33.33	—	3
Labour MPs	43.45	18.19	36.36	—	11
Religious figures	100.00	—	—	—	3
US politicians	75.00	25.00	—	—	4
Ian McDonald	58.82	5.88	29.41	5.88	17
Falklanders	9.09	36.36	54.55	—	11

managed to uphold the principle of neutrality of language is applicable only to the London end of operations. Nevertheless the findings of Tables 11.4 and 11.5 do demonstrate, given the context within which the Task Force journalists were filing, a quite remarkable discipline and success in not allowing patriotic language to contaminate their despatches. The critics in one sense therefore had a right to be annoyed; the broadcasters did indeed reject the use of patriotic language during the war.

Although members of the Government may have complained about the lack of patriotic language used by broadcasters, they were not shy about introducing patriotic language themselves onto the screen. The access gained and the language used by members of the Government would not appear to have been taken into account by those critics who accused television of acting as a vehicle for Argentine propaganda. For example, and not too surprisingly, members of the Government used possessive terms the most when describing their own Government, but more importantly in terms of demonstrating patriotic enthusiasms they used such terms only slightly less frequently when referring to the country and military equipment.

Apart from the Falklanders, who it must be remembered were at the sharp end of Argentinian aggression, no other group used the possessive term to the same extent as members of the Government. Labour Members of Parliament tended to be less patriotic in their use of language than members of the Government when referring to

British military equipment – 33 percent compared to 49 percent in the use of the possessive term. And similarly in their description of the British Government – 25 percent compared to 61 percent. Yet, in referring to Britain, Labour Members of Parliament used the possessive term in over 60 percent of cases. The war undoubtedly placed many members of the Opposition in a difficult position. Although some might have supported Argentina's claim to the Falklands they did not support the manner in which it staked its claim. It may be therefore that the type of language adopted is explained by the schism of the desire to support Britain, but reluctance to support the British Government. In other words, war with Argentina was one thing, but peace with Mrs Thatcher's Government another.

It is not from the analysis of language alone that the values behind the news can be pieced together. Examining the types of people interviewed – their status and positions held – and detecting the themes and references occurring in news reports adds assistance.

The questions of balance and truth were obvious points of tension during the Falklands Conflict: politicians criticizing the broadcasters for continuing with their attempts at balance rather than taking sides, and broadcasters complaining about the difficulty of establishing simple truths due to the unwillingness of Government to provide the necessary facts and at times objecting that the information if given served to confuse rather than clarify matters.

During a crisis such as war the necessity for broadcasters to operate the concept of balance lessens, for the simple reason that balance is not a method by which to arrive at truth, although in journalistic circles it is taken to be so, but a practical device by which to defend against political attack. The idea of balance when all appear to be on the same side loses its meaning. In fact one can go so far as to establish a general rule: the greater the social consensus on issues, the less the need for broadcasters to operate the concept of balance.

Although there may not have been universal approval for the sending of the Task Force such crisis periods like that of the Falklands Conflict tend to produce a consensus about the government's authority. The Government of Mrs Thatcher was accorded a legitimacy of speech rarely given to any government during more normal times. These moments of national agreement make it politically unwise for any opposition to launch outright attacks on the government of the day. It is this suspension of vigorous opposition that slightly alters the rules of how broadcasting institutions engage the political world. Only after the war was over and balance returned as a strong operating procedure, were other voices raised in discussions about, for example, the sinking of the Argentinian ship, the *Belgrano*. Clearly more information came to light after the war to create dissenting voices, but such knowledge was a determinant of the loosening of authority, both psychologically and materially.

Whilst the war was in progress the automatic assumption by broadcasters that interviews with ministers required responses from others of similar but oppositional status was suspended. We are not arguing that this was a manifest and conscious act, but that broadcasters along with the general public accepted the natural authority of government special to the times. Some evidence for the workings of this process can be seen by the results in Table 11.6 which shows a predominance of interviews with representatives of the Government.

Table 11.6   *Frequency of actors interviewed – both channels*

Actors	Total no. of interviews
Government (incl. ambassadors and backbenchers)	45
Labour MPs	19
Liberal/SDP MPs	7
Religious figures	4
Military officers	40
Marines – soldiers	8
US politicians	20
Argentine politicians and military	16
Falklanders	17
Total	176

Despite this natural authority the Government failed to take maximum advantage if its position. For example, if the Ministry of Defence had been more adept at news management it would not have refused to provide the type of information, or at least a realistic minimum of information, necessary to satisfy the demands of the defence correspondents.

Despite the tactical mistakes made by the Government in 'controlling' the news, the advantage in regulating the flow of information was all on its side. However, whilst it was possible for the Government to control the release of official information, its power did not stretch to controlling other sources of information. Concern was expressed by the Government over the type of informed military speculation given by retired senior Service personnel. It is perhaps ironic that individuals who could be expected to support military venture would be such a thorn in the side of the Government. But given the absence of pictures it is not surprising that retired and often just recently retired senior military personnel were wheeled on to give their professional judgement about events that could not be seen. As a category of actors military figures appeared as frequently as members of the Government (Table 11.6).

What was obvious to those within broadcasting during the conflict was that for once in its life television would have to look to its merit as a provider of news without the benefits of picture support. What we have done so far therefore is to look at the exact composition of the bulletins and a particular aspect of content – language used. Now we wish to examine the themes within the bulletins to determine the image presented.

Once the Task Force had sailed the principal questions were, first, whether there would be an engagement – asked during the period of the content analysis covering the diplomatic manoeuvres – and then, after South Georgia was retaken, how extensive the fighting would be. But, if we take the content analysis period as a whole then what is strikingly apparent from the results is that as a theme the possibility that 'Britain might lose the war' hardly entered the frame at all. It had in fact the lowest frequency score of all the themes identified with a percentage distribution of under 1 percent (Table 11.7). The news therefore even before battle commenced was not pessimistic about the outcome.

Table 11.7   *Main themes in order of relative frequency. Percentage distribution of items (bulletins) by themes (both channels)*

Theme	N	% of items
Diplomacy as a way of solving problem	95	65.07
Military equipment – capacity, ships, planes (British)	92	63.01
Possibility of fighting	92	63.01
Task Force preparations, training, equipment	82	56.16
Conditions of Conflict – weather, terrain	82	56.16
Details of operations, battles	77	52.74
Sovereignty – Argentinian	70	47.95
Tactical discussions – military, battle plans	62	42.47
Sovereignty – British	61	41.78
Diplomacy – as a way of not solving problem	55	37.67
Military equipment – capacity, ships, planes (Argentina)	54	36.99
Support for British position – UN, EEC, world (except USA)	53	36.30
Peace plans – UN – likelihood of failure	53	36.30
US support for British position	49	33.56
State of British armed forces – ready – positive	49	33.56
Aggression as a way of solving problem	48	32.88
Peace plans – Haig – likelihood of failure	48	32.88

Theme	N	% of items
Skill of troops – British	46	31.51
Military equipment during war – e.g. Exocet	46	31.51
Self-determination for Falklanders (refs. to)	41	28.08
Morale of troops – British – positive	41	28.08
Aggression – the need to combat	40	27.40
Future of Falklands after war – political	38	26.03
US neutral	36	24.66
Falklanders' reaction to invasion	36	24.66
Support for war within Argentina	36	24.66
Patriotism – British honour at stake	35	23.97
Lack of support for British position – UN, EEC, world (except USA)	35	23.97
State of war – British winning	35	23.97
Bravery of troops – British	35	23.97
Argentine claim to Falklands	34	23.29
Belief of British reinvasion of Falklands	33	22.60
Support for invasion within Argentina	30	20.55
State of Argentine armed forces	30	20.55
Political control of Argentine mass media	30	20.55
Symbols of British nationalism	29	19.86
Treatment of Argentine prisoners – positive	29	19.86
South American support for Argentina	28	19.18
Aggression as a way of not solving problem	26	17.81
Argentine treatment of Falklands – negative	26	17.81
Falklands – Englishness, love for Britain	24	16.44
Peace plans – Haig – likelihood of success	24	16.44
Morale of troops – Argentine – negative	23	15.75
Peace plans – UN, likelihood of success	23	15.75
Political system – Argentinian fascist, Junta unrepresentative, critical	22	15.07
Moral arguments against conflicts	22	15.07
Pope's visit – decision to visit Britain, should come	22	15.07
Tactical discussions during war	22	15.07
State of Argentine armed forces – negative	22	15.07
Legal position – status of Falklands	21	14.38
Lack of support for Argentine position, UN, EEC, world (except USA)	21	14.38
Communications difficulties	21	14.38
State of war – Argentina might lose	21	14.38
US aid to Britain – military, communication, intelligence	20	13.70
Support for sending Task Force – Parliamentary	20	13.70
Possibility of casualties – British, heavy	20	13.70
Conflict over name – Malvinas or Falklands	19	13.01
Criticism of British Gov. for not realizing invasion	19	13.01
Opposition in Britain to sending of Task Force – Parliamentary	19	13.01
Censorship – British references to reporting restrictions	18	12.33
Democracy	18	12.33

Theme	N	% of items
Political system – Argentinian, fascist, Junta – unrepresentative – descriptive	18	12.33
Lack of support for British position, UN, EEC, world (except USA)	18	12.33
Neutral position – Ireland, Italy	18	12.33
Arms trade – supplies, trade with Argentina	18	12.33
Morale of troops – Argentine, positive	18	12.33
Symbols of Argentine nationalism – self-sacrifice	18	12.33
Falklands reaction to invasion	17	11.64
Possibility of casualties – Argentine, heavy	17	11.64
Possibility of casualties – British – light	17	11.64
Colonialism – relic of the past	16	10.96
Prince Andrew	16	10.96
Political capital being made by Thatcher and Gov.	16	10.96
Pope's visit to Britain	16	10.96
Censorship – Argentine lack of freedom	16	10.96
US links with South America – political	15	10.27
British in Argentina – links, history	15	10.27
Trade, British–Argentine – economic	15	10.27
East–West conflict	14	9.59
Political/military comparison without the conflicts – Hitler/Ruhr, Cuba, Berlin	14	9.59
Support for sending Task Force – public display – opinion polls	14	9.59
Recall of Task Force – calls for	14	9.59
Bravery of troops – Argentina	14	9.59
Funerals – British	14	9.59
Support for Argentine position – UN, EEC, world (except USA)	14	9.59
State of British armed forces – cuts – negative	12	8.22
Skill of troops – Argentine	12	8.22
Military mistakes – Argentina – unexploded bombs	12	8.22
Pope's visit – decision to visit Britain – should not come	12	8.22
Importance of media in context of communications war	12	8.22
South American disputes with Argentina	11	7.53
South American support for Britain	11	7.53
History of Falklands	11	7.53
Falklands – they are Argentina's	11	7.53
Pope's visit in Argentina	11	7.53
Condition of Argentine prisoners – positive	11	7.53
Peace plans – Peru – likelihood of failure	11	7.53
State of war – Argentina winning	11	7.53
British treatment of Falklanders – positive	10	6.85
Previous British conflicts – Suez, World War II, Cyprus	10	6.85
Colonialism – Britain's responsibility	9	6.16
Arms trade – world, general	9	6.16
Condition of Argentine prisoners – negative	9	6.16
Unfair fighting tactics – napalm (British)	9	6.16
Discipline of troops, looting etc. – Argentine	9	6.16

Theme	N	% of items
S. American criticism of Argentina (lack of support)	8	5.48
Whole escapade is madness	8	5.48
Political control of British mass media	8	5.48
Funerals – Argentina	8	5.48
British in Argentina – lack of support for British case	8	5.48
Invasion – reasons for Argentina – Galtieri's personal position	7	4.79
Argentine treatment of Falklands – positive	7	4.79
Future of Falklands after war – economic	7	4.79
British–Argentine relationship after war	7	4.79
Lack of support in Britain – opinion polls, public	7	4.79
Ridicule/comment of British figures in Argentine media display	7	4.79
Unfair fighting tactics, napalm, white flags (Argentina)	7	4.79
Lack of equipment – i.e. flash masks (Argentina)	7	4.79
Military mistakes – British	7	4.79
Possibility of casualties – Argentina – light	7	4.79
Fascism	7	4.79
Political system – British parliamentary democracy – representativeness	6	4.11
US links with South America – economic	6	4.11
Invasion – reasons for Argentina – economic problems	6	4.11
Invasion – reasons for Argentina – social and political	6	4.11
Religious reactions – British position – support for	6	4.11
Religious reactions – British position – lack of support for	6	4.11
Religious reactions – Argentine position, support for	6	4.11
British treatment of Falklanders, negative	5	3.42
Recall of Task Force – impractical, present/future	5	3.42
Ridicule/comment of Argentine figures in British media	5	3.42
Peace plans – Peru – likelihood of success	5	3.42
World Cup – British should not participate	5	3.42
US aid to Argentina	4	2.74
Falklands – links with Argentina, trade, medical, tourism, education	4	2.74
Invasion – reasons for Argentina, legal entitlement	4	2.74
Lack of support for war within Argentina	4	2.74
Argentine political system, history etc.	4	2.74
Opposition within Argentina to Government	4	2.74
Previous Argentine conflicts – external	4	2.74
Opposition in Britain to sending of Task Force – public display, opinion polls	4	2.74
Pooled despatches	4	2.74
Terrorism	4	2.74
Treatment of Argentine prisoners – negative	4	2.74
World Cup – British should participate	4	2.74
Condition of British prisoners – positive	4	2.74
Discipline of troops, looting, etc. – British	4	2.74
Arms trade – supplies, trade with Britain	4	2.74

Theme	N	% of items
US support for Argentine position	3	2.05
British links with S. America – economic and political	3	2.05
Disbelief of British invasion of Falklands	3	2.05
Trade British–Argentine – arms, training	3	2.05
Religious reactions – Argentine position, lack of support for	3	2.05
Conditions of British prisoners – negative	3	2.05
Special terms during Conflict – i.e. yomping	3	2.05
Repatriation of bodies	3	2.05
Previous Argentine conflicts – internal	2	1.37
Lack of support for invasion within Argentina	2	1.37
Recall of Task Force – impractical, present/future	2	1.37
Treatment of British prisoners – positive	2	1.37
Lack of equipment – i.e. flash masks – British	2	1.37
Possibility of casualties – Falklands, light	2	1.37
Britain's international standing viz other colonies, i.e. Hong Kong	1	0.68
Invasion – reasons for Argentina, geographical	1	0.68
British in Argentina – support for British case – positive	1	0.68
Treatment of British prisoners – negative	1	0.68
Possibility of casualties – Falklanders – heavy	1	0.68
Morale of troops – British – negative	1	0.68
State of war – British might lose	1	0.68
Total responses	3238	

Percentages in excess of 100 because more than one theme could be coded for a given item

The themes achieving the highest frequency scores, on the other hand, were those concerning diplomatic moves and those of the military aspects of the campaign. What is surprising in the light of these scores is the criticism made of television for failing to give sufficient regard to peace proposals and instead roll with the juggernaut of war. However, as Table 11.7 shows, diplomatic themes were strongly represented: 'diplomacy as a way of solving the problem' received the highest frequency of all themes, having a percentage distribution (65 percent) in all bulletins; 'diplomacy as a way of not solving the problem' had a percentage distribution of just under 38 percent. Furthermore, the frequency of 'diplomacy as a way of solving' was fairly consistent through the first four periods of the conflict but for the final period (1 May–15 June) the frequency dropped to less than half of the overall score.

Given the criticism made against the news for its failure to pay attention to diplomatic activity, it is worthwhile to examine the issue in more detail, and begin with the coverage of the actual peace plans. Table 11.7 includes the frequencies and percentage distribution of the different peace plans as themes in terms of the perceived likelihood of success or failure. Both the Haig and the United Nations plans were mentioned with approximately the same frequency, and in both cases stress was laid on their likely failure. Adding the frequencies for success and failure for each plan respectively then, the combined total for the Haig plan gives a percentage distribution of 49 percent and for the UN plan 52 percent. These combined totals make the UN and the Haig peace plans the seventh and eighth highest in terms of frequencies of the themes we identified. The Peruvian peace plan on the other hand, to which so much attention was given after the war, with criticism heaped on television for not according it greater attention, did receive a lower frequency than either the Haig or UN plans. Again failure rather than success achieved a higher frequency.

Compared with either the Haig or the UN attempts at peace the Peruvian plan did receive lack of coverage. This lower frequency however must be set in the context of the movement of events themselves. The Peruvian peace initiative was made at a later stage in the crisis than the other two attempts at peace. Hardly had the plan emerged when it was scuppered by the sinking of the *Belgrano*, and not surprisingly therefore had little chance to gain much coverage.

In analysing any news the actual movement of events should not be ignored. For instance Britain did not sit by idly following Argentina's takeover of the Falklands. The opening rounds of the conflict saw a flurry of diplomatic activity as Britain sought to gain support and sympathy for its position from the UN, the EEC and any one else for that matter whom it thought likely to come to its aid. The events helped to dictate the news, and the type of diplomatic efforts made were reflected in the news. Apart from the peace plans themselves, the other aspect of diplomacy which achieved high notification within the themes was 'support of the British position' with a percentage distribution of 36 percent (Table 11.7). The theme 'US support for British position' reached just under 34 percent, which, when combined with 'support for British position by the rest of the world', scored the second highest frequency.

Thus, whilst military aspects of the conflict are perhaps the most clearly remembered, viewed as a whole a great deal of attention was paid by the news to the political manouvrings of the Government – not just its efforts to secure peace.

If we turn to coverage of Argentina itself within the relative frequency of themes, then the main item to emerge was its sovereign rights, followed by support for the invasion and support for the resulting war (see Table 11.7). For example, the theme 'sovereignty – Argentinian' achieved a percentage distribution of 48 percent. This was the seventh highest score of any theme within the total schedule and achieved a higher rating than the theme 'sovereignty – British' which came ninth with a score of just under 42 percent. A word of caution is necessary. The greater number of references to Argentinian sovereignty do not mean that British television displayed particular sympathy towards Argentina. It simply means that the question of sovereignty was not ignored. Indeed, if we examine the scores for the number of times an explanation was given of Argentinian actions we see that it fared less well than these absolute figures would suggest. That is, although the question of Argentina's sovereign rights was given frequent coverage, comparatively little attention was given to any reasons for its claims. We divided the theme 'invasion – reasons for Argentina' into five categories of explanation: 'Galtieri's personal position', 'economic problems', 'social and political', 'legal entitlement' to the Falklands and 'geographical' claims. Even when all these themes are taken together their frequency of appearance in the news bulletins was relatively low with a percentage distribution of just over 16 percent.

This relative lack of attention given to themes dealing with analysis and explanation for Argentina's invasion of the Falklands is not specific to the way in which television covered that particular conflict, but part of a general condition characterizing television news – a deficiency as a provider of explanation accompanied by analysis. In an area where television news is supposedly strong – the covering of visible action – it was found sadly lacking when fighting did occur. Instead of pictures it had to rely on voice reports for immediate happenings.

The absence of pictures of men at war did not stop the featuring of the combatants. Their treatment in the news throws up some interesting questions, and gives some support to our earlier comments about the identification of the Task Force journalists with the men on whom they reported. Taking the themes dealing with troops then, Table 11.7 shows the percentage distribution of the skill (31 percent), morale – positive (28 percent) and bravery (24 percent) themes, which when taken together demonstrate the extremely positive picture the news painted of the Task Force's performance. This positive image can also be seen by comparing the themes for 'treatment of Argentinian prisoners – positive' which achieved a percentage distribution of just under 20 percent with 'treatment of Argentinian prisoners – negative' which scored just under 3 percent.

Whilst the image of the British troops carried by the news may have been positive and therefore gave the Government no grounds for concern, other aspects of the war did. One of the main areas of controversy during the conflict related to the release of casualty figures. The confusion about the numbers of casualties sustained at Bluff Cove provoked particular alarm amongst broadcasters and Government alike. The details of the release of information relating to military losses have been discussed in previous chapters but Table 11.8 lists the frequency of the announcements of casualties presented by the news bulletins.

Table 11.8   *Casualties – frequency and percentage distribution of references*

Announcement	N	% of items
British military casualties by British source – i.e. planes, ships etc. Precise	41	28.08
British military casualties by British source – i.e. planes, ships etc. Imprecise	10	6.85
Argentine military casualties by British source – i.e. planes, ships etc. Precise	42	28.77
Argentine military casualties by British source – i.e. planes, ships etc. Imprecise	19	13.01
British military casualties by Argentine source – i.e. planes, ships etc. Precise	12	8.22
British military casualties by Argentine source – i.e. planes, ships etc. Imprecise	10	6.85
Argentine military casualties by Argentine source – i.e. planes, ships etc. Precise	8	5.48
Argentine military casualties by Argentine source. Imprecise	9	6.16
British troops casualties by British source. Precise	34	23.29
British troops casualties by British source. Imprecise	24	16.44
Argentine troops casualties by British source. Precise	21	14.38
Argentine troops casualties by British source. Imprecise	24	16.44
British troops casualties by Argentine source. Precise	3	2.05
British troops casualties by Argentine source. Imprecise	3	2.05
Argentine troops casualties by Argentine source. Precise	6	4.11
Argentine troops casualties by Argentine source. Imprecise	4	2.74
Total responses	270	

Percentages in excess of 100 because more than one theme could be coded for a given item

Two main points emerge. First, the overwhelming reliance on British sources of information for quotation of casualties compared to Argentine sources. Second, the amount of imprecise information that was contained in the announcements. For example, it was as likely that the news said, 'A number of losses were sustained' as it was to give actual figures of the losses. In fact, as Table 11.8 shows, the announcements of the number of casualties were as likely to be imprecise as they were to be precise.

There was little possibility of swift, accurate, independent verification of casualty figures. Thus the broadcasters, like the rest of the media, were forced into reliance on government sources, either British or Argentinian. In the case of troop casualties the Argentinian Government was not in a position to possess intelligence about British troops. British Government sources therefore had to be used by the British media, and in doing so the broadcasters at times transferred into the news official uncertainty, but at other times carried deliberate attempts by officials, as in the case of Bluff Cove, to mislead the public.

Perhaps more than any other issue the Government's attempt to mislead broadcasters captures the tension between open reporting and the desire by government to influence and control opinion. It is something which all broadcasters have to live with and struggle against, but in the conditions of war the balance tips steeply in the government's favour. Such was the closure of usual sources that even junior ministers and backbenchers, normally well informed, found their traditional avenues of information closed during the Falklands war. Like the broadcasters they had to depend on the Government's official public statements. In such a situation it was easy for the Government to have its version of events accepted as true: there was nothing to check its version against, and in the case of casualty figures it was impossible to do so. After Bluff Cove the knowledge that the Government had deliberately misled the media at least confirmed the broadcasters' suspicions of the Government's unwillingness to take them into its confidence. Peter Snow's professional caution, when earlier in the war he questioned the Government's right to have its figures automatically accepted, was vindicated.

Journalists do not always expect complete honesty from their sources, but the shock to their nervous systems during the Falkland war was the brazen attempt by the Government to treat them as a pure extension of its information arm. Not only were the broadcasters and other media personnel subjected to this pressure in the course of their work but they also found the results of their efforts the subject of attack. The accuracy of those criticisms – particularly with respect to language, use of Argentinian film, representation of various actors – has been demonstrated in the content analysis.

The next question, and the basis of the following chapter, is what did the general public think about such issues? Did they stand with the critics or with the broadcasters? Did they support the broadcasters in their attempt to preserve the professional norm of neutrality or did they wish for a partisan news? Did they support the Government's attempts to turn the Fourth Estate into a Fourth Service?

12

The audience's response

During and after the Falklands campaign, much was said about the public's attitude to the way in which the conflict was reported and, indeed, to the war itself. We believe it to be important to look more closely at the basis for these observations; while it is unwise to claim that such research can ever give a complete and precise account of how people actually felt and what they thought, investigation is more rewarding than mere supposition. We did not, however, set out to measure changes in attitudes, not least because survey by questionnaire is too blunt an instrument to measure what may be very small changes over a long period of time. Nor did we seek to assess the effect of the mass media on the attitudes of readers, listeners and viewers, but simply to ask the audience what it thought of what it read, heard and saw. We did not look for information which predicted attitudes or behaviour, confining ourselves to enquiries about attitudes at one particular time – taking, as we would describe it, the pulse of the audience at a single point.

Our survey was conducted after the conflict was over. This does not necessarily mean that the attitudes we found were not held by the audience during the conflict. Indeed, we have reason to believe that they were, not least because our questions represented an exploration not just of detailed but also of general attitudes. (Furthermore we found from our own checks in the questionnaire and from our field workers' reports that respondents had little difficulty in recalling the history of the conflict and their own experience while it lasted.) We also believe that respondents who were questioned after the heat of the moment had cooled were then able to give a clearer, more considered account of their views. We did ensure, however, that the survey was completed before Parliament discussed the report of the House of Commons' Select Committee on Defence on the Government's handling of the mass media, since we wished to avoid the possibility that our respondents' views might be influenced by extensive press coverage of that debate.

This sharply focused, retrospective approach also allowed us to include in our survey a particularly important theme – the exploration of attitudes to the complex and elusive subjects of censorship and bias. We sought our respondents' views as to the nature of television's role in society and tried to discover whether they believe that television coverage seeks, and manages, to be 'fair', balanced and impartial, or whether they believe that it reflects only the outlook and beliefs of those who make programmes. We wished to know the beliefs and expectations that the audience has of television reporting, both generally and in relation to this particular conflict and the issues it raised. What are the attitudes, political and otherwise, of the audience? How are they related to the programme-makers' nervousness or boldness in questioning and replying to the questions of politicians and officials? Is the programme-makers' performance shaped to take account of audiences' attitudes and, if so, are they gauged at all accurately? Our survey, then, was as much about news-reporting generally as about the Falklands Conflict in particular. (See Appendix III for technical details of the survey.)

Statistical analysis can squeeze data only so far, however impressive statistics may look. Like the journalists quoted in an earlier chapter, we are aware that 'facts do not speak for themselves'. We have therefore drawn on our own interpretations of the figures here but, since we are aware that others might quarrel with our conclusions, we have included a great many tables in our text. The data on which our analysis is based is open to inspection; readers can make their own judgement of the plausibility of our conclusions.

The data itself is not, however, sterile. It provides evidence sometimes to disprove, sometimes to question, accepted assumptions. By combining survey data, statistical analysis, content analysis and judgement, we can derive general and useful insights from specific answers to our questionnaire. The first example – an examination of the public's attitude to the sailing of the Task Force, with the media's depiction of it, is typical and instructive.

At 10.45 a.m. on Monday 5 April 1982, television pictures showed *Hermes*, the flagship of the fleet, pushing away from the quayside at Portsmouth, out into the Solent. *Invincible*, the other carrier, steamed ahead exchanging signals. Lining the guardrail were the ship's company and the Royal Marines; drawn up on deck were Sea King helicopters and Harrier jets. It was a formidable display of strength and resolve, spectacular and moving. A huge crowd spilled out over the quay, waving Union Jacks, holding children high, displaying banners with exhortations and instructions: 'Give 'em Hell'. One woman bared her breasts. The crowd cheered, the ships' sirens shrieked. In the background, caught by the TV cameras, was HMS *Victory,* Nelson's flagship. The mood, as television showed it that spring morning, was jolly and supportive. From the television pictures, the impression was of some mass jaunt, an expedition, launched on a wave of popular support, to teach the Argentinians a lesson – jingoism, passionate and rampant. Nor was this simply an impression; formal content analysis of those pictures, when interpreted, would say the same. The crowd were cheering and waving. What content analysis, on its own, cannot tell us is why they did so or whether the public mood, as it was depicted, represented more widespread, deep-rooted popular feeling. Were these reactions, as some critics would have it, the result of manipulation of the public by the media or by politicians? Our inquiries started with an exploration of these questions.

The Argentinians' claim

We investigated, first, what members of the public thought they knew about the Falklands and whether they felt the Argentinians' claim was justified. The answers, as shown in our tables, are interesting and perhaps surprising.

When we asked our respondents if, before the Conflict, they knew where the Falklands were, 46 percent *claimed* that they did, whilst 22 percent did not, but said they had heard of them. A further 29 percent did not know where they were and had never heard of them. It is therefore safe to say that, to the bulk of the population, some 54 percent of individuals (including 'don't knows'), the Islands were, to put it bluntly, some God-forsaken place of which they could hardly have had any real knowledge whatsoever. It is therefore particularly interesting that, when asked how much justification the Argentinians had for their claim, 14 percent of our sample considered they had a lot, 36 per cent a little, and 41 percent none at all. This is shown in Tables 12.1a and 12.1b.

In other words, adding the responses together and ignoring the 9 percent 'don't knows', the majority of the population, some 50 per cent, considered that the Argentinians had at least some legitimate right to the Falklands.

It is reasonable to assume that, even among those who knew where the Islands were, it is unlikely that their knowledge included an understanding of the complex historical relationship between the Falklands, Britain and Argentina. On what, then, did the majority of our respondents base their view that Argentina's claim was, at least in part, legitimate? Presumably there had been no sudden run on the contents of the relevant shelves of public libraries, yet more than 50 percent of the public appears to have held a view contrary to that which might have been expected to be the 'national' position. Their information must have come from the mass media. It was inevitably affected by, and in turn affected, existing assumptions

Table 12.1a   *Argentina claimed that the Falkland Islands really belonged to them. How much justification do you think they have for this claim?*

| | Total | Voted 1979 | | Age group | | | | | | |
		Con.	Labour	18–24	25–34	35–44	45–54	55–64	65+
Total	1076	410	291	109	254	225	129	166	193
	100%								
A lot	147	36	65	15	35	37	22	19	19
	14%	9%	22%	14%	14%	16%	17%	11%	10%
A little	382	150	89	45	101	83	49	50	54
	36%	37%	31%	41%	40%	37%	38%	30%	28%
None at all	446	197	108	32	94	87	47	84	102
	41%	48%	37%	29%	37%	39%	36%	51%	53%
Don't know	101	27	29	17	24	18	11	13	18
	9%	7%	10%	16%	9%	8%	9%	8%	9%

Base – all

Table 12.1b   *Argentina claimed that the Falkland Islands really belonged to them. How much justification do you think they have for this claim?*

	Total	Express	Mail	Mirror/Record	Telegraph	Financial Times	Guardian	Star	Sun	Times
						Readership				
Total	1076 100%	224	210	314	149	14	62	107	317	42
A lot	147 14%	22 10%	23 11%	56 18%	20 13%	1 7%	19 31%	13 12%	39 12%	6 14%
A little	382 36%	79 35%	85 40%	102 32%	59 40%	5 36%	26 42%	28 26%	107 34%	17 40%
None	446 41%	108 48%	91 43%	129 41%	61 41%	6 43%	13 21%	54 50%	143 45%	16 38%
Don't know	101 9%	15 7%	11 5%	27 9%	9 6%	2 14%	4 6%	12 11%	28 9%	3 7%

Base – all

and dispositions, of which, since the question of sovereignty was central, political affiliation was one of the most important. We therefore examined this more closely, asking our respondents how they had voted in the most recent (1979) General Election. It is clear, as Table 12.1a indicates, that there was a marked difference in attitude between Conservative and Labour voters.

We also asked our respondents which newspapers they read, to see whether and to what extent this filter may have influenced their view of the legitimacy of Argentina's claim. The spread of opinion is remarkably similar among readers of each national newspaper.

For example, of those who considered that the Argentinians had a strong claim to the Falklands, only *Financial Times*, *Guardian* and *Mirror* readers departed very much from the general spread and, on the whole, only *Guardian* readers did so to any notable extent. (Throughout our analysis due caution is paid to the sample size of both *Guardian* and *Times* readers. The sample of *Financial Times* readers is too small a number from which to draw any firm conclusions and is thus ignored throughout.)

Table 12.1b supports the generally held notion that *Guardian* readers tend to be 'liberal', showing a 31 percent figure, as against the national total of 14 percent, for those believing in a strong legitimate Argentine claim, and 21 percent, compared to the total national figure of 41 percent, considering that the claim was totally . unfounded. Only the proportion believing that the Argentinians had 'little claim' matched that among readers of other papers. If, however, the category of 'a lot' is combined with 'a little' to supply the category believing that the Argentinians 'had some justification for their claim', only *Guardian* readers stand out dramatically, with 73 percent. The next highest total is *Times* readers, with 54 percent. It is interesting that readers of the *Sun,* the newspaper most vociferously indignant at the seizure of the Islands, show 46 per cent believing 'some' (combined scores of 'a lot' and 'a little') claim was justified, little different from readers of the other tabloids. The *Express* has 45 percent, the *Mail* 51 percent, the *Mirror* 50 percent, and the *Star* 38 percent. *Sun* readers felt, for that matter, much the same as those of the 'heavies', with 53 per cent for the *Telegraph* and 54 percent for *The Times*.

The most interesting responses, however, are in the two extreme categories, of those believing the Argentinians had a substantial claim, 'a lot', or 'none at all'. Excluding the *Guardian*, the most divergent views are among *Mirror* readers, with 18 percent considering the Argentinians had substantial justification and 41 percent seeing none. The *Telegraph* matches the proportion of *Mirror* readers seeing no claim, with *The Times* roughly the same. More remarkably, readers of both the *Telegraph* and *The Times* are, respectively, only 5 percent and 4 percent less inclined than *Mirror* readers to believe that the Argentinians' claim was substantially legitimate.

Even that small difference, however, makes *Mirror* readers, as well as *Guardian* readers, stand out from the rest. These were, of course, the two papers blasted as traitors by the *Sun*.

We have also correlated political affiliation and choice of newspaper. As Table 12.2 shows, 2 percent more of the *Sun*'s readers voted Labour at the last General Election prior to the invasion than voted Conservative, though the level of Labour support falls below that among *Guardian* and *Mirror* readers and is the same as that of the *Star*. In terms of readership, the rest of Fleet Street may all be considered Conservative, with some interesting differences. A higher proportion of *Telegraph* readers vote Conservative than do readers of other papers, followed by the *Mail*, with the *Express* running a close third. Although *The Times* is clearly not a Labour paper, its support running exactly the same as the *Telegraph*, it does differ from the rest in that group because of its Liberal support. *Guardian* readers also support the Conservatives slightly more than *Mirror* readers, but also have a reasonably high Liberal attachment.

From Tables 12.1 and 12.2, therefore, we can judge that – apart from the fact that *Guardian* and *Mirror* readers differ strikingly from the rest – newspaper readership goes only a little way towards explaining attitudes to Argentina's claim – and indeed, readers' satisfaction or dissatisfaction with newspaper coverage.

Combining data on voting behaviour with respondents' views of the claim, gives a much fuller picture. Putting the 'a lot' and 'a little' categories together, to make 'some' justification, gives us 53 percent who voted Labour, compared with 46 percent who voted Conservative. Liberal voters, with a total of 57 percent, were, as we have seen, more inclined than Conservatives to support Argentina's claim.

The evidence of Tables 12.1a and b, and 12.2 helps explain the material in Table 12.3, showing the extent to which readers were satisfied with the line their newspapers took in covering the war. The *Sun* produced 22 percent who were dissatisfied with its coverage.

The *Mirror* seems more unpopular than might be expected given its sympathy towards the Argentinian claim by its readers, its Labour support, and its restrained reportage when compared to the *Sun*'s. The explanation for this rests in the rather untidy nature of newspaper readership as shown in Table 12.4.

So far our analysis of readership and satisfaction has been based on the figure derived by adding those who read the newspaper in

Table 12.2   *Which party did you vote for in the last election?*

	Total	Readership									Arg. claim just		
		Express	Mail	Mirror/ Record	Telegraph	Financial Times	Guardian	Star	Sun	Times	Lot	Little	Not at all
Total	1076	224	210	314	149	14	62	107	317	42	147	382	446
	100%	21%	20%	29%	14%	1%	6%	10%	29%	4%	14%	36%	41%
Conservative	410	112	113	75	87	7	16	33	94	19	36	150	197
	38%	50%	54%	24%	58%	50%	26%	31%	30%	45%	24%	39%	44%
	100%	27%	28%	18%	21%	2%	4%	8%	23%	5%	9%	37%	48%
Labour	291	43	31	123	15	–	25	34	103	4	65	89	108
	27%	19%	15%	39%	10%	–	40%	32%	32%	10%	44%	23%	24%
	100%	15%	11%	42%	5%	–	9%	12%	35%	1%	22%	31%	37%
Liberal	83	14	19	23	9	2	7	10	23	7	12	36	30
	8%	6%	9%	7%	6%	14%	11%	9%	7%	17%	8%	9%	7%
	100%	17%	23%	28%	11%	2%	8%	12%	28%	8%	14%	43%	36%

Base – all

Table 12.3   *Newspaper coverage of the Falklands, and readers' satisfaction*

	Express	Daily Mail	Mirror/ Record	Telegraph	Guardian	Star	Sun	Times
Total	224	210	314	149	62	107	317	42
	100%	100%	100%	100%	100%	100%	100%	100%
Very satisfied	54	50	55	36	18	22	62	10
	24%	24%	18%	24%	29%	21%	20%	24%
Fairly satisfied	116	111	170	84	32	54	148	20
	52%	53%	54%	56%	52%	50%	47%	62%
Neither	16	18	30	11	3	10	31	1
	7%	9%	10%	7%	5%	9%	10%	2%
Fairly dissatisfied	18	20	39	12	4	9	40	1
	8%	10%	12%	8%	6%	8%	13%	2%
Very dissatisfied	14	4	6	2	3	7	27	1
	6%	2%	2%	1%	5%	7%	9%	2%
Don't know	6	7	14	4	2	5	9	3
	3%	3%	4%	3%	3%	5%	3%	7%

Table 12.4   *Frequency of readership*

Frequency	Express N=224	Daily Mail N=210	Mirror/ Record N=314	Telegraph N=149	Guardian N=62	Star N=107	Sun N=317	Times N=42
Every day	140	129	210	92	27	57	217	12
	63%	61%	67%	62%	44%	53%	68%	29%
Frequently	27	27	37	19	15	19	41	6
	12%	13%	12%	13%	24%	18%	13%	14%
Occasionally	57	54	67	38	20	31	54	24
	25%	26%	21%	26%	32%	24%	19%	57%

question every day to those who read it frequently and those who do so occasionally. This, however, masks the subtleties of the data. Thus, by examining frequency of readership and levels of satisfaction together, we can understand, in theory at least, why the *Sun* was unpopular and the Mirror satisfied its readers only to a limited degree.

The *Mirror* and the *Sun* see each other as arch-rivals. Both have a high circulation, the *Sun,* with over 4 million readers, enjoying the largest of any British newspaper. In our sample they have, correspondingly, the two highest returns – the *Mirror* ($N = 314$), and the *Sun* ($N = 317$) – giving a good statistical base. Data for the *Mirror* and the *Sun* combined with details of frequency of reading, tell us more in Table 12.5.

The spread of readership frequency percentages is much the same for both papers, but satisfaction scores based on frequency are not. For example, there is practically no difference in the dissatisfaction scores, only 1 percent, between the two papers' everyday readers, while among frequent and occasional readers the difference in popularity is dramatic: only 11 percent of *frequent Mirror* readers were dissatisfied, compared to 32 per cent of *frequent Sun* readers, and, of *occasional* readers 14 per cent for the *Mirror* compared to 34 percent for the *Sun.*

Given that the *Sun* speaks of itself as a campaigning paper, and that during the Falklands campaign its voice was the loudest and the most nationalistic, we may ask what this tells us about the claim that news represents readers' views. The *Sun* scathingly attacked the *Mirror* for failing to support the Falklands campaign, but the *Mirror* spoke for its readers in a way that the *Sun* did not. *Mirror* readers, as Table 12.5 indicates, showed a more uniform level of satisfaction. In fact, despite its bullying tone, the *Sun* could not win. It was bound to be unpopular with a large section of its readers in that, the less it sympathised with the Argentine claim and, therefore, struck a chord with Conservative voters, the more it offended its Labour readers. It is therefore incorrect to judge from the *Sun*'s editorial line that a substantial number of people (approximately 4 million sales) privately agreed with the sentiments the paper expressed. Just as it is wrong to judge the sentiments of a nation from the quayside pictures of the farewell to the Task Force.

We now turn to a closer inspection of public attitudes towards the Conflict. Beneath the outward enthusiasm for the sailing of the Task Force, what concerns were felt by the population as a whole?

To much of the public, the way in which the Argentinian invasion of the Falklands, on Friday, 2 April, affected British interests was not immediately apparent. The Islands' importance to Britain –

Table 12.5 *Mirror/Record and Sun's coverage of the Falklands: satisfaction and frequency of readership*

	All Mirror/Record readers				All Sun readers			
	Total	Occasionally	Frequently	Daily	Total	Occasionally	Frequently	Daily
Total	314 100%	67 21%	37 12%	210 67%	317 100%	59 19%	41 13%	217 68%
Very satisfied	55 18%	– –	9 24%	46 22%	62 20%	1 2%	6 15%	55 25%
Fairly satisfied	170 54% 100%	43 64% 25%	22 59% 13%	105 50% 62%	148 47% 100%	23 39% 16%	18 44% 12%	107 49% 72%
Combined satisfaction	72%	64%	83%	72%	67%	41%	59%	74%
Neither	30 10% 100%	10 15% 33% 100%	1 3% 3% 100%	19 9% 63% 100%	31 10% 100%	10 17% 32% 100%	4 10% 13% 100%	17 8% 55%
Fairly dissatisfied	39 12% 100%	7 10% 18%	3 8% 8%	29 14% 74%	40 13% 100%	14 24% 35%	7 17% 18%	19 9% 48%
Very dissatisfied	6 2% 100%	3 4% 50%	1 3% 17%	2 1% 23%	27 9% 100%	6 10% 22%	6 15% 22%	15 7% 56%
Combined dissatisfaction	14%	14%	11%	15%	22%	34%	32%	16%
Don't know	14 4% 100%	4 6% 29%	1 3% 7%	9 4% 64%	9 3% 100%	5 8% 100%	– –	4 2% 44%

even, as we have seen, their location – was only vaguely apprehen-
ded, if at all. The story, however, was dramatic and its 'human
interest' lay in the fact that Major Mike Norman, the Commanding
Officer of the Falklands garrison, was battling against overwhelming
Argentinian odds, with only a handful of Royal Marines to help
him. The issue of sovereignty soon materialized. The Islands were
British and whether they were to remain so was not to be determined by armed foreign aggression. What is clear from our data,
however, is that the British people were concerned about Argentina's action.

For example, 52 percent of our respondents stated that they were
very concerned, with a further 33 percent declaring themselves
concerned. Only 9 percent considered that they were not very
concerned and a very small proportion, 5 percent, not concerned at
all. Such answers are, on their own, largely useless, since it is
difficult to say what 'being concerned' actually means. (It could be –
though this is facetious – that people were concerned for the welfare
of the indigenous penguin population.) It is reasonable to assume
that concern arose, no matter how vaguely, from the expectation of
armed conflict. Certainly, the nature of their anxiety becomes much
clearer when respondents were asked whether they thought at the
time of the invasion that the issue might be 'resolved by diplomatic
means alone', or whether they thought it could be 'resolved only by
fighting', their replies being cross-tabulated with their estimates of
'concern'. Those who considered that only fighting would resolve
the issue expressed a much higher degree of concern than those who
thought diplomacy would resolve matters. At the extreme, although
the pattern is the same throughout of those who thought there
would be fighting, as opposed to diplomacy, 66 percent were 'very
concerned', compared to 42 percent, respectively.

Clearly that level of concern was directly related to the expectation of fighting. What is intriguing is why some people rather than
others should take a less optimistic view of the possibility of diplomatic resolution. It could be, of course, that their reasoning was
based on no more than a simple estimation of the Prime Minister's
character, so that, on hearing of the invasion, the automatic
response was: 'I can't see Thatcher putting up with that'. Table
12.6, however, shows that the older the person, the more likely he
or she was to believe that matters would lead to a fight, a view held
by more men than women and more Conservative than Labour
voters.

Conservative voters may have taken this view because what they
admired about their party was its tough and determined leadership.
On the other hand, they might equally well have felt that, as a

Table 12.6 Did you think at the time (invasion) that the situation could be solved by diplomatic means alone with no fighting or did you think it could only be solved by fighting?

| | Total | Age group | | | | | | Sex | | Voted 1979 | | Arg. claim just | | |
		18–24	25–34	35–44	45–54	55–64	65+	Male	Fem.	Con.	Lab.	Lot	Little	Not
Total	1076 100%	109	254	225	129	166	193	513	563	410	291	147	382	446
Diplomacy	576 54%	68 62%	162 64%	121 54%	60 47%	80 48%	85 44%	253 49%	323 57%	187 46%	186 64%	108 73%	220 58%	195 44%
Fighting	442 41%	33 30%	84 33%	94 42%	59 46%	74 45%	98 51%	245 48%	197 35%	199 49%	94 32%	32 22%	145 38%	235 53%
Don't know	54 5%	6 6%	6 2%	10 4%	10 8%	12 7%	10 5%	14 3%	40 7%	23 6%	11 4%	7 5%	15 4%	16 4%
Can't remember	4 *	2 2%	2 1%	–	–	–	–	1 *	3 1%	1 *	–	–	2 1%	–

*less than 0.5. Base – all

resourceful and skilled politician, the Prime Minister would be able both to retrieve the Falklands and avoid a war. If that were so, we might expect Labour voters, antagonistic to Mrs Thatcher and dismissive of her competence, to consider that under her direction war was the more likely outcome.

Analysing the data often shows what is *not* likely and, in this case, an examination suggests other explanations. For example, Table 12.6 shows a clear relationship between age and the expectation of war.

There is a sharp climb from the age band 25–34, early adulthood to 35–44 and another from 55–64 to 65+, the onset of old age. We can conclude that, the longer a person has lived, the less likely he or she is to believe in the peaceful resolution of such disputes; indeed, we can suppose that the greater the number of attempts at peaceful diplomacy a person has witnessed, the more politically disillusioned he or she may be. There may, however, be another explanation.

As Table 12.6 shows, those who believed Argentina's claim was justified displayed more confidence in diplomatic resolution of the Conflict than those who did not believe the claim just.

Looking back at Table 12.1a shows us that younger people were more inclined than older people to feel that Argentina's claim was justified. It might be, then, that attitudes toward the way in which the dispute would be resolved were not a simple question of age of respondents, but was linked with the judgement of the legitimacy of Argentina's claim. Those who thought it legitimate might hope, as well as expect, that negotiations would be the correct response, and vice versa.

Table 12.7 shows the relationship between attitudes and the sex of respondents.

When those believing Argentina to have 'a lot' of justification for her action are combined with those finding 'a little' to make together those finding 'some' justification, the score is, at 49 per cent, equal for both sexes. More women, 57 percent, than men, 49 percent, believed the issue would be resolved diplomatically, yet more women, 87 percent, showed, though marginally, a high level of concern than men, at 83 percent. These differences may have one, or all of several explanations. From Table 12.7 we can see that it may well be the fact that when it came to expressing strong views – for example 'a lot of justification' and 'none at all' – women scored lower than men, perhaps reflecting their greater uncertainty about the whole affair. Twice as many women (39 percent) as men (19 percent), for example, admitted that they had never heard of the Falklands before the crisis, and twice as many (13 percent to

Table 12.7 *Sex, Argentinian justification, level of concern and belief in diplomatic solution*

	Total	Arg. claim just			Solution			Concern			
		Lot	Little	None at all	Dipl.	Fight	Very	A little	Not very	Not at all
Total	1076										
	100%										
Male	513	79	174	230	253	245	261	162	51	34
	48%	15%	34%	45%	49%	48%	51%	32%	10%	7%
Female	563	68	208	216	323	197	296	189	49	23
	52%	12%	37%	38%	57%	35%	53%	34%	9%	4%

Base – all

6 percent) that they did not know whether the Argentinians had any justification for their claim. Similarly, twice as many women (7 percent) as men (3 percent) admitted that they did not know one way or the other how the situation would be resolved. Looking back to Table 12.7, too, the higher level of concern on the part of the women in our sample may simply be explained by the fact that the possibility of violent conflict, however remote, worries them in any situation more than it does men. The figures are interesting, their lessons unclear. In any case, the influence of sex on attitudes is in this case small, especially relative to the influence of political allegiance.

So far, we can conclude that Conservative voters, rather than spoiling for a fight, were more concerned than Labour voters, because the issue could lead to war. So were older people, whose concern was perhaps greater because they were more likely to remember what war was like. Why, though, were younger people and Labour voters more likely than older people and Conservative voters to believe the Argentinian claim legitimate? Perhaps the Labour Party's anti-colonialist history influenced its supporters' attitudes. Perhaps younger voters did not share nostalgia for the traditions of Empire and Commonwealth.

In the case of Labour voters, however, this argument is shaky, since the Party's anti-colonialist tradition is matched equally sincerely by its anti-Fascist outlook. The Argentinian regime that had ordered the invasion of the Falklands was hardly one to which Labour voters might be expected to hand over a British possession, however anti-imperialist the gesture.

In summary then, our survey clearly shows that attitudes to the Falklands war were diverse and fragmented, according to several variables, political allegiance being one of the most crucial. So far, however, the evidence of the survey is chiefly useful in that it gives us a yardstick against which to consider public attitudes towards the reporting of the war. Those reactions were, obviously, confirmed by the views which each individual held of those more general questions. The principal points to keep in mind are, therefore: that, of those having any opinion at all, the majority accepted that Argentina had some claim to what was nonetheless considered a British possession; and that most people, 54 percent, thought at the time of the invasion that matters would be resolved peacefully.

We can now look behind the picture of cheering at the quayside as the Task Force set sail. When the categories of respondents 'approving' and 'approving strongly' are combined (Tables 12.8a and 12.8b), it appears that 72 percent of the country supported the decision to send a Task Force, with 17 per cent, 'disapproving' and

Table 12.8a *Approval and disapproval of decision to send the Task Force*

	Total	Age group						Sex		Voted 1979		Arg. claim just			Solution	
		18–24	25–34	35–44	45–54	55–64	65+	Male	Fem.	Con.	Lab.	Lot	Little	None	Dipl.	Fight
Total	1076 100%	109	254	225	129	166	193	513	563	410	291	147	382	446	576	442
Approved strongly	361 34%	23 21%	70 28%	78 35%	36 28%	76 46%	78 40%	222 43%	139 25%	199 49%	57 20%	23 16%	101 26%	224 50%	125 22%	218 49%
Combined	72%	65%	66%	76%	72%	79%	69%	76%	67%	86%	53%	45%	68%	87%	58%	89%
Approved	404 38%	48 44%	96 38%	93 41%	57 44%	54 33%	56 29%	170 33%	234 42%	152 37%	97 33%	42 29%	160 42%	165 37%	207 36%	179 40%
Neither	116 11%	20 18%	32 13%	21 9%	11 9%	13 8%	19 10%	40 8%	76 13%	25 6%	42 14%	15 10%	46 12%	30 7%	80 14%	27 6%
Disapproved	115 11%	11 10%	39 15%	18 8%	15 12%	14 8%	18 9%	38 7%	77 14%	22 5%	53 18%	31 21%	52 14%	14 3%	96 17%	12 3%
Combined	17%	15%	21%	13%	20%	12%	18%	15%	19%	8%	31%	44%	19%	6%	28%	4%
Disapproved strongly	69 6%	5 5%	15 6%	14 6%	10 8%	7 4%	18 9%	40 8%	29 5%	11 3%	39 13%	34 23%	18 5%	12 3%	61 11%	5 1%
Can't remember	11 1%	2 2%	2 1%	1 *	– –	2 1%	4 2%	3 1%	8 1%	2 *	3 1%	2 1%	5 1%	1 *	7 1%	1 *

*=less than 0.5. Base – all

Table 12.8b   *Readership*

	Express	Mail	Mirror/ Record	Telegraph	Guardian	Star	Sun	Times
Total	224	210	314	149	62	107	317	42
Approved	98	97	91	63	12	44	108	16
strongly	44%	46%	29%	42%	19%	41%	34%	38%
Combined	82%	83%	66%	80%	53%	73%	72%	86%
Approved	84	77	117	56	21	34	121	20
	38%	37%	37%	38%	34%	32%	38%	48%
Neither	18	13	42	13	6	12	40	1
	8%	6%	13%	9%	10%	11%	13%	2%
Disapproved	14	12	31	9	12	6	26	1
	6%	6%	10%	6%	19%	6%	8%	2%
Combined	10%	11%	19%	11%	37%	15%	14%	12%
Disapproved	10	11	29	7	11	10	18	4
strongly	4%	5%	9%	5%	18%	9%	6%	10%
Can't remember	–	–	4	1	–	1	4	–
	–	–	1%	1%	–	1%	1%	–

'disapproving strongly', disagreeing with it. The lack of support was overwhelmingly concentrated among Labour voters: 86 percent of Conservatives approved of the decision to some extent, but only 53 percent of Labour voters did. The most interesting split, however, is found when we looked at the figures for those who disagreed with the decision. Four times as many Labour voters as Conservatives, 31 percent compared to 8 percent, disapproved of the decision to send the Task Force. When we look at extremes of opinion the difference is even more striking. Forty-nine percent of Conservatives 'strongly approved' of the decision, for example, compared to only twenty percent of Labour voters.

Taken to extremes, Tables 12.8a and 12.8b confirm our suggestion as to why the *Sun* was unpopular with its readers.

Their disinclination to support the sending of the Task Force was outstripped only by that of *Guardian* and *Mirror* readers. The latter, strongly Labour, showed only 66 percent in favour of the expedition; *Guardian* readers were 53 percent in favour. The *Sun* and *Star*, with many Labour-voting readers, produced 72 percent and 73 percent, respectively, while the staunchly Conservative papers showed, not surprisingly, strong support: 86 percent among *Times* readers, 83 percent for the *Mail*, 82 percent for the *Express* and 80 percent for the *Telegraph*.

Political allegiance was by far the most important influence on respondents' views as to whether or not the Task Force should be despatched. More than anything else, political allegiance also explained the degree to which readers were satisfied with the attitudes adopted in the newspapers they read. As Tables 12.8a and 12.8b also indicate, the greater their belief that Argentina had little or no claim to the Islands, the more firmly people were inclined to support the sending of the Task Force. Equally predictably, enthusiasm for the despatch of the Task Force was greater among people who believed the dispute would be resolved by fighting.

All in all, the pattern of support for the sending of the Task Force was far from straightforward. As Tables 12.8 and 12.8b show, however, of those who neither approved nor disapproved of the Task Force's being sent, younger people adopted this position more than older. This may indicate a degree of apathy among the young, and it may suggest that, once the Task Force had departed, the young, formerly 'liberal' in their attitude to Argentina's claim, were then ready to accept the course of events as they unfolded. From Tables 12.1 and 12.6 too, we can see that, for older people the opposite was true. Believing Argentina's claim illegitimate and being cynical about the prospects of a diplomatic settlement, they nonetheless showed little enthusiasm for the despatch of the Task Force. It seems that their very concern at the news of the invasion overrode their feelings that Argentina's action had been unjustified. They were reluctant to endorse their own view that the Islands could be retrieved only by force.

But, as Table 12.9 shows, when the Task Force set sail, a considerable part of the population did not really think that it would end in war. Only 46 percent were certain of it. Excluding the 1 percent who could not remember what they thought, more than 50 percent thought there might not be a fight or said they did not know or were unsure.

Table 12.9 also shows that, of those who thought the Task Force would definitely see action, 77 percent approved of its departure. Fifteen percent of those, however, disapproved, with a further 7 percent ambivalent.

Thus when the Task Force actually left anchorage 23 percent who thought it would engage the Argentinians did not support its departure. However, of those who thought it would not be involved in action 64 percent also approved its departure. It would appear that a hard core (21 percent) not only thought that it would not be engaged in action but still objected to its leaving, which, when added to the 14 percent who neither approved nor disapproved, means that 35 percent (or 14 percent of the total population) did not actively approve even though its mission was that of a diplomatic show of strength. Of those who actively disapproved even though they did not believe it would see action, the proportion is 7 percent.

Although it might be considered wrong to include those who

Table 12.9 *Opinion of whether at the time of sailing thought Task Force would or would not be involved in fighting*

	Total	Age group						Sex		Voted 1979		Task Force approval			
		18–24	25–34	35–44	45–54	55–64	65+	Male	Fem.	Con.	Lab.	Appr. str.	Appr.	Neither	Disappr.
Total	1076	109	254	225	129	166	193	513	563	410	291	361	404	116	184
	100%	10%	24%	21%	12%	15%	18%	48%	52%	38%	27%	34%	38%	11%	17%
Thought it would	500	30	96	101	63	93	117	273	227	203	125	214	168	37	77
	46%	28%	38%	45%	49%	56%	61%	53%	40%	50%	43%	59%	42%	32%	42%
	100%	6%	19%	20%	13%	19%	23%	55%	45%	41%	25%	43%	34%	7%	15%
Thought it might	118	14	24	25	12	18	25	54	64	51	27	39	48	15	16
	11%	13%	9%	11%	9%	11%	13%	11%	11%	12%	9%	11%	12%	13%	9%
	100%	12%	20%	21%	10%	15%	21%	46%	54%	43%	23%	33%	41%	13%	14%
Thought it would not	423	63	128	90	51	50	41	173	250	147	127	101	170	60	88
	39%	58%	50%	40%	40%	30%	21%	34%	44%	36%	44%	28%	42%	52%	48%
	100%	15%	30%	21%	12%	12%	10%	41%	59%	35%	30%	24%	40%	14%	21%
Don't know	29	2	3	9	3	5	7	11	18	7	12	7	16	3	3
	3%	2%	1%	4%	2%	3%	4%	2%	3%	2%	4%	2%	4%	3%	2%
	100%	7%	10%	31%	10%	17%	24%	38%	62%	24%	41%	24%	55%	10%	10%
Can't remember	6	–	3	–	–	–	3	2	4	2	–	–	2	1	–
	1%	–	1%	–	–	–	2%	*	1%	*	–	–	*	1%	–
	100%	–	50%	–	–	–	50%	33%	67%	33%	–	–	33%	17%	–

* = Less than 0.5. Base – all

neither approved nor disapproved of the Task Force in figures for non-support of the embarkation, it is perfectly reasonable to do so; our purpose is to show and make the important point that the quayside scenes of apparent untrammelled delight and cheering do not necessarily represent a nation of bloodcurdling enthusiasts, wide-nostrilled for the onslaught of battle.

The reality behind the picture on the screens, as the survey returns show, is far more complex than that, or at least insofar as the general populace is concerned. It may, of course, be that those who congregated at Portsmouth were different from the rest of the country and that they did look forward to the coming battle. From our survey, however, it would be a fundamental mistake to read too much into the televised scenes alone and, more importantly, to use them as a visual yardstick of sentiments in the country at large. In fact, intuitively it would be reasonable to argue that since most of those lining the quayside were from Portsmouth, a naval town, and would have had husbands and relatives sailing with the fleet, they would be less likely than the rest of the population to want an armed conflict to break out. From our data, however, there is no reason to presume that the cheering from the quay was a jingoistic cry for war. In fact, Table 12.9 shows that if one takes those who thought the Task Force *would* do battle and who also *approved strongly* of the decision the figure, as a percentage of total population, is only 20 percent.

And what of the outcome? Table 12.10 shows that, of those who expected a fight, 86 percent considered Britain would win compared to 77 percent of those who thought the outcome would be a diplomatic resolution.

The more a person approved of the expedition the more likely he or she was to think that Britain would win: 89 percent of those who strongly approved compared with 68 percent of those who disapproved. Labour voters were slightly less confident of victory than Conservatives.

Comparing what we have learnt about attitudes to the Argentinian claim with what respondents said they thought the outcome would be, we see that those who disapproved of the Task Force's sailing might have done so partly because they felt Britain would not win any eventual war. Those who had thought matters might be resolved peacefully believed, when it appeared the war was inevitable, that Britain would lose. In part, then, their belief in a diplomatic solution was probably wishful thinking. The Prime Minister, Margaret Thatcher, herself considered both questions together. One of her first questions to the Chief of Staff before the Task Force was to sail, was whether, if it came to a fight, Britain could win.

Table 12.10   *At the time before any fighting started, opinion of whether Britain would win or lose if there was fighting*

	Total	Sex		Voted 1979		Arg. claim just		
		Male	Fem.	Con.	Lab.	Lot	Little	Not
Total	1076	513	563	410	291	147	382	446
	100%	48%	52%	38%	27%	14%	36%	41%
Britain win	866	442	424	342	231	111	304	377
	80%	86%	75%	83%	79%	76%	80%	85%
	100%	51%	49%	39%	27%	13%	35%	44%
Argentina win	41	19	22	11	17	10	22	6
	4%	4%	4%	3%	6%	7%	6%	1%
	100%	46%	54%	27%	41%	24%	54%	15%
Neither side	17	9	8	4	6	6	4	7
win	2%	2%	1%	1%	2%	4%	1%	2%
	100%	53%	47%	24%	35%	35%	24%	41%
Didn't know at	141	41	100	50	35	20	47	54
the time	13%	8%	18%	12%	12%	14%	12%	12%
	100%	29%	71%	35%	25%	14%	33%	38%
Can't	11	2	9	3	2	–	5	2
remember	1%	*	2%	1%	1%	–	1%	*
	100%	18%	8%	27%	18%	–	45%	18%

*=Less than 0.5. Base – all

In the spirit of this type of analysis, adding subtlety to the complex process involved in opinion formation, why more Labour than Conservative voters nurtured doubts about Britain's military capacity is less easily resolved; it might rest around a general lack of confidence in a part of the state apparatus, based on class scepticism of competent management. Examining Table 12.10 it does look as if such theorizing might have some basis in fact: the higher classes did show slightly more confidence in a British military victory.

Overwhelmingly, there was little doubt in the minds of the British public that victory was assured, but it is by examining small departures from the norm that the more general movement can better be understood. For example, Table 12.10 lends support to the notion raised earlier when discussing Table 12.7 that the higher concern amongst women was to some extent a possible product of their greater confusion: that they claimed less geographical knowledge of the Falklands, were more uncertain about whether Argentina had justifiable claims or not, and were less certain one way or the other about how it would be resolved. It is again clear from Table 12.10 that when the Task Force actually set sail the confusion continued: 18 percent of women compared to 8 percent of men did not know how the situation would be resolved, by fighting or diplomacy. Providing that confusion or uncertainty is a reasonable supposition

Table 12.10 (continued)

Solution		Task Force approval				Class			
Dipl.	Fight	Appr. str.	Appr.	Neith.	Disappr.	AB	C1	C2	DE
576	442	361	404	116	184	182	224	375	295
54%	41%	34%	38%	11%	17%	17%	21%	35%	27%
446	379	320	326	89	126	153	182	298	233
77%	86%	89%	81%	77%	68%	84%	81%	79%	79%
52%	44%	37%	38%	10%	15%	18%	21%	34%	27%
28	12	4	13	7	17	6	4	16	15
5%	3%	1%	3%	6%	9%	3%	2%	4%	5%
68%	29%	10%	32%	17%	41%	15%	10%	39%	37%
15	2	2	5	2	7	1	4	6	6
3%	*	1%	1%	2%	4%	1%	2%	2%	2%
88%	12%	12%	29%	12%	41%	6%	24%	35%	35%
80	47	34	56	17	322	21	33	51	36
14%	11%	9%	14%	15%	17%	12%	15%	14%	12%
57%	33%	24%	40%	12%	23%	15%	23%	36%	26%
7	2	1	4	1	2	1	1	4	5
1%	*	*	1%	1%	1%	1%	*	1%	2%
64%	18%	9%	36%	9%	18%	9%	9%	36%	45%

as a contributory explanation of the different levels of concern between the sexes then to discover this further area of uncertainty does lend it support in understanding the processes at work in attitude formation.

It also raises the consideration that perhaps *some* of the declared difference between Labour and Conservative voters is in some way related to a greater 'confidence' by Conservatives about the world. We have already argued that differences in the responses are due not to the specifics of ideology, but to the general attitudinal framework or world outlook, upon which voting choice rested; thus, part of the *weltanshauung* could well have embraced a greater certainty or confidence in forming views on matters which did not relate to them directly. For example, taking the 'don't know' as an indication of a lack of certainty/confidence, then apart from the question relating to whether at the time of the Argentinian invasion of the Falklands the situation would be resolved by war or diplomacy, Conservative voters consistently scored lower than Labour voters.

Of particular interest is the fact that only 6 percent of Conservative voters as opposed to 14 percent of Labour voters answered that they neither approved nor disapproved of the decision to send the Task Force. In Tables 12.8a and 12.8b it was noted that whilst the youngest age group had moved more in line with the rest of the age population in supporting the Task Force they nevertheless included the largest number of individuals (18 percent) who neither approved nor disapproved and which we labelled as apathetic. To be apathetic however is not to bother or care and is often associated with the disengagement of youth in anything other than their immediate surroundings or interests: an egocentricity precluding interest in matters which do not obviously affect them. It is also a condition out of which flows a lack of confidence or certainty of opinion about matters removed from oneself for the exact reason that they are of no concern.

It does look as if the Conservative voter was not so apathetic about the world or rather those spheres of it distant from his or her own world of everyday living, and thus had a greater confidence and certainty of position. This is not unrelated to class as Table 12.11 shows. Although the relationship is not absolute, the trend is that the higher the class the lower was the score on uncertainty. That is especially clear in terms of approval or disapproval of the Task Force: perhaps the best test of involvement. This relative lack of interest/involvement on the part of Labour voters and their consequent uncertainty is reflected also in the level of attention paid to both radio and television news of the conflict. For example, of those who voted Conservative, 30 percent listened to more radio news during the conflict than they did before compared to 24 percent of those who voted Labour. The pattern is repeated in terms of viewing news on television. Fifty seven percent of those who voted Conservative watched more TV news during the conflict than they did before as against 46 percent of those who voted Labour. From Table 12.11 it is clear that class is again at work as a factor of influence. For both radio and television news the top two classes, AB and C1, scored equally in listening to more news than they did before the conflict and more than the two lower classes, C2 and DE, who in turn both watched and listened less, in line with decreasing social status.

These figures should not be surprising. Other studies have shown that economic and, in the case of women, domestic constraints prevent people from perceiving the relevance of affairs in the wider world to their own local preoccupations. This, in turn, prevents the development of confidence and the growth of knowledge which, together, increase interest in issues of more than parochial concern.

If, as our survey suggests, the crowd on Portsmouth quay was not, on the whole, cheering the fleet as it sailed off to war – because for the most part its members did not believe there would be a war – what, then, were they cheering? It was, we must conclude, simply the predictable response to a pageant.

Table 12.11 Class and uncertainty over issues and levels of interest

	Total	Class				Sex		Voted 1979	
		AB	C1	C2	DE	Male	Female	Con.	Lab.
Total	1076 100%	182	224	375	295	513	563	410	291
Neither approved nor disapproved of decision to send Task Force	116 11%	12 7%	19 8%	44 12%	41 14%	40 8%	76 13%	25 6%	42 14%
Didn't know at time of invasion if it could be solved dipl. or by fighting	54 5%	8 4%	13 6%	16 4%	17 6%	14 3%	40 7%	23 6%	11 4%
Didn't know how justified Argentina was in its claim to the Falklands	101 9%	10 5%	21 9%	32 9%	38 13%	30 6%	71 13%	27 7%	29 10%
Didn't know at time of Task Force sailing if it would be involved in fighting	29 3%	5 3%	5 2%	5 1%	14 5%	11 2%	18 3%	7 2%	12 4%
Listened to radio news more often during the Conflict than before	290 27%	56 31%	70 31%	108 29%	56 19%	158 31%	132 23%	122 30%	71 24%
Base – all who watch news on TV Total	1052	177	221	363	291	499	533	405	285
Watched news more often on TV during conflict than before	547 52%	103 58%	128 58%	180 50%	136 47%	258 52%	289 52%	229 57%	132 46%

We can take it: give us the news

The British public may have had little knowledge, and mixed feelings, about Argentina's military capabilities; overwhelmingly, however, they believed that, if there were to be a war, Britain would win. As Table 12.10 shows, a mere 4 percent forecast an Argentinian victory. Those who approved most strongly of the despatch of the Task Force were most confident of British victory; conversely, those who disapproved most were the most likely to predict a British defeat. It is less easy to discover why people thought as they did, especially in the case of the pessimists, for here the figures are very small. It could be that some of those who disapproved of the Task Force's sailing did so simply because they thought that Britain would lose. On the other hand – motives being complex and people perverse – it might have been the case that some of those who forecast a British defeat nonetheless approved of the Task Force's departure, either because they hoped that the Government and particularly the Prime Minister might thus be humiliated, or because they imagined that this might boost the call for reductions in defence cuts. We indicate these various lines of thought to emphasize the variety of ways in which statistics and tables may be interpreted.

Our findings do, however, give a clear picture of trends. One of these is the change in the degree to which the public felt confident that the outcome of the war would be a British victory. When the *Atlantic Conveyor* was lost with its valuable cargo of helicopters, spare parts and equipment, some 5 percent of our repondents believed that the power of the Argentinian air force should not be underestimated and that Britain might yet lose the war. When HMS *Sheffield* was hit, on 4 May, and abandoned with the loss of 20 lives, that figure rose to 12 per cent. The news that the Argentinians possessed Exocet missiles and that the Task Force was inadequately protected against them undoubtedly helped sap the public's confidence.

These facts were covered extensively in the British press. Some comfort was drawn from reports that Argentina's supply of the missiles was limited, that the embargo on arms sales imposed by European Community countries had closed off their major source of supply and that Argentina's world-wide search for replacements was proving difficult. It was, still, now all too plain that the British fleet might not be indomitable.

There were, and are, those who felt that it was unwise to publish news of such setbacks or publicly to discuss the nature, even the very existence, of Exocet missiles, not just because such reports might give comfort and aid to an enemy but also because they undermined national morale. Others believed that, if such news had to be reported, it should be presented in a way that would maximize domestic support for the war and boost, rather than diminish, confidence. Some Conservative newspapers and some Conservative Members of Parliament certainly deplored what they saw as insufficient partisanship in the televison news coverage of the war. We therefore asked our respondents their opinion: specifically, whether the news should have referred to the soldiers with the Task Force as 'our forces' or as 'the British forces', and whether their opponents should have been described as 'the Argentinians' or as 'the enemy'. We asked three sets of questions; the results are set out in Tables 12.12, 12.13 and 12.14.

It is overwhelmingly clear that the public preferred non-partisan language in their news bulletins. As Table 12.12 shows, for instance, 74 percent preferred references to 'the Argentinian forces surrendered today' and only 13 percent preferred 'the enemy'.

Furthermore, as Table 12.12 demonstrates, 72 percent of those who knew someone in the Task Force preferred to hear references to 'the Argentinians'. Considering the emotional strain of the episode, these figures are evidence of remarkable discrimination on the part of the public and, we believe, a striking sensitivity to the value of impartiality in news broadcasting.

It is interesting, too, that by and large, neither the sex nor the political opinions of respondents seems to be a guide to their views on this point (whereas, looking back, they were guides to attitudes to the conflict itself). Table 12.12 shows this clearly. We also see this closing of political divisions when we break down the overall figures among readers of different newspapers. Thus 77 percent of *Sun* readers and of *Mail* readers preferred the term 'Argentinian forces', compared to 74 percent of *Express* readers, 73 percent for the *Mirror* and 71 percent for the *Star*. For the more serious papers, the figures are, perhaps predictably, even higher: 89 percent for the *Guardian*; 82 per cent for the *Telegraph* and 81 percent for *The Times*.

Similarly, looking at Table 12.13, the public preferred the non-partisan term 'the British forces' to that of the term 'our forces'.

The preferential scores however do shift somewhat with 54 per cent preferring 'British forces' as opposed to 29 percent opting for 'our forces'. Again there is hardly any difference between the sexes or between political allegiances, and consequently there are no great differences in terms of readership responses. Although there is undoubtedly a shift towards the use of the more personalized identification referent in Table 12.13 of 'our forces', when

Table 12.12a   'Argentinian forces surrendered today' or 'The enemy forces surrendered today'

	Total	Readership								Armed Forces connection				Arg. claim just		
		Expr.	Mail	Mirror/ Record	Telegr.	Guard.	Star	Sun	Times	Been in	Knew T.F.	Knew Forces	None	Lot	Little	None
Total	1076 100%	224	210	314	149	62	107	317	42	259	239	205	488	147	382	446
Argentinian forces	801 74%	165 74%	162 77%	230 73%	122 82%	55 89%	76 71%	244 77%	34 81%	183 71%	173 72%	154 75%	372 76%	111 76%	311 81%	311 70%
Enemy forces	138 13%	32 14%	24 11%	48 15%	12 8%	4 6%	23 21%	44 14%	2 5%	39 15%	40 17%	26 13%	50 10%	11 7%	31 8%	86 19%
Don't know/ Don't mind	137 13%	27 12%	24 11%	36 11%	15 10%	3 5%	8 7%	29 9%	6 14%	37 14%	26 11%	25 12%	66 14%	25 17%	40 10%	49 11%

Base – all

Table 12.12b

	Sex		Voted 1979		Task Force approval			
	Male	Fem.	Con.	Lab.	Appr. str.	Appr.	Neither	Disapr.
Total	513	563	410	291	361	404	116	184
Argentinian	382	419	309	220	259	307	84	145
forces	74%	74%	75%	76%	72%	76%	72%	79%
Enemy forces	71	67	52	32	60	48	13	13
	14%	12%	13%	11%	17%	12%	11%	7%
Don't know/	60	77	49	39	42	49	19	26
Don't mind	12%	14%	12%	13%	12%	12%	16%	14%

compared to Table 12.12 of labelling Argentina as 'the enemy', the clear preference is still for the news to adopt a more neutral description. Perhaps surprisingly, even those who knew someone within the Task Force did not especially wish to have the news identify with the troops to the extent of using 'our forces'. Only 32 percent did so compared with 33 percent who had been in the Forces at some time, but slightly more so than those who merely knew someone in the Services (27 percent) and those who had no connection (28 percent).

Finally, we decided to ask a much more testing question to elicit responses as to whether the fleet's departure should have been notified by the phrase 'The British Task Force sailed south today' or just 'The Task Force sailed south today'. The fact that a quarter of the total population considered that the most appropriate form was that of pure military description rather than one of national attachment demonstrates the fervour with which the public favoured neutral over partisan language. That 60 percent opted for the title 'the British Task Force' matters little to the general point because that itself is not a category of strong partisanship in the same way that 'the enemy' or 'our forces' is. After all, it was not the Irish Task Force, it was British, and on that ground a perfectly reasonable way of referring to the fleet. It is not, in other words, any different in connotation from the use of the description of 'the Task Force' and ably represents the strong preference for neutral language on television news. Throughout the three tables the absence of differences between those who voted Conservative and those who voted Labour which is then reflected in the absence of differences in attitudes between the various newspaper readerships means two basic things. To begin with, the fact that the *Sun* boasted that it was the paper that supported 'our boys' does not appear to have had any appreciable effect on its readers in terms of preparation to support its patriotic stance when transferred to television news: the paper may have voraciously supported 'our boys' but its readers (Table

Table 12.13a   'The British Forces moved 5 miles towards Port Stanley' or 'Our Forces moved 5 miles towards Port Stanley'

	Total	Readership								Armed Forces connection				Arg. claim just		
		Expr.	Mail	Mirror/Record	Telegr.	Guard.	Star	Sun	Times	Been in	Knew T.F.	Knew Forces	None	Lot	Little	None
Total	1076	224	210	314	149	62	107	317	42	259	239	205	488	147	382	446
British Forces	586	126	112	178	80	39	58	184	20	132	133	112	266	88	205	237
	54%	56%	53%	57%	54%	63%	54%	58%	48%	51%	56%	55%	55%	60%	54%	53%
Our Forces	311	72	56	95	41	16	39	98	15	85	76	56	136	31	109	148
	29%	32%	27%	30%	28%	26%	36%	31%	36%	33%	32%	27%	28%	21%	29%	33%
Don't know/	179	26	42	41	28	7	10	35	7	42	30	37	36	28	68	61
Don't mind	17%	12%	20%	13%	19%	11%	9%	11%	17%	16%	13%	18%	18%	19%	18%	14%

Base – all

Table 12.13b

	Sex		Voted 1979		Task Force approval			
	Male	Fem.	Con.	Lab.	Appr. str.	Appr.	Neither	Disappr.
Total	513	563	410	291	361	404	116	184
British	275	311	223	167	182	236	59	104
Forces	54%	55%	54%	57%	50%	58%	51%	57%
Our Forces	162	149	119	81	118	111	31	48
	32%	26%	29%	28%	33%	27%	17%	26%
Don't know/	76	103	68	43	61	57	26	32
Don't mind	15%	18%	17%	15%	17%	14%	22%	17%

12.14) had no desire for television news to refer to them as 'our forces'. They preferred 'British forces'. Once more therefore the *Sun*'s attack on television looks decidedly misplaced even amongst its own readers.

What is more important, however, and particularly vital in terms of the calls for political interference with television news, so that it would more openly side with Government policies by taking a nationalistic stance, is that the idea of its neutrality as represented by the language it uses appears to be strongly embedded in the principle of British broadcasting culture in the widest sense: supported not just by the practitioners, but by the public it serves. Judging by Tables 12.12 and 12.13 the only influence on preferring a more nationalistic language, and a less neutral form of expression, appears to be the personal one of belief in Argentinian claims to the Falklands, and the strength of approval of the decision to send the Task Force, both of which are related to each other. For example, the less justification the Argentinians were held to have for their claim and the more the Task Force was approved of, the greater the degree to which the individual preferred a language of identification. At the margins, therefore, it may be that given the specific nature of the issues some form of outrage expressed itself in preference for a combative appeal, but it is obvious that such sentiment is not by any means dominant.

If, as it would appear, broadcasting culture within Britain is one which prefers those responsible for television news to adopt a neutral language, it is not one which naively accepts that outside political interference with the news will not occur. When asked for example, 'Do you think the news was censored at all during the Falklands Conflict?', 85 percent of the population thought it was. There was no difference in expectation in relation to political allegiance. However, after informing all the respondents that the news was in fact censored by the Ministry of Defence in London, differences did occur in strength of approval.

Table 12.14a   'The British Task Force sailed south today' or 'The Task Force sailed south today'

	Total	Readership								Armed Forces connection				Arg. claim just		
		Expr.	Mail	Mirror/Record	Telegr.	Guard.	Star	Sun	Times	Been in	Knew T.F.	Knew Forces	None	Lot	Little	None
Total	1076 100%	224	210	314	149	62	107	317	42	259	239	205	488	147	382	446
British Task Force	646 60%	141 63%	128 61%	196 62%	81 54%	36 58%	72 67%	207 65%	22 52%	145 56%	145 61%	131 64%	292 60%	71 48%	224 59%	287 64%
The Task Force	265 25%	60 27%	54 26%	78 25%	38 26%	17 27%	27 25%	79 25%	10 24%	76 29%	59 25%	51 25%	111 23%	44 30%	99 26%	105 24%
Don't know/ Don't mind	165 15%	23 10%	28 13%	40 13%	30 20%	9 15%	8 7%	31 10%	10 24%	38 15%	35 15%	23 11%	85 17%	32 22%	59 15%	54 12%

Base – all

Table 12.14b

	Sex		Voted 1979		Task Force approval			
	Male	Fem.	Con.	Lab.	Appr. str.	Appr.	Neither	Disappr.
Total	513	563	410	291	361	404	116	184
British Task	290	356	247	185	214	252	66	108
Force	57%	63%	60%	64%	59%	62%	57%	59%
The Task	141	124	104	67	98	98	21	45
Force	27%	22%	25%	23%	27%	24%	18%	24%
Don't know/	82	83	59	39	49	54	29	31
Don't mind	16%	15%	14%	13%	14%	13%	25%	17%

The differences in approval of censorship are quite pronounced. The younger the person, for example, the less they approved. The only slight falter in the trend is the 45–54 age band. Men more than women and Conservatives more than Labour voters approved (of the latter 78 percent against 52 percent). Viewed one way this could be interpreted that the younger the person the more 'liberal' he or she was likely to be, and similarly for Labour more than Conservative, and women more than men. On the other hand, given that this was a war it could be taken that the young, women and Labour voters were just more naive than the old, men and Conservatives. However, on the basis of Table 12.15, it looks as if what is really at work is 'liberality'. For example, of those who strongly approved of censorship, 63 percent also strongly approved of the decision to despatch a Task Force followed by 25 percent who simply approved, with a dramatic drop to only 6 percent who disapproved. It might therefore be that those who so strongly approved of what was, after all, a military as well as political decision, embraced censorship as a corollary of military activity. In other words, if they were more prepared to accept a military response to the news of the Argentinian invasion, they were also more prepared to accept a 'militarization' of broadcasting as a 'reasonable' continuation of a particular policy. It is not the liberal's response. Working from the same category they would be amongst the 18 per cent of individuals who strongly disapproved of censorship yet strongly approved of a Task Force. That is, whilst accepting a military response to the Argentinian invasion they nevertheless, whatever the dictates of the military situation, did not acquiesce to the overthrow of the liberal democratic value of the independence of the media from state interference.

From Table 12.15 it was suggested that the responses in approving or disapproving of censorship were based on an appreciation of 'liberal' values, or more precisely some of the responses were taken as demonstrating a lack of appreciation. If Tables 12.16

Table 12.15   *All the news reports from the Falklands were censored by the MoD in London. How much do you approve or disapprove of this?*

	Total	Age group						Sex		Voted 1979		Task Force Approval			
		18–24	25–34	35–44	45–54	55–64	65+	Male	Fem.	Con.	Lab.	Appr. Str.	Appr.	Neither	Disappr.
Total	1076	109	254	225	129	166	193	513	563	410	291	361	404	116	184
	100%	10%	24%	21%	12%	15%	18%	48%	52%	38%	27%	34%	38%	11%	17%
Strongly approve	200	9	38	37	21	37	58	121	79	108	38	126	50	11	11
	19%	8%	15%	16%	16%	22%	30%	24%	14%	26%	13%	35%	12%	9%	6%
	100%	5%	19%	19%	11%	19%	29%	61%	40%	54%	19%	63%	25%	9%	6%
Approve	500	46	113	111	61	77	92	250	250	213	113	154	229	43	71
	46%	42%	44%	49%	47%	46%	48%	49%	44%	52%	39%	43%	57%	37%	39%
	100%	9%	23%	22%	12%	15%	18%	50%	50%	43%	23%	31%	46%	9%	14%
Neither	91	18	27	22	7	9	8	26	65	26	31	12	30	23	23
	8%	17%	11%	10%	5%	5%	4%	5%	12%	6%	11%	3%	7%	20%	13%
	100%	20%	30%	24%	8%	10%	9%	29%	71%	29%	34%	13%	33%	25%	25%
Disapprove	191	22	55	35	27	26	26	74	117	40	70	46	75	24	44
	18%	20%	22%	16%	21%	16%	13%	14%	21%	10%	24%	13%	19%	21%	24%
	100%	12%	29%	18%	14%	14%	14%	39%	61%	21%	37%	24%	39%	13%	23%
Strongly disapprove	62	9	13	16	9	8	7	29	33	13	29	11	10	11	29
	6%	8%	5%	7%	7%	5%	4%	6%	6%	3%	10%	3%	2%	9%	16%
	100%	15%	21%	26%	15%	13%	11%	47%	53%	21%	47%	18%	16%	18%	47%
Don't know	32	5	8	4	4	9	2	13	19	10	10	12	10	4	6
	3%	5%	3%	3%	3%	5%	1%	3%	3%	2%	3%	3%	2%	3%	3%
	100%	16%	25%	13%	13%	28%	6%	41%	59%	31%	31%	38%	31%	13%	19%

Base – all

and 12.17 are now examined, further support is provided. But first to look at the overall picture. To the question of approval of the Government providing false information to the media, then combining the numbers who 'strongly approve' with those who 'approve', 34 percent of the population were favourably disposed towards it and 6 percent were neutral with 56 percent disapproving or strongly disapproving of such a practice.

If, therefore, the principle of democracy is that government as an elected assembly of the people ought not to lie to those it represents, Table 12.16 is a somewhat chilly sign. However, dishonesty amongst politicians, or the desire to mislead, is viewed by most people, one would suspect, as an occupational trait and therefore to be expected as part of the same magic performance of suddenly appearing on one's doorstep at election time. Thus Table 12.16 is the vital table to understand.

When compared with Table 12.16, what is interesting in terms of liberal attitudes about Table 12.17 is the proportional drop in numbers of those approving of the media 'broadcasting' false information. For example, whereas 34 percent considered it right for the Government to lie (Table 12.16), only 21 percent considered it right for the media to do so (Table 12.17). Whatever the expectations the public has, therefore, of politicians' propensity for truthfulness it would seem that the overwhelming wish is that the media should not follow suit, but instead be bound by honest principles. However, while it may seem impressive that a combined 70 percent of the public 'disapprove' of the media deliberately putting out false information, of which 33 percent did so strongly, it still remains the case that 21 per cent show little appreciation of what a liberal democracy is supposed to entail either theoretically or in practice. To those concerned with truth within the media industry, and those concerned with the support of liberal democratic values, Table 12.17 makes bleak reading.

It is impossible to say from Table 12.17 whether the 21 percent do not understand the structures of a liberal democracy, or whether they do but fail to appreciate democracy as a value. Whichever way, however, it is a problem for civic education. But matters are not quite as they appear, or at least they offer room for the consideration that democratic values are more strongly embedded in terms of the social system than that figure of 21 percent might suggest in that the values are not the property of any specific political party. For example, on the question of whether the Government should issue false information, more Conservative (41 percent) than Labour voters approved (30 per cent) (Table 12.16); but as we have argued the real test of democratic values rests with Table 12.17 and

Table 12.16   *How strongly would you approve or disapprove if the Government gave out false information to the British news media in the hope that it would help the conflict?*

	Total	Readership								Sex		Voted 1979		Task Force approval			
		Express	Mail	Mirror/ Record	Teleg.	Guard.	Star	Sun	Times	Male	Fem.	Con.	Lab.	Appr. str.	Appr.	Neither	Disappr.
Total	1076 100%	224	210	314	149	62	107	317	42	513	563	410	291	361	404	116	184
Strongly approve	69 6%	25 11%	19 9%	21 7%	10 7%	2 3%	8 7%	22 7%	4 10%	44 9%	25 4%	36 9%	15 5%	45 12%	16 4%	2 2%	6 3%
Approve	303 28%	66 29%	66 31%	95 30%	48 32%	15 24%	30 28%	100 32%	16 38%	172 34%	131 23%	130 32%	72 25%	115 32%	121 30%	26 22%	39 21%
Neither	64 6%	12 5%	14 7%	14 4%	9 6%	3 5%	1 1%	15 5%	2 5%	26 5%	38 7%	22 5%	17 6%	17 5%	24 6%	14 12%	8 4%
Disapprove	371 34%	66 29%	58 28%	111 35%	48 32%	23 37%	33 31%	90 28%	12 29%	164 32%	207 37%	130 32%	104 36%	101 28%	160 40%	44 38%	62 34%
Strongly	238 22%	51 23%	52 25%	66 21%	28 19%	19 31%	32 30%	87 27%	8 19%	100 19%	138 25%	82 20%	76 26%	77 21%	70 17%	26 22%	62 34%
Don't know	31 3%	4 2%	1 *	7 2%	6 4%	– –	3 3%	3 1%	– –	7 1%	24 4%	10 2%	7 2%	6 2%	13 3%	4 3%	7 4%

* = less than 0.5. Base – all

Table 12.17 *How strongly would you approve or disapprove if the British news media deliberately put out false information in the hope that it would help the conflict?*

	Total	Readership								Sex		Voted 1979		Task Force approval			
		Express	Mail	Mirror/Record	Teleg.	Guard.	Star	Sun	Times	Male	Fem.	Con.	Lab.	Appr. str.	Appr.	Neither	Disappr.
Total	1076 100%	224	210	314	149	62	107	317	42	513	563	410	291	361	404	116	184
Strongly approve	43 4%	14 6%	11 5%	17 5%	5 3%	2 3%	4 4%	15 5%	2 5%	30 6%	13 2%	22 5%	14 5%	27 7%	11 3%	1 1%	4 2%
Approve	186 17%	46 21%	38 18%	63 20%	32 21%	6 10%	24 22%	68 21%	12 29%	115 22%	71 13%	76 19%	51 18%	78 22%	68 17%	13 11%	24 13%
Neither	51 5%	8 4%	11 5%	11 4%	6 4%	2 3%	2 2%	11 3%	2 5%	17 3%	34 6%	15 4%	15 5%	16 4%	13 3%	13 11%	8 4%
Disapprove	402 37%	80 36%	78 37%	115 37%	58 39%	22 35%	26 24%	104 33%	12 29%	178 35%	224 40%	150 37%	103 35%	108 30%	174 43%	47 41%	69 38%
Strongly disapprove	360 33%	70 31%	70 33%	102 32%	43 29%	29 47%	47 44%	114 36%	14 33%	164 32%	196 35%	135 33%	102 35%	126 35%	120 30%	38 33%	74 40%
Don't know	34 3%	6 3%	2 1%	6 2%	5 3%	1 2%	4 4%	5 2%	–	9 2%	25 4%	12 3%	6 2%	6 2%	18 4%	4 3%	5 3%

Base – all

the views on the media and false information. When it comes to that test the political ranks close, and there is hardly any difference whatsoever between Conservative and Labour voters, a mere 1 percent.

This in effect means that the 21 percent fall outside representative political grouping in that their approval of being lied to by the media is not a product of party political ideology, but an attitude towards the war. From both Tables 12.16 and 12.17, but more importantly in this case, Table 12.17, the stronger the approval for the Task Force the greater the approval of being lied to. It would seem, therefore, that it was these individuals who approved of the *militarization of the media* to turn public information into an extension of the war effort to go beyond *negative censorship* to a desire for *positive censorship*.

Moving away from censorship as such to the question of desire for open reporting it is clear from Table 12.18 that the overriding mass of the population, three quarters in fact, are in favour of reporting information even though it might reflect unfavourably on British troops. Not surprisingly, perhaps, most of those would prefer such damaging stories to be made public only after the conflict – 49 percent of the total population. Nevertheless, 26 percent thought journalists ought to include such material in the despatches even whilst the conflict was in progress, 8 percent more than those who considered that it should *never* come to light. It does represent a very strong desire on the part of the public for a truthful media. What is interesting is that those who actually knew someone with the Task Force were as prepared to have unfavourable material published as anyone else: 77 percent compared to 76 percent who had no connection with the Armed Forces, 75 percent who knew someone in the Services and 72 percent who had been a member of the Forces themselves. Even as the war was in progress, 27 percent of them wished that unfavourable material, if it existed, should not be hidden.

The split between Conservative and Labour voters appears as a return to pattern, but there is a difference which is easily over-looked. For example, (36 percent) of those who voted Labour and considered that a journalist, if in possession of unfavourable material, ought to file it at the time of engagement compares with only 17 percent of Conservatives who thought so. However, when combined with a preference for publishing after the war there is only a 3 percent difference. What this suggests is a basic commit-ment to the democratic values reported in the previous section. The support for publishing whilst the war was in progress is a *tactical consideration*, but the lack of desire to withold information once

Table 12.18 *If a journalist with the Task Force discovered something very unfavourable about the conduct of the British troops should he disclose it?*

	Total	Readership								Vote 1979		Armed Forces connection			
		Express	Mail	Mirror/Record	Telegr.	Guard.	Star	Sun	Times	Con.	Lab.	Been in	Knew T.F.	Knew Forces	None
Total	1076 100%	224	210	314	149	62	107	317	42	410	291	159	239	205	488
Publish while Conflict going on	284 26%	44 20%	48 23%	102 32%	30 20%	17 27%	37 35%	111 35%	12 29%	69 17%	105 36%	54 21%	64 27%	50 24%	136 28%
Not publish until Conflict over	523 49%	120 54%	111 53%	149 47%	85 57%	37 60%	47 44%	133 42%	22 52%	239 58%	123 42%	132 51%	119 50%	104 51%	232 48%
Not even publish after Conflict	193 18%	42 19%	39 19%	42 13%	27 18%	5 8%	16 15%	53 17%	5 12%	83 20%	46 16%	60 23%	40 17%	40 20%	80 16%
Don't know	76 7%	18 8%	12 6%	21 7%	7 5%	3 5%	7 7%	20 6%	3 7%	19 5%	17 6%	13 5%	16 7%	11 5%	40 8%

Base – all

hostilities were over is a *preference for truth* and on that Conservative and Labour voters hardly differ.

It is this difference between *tactical considerations* and *truth preferences* which may be the answer in explaining why *Guardian* readers do not, as might be expected from previous performances, outdistance readers of other papers in their approval for publishing unfavourable reports whilst the war was in operation.

These findings were then compared with answers to our earlier questions about preferences for one sort of language or another. The comparison is important; those who favour the publication of material that might reflect badly on the Forces are showing that they prefer to be given information rather than have it kept from them, indicating an independence of mind and a wish for material on which to make well-informed judgements. We would expect such people to prefer that information be given in neutral, rather than partisan, language. The information in our survey showed that there is indeed such a connection. Table 12.19 shows that among those favouring publication of possibly embarrassing material during a conflict, fully 80 percent preferred the use of the term 'Argentinian forces' to that of 'enemy', dropping to 76 percent preferring 'Argentinian forces' amonst those who wish publication only after the war was over, falling to the low of 71 percent preferring 'Argentinian forces' amongst those who did not want such material published at all.

The information obtained in previous chapters concerned the procedures by which governments and broadcasters operated, in deciding what to publish, and in what form, at a time of crisis. We were, however, equally interested in the general climate in which such decisions were made. Were they taken against a – possibly assumed – background of opinion which was tolerant or intolerant of criticism of public institutions, eager or reluctant to hear, see and read diverse and critical views? We therefore included in our survey two questions about the behaviour of television programmes, in times of conflict and, as a control, in normal times.

Tables 12.20 and 12.21 give our findings. It is clear that there is a great deal of popular support for critical current affairs programmes. In Table 12.20, for example, we see that 61 percent of those who watch such programmes believe that in times of conflict they should, if necessary, be critical.

If we then take those who do not hold this view, plus 'don't knows', and ask their opinion of programmes broadcast during 'normal' times, we find that only 27 percent still regard criticisms as wrong. Table 12.21 shows this clearly.

Table 12.19 *If a journalist with the Task Force discovered something very unfavourable about the conduct of British troops should he disclose it?*

	Total	Wording preferred				Censorship		Gov. false inf.		Media false inf.	
		Argent. Forces	Enemy Forces	British Forces	Our Forces	App.	Disap.	App.	Disap.	App.	Disap.
Total	1076 100%	801 74%	138 13%	586 54%	311 29%	700 65%	253 24%	372 35%	609 57%	229 21%	762 71%
Would publish it while Conflict going on	284 26% 100%	227 28% 80%	28 20% 10%	178 30% 63%	74 24% 26%	122 17% 43%	125 49% 44%	63 17% 22%	201 33% 71%	37 16% 13%	228 30% 80%
Not publish until Conflict over	523 49% 100%	397 50% 76%	70 51% 13%	285 49% 54%	150 48% 29%	384 55% 73%	88 35% 17%	214 58% 41%	269 44% 51%	131 57% 25%	359 47% 69%
Not publish even after Conflict	193 18% 100%	137 17% 71%	29 21% 15%	90 15% 47%	70 23% 36%	149 21% 77%	25 10% 13%	77 21% 40%	97 16% 50%	49 21% 25%	127 17% 66%
Don't know	76 7% 100%	40 5% 53%	11 8% 14%	33 6% 43%	17 5% 22%	45 6% 59%	15 6% 20%	18 5% 24%	42 7% 55%	12 5% 16%	48 6% 63%

Base – all

Table 12.20 *Should current affairs programmes criticize government in times of conflict?*

	Total	Readership								Sex		Voted 1979	
		Express	Mail	Mirror/Record	Telegr.	Guard.	Star	Sun	Times	Male	Fem.	Con.	Lab.
Total	751	167	165	223	113	49	82	225	36	376	375	293	198
	100%												
Should criticize if necessary	455	91	99	151	61	39	52	142	28	235	220	144	142
	61%	54%	60%	68%	54%	80%	63%	63%	78%	63%	59%	49%	72%
Should avoid criticism	264	72	62	60	48	9	27	73	8	130	134	140	49
	35%	43%	38%	27%	42%	18%	33%	32%	22%	35%	36%	48%	25%
Don't know	32	4	4	12	4	1	3	10	–	11	21	9	7
	4%	2%	2%	5%	4%	2%	4%	4%	–	3%	6%	3%	4%

Base – all who ever watch current affairs programmes

Table 12.21 *Should current affairs programmes criticize government in normal times?*

	Total	Readership								Sex		Voted 1979	
		Express	Mail	Mirror/Record	Telegr.	Guard.	Star	Sun	Times	Male	Fem.	Con.	Lab.
Total	296	76	66	72	52	10	30	83	8	141	155	149	56
	100%												
Should criticize if necessary	198	52	52	54	38	7	22	54	7	110	88	108	36
	67%	68%	79%	75%	73%	70%	73%	65%	88%	78%	57%	72%	64%
Should avoid criticism	80	21	14	13	12	2	8	25	1	26	54	34	17
	27%	28%	21%	18%	23%	20%	27%	30%	13%	18%	35%	23%	30%
Don't know	18	3	–	5	2	1	–	4	–	5	13	7	3
	6%	4%	–	7%	4%	10%	–	5%	–	4%	8%	5%	5%

Base – all who think current affairs programmes *should not criticize government in times of crisis*

Thus we find that a mere 11 percent of the total population who watch current affairs programmes consider it wrong to criticize the Government during normal times. Broadcasters who wish to take a critical stance therefore do so in the light of strong popular support for the principle of journalistic independence, in both normal and conflict times.

Since it was in some of the newspapers that accusations of 'treachery' on the part of the broadcasters first appeared, it is particularly interesting to see whether their readers themselves shared the view that television programmes should not criticize the Government in times of conflict. In fact, as Table 12.20 shows, not one set of readers agrees with such an editorial line. In the case of the *Sun*, for example, 63 percent of readers support the broadcasters' right to criticize. As for 'normal' circumstances, Table 12.21 shows that support is even stronger. It would appear that the public distinguishes between the role of journalists and that of opposition parties in Parliament at a time of conflict. For example as many as 50 percent of our respondents maintained that, in such times, Members should refrain from criticizing the Government's handling of a conflict like the Falklands war. Five percent did not know and 45 per cent considered criticism appropriate. The explanation for the difference seems likely to revolve around attitudes towards representation. That is, that the current affairs programmes represent journalistic values whilst Parliament represents the nation.

Those tables tell us much about the principles which give a guide to people's reactions. Next we looked at opinion in practice. What did people think of the current affairs programmes they watched during the Falklands war itself? Table 12.22 shows that while 19 per cent considered them over-critical of the Government and 14 per cent saw them as insufficiently critical, 60 percent believed them to be 'about right'.

Comparing information acquired from our earlier questions with these later replies produces some revealing findings. For example, of the 61 percent who said they thought current affairs programmes should be critical in times of crisis, 8 percent believed that in the Falklands case they went too far. Twenty-one percent of the same group, however, thought programmes insufficiently critical.

Such a high level of dissatisfaction, 21 percent, might, we thought, indicate something more: the belief, perhaps, that the Government deserved more criticism. Sure enough, Table 12.22 indicates that more Labour voters, 29 percent, than Conservatives, 5 percent, fell into this category of the disappointed. Our figures hold, however, much more than this. The clue lies in our findings as to whether people approved or disapproved of the sending of the

Table 12.22   *Thinking back to the Falklands crisis, would you say that the TV current affairs programmes you saw were:*

	Total	Readership							
		Express	Mail	Mirror/ Record	Teleg.	Guard.	Star	Sun	Times
Total	699	161	153	210	105	45	76	210	34
	100%	23%	22%	30%	15%	6%	11%	30%	5%
Too critical	136	40	35	30	16	4	12	37	1
of gov.	19%	25%	23%	14%	15%	9%	16%	18%	3%
	100%	29%	26%	22%	12%	3%	9%	27%	1%
Not critical	99	20	15	44	9	15	16	31	6
enough	14%	12%	10%	21%	9%	33%	21%	15%	18%
	100%	20%	15%	44%	9%	15%	16%	31%	6%
About right	418	90	95	120	72	25	44	134	25
	60%	56%	62%	57%	69%	56%	58%	64%	74%
	100%	22%	23%	29%	17%	6%	11%	32%	6%
Other answer	6	2	2	–	2	–	–	–	1
	1%	1%	1%	–	2%	–	–	–	3%
	100%	33%	33%	–	33%	–	–	–	17%
Can't	17	4	3	7	5	1	3	3	–
remember	2%	2%	2%	3%	5%	2%	4%	1%	–
	100%	24%	18%	41%	29%	6%	18%	18%	–
Don't know	23	5	3	9	1	–	1	5	1
	3%	3%	2%	4%	1%	–	1%	2%	3%
	100%	13%	13%	39%	4%	–	4%	22%	4%

Base – all who watched current affairs programmes during the conflict

Task Force, or, most importantly, whether they cared at all, either way. We matched this information to respondents' views about the quality of current affairs programmes. It appeared that, of those who strongly approved of the despatch of the Task Force, 8 percent considered such programmes insufficiently critical; of those who merely approved, 8 percent again; and of those who neither approved nor disapproved, 10 percent. Of those who disapproved of the sailing, however, as many as 44 percent thought the programmes insufficiently critical. It would appear that there is a strong correlation between attitudes to the policy with which such programmes deal and attitudes to the programmes themselves. Those who found programmes insufficiently critical were talking less about questions of 'impartiality', 'balance' or 'bias' and more about the degree to which the policy that was being discussed was questioned and challenged. We would suggest that, the greater the division in public opinion on any issue, the greater will be the argument as to what is, or is not, a 'critical' programme.

The acceptance of criticism as a legitimate principle of current

Table 12.22 (continued)

	Current affairs			Voted 1979		Task Force approval			
	Crisis		Normal						
Crit.	Not crit.	Crit.	Not crit.	Con.	Lab.	Appr. str.	Appr.	Neither	Disap.
424	249	186	76	274	183	248	276	52	118
61%	36%	27%	11%	39%	26%	26%	35%	7%	17%
36	95	66	32	73	21	73	46	10	7
8%	38%	35%	42%	27%	11%	29%	17%	19%	6%
26%	70%	49%	24%	54%	15%	54%	34%	7%	5%
87	11	11	1	14	53	19	23	5	52
21%	4%	6%	1%	5%	29%	8%	8%	10%	44%
88%	11%	11%	1%	14%	54%	19%	23%	5%	53%
277	125	95	31	172	100	133	193	32	55
65%	50%	51%	49%	68%	55%	55%	63%	62%	47%
66%	30%	23%	9%	41%	24%	53%	45%	8%	13%
5	1	1	–	2	1	2	2	1	1
1%	*	1%	–	1%	1%	1%	1%	2%	1%
83%	17%	17%	–	33%	7%	33%	33%	17%	17%
9	7	4	4	6	4	8	6	1	2
2%	3%	2%	5%	2%	2%	3%	2%	2%	2%
53%	41%	24%	24%	35%	24%	47%	35%	5%	12%
10	10	9	2	7	4	8	11	3	1
2%	4%	5%	3%	3%	2%	3%	4%	6%	1%
43%	43%	39%	9%	30%	17%	35%	48%	13%	4%

affairs programming would appear from Table 12.23 to be linked with notions of fairness, if fairness is taken to mean equal coverage for the participants in a dispute. On that basis, then the majority of those who actually watch current affairs programmes expect them to be fair. For example, 55 percent considered that the Argentinians ought to have been given equal coverage with Britain. Given the nature of the dispute, it is a remarkable testament to the extent to which the concept of fairness, which the public holds towards current affairs programmes, is embedded within British broadcasting culture. However, any single attitude is not something which is struck *ex nihilo* in isolation from a totality of attitudes collectively viewed as a disposition. Thus, it is interesting that of those who considered that current affairs programmes ought to be critical of the Government even in a crisis situation, more (62 percent) considered that equal coverage should be afforded to Argentinian than those who thought current affairs programmes ought not to criticize at such times (45 percent) (Table 12.23). The same also holds true for those who in normal times considered that current affairs

Table 12.23   *Should current affairs programmes have given Britain and Argentina equal coverage during Falklands Conflict?*

	Total	Readership							
		Express	Mail	Mirror/ Record	Teleg.	Guard.	Star	Sun	Times
Total	751	167	165	223	113	49	82	225	36
	100%								
Equal	414	81	83	134	53	33	39	119	16
coverage	55%	49%	50%	60%	47%	67%	48%	53%	44%
Concentrate	313	79	78	84	57	15	39	103	19
on Britain	42%	47%	47%	38%	50%	31%	48%	46%	53%
Don't know	24	7	4	5	3	1	4	3	1
	3%	4%	2%	2%	3%	2%	5%	1%	3%

Base – all who ever watch current affairs programmes

programmes ought to be critical – 56 percent wanted equal coverage as opposed to 51 percent of those who opposed criticism even in routine times. (The score is a combined one with 'critical in crisis times' included because they were excluded from the 'normal times' question on the grounds that they would automatically agree and therefore must be transferred over.) Whilst the preference, or, more accurately, agreement, that criticism is a rightful part of current affairs programmes is associated with fairness, the issue itself ought not to be overlooked in framing attitudes towards coverage, and is related to our earlier point about the primacy of the topic when judging reaction in terms of the perceived critical approach to it.

Furthermore, opinions about 'fairness' were affected by respondents' views of the issue itself. People who believed that Argentina's claim had 'a lot of justification' tended to think that equal coverage should be given (79 percent), while those considering that Argentina had no rightful claim at all tended to be less keen on equal coverage (41 percent). However firmly the public holds to the notion of 'fairness' in general, and however carefully broadcasters try to satisfy it, programme-makers apparently cannot win: the actions and claims of the participants in any dispute will themselves shape popular attitudes to what is 'fair' treatment.

We then looked more closely at different notions of what was and what was not 'fair', by asking the public whether certain groups should or should not have access to television programmes to make their case. From Tables 12.23 and 12.24 it appeared that those who believed Argentina to have no claim to the Falklands also felt that other parties and factions with whom they disagreed should receive only restricted coverage. For instance, as Table 12.24 shows, the

Table 12.23 (continued)

	Current affairs				Voted 1979		Arg. claim just		
	Crisis		Normal						
	Crit.	Not	Crit.	Not	Con.	Lab.	Lot	Little	Not
	455	264	198	80	293	198	112	284	298
	284	119	81	41	134	126	89	164	122
	62%	45%	41%	51%	46%	64%	79%	58%	41%
	157	138	110	37	149	67	21	113	166
	35%	52%	56%	46%	51%	34%	19%	40%	56%
	14	7	7	2	10	5	2	7	10
	3%	3%	4%	3%	3%	3%	2%	2%	3%

less an individual thought of Argentina's claim, the less willing he or she was to see on television coverage of the cause of the Communist Party, the National Front, the IRA or the Red Brigade.

Table 12.24 suggests that a broader measure of 'tolerance' was to be found among Labour voters than among Conservative voters – not just as far as the Falklands coverage was concerned but as regards all five topics on which we questioned respondents.

From the evidence so far we can draw some simple conclusions about the nature of 'balance' in television current affairs programmes and about viewers' perceptions. In an effort to provide 'balanced coverage', television programme-makers seek on each issue to give fair coverage to both sides. To their surprise this does not protect them from criticism. The fact that in each case criticism generally comes *from* both sides is taken, carefully, to be evidence that coverage must have been 'fair'. In fact, as we have seen, views as to what is or is not fair are shaped by more complex influences than, for example, political allegiance or attitudes to a particular dispute. By striving even harder to achieve, say, political balance, broadcasters simply draw further accusations of 'unfairness' upon themselves. What is much harder, perhaps impossible, for them to do is to suit many constituents who display various degrees of tolerance.

As Table 12.25 shows, during the Falklands dispute 51 percent of viewers who felt current affairs programmes should concentrate on Britain, did not believe that Argentina's case was overemphasized. This suggests, we think, a remarkably high level of 'tolerance' among the British public.

As far as perceptions go, a majority of the public did not think television current affairs coverage 'unfair'.

Our questions about television coverage have so far been concentrated on the public's views of current affairs programmes. Since even more of the population, 98 percent of our sample, watch the television news than watch current affairs programmes (70 percent), we thought it useful in the next stage of our survey to turn our attention to news coverage. All in all, most replies confirm the trends we have seen so far: for instance, as Table 12.26 indicates, where the news is concerned, there is a positive correlation between belief in the justice of Argentina's claim and the desire for equal television coverage.

We also explored the relationship between questions of 'fairness' and attitudes to a specific issue, the sending of the Task Force. Table 12.26, for example, shows the relationship very clearly. Seventy-one percent of those who disapproved of the Task Force's despatch wanted equal coverage; only 44 percent of those who strongly approved of the sailing of the Task Force wished for equal coverage. From Table 12.27, however, we see that, of those who believed that the news ought to have concentrated on Britain's point of view, the overwhelming majority, 73 percent, thought that 'in normal times' there should be equal coverage given to the participants of a dispute.

There is among this group little difference between those who strongly approved of the Task Force's sailing and those who did not (67 percent: 69 percent). In 'normal times' they believe in the principle of fairness.

From this evidence it would be easy to deduce that, whereas some people adhere to the principle of 'fairness' when it is in line with their beliefs about specific issues (i.e. those who approved of the sending of the Task Force), others will adhere to it at all times. Those who disapproved of the Task Force's departure *and* wanted equal coverage fall into the latter category. Let us now however look at people's reactions to television news coverage of war. Table 12.28 reveals that 65 percent found nothing to worry about in the news coverage; these non-worriers were drawn equally from those who approved strongly and those who disapproved of the sending of the Task Force. But what about the people who did find things to worry about? One criticism was, for instance, that the news 'glorified war'; 10 percent of those who strongly approved the Task Force's sailing and also were worried by TV news reporting felt this compared to 24 percent who had disapproved of the Task Force sailing. Another worry was that the news showed too much blood and horror; here the position was reversed. Of those who strongly approved of the Task Force sailing 7 percent were worried

Table 12.24   *Should be on television*

		Total	Vote 1979		Arg. claim just		
			Con.	Lab.	Lot	Little	Not at all
Total		1076	410	291	147	382	446
		100%					
Communist	Yes	663	229	198	114	256	237
		62%	56%	68%	78%	67%	53%
	No	352	158	80	29	103	190
		33%	39%	27%	20%	27%	43%
National Front	Yes	555	200	150	95	228	183
		52%	49%	52%	65%	60%	41%
	No	455	189	126	46	130	241
		42%	46%	43%	31%	34%	54%
IRA	Yes	326	107	96	71	130	96
		30%	26%	33%	48%	34%	22%
	No	698	292	178	67	237	323
		65%	71%	61%	46%	62%	75%
Red Brigades	Yes	256	79	78	53	106	73
		24%	19%	27%	36%	28%	16%
	No	763	315	201	85	259	356
		71%	77%	69%	58%	68%	80%

Base – all

Table 12.25   *Thinking back to the Falklands crisis do you think any of the current affairs programmes gave too much emphasis to Argentina's point of view or not?*

	Total	Voted 1979		Arg. claim just		
		Con.	Lab.	Lot	Little	None
Total	320	152	69	20	115	170
	100%					
Yes	121	60	24	7	36	74
	38%	39%	35%	35%	31%	44%
No	164	73	36	11	72	74
	51%	48%	52%	55%	63%	44%
Didn't see any	3	2	1	–	–	3
	1%	1%	1%	–	–	2%
Don't know	32	17	8	2	7	19
	10%	11%	12%	10%	6%	11%

Base – all those who think current affairs programmes should have concentrated on Britain

Table 12.26 *During the Falklands crisis do you think TV news should have given equal coverage to both Argentina's and Britain's points of view or should it have concentrated more on Britain's point of view?*

	Total	Armed Forces connection				Arg. claim just			Task Force approval			
		Been in	Know T.F.	Know Forces	None	Lot	Little	None	Appr. str.	Appr.	Neither	Disappr.
Total	1052	254	233	202	475	143	377	437	355	396	112	179
	100%	24%	22%	19%	45%	14%	36%	42%	34%	36%	11%	17%
Equal coverage	545	119	108	99	262	95	194	190	155	192	66	127
	52%	47%	46%	49%	55%	66%	51%	43%	44%	48%	59%	71%
	100%	22%	20%	18%	48%	17%	36%	35%	28%	35%	12%	23%
Concentrate on Britain	471	128	117	98	193	42	169	240	190	195	39	43
	45%	50%	50%	49%	41%	29%	45%	55%	54%	49%	35%	24%
	100%	27%	25%	21%	41%	9%	36%	51%	40%	41%	8%	9%
Don't know	36	7	8	5	20	6	14	7	10	9	7	9
	3%	3%	3%	2%	4%	4%	4%	2%	3%	2%	6%	5%
	100%	19%	22%	14%	56%	17%	39%	19%	28%	25%	19%	25%

Base – all who watch news on TV

Table 12.27 *In normal circumstances when there is no national crisis do you think TV news should always give equal coverage to both sides in a dispute or is it sometimes right to take sides?*

	Total	Armed Forces connection				Arg. claim just			Task Force approval			
		Been in	Know T.F.	Know Forces	None	Lot	Little	None	Appr. str.	Appr.	Neither	Disappr.
Total	507	135	125	103	213	48	183	247	200	204	46	52
	100%	27%	25%	20%	42%	9%	36%	49%	39%	40%	9%	10%
Always give equal coverage	368	99	91	82	148	35	139	173	133	163	33	36
	73%	73%	73%	80%	69%	73%	76%	70%	67%	80%	72%	69%
	100%	27%	25%	22%	40%	10%	38%	47%	36%	44%	9%	10%
Sometimes take sides	79	22	20	9	36	7	27	42	39	25	4	10
	16%	16%	16%	9%	17%	15%	15%	17%	20%	12%	9%	19%
	100%	28%	25%	11%	46%	9%	34%	53%	49%	32%	5%	13%
Depends on dispute	52	12	12	12	24	5	15	28	26	13	8	4
	10%	9%	10%	12%	11%	10%	8%	11%	13%	6%	17%	8%
	100%	23%	23%	23%	46%	10%	29%	54%	50%	25%	15%	8%
Don't know	8	2	2	–	5	1	2	4	2	3	1	2
	2%	1%	2%	–	2%	2%	1%	2%	1%	1%	2%	4%
	100%	25%	25%		63%	13%	25%	50%	25%	38%	13%	25%

Base – all who think TV news should have concentrated on Britain's point of view

Table 12.28   *What things worried you about TV news reporting?*

	Total	Readership							
		Express	Mail	Mirror/ Record	Teleg.	Guard.	Star	Sun	Times
Total	331 100%	84	77	92	57	33	36	87	21
Too much information/ details: could help Argentinians	105 32%	32 38%	28 36%	22 24%	18 32%	4 12%	12 33%	28 32%	4 19%
Totally neutral: should have been more pro-British	18 5%	7 8%	5 6%	5 5%	3 5%	2 6%	2 6%	3 3%	1 5%
Too pro-British: should have been more neutral	24 7%	3 4%	3 4%	9 10%	5 9%	8 24%	2 6%	6 7%	3 14%
Too gory/ shocking – showing injuries	27 8%	6 7%	6 8%	7 8%	3 5%	– –	2 6%	6 7%	1 5%
Glorifying war/ sensationalism	46 14%	10 12%	6 8%	20 22%	7 12%	9 27%	7 19%	10 11%	5 24%
Not enough pictures/no live pictures	29 9%	9 11%	4 5%	7 8%	6 11%	3 9%	2 6%	5 6%	5 24%
Other	124 37%	30 36%	32 42%	36 39%	24 42%	15 45%	13 36%	33 38%	10 48%
Don't know	7 2%	5 6%	3 4%	4 4%	1 2%	1 3%	– –	2 2%	– –

Base – all worried by TV news reporting

compared to 3 percent of 'Task Force disapprovers'.

What this suggests is at work is the issue raised at various points in the book concerning the belief that televised war ought to show gore in order to discourage such activity. In other words, news should not so much carry information about *the war* but carry information about *war* as a statement of the condition of humanity. In this context it is not surprising that those who were against the Task Force and the use of force, should not be so worried about the portrayal of vileness of battle as those who supported the Task Force. If anything, the vivid portrayal of slaughter could be con-

Table 12.28 (continued)

	Armed Forces connection			Task Force approval			
Been in	Knew T.F.	Knew Forces	None	Appr. str.	Appr.	Neither	Disappr.
79	82	69	136	139	101	21	70
30	19	25	44	61	27	4	13
38%	23%	36%	32%	44%	27%	19%	19%
4	6	6	5	13	4	–	1
5%	7%	9%	4%	9%	4%	–	1%
1	7	5	11	3	4	2	15
1%	9%	7%	8%	2%	4%	10%	21%
5	7	6	11	10	13	2	2
6%	9%	9%	8%	7%	13%	10%	3%
10	11	9	19	14	12	3	17
13%	13%	13%	14%	10%	12%	14%	24%
12	6	7	10	12	10	3	4
15%	7%	10%	7%	9%	10%	14%	5%
30	35	21	53	40	41	9	34
38%	43%	30%	39%	29%	41%	43%	49%
–	2	3	2	3	4	–	–
–	2%	4%	1%	2%	4%	–	–

sidered the best to come out of a bad situation. Futhermore, the fact that those who disapproved of the Task Force were also by far the most worried that the news glorified and sensationalized war fits the moralistic pattern. The fact, therefore, that those who disapproved of the Task Force only differ from those who approved by demanding equal coverage in times of war, not normal times, suggests that the wish for fairness is based on grounds other than 'pure' concern for the impartiality of television news as a principle of broadcasting. It is a moral principle about war, and one which the principle of fairness simply facilitates. 'Fairness' means that it is not a British position that is given nor an Argentinian one, but the method by which war can best be seen for what it is – horrific destruction which should not be obscured by national pride or partisanship. Judging from Table 12.27, *Guardian* readers would appear to be exceptionally well-represented amongst this group. They worried the most that the news was too pro-British, again fitting the notion that nationalism ought not to detract from the moral purpose of covering war. Admittedly we cannot be certain about this explanation. Nevertheless it is clear that the demand for fairness in coverage should be viewed as problematic of social explanation rather than be seen simplistically as an intellectual attitude towards information, as if attitudes to one thing are not formed from positions in other areas. What we are suggesting then is that the broadcasters can take some comfort in the extent to which there is popular support for some of the central canons of their professional ideology. They should not, however, imagine that the roots of such support are unitary nor that for quite substantial numbers of people their understanding of the nature and function of fairness and balance is the same.

It is the emotional component of the perceptions and demands made of the news that the coverage of the Falklands highlights. One can talk as we have done of a commitment to the principle of fairness, but one needs to know what being fair means when confronted by news which emotionally engages the viewer. It is essential, therefore, to understand the framework of reasoning surrounding individual responses. For example, it is quite clear that collectively the single most worrying aspect of the news was that it provided too much detailed information which might be of assistance to the Argentinians.

As Table 12.28 shows, of those who were worried by the news coverage, the least-worried were *Guardian* readers (only 12 percent concerned) and *Times* readers (only 19 percent concerned). These were also the groups who felt most keenly that television news was too pro-British. The *Sun* accused these newspapers of being 'unpatriotic'; we suspect, rather, that *Guardian* and *Times* readers were not careless of British lives but hungry for information. Indeed, Table 12.28 shows that there is no simple correlation between a concern to protect British lives and the desire for more information. Of those worried by TV news reporting, people who knew members of the Task Force, though perhaps worried by some aspects of the news, were the least anxious about the possibility that information might be given to the enemy than others. Only 23 percent found this a danger. It is likely that their desire for as much news as possible outweighed their fears. Table 12.26 shows that they did not particularly wish for a concentration on a British point of view and Table 12.27, as a control, shows that they are no different from others in their attitude towards news during normal non-crisis times. Emotional ties with members of the Forces seemed to feed an appetite for information, rather than 'patriotic' reporting which might obscure accuracy.

We have considered notions of 'balance' in relation to television current affairs programmes; now we will attempt to do the same for news. Since most of the controversy over news coverage concerned BBC, rather than ITN, broadcasts, we asked our respondents about their perceptions of each channel separately. We should bear in mind, however, that people are prone to confuse their recollections of the differences between stations and some misremembering is to be expected.

Our findings echo our earlier discoveries. Table 12.29, for example, which examines the opinion of people who thought that television news ought to have concentrated more on Britain's position, indicates that only 26 percent thought that too much emphasis was given to the Argentinian's point of view by the BBC and only 19 percent by ITV.

The largest category which perceived the news in those terms was those who approved the most strongly of the Task Force, 37 percent and 28 percent respectively for the BBC and ITV, compared to 17 per cent and 15 percent of those who disapproved. The interesting point, however, is that as shown by Table 12.26 the more an individual supported the Task Force the less he or she wanted equal coverage.

In other words, judging by Table 12.29, it was these latter who were likely to be most disappointed by the news coverage of the war. Remembering that those in Table 12.26 did not wish for equal coverage, what this probably means is that strong support for the Task Force prompted them to view the news as supporting Argentina more readily than did those who were not so certain in their support of a military venture. In understanding the news, it is not sufficient, therefore, to state via some form of content analysis what the news was if that very same content was not the same for different groups and individuals. It is not the same because of the different emotional attachments to the facts the news covers. In only the most formalistic sense is the news the same for everyone.

What about people who wanted 'equal coverage'? Table 12.30 shows that most thought it was not achieved.

Forty-two percent (42 percent BBC: 41 percent ITN) saw the news as favouring Britain and 2 percent (3 percent BBC: 2 per cent ITN) saw it as favouring Argentina, while 37 percent (37 percent BBC: 36 percent ITN) thought it evenly balanced.

Table 12.29   *During the Falklands crisis do you think the news on BBC/ITV gave too much emphasis to Argentina's point of view or not?*

	Total	BBC Task Force approval				Total	ITV Task Force approval			
		Appr. str.	Appr.	Neither	Disappr.		Appr. str.	Appr.	Neither	Disappr.
Total	507	200	204	46	52	507	200	204	46	52
	100%					100%				
Yes – too much	131	73	45	4	9	98	56	31	3	8
	26%	37%	22%	9%	17%	19%	28%	15%	7%	15%
No	290	99	130	28	30	312	109	137	32	30
	57%	50%	64%	61%	58%	62%	55%	67%	70%	58%
Didn't see BBC	15	3	7	–	5	26	8	9	2	7
	3%	2%	3%	–	10%	5%	4%	4%	4%	13%
Don't know	71	25	22	14	8	71	27	27	9	7
	14%	13%	11%	30%	15%	14%	14%	13%	20%	13%

Base – all who think TV news should have concentrated on Britain's point of view

The audience's response 341

Table 12.30 During the Falklands crisis do you think the news on BBC/ITV did give equal coverage to both sides' points of view or did it concentrate more on one side?

| | BBC | | | | | ITV | | | | |
| | Total | Task Force approval | | | | Total | Task Force approval | | | |
		Appr. str.	Appr.	Neither	Disappr.		Appr. str.	Appr.	Neither	Disappr.
Total	545 100%	155	192	66	127	545 100%	155	192	66	127
Did give equal coverage	202 37%	70 45%	75 39%	21 32%	34 27%	198 36%	71 46%	70 36%	19 29%	35 28%
More of Britain's point of view	230 42%	53 34%	74 39%	30 45%	72 57%	224 41%	54 35%	77 40%	30 45%	62 49%
More of Arg. point of view	15 3%	6 4%	6 3%	2 3%	1 1%	10 2%	4 3%	5 3%	1 2%	–
Varied too much to say	6 1%	1 1%	3 2%	–	2 2%	11 2%	2 1%	4 2%	–	5 4%
Didn't see any BBC	30 6%	8 5%	10 5%	4 6%	7 6%	26 5%	6 4%	5 3%	2 3%	13 10%
Don't know	62 11%	17 11%	24 13%	9 14%	11 9%	76 14%	18 12%	31 16%	14 21%	12 9%

Base – all who thinks TV news should have given equal coverage to Britain and Argentina

One curious aspect of the Falklands Conflict was that the British public had access to Argentinian news film, something which became highly controversial. However, only 13 percent of the population actually objected to seeing Argentinian film on their television screens (Table 12.31), while a further 4 percent considered there was too much of it although they did not object. The majority of the viewing public – 58 percent – did not object to such film, or the amount, believing it to be 'about right', with a further 7 percent wishing for more than was actually shown.

Those who did object came equally from both of the main political parties; more interestingly, and now, perhaps, predictably, the greater the belief in the legitimacy of the Argentinian claim, the less the objection, and vice versa.

To an appreciable extent, it seems altogether that a large proportion of the British public hardly felt that Britain was at war with Argentina at all. The desire to transform a battle into a national struggle appears to have been missing. This may in part account for the *Sun*'s unpopularity with its readers, who as Table 12.31 indicates were prepared as much as most, to see Argentinian film on their television screens. More generally, it may be that our findings themselves reflect the nature of this particular case. In a different setting, where people do feel engaged in a vital national struggle, there may be less readiness to have equal coverage or to see 'enemy' film.

We have attempted in this chapter to give some empirical understanding of how the audience for the news of the Falklands Conflict received or rather perceived it. The basic theoretical position taken, however, is that any attempt at such understanding is valueless without knowing something about the audience – its social composition, attitudes to the war, and attitudes to the media in general. The argument behind this is that the audience does not stand in relation to the media independently of other relationships which have shaped opinion and are brought into play when viewing, listening or reading the news. The audience for the modern communication of news is a mass only in the sense of size, not in terms of differentiation, and it is the differences which give the content different meanings.

To understand, therefore, from some formal construction what the news is, only informs what imagery is on offer on the construction as presented; it does not say how it is accepted.

Information – neutral and open – was wanted. Though some, informed by their views about war in general and this war in particular, were unhappy with its coverage, there was no surge of discontent on the part of the public. Indeed, it was the critics –

Table 12.31a *Reaction to Argentinian film*

	Total	Voted 1979		Arg. claim just			Task Force approval			
		Con.	Lab.	Lot	Little	None	Approve strongly	Approve	Neither	Disapprove
Total	1052 100%	405	285	143	377	437	355	396	112	179
Objected	137 13%	54 13%	39 14%	13 9%	40 11%	76 17%	61 17%	45 11%	13 12%	16 9%
Didn't object too much	46 4%	23 6%	10 4%	3 2%	13 3%	27 6%	23 6%	16 4%	2 2%	5 3%
About right	608 58%	243 60%	157 55%	78 55%	234 62%	246 56%	205 58%	251 63%	58 52%	88 49%
Too little	76 7%	23 6%	22 8%	25 17%	25 7%	17 4%	15 4%	25 6%	8 7%	26 15%
Don't know	185 18%	62 15%	57 20%	24 17%	65 17%	71 16%	51 14%	59 15%	31 28%	44 25%

Base – all who saw TV news

Table 12.31b   *Readership*

	Express	Mail	Mirror/ Record	Telegraph	Guardian	Star	Sun	Times
Total	219	207	308	142	61	107	312	41
Objected	35	25	37	9	–	15	47	–
	16%	12%	12%	6%	–	14%	15%	–
Did not object	16	10	12	10	1	2	10	1
too much	7%	5%	4%	7%	2%	2%	3%	2%
About right	123	123	186	88	37	64	184	32
	56%	59%	60%	62%	61%	60%	59%	78%
Too little	17	18	24	15	10	8	21	5
	8%	9%	8%	11%	16%	7%	7%	12%
Don't know	28	31	49	20	13	18	50	3
	13%	15%	16%	14%	21%	17%	16%	7%

politicians and newspapers like the *Sun* – who were isolated. Their intolerance contrasted sharply with the general tolerance of the public. Perceptions of bias do not necessarily reflect political allegiance; they refelect a whole variety of opinions and attitudes.

In terms of individual news items or programmes what this means is that the charge of bias may be levied by individuals who consider other items and other programmes fair, and this, as we have endeavoured to point out, does not follow a strictly political divide but stems from subtleties of attitudes to a whole variety of items in the news which individuals have opinions about. Such analysis does not mean that the broadcaster can cavalierly discount criticism as being no more than the expected complaints of coloured emotional interest; but it is to place the charge of bias over individual topics into some kind of operative, protective framework of defence. It is the criticism over time, and over a variety of topics, and the emergence of any consensus of feelings that desired principles are not being adhered to which requires the most serious attention, not individual coverage.

It is fundamental for the broadcasters to appreciate from the survey returns the basic freedom which the public gives them to operate independently to attempt to display opposing positions, to criticize government policies if considered necessary in current affairs programmes, and not to collude in misinformation. From this appreciation should come some understanding of the type of ground which is the popular broadcasting culture within which they operate. The war in the Falklands tested not just battle might in the South Atlantic, but also that culture.

Conclusion

By calling this book *Journalists at War* we meant to signify that our study was about the gathering of war news and also to denote a battle for information. This hopefully we have done. In particular we wanted to show journalists at work in a situation that allowed clear vision of the practices that they are likely to employ, whether covering a war or not. It is not our intention in the conclusion to go over old ground and draw out the salient features of what it is to be a journalist. They have told their own story and we have made our interpretations of their behaviour as the story unfolded.

Yet *Journalists at War* is also about the battle for information, and of how a society tells a story about itself. That battle, however, is far from simple. Some of the ingredients have already been illustrated in our story, but it is the political climate surrounding news that we now wish to discuss. Our conclusion therefore is not so much a closing statement about the study, but the opening of further discussion on the role of information in society. The points we make are not drawn from the empirical data of the study, but based on issues which in the course of our research required consideration.

The British Government attacked sections of the media for its coverage of the Falklands Conflict, but does attack signify a lack of appreciation for the free flow of information? It may, but all governments will, to some extent, attempt to control the media and none more so than at a time of crisis. The attempt to manage the news is in the nature of the beast, as it is for other animals to resist the attempt at control. That struggle is a political one but, because the Falklands crisis offers an old lesson, it does not mean there are no new ones to be learnt.

We have pointed to the battle for information and pointed to the extent of the effort at control, but were the attacks on the media, the BBC in particular, simply part of that general effort at control or did they demonstrate other more malignant features? We think they did, and if our analysis is correct, they have much wider implications than the control of information. First however, we need to dispel some myths about the media and war.

After the war, came enquiry. The Ministry of Defence established a study group under the leadership of General Sir Hugh Beach to inquire into new information measures that might be adopted in the light of the Falklands experience. Because other studies have discussed this enquiry at length we will not go into the resulting report, but the line contained in the Beach Report, 'It is important for public morale that as much news as possible reaches the people', requires some comment. As a statement it scarcely disguises the view that the public could be a problem in the achievement of some administrative end.

News organizations, like any organ of enquiry, make judgements concerning what facts are necessary to enable the audience to understand events, and as such the construction of the news involves an intellectual task. The type of logic displayed by the Beach Report, however, is light years away from appreciating that *type* of excercise: its thinking is more part of a therapeutic exercise to produce a state of psychological well-being, in which the individual is to have no say over the development of his own condition. Yet if the managing of public morale (and reading the Beach Report carefully, that would involve giving very little unsupervised news indeed) forces the government to concern itself with news, one needs to know on what that concern is based. Is it based on muddled thinking about the effects of war news and the wrong lessons of the Americans' experience of Vietnam? The failure to understand the nature of war threatens to damage the cause of open reporting.

The demand that wars should be fully and openly reported is not necessarily wrong, but the belief that showing its full horror will affect the continuation of war is misplaced. It is also a dangerous idea to place in the heads of government. The belief that the media's portrayal of war possesses the power to affect the course of war, if accepted, is bound to worry any government committed to the armed resolution of a political difficulty. For example, the USA, drawing on the wrong lessons of the Falklands Conflict and of Vietnam, took no chances with their invasion of Grenada. No television coverage was allowed except for the military's own cameramen. It is one thing therefore to state out of ideological righteousness that governments have no right to interfere with the news when security is not involved, but another to ignore the fact that worried governments will interfere and make their own ideological justifications for doing so.

Even though the cry that the Falklands war was deliberately sanitized by not allowing immediate television pictures has no foundation, the belief persists that had 'gore news' been shown the effect would have been to lessen the public's resolve to see the war through. Historically, there is no evidence to suggest that showing the horrors of war act as a brake on existing wars or indeed make wars in the future less likely. Wars are ended by defeat and begun with the sure certainty that much horror will follow. The horror of war is not some closely guarded military secret: civilians through the ages who have experienced war know its full horror and, more recently, through the visual media of television, so does most of the world. The point is that whether war is at close quarters or removed, the knowledge and portrayal of it makes no difference to a course whose causes rest outside the shock of events as they unfold. Certainly, the increased destructive power of modern weaponry may add fear, it may even add caution, but there is nothing in the past to suppose the imagined horror will stop war, and the destructive capacity of opposing forces are not horrors to military consideration so much as technical factors to be catered for. Political and power arrangements make war more or less likely, not sentimentality.

Yet the belief persists that the graphic portrayal of horror has the power to stop war and is given tremendous currency and apparent support by the American experience of the coverage of Vietnam. In fact, from historical evidence the counter-hypothesis, that the graphic portrayal of destruction is more likely to stiffen resolve to fight and foster the revengeful desire to inflict further destruction, is a stronger candidate for support.

Provided the justice of the cause is believed in then horror stories through the ages have been good for resolve. For example, the atrocity stories during the First World War of German troops raping Belgium nuns were meant precisely to fuel hatred for the enemy and stiffen the will to fight. Similarly, the International Brigade was raised to fight in Spain by sympathetic Republican writers and journalists who detailed the destruction and savagery of Franco's forces.

The mistaken belief in the power of information to alter the course of war has undoubtedly been fed by the sheer hope that if only the inhumanity of such events were given greater coverage, the acts of barbarity which war involves would be unthinkable. It shows a touching faith in mankind's sensibilities and an acceptance that there is not much wrong with human affairs that cannot be put right by better communication. Why better communication and understanding of other peoples should lead to a reduction in aggression, all of which is implied in the wish to show the deliberately designed mass death of war, is a belief bordering on the mystical.

Another more 'scientific' belief is that the mass media, and television in particular, has a tremendous effect on people's attitudes and behaviour. There is not much research evidence to support such a case. The effects attributed to television on attitude change and behaviour require extreme qualification. The media are only part of an individual's social world and in terms of attitudes and behaviour not a primary influence: mass-media information works within a tightly bounded framework of other influences. Although disagreements exist within the academic community as to the precise influence of television, this is the basic conclusion of most social research in the area of effect studies. Yet when it comes to war scant regard is paid to what is known about television and its effects. The pictures we see of war do not come unhinged from the rest of our knowledge, experience, values and attitudes, but work on and with the existing meanings people have of war and political policy.

This may be a reality not easy to accept by political groups who, unable to influence political decisions about war, place their hope in the direct popular appeal of pictures to produce the type of policy decisions they would like to see. Some of the confusion may well be drawn from the experiences of artistic anti-war statement cinema. If that is the case then it is to misunderstand the context within which not just 'agitprop' works, but also the nature of anti-war statement cinema as compared to the news.

To be shocked and outraged by anti-war sentiments of films such as *All Quiet on the Western Front* or the *Grand Illusion* entails a different emotional development from that fostered by television news, or even the most proximate genre, the war documentary, with its often implied commentary on war's shocking nature. However, the film genre does not present nations or armies, but feelings and people. In some ways such cinema de-contextualizes and offers instead the immediacy of suffering as a shared attribute, capable of universal understanding. The possibility of this emotional tug, and the power of such cinema to create a belief that if only people understood the horror, the wasteful shame of war, war would become unthinkable, derives in part from placing issues in the background, stripping them of political life and bringing biography to the fore. No matter what the nationality of the participants, the development of character can summon up pacifist sentiments. It is the concentration within anti-war statement cinema on the individual which creates sympathetic identification.

The news, however, unless its practice is radically altered to include characterization beyond the 'home boy story', or beyond the type of close sympathetic writing of Ernie Pyle during the Second World War, is severely limited in its possibility of developing the kind of emotional state managed by such films. News is best seen as a first rough draft of history, not the making of a sentiment. Yet, the 'lessons' of Vietnam stay to haunt governments and to fuel the mistaken beliefs of others. During the Falklands Conflict it was feared by the Government that pictures of suffering would be brought into the living rooms of the nation and produce an outcry against the war. Both the hope and fear are premised on scantily understood lessons of American experience in Vietnam, and misunderstanding about the portrayal of horror. Certainly, it was the Government's political hope during the Falklands Conflict that when bodies started piling up on the beaches, a not-unexpected eventuality, the country would stand solid, not waver, and accept such costs as a legitimate price for a correct political policy. And that is precisely what the American television networks could not deliver to their audience with Vietnam – death with sense.

If there is a media lesson to be drawn from Vietnam, it is not the effect of pictures on American morale, but the shattering effect of information on an unprepared public, because it was uninformed about the course and nature of the struggle in South East Asia. Of course, the pictures were unpleasant because the policy was seen to be unpleasant. The setting fire to a peasant's hut by a G.I. with a Zippo lighter, if he has no right to set fire to it, looks and feels odd, but as long as the policy upon which war is fought is accepted as correct such news pictures, while disturbing, will not posses the power of social disruption. It is only if genuine questioning of policy is taking place, sufficient to enquire over the legitimacy of the exercise, that the news, indeed all news, even battle victories, becomes bad news. The acceptance level may differ depending on who is doing the dying, friend or foe, but graphic misery will upset; it does not necessarily need to be bloody to do so once the frame-work of the operation is placed in doubt. The captured hopelessness by the news of a refugee camp could be deeply disturbing to a public that does not accept the justice of its own case.

It is wrong, therefore, to invest the news with greater power than it actually possesses. To do so is to draw the wrong lessons from history, wrong lessons from effects studies, and worse, give hostage to those who would wish to restrict the free flow of communications.

Although our argument may go against the commonsense under-standing of the role of the media and the portrayal of war, it does not mean that the news by its portrayal of suffering can never disturb and weaken support for war. It can, but only, within a certain context. Nothing is static, and the news can become an articulator of concern when the images presented interact with other information which questions the validity of policy.

It is current affairs, with its tradition of challenge and discussion, the airing of opinion and dissenting voices, which has the capability of assembling the pictures shown by the news into a different framework of reception. The political outcry made during the Falk-lands against *Newsnight* and *Panorama* therefore, while ostensibly relating to the question of patriotic disloyalty, had a validity not fully realized by those bringing the charges. The danger posed by current affairs to the Government's standing was that, if policy was seen to be askew, the news pictures would have been perceived very differently indeed. Battlefield death would have become senseless slaughter. It is only with such shifts that the news can come into its own as a force for social distruption and fulfill the function accredited to it by those who believe the graphic portrayal of violence alone is its own argument for non-acceptance. The Government had reason to be nervous of current affairs programmes because had criticism promoted the questioning of policy the news would have become massively uncontrollable *vis* the Americans experience of Vietnam. The images of horror would then have offered a different moral tale, especially if the war went badly.

It is not the control of information therefore that is the problem for government, but the control of opinion. From our survey, it is quite clear that the public did not wish the 'fourth estate' to become the 'fourth service': it expected current affairs to be critical of government policy. The evidence is that the public want an independent media. Now we come to the second discussion point of our conclusion: the nature of the attack made on the broadcasting media during the Falklands crisis.

It is to be expected that no government, especially during a war, would have its policy criticized or challenged without fighting back. Despite the fact that criticism is predictable, it is essential to understand the precise nature of the attacks made during the Falklands if headway is to be made in assessing the threat they offered to media independence. Such understanding is even more important if those attacks hold lessons for the future.

The question is, therefore, whether the attacks were caused by the political desire to have the media toe the line of Government thought, an extension of the tension between the media and government during normal times, or whether they represented something more. Our answer is they did, and in doing so, offered warning about the delicate state of broadcasting in British society.

All cultural production is a contest for meaning, but there is a difference between the struggle for meaning in the sense of establishing an understanding of the world such as that engaged in by the journalists with the Task Force, and a struggle between cultures to have their own meanings of the world established. The latter is a political power struggle, and the attack on the media during the Falklands was just that; not in the ordinary sense of the attempt by government to control the media, but to settle permanently the cultural landscape. It would be a mistake, in other words, to see the attacks on the media merely as government acting like government, or one more twist in the disregard for the legitimacy of opposing views. The criticism this time had a more significant dimension.

What the attacks exposed was not so much the fear of information, but the dislike of certain social groups which traditionally have been either the brokers of ideas or formed the receptive cultural fabric for creative expression. Broadcasting culture forms part of a wider creative culture, and what was up for attack during the Falklands was the very base upon which the independence necessary for intellectual life depends: freedom from the political-economic base of society. The focus of our analysis is that of symbolic protest.

The whole idea of an independent media is that the news will be, or at least will possess the possibility of being, free from the desires of those it reports on and about. It is an ideal, and as with many ideals not always realized in practice. But the value of a principle is not necessarily its continual success so much as a standard by which to judge performance. Yet the independence of thought necessary for critical evaluation of government policy is not something which can readily be created. The confidence for critique operates within a developed ethos and tradition of performance and therefore, even though war presents new conditions, any damage to that ethos is to be viewed with concern. It is one thing, for example, for the media to struggle for access to information during a conflict and reasonable, based on experience, to expect difficulties, but it is quite another matter to struggle against a style of criticism which by its very temper is inimicable to the atmosphere necessary for broadcasting freedom. What characterized the attacks on the media during the Falklands Conflict was an intolerence rarely, if ever, seen in British broadcasting culture. It took a form beyond that which the media might expect to meet and answer in the course of general production and revealed an antagonism striking at the very heart of the principles of broadcasting which no defence of practice, and hence content, could hope to pacify.

The attacks on the BBC during the Falklands Conflict were not simply made on the principles of broadcasting but also on the cultural groups which were seen to embody those principles – the professional liberal classes which in Europe could more easily be referred to as the 'intelligentsia'. The attacks fell on the liberally educated, associated in the minds of the assailants with broadcasting personnel and the readers of the *Guardian*. It was an exhibition not just of political intolerance, but of the cultural resentment of position, beautifully captured by the MP Alan Clarke, present at the meeting of the Conservative Back Bench Media Group, when (as mentioned in Chapter 10) in referring to the onslaught on George

Howard, Chairman of the Board of Governors of the BBC and Alastair Milne, the Director General designate, he informed us: 'it is good for people in those sorts of positions to be roughed up. We have to go through it. It's quite funny, you know, those sort of self-satisfied creeps on big salaries and fixed contracts when they have a nasty time'.

In terms of background Milne and Howard came from different worlds: thus it is the reference to 'position' as an occupational marker and Clarke's note, 'We have to go through it', that is revealing. What Clarke has done, which is typical of the type of thinking involved in cultural symbolic protest, is to take two different species, bracketed them together as part of the same institution, and then placed that institution as somehow separate from other organizations in terms of pressures and practices. No doubt the BBC has practices special to itself, but for anyone in Milne's position, as head of a corporation as enormous as the BBC, life can be as rough as in many boardrooms of corporate organizations in the commercial world. The idea therefore that it was good for Milne 'to be roughed up' as an allegium for a protected life is diagnostically mistaken.

What Clarke's sentiments betray is a cultural dislike of a specific occupational group. Thus while the attack by the Conservative Back Bench Media Group on Milne and Howard was an attempt to remind the BBC of its supposed place, the bitterness of the dislike was based on the refusal of individuals within the organization to recognize that place. After all, the BBC is a very respectable institution possessing the type of establishment aura attractive to most conservative thought, but that it should be seen to turn with critical gaze against the establishment was taken as an act of gross misbehaviour requiring control. The attack, however, represented more than that. The back benchers may have been able to get their hands on Milne and Howard for one brief moment, but there were others they would also have liked to throttle.

The service value, expressed by the social worker's responsibility to his client, the educationalist's to his pupil, or the broadcaster's to his audience, rather than the broader social political system, is potentially always a point of political tension. How great the tension becomes depends on the degree to which the external governing forces wish to make such groups accountable beyond a point where the independence necessary to perform the role, within the ideology developed by the occupational group, is threatened. The ability to resist is a question of power, but given their weak position in the economic structure that power is largely determined by the value given, and the respect accorded to such groups. What has changed in recent years, however, marked by the coming to power in 1979 of the Conservative Government, is the relationship between non-productive creative groups and the economic base. The triumph of business and the tightening of the market mentality means such groups now sit in a disadvantaged and uncomfortable political position.

Although the principal power and economic structure of Britain has not changed since the coming to power of the Conservative Government in 1979, the political expression of its interests have. The resulting atmosphere is a reduction in tolerence to the realm of public service values in broadcasting, education, welfare, the arts and disdain for the values of the groups who occupy those sectors of employment. It is no longer feasible for the liberal intelligentsia to act as a superior kind of conscience (organized labour, seen to be based on sectional economic interest, never truly occupied that position) and remind its paymasters of higher matters than economic value or pragmatic worth, when the authority to do so is missing.

The BBC, unable to demonstrate its social benefit in terms of the understood principles of economic costing, proved itself a nuisance by sticking to its discredited values at a precise moment in time when it was seen to be needed the most. At the very least it should have cashed in on its privileged position to the service of Government.

What the excitement of the Falklands Conflict managed to do was to bring long simmering resentment against liberal groups who have failed to support the new economic values. That resentment had long been present, but the Falklands presented the opportunity to discredit liberal thought in a way not possible during a non-crisis. It is not suggested that this was an especially conscious manoeuvre, in the manner of McCarthy during the Cold War period of the fifties in America, more that it grew out of absolute dislike of groups whose values place principles of independence and criticism as key features of national life. To those within broadcasting, independence is not a gracious priviledge but a fundamental right to be defended. The stance the attackers were capable of taking therefore was one of criticizing types of individuals whose place in the economic political structure had been weakened to the point of disqualification of their values and to turn that demise into an open onslaught by suggesting they had a weakened allegiance to Britain.

We are not suggesting that the outcry against media content was ingenuous and that the real motive had nothing to do with their stated protestations. Nothing could be further from the truth. Sections of the Government, the Conservative Back Bench, the *Sun* newspaper, along with the *Express* and *Mail*, were annoyed at the type of coverage given to the Falklands Conflict by television and the *Guardian*. But the value of using our type of framework of analysis is that it allows an understanding of the vehemence of the attacks; an understanding of how the attacks came about; the historical placement of the symbols that were represented by the BBC and the relationship of the attackers and defenders to these. It also, in this instance, allows an understanding of why the attacks did not, as our survey shows, have popular resonance.

Culture involves both a political and intellectual struggle. What is at issue in cultural attack is not simply form, but the political base upon which the culture rests. A party wedded to a particularly muscular economic philosophy is not one that values highly the social contribution of the liberal intelligentsia. Seen as an economic luxury, they are also held as part of the political opposition to the 'new Conservatism'. Thus the objection to broadcast content was genuine enough; it was disliked for its failure to embody sufficiently national symbols, but the real protest and passion focused on individuals such as Milne and his associates as representatives of certain cultural groups. It was this dislike, on the part of the 'new order', of the cultural groups lodged within television (and one can also include readers of the *Guardian*, seen to be sheltering behind its pages in public sector services, the arts and education), that provided the vicious element to proceedings, and allowed the *Sun*, and to a lesser extent the *Mail* and *Express*, to join the attack as the popular brokers of the associated new mood, but the struggle itself was part of the wider political struggle to determine the contours of how society sees itself and the values by which it is to perform.

The groups we have labelled the intelligentsia are the holders of values created out of a time when their erstwhile predecessors were in respectful ascendency and sufficiently politically powerful to have their values socially established. They are now to be put in their place along with their ideas, and the attack on independent broadcasting should be seen in the context of sorting out wider power arrangements in the form of loosening the grip on public symbolic life by those cultural groups already defeated economically and politically. The 'new order', in their effort to finish or curtail the defeated groups by removing them from the stage of public performance, do so by suffocating their expressive creativity, one part of which is to alter the climate conducive to independent judgement. Abuse is one tactic to this achievement, the stiffling of funds is another.

The new cultural intolerance, with its vicious vocalization, is specific to the Conservatives, but in terms of process is not the preserve of any single political alignment. Each case of cultural protest requires separate study. A Labour Government could be as equally unfriendly to broadcasting as a Conservative one, but the roots would be different. A stridently class-bound Labour party might well separate off social workers as a group for appreciation, on the grounds that they give assistance to the poor and under-priviledged damaged by the productive processes they dislike, but turn on other liberal groupings such as broadcasters as middle class individuals, uncommitted by their independence to working class struggle.

Whether the type of attack on broadcasting during the Falklands and since is capable of containment is difficult to say, but it helps to see the attacks as a symbolic protest. The only real comfort that broadcasters can draw, and it is a very real one, is that the attackers' association of values with specific cultural groups – the notion of the liberal as traitor – to provide a focus for protest and collective front of attack, fell short of a popular movement. Indeed, the attacks, as our survey shows, removed the attackers from the mainstream of popular support. Why this should be so is intriguing; after all, the new conservatism has a popular mandate for its mood, but it is important, perhaps even annoying, to the new regime that it has not managed to alter the climate conducive to independent judgement. The block to success was that although the attacks were directed against recognizable groups, those groups were only truely recognized by those at the forefront of determining the new cultural landscape. To the general public, such groups are not clear social entities to be approved of or disliked, or at least not as carriers of a certain culture and cultural political power.

Furthermore the general public does not come into contact with cultural expressors as antagonists in the struggle for political position. Thus, the right of current affairs programmes to criticize government policy, or the lexical choice in the presentation of news, are not issues identifiable with class, party or status groups in the same way that private education, nationalization, private medicine, the selling of council houses or any other inumerable issues; they remain for the most part at the level of unattached preferences. Where controversy does ensue, it is as a matter of principles unrelated to social position. It is very difficult, in other words, to, turn the liberal as traitor into a product of social position. The fact, therefore, that the general public could not associate the principles involved in independent broadcasting with cultural groupings meant that they remained loyal to those principles. Broadcasting independence was not viewed as the property of any group, but held as the occupied territory of a national heritage.

That the 'new order' or some of its spokesmen, since it is not without opposition within its own ranks, did not take the bulk of the population into the fray with them was not the failure of muscle, merely a pointer to the fact that it has yet some way to go before embracing more of the body politic. The outcome cannot be certain, but the lack of general support for the attack rested, we would argue, on the ability of the public to disassociate the values of independent broadcasting with specific cultural groups and instead to hold them as valuable national values, the preserves of no one. That, however, is the battle. Once values, like religious beliefs, are separated off from general inheritance to be seen as the property of an identifiable class of individuals, they are open to attack on the grounds that have little to do with the internal merits of the beliefs and values. The task, therefore, for those who wish to preserve independent broadcasting is not to allow the values to become isolated, which at the moment, or at least as shown by the severe testing of the Falklands Conflict, they are not.

Appendix I

Dramatis Personae

The journalists

Brian Hanrahan	BBC TV News	*Hermes*
John Jockell	BBC TV News (Soundman)	*Hermes*
Bernard Hesketh	BBC TV News (Cameraman)	*Hermes*
Michael Nicholson	ITN	*Hermes*
Peter Archer	Press Association	*Hermes*
Martin Cleaver	Press Association (Photographer)	*Hermes*
Peter Heaps	ITN (Engineer)	*Hermes*
Mark Singleton	BBC TV News (Engineer)	*Hermes*
John Witherow	*The Times*	*Invincible*
Gareth Parry	The *Guardian*	*Invincible*
Alfred McIlroy	The *Daily Telegraph*	*Invincible*
Tony Snow	The *Sun*	*Invincible*
Mick Seamark	The *Daily Star*	*Invincible*
Richard Saville	Press Association	*Canberra*
John Shirley	The *Sunday Times*	*Canberra*
Patrick Bishop	The *Observer*	*Canberra*
Charles Lawrence	The *Sunday Telegraph*	*Canberra*
Max Hastings	The *Standard* (London)	*Canberra*
Ian Bruce	The *Glasgow Herald*	*Canberra*
Derek Hudson	The *Yorkshire Post*	*Canberra*
Leslie Dowd	Reuters	*Canberra*
Robert Fox	BBC Radio News	*Canberra*
Kim Sabido	Independent Radio News	*Canberra*
Jeremy Hands	ITN	*Canberra*
John Martin	ITN (Soundman)	*Canberra*
Bob Hammond	ITN (Cameraman)	*Canberra*
Alastair McQueen	The *Daily Mirror*	*Canberra*
Robert McGowan	The *Daily Express*	*Sir Lancelot*
Tom Smith	The *Daily Express*	*Sir Lancelot*
David Norris	The *Daily Mail*	*Stromness*

Ministry of Defence Chiefs of Staff Committee

Admiral of the Fleet – Sir Terence Lewin – Chief of Defence Staff
Admiral Sir Henry Leach – First Sea Lord
General Sir Edwin Bramall – Chief of the General Staff
Air Chief Marshall Sir Michael Beetham – Chief of the Air Staff
Vice Admiral Sir William Staneley – Vice Chief of Naval Staff (Operational Planning for Task Force)
Admiral Sir John Fieldhouse – Commander-in-Chief of Fleet (in charge of Combined Operations Headquarters, HMS *Warrior*, Northwood)

Rear Admiral Sir John F Woodward – Commander, Task Group
Major General Sir Jeremy Moore – Commander, Land Forces
Captain LE Middleton – Captain, HMS *Hermes*
Captain JJ Black – Captain, HMS *Invincible*
Captain C Burne – Senior Naval Officer on Canberra
Commander PH Longhurst – Directorate of Naval Operational Requirements

Sir Geoffrey Johnson Smith MP, Conservative
John Page MP, Conservative
Alan Clark MP, Conservative
Dafydd Elis Thomas MP, Welsh Nationalist
Robert Adley MP, Conservative
Sir Peter Mills MP, Conservative
Eldon Griffiths MP, Conservative
Sir Anthony Grant MP, Conservative
Kenneth Warren MP, Conservative
Sir Geoffrey Rippon MP, Conservative
Sally Oppenheimer MP, Conservative
Sir Bernard Braine MP, Conservative
Michael Foot MP, Leader, Labour Party
David Winnick MP, Labour
Winston Churchill MP, Conservative
Angus Maude MP, Conservative
John Stokes MP, Conservative
Dr Brian Mawhinney MP, Conservative
David Crouch MP, Conservative
William Rogers MP, SDP
David Steel, Leader, Liberal Party
Nicholas Winterton MP, Conservative
Gregor Mackenzie MP, Labour
Tam Dalyell MP, Labour
Sir Anthony Meyer MP, Conservative

George Foulkes MP, Labour
Sir Anthony Buck MP, Conservative

Senior media figures

George Howard	Chairman, BBC
Ian Trethowan	Director-General, BBC
Alastair Milne	Director-General Elect, BBC
Alan Protheroe	Assistant Director-General, BBC
Bob Kearsley	News Editor, BBC Radio News
Ken Brazier	Editor, BBC News External Services
David Lloyd	Editor, BBC TV *Newsnight* (from 7 May 1982)
Ron Neil	Editor, BBC TV *Newsnight* (up to 6 May 1982)
George Carey	Editor, BBC TV *Panorama*
Peter Woon	Editor, BBC TV News
Rik Thompson	Foreign Editor, BBC TV News
Ken Oxley	Chief Engineer, BBC TV News
Peter Snow	Presenter, BBC TV, *Newsnight*
David Nicholas	Editor, Independent Television News
Michael Cockerell	Reporter, BBC TV *Panorama*
Christopher Wain	Defence Correspondent, BBC TV News
Robert Hutchinson	Defence Correspondent, Press Association
Simon Jenkins	Political Editor, *The Economist*
Robert Kee	Presenter, BBC TV *Panorama*
Sir Brian Young	Director General, IBA
David Glencross	Deputy Director, IBA

Ministry of Defence Public Relations Officers

Graham Hammond	*Hermes*
Martin Helm	*Canberra*
Alan George	*Canberra*
Robin Barrett	*Hermes*
Roger Goodwin	*Invincible*
Alan Percival	*Canberra*
Brian Barton	*QE2*

Ministry of Defence officials, London

Sir Frank Cooper	Permanent Under-Secretary of State
Neville Taylor	Chief of Public Relations
Ian McDonald	Deputy Chief of Public Relations
Brigadier	
DJ Ramsbotham	Director of Public Relations (Army)
Captain Sutherland	Director of Public Relations (Navy)

The War Cabinet

Margaret Thatcher	Prime Minister
William Whitelaw	Home Secretary
John Nott	Defence Secretary
Francis Pym	Foreign Secretary
Cecil Parkinson	Paymaster General

Principal advisers

Sir Robert Armstrong	Cabinet Secretary
Sir Anthony Acland	Permanent Secretary, Foreign Office
Sir Frank Cooper	Permanent Under-Secretary, Ministry of Defence
Sir Terence Lewin	Admiral of the Fleet, Chief of Defence Staff
Sir Michael Palliser	Ex-permanent Secretary, Foreign Office (Special Consultant)
Bernard Ingham	Chief Press Secretary, No. 10 Downing Street

Appendix II

A chronology of the 1982 Falklands Conflict

26 February: Anglo-Argentine talks in New York

19 March: Argentine scrap merchants land at Leith, South Georgia

22 March: Foreign Office says landing was illegal

27 March: Reports of Argentine naval movements

29 March: Britain states its concern about a 'potentially dangerous situation'

1 April: Prime Minister told Argentine invasion of Falklands imminent

2 April: Argentina invades Falkland Islands. Royal Marines surrender

3 April: Argentina invades South Georgia. First House of Commons Saturday sitting since Suez. UN Security Council passes Resolution 502 calling for an end to hostilities, the withdrawal of Argentine troops and settlement by peaceful means. First RAF Transport Aircraft deploy to Ascension Island

5 April: Lord Carrington resigns as Foreign Secretary. Task Force sails

7 April: Britain declares a 200-mile military exclusion zone around the Falklands (effective 12 April)

8 April: Alexander Haig, US Secretary of State, arrives in London to begin diplomatic shuttle

9 April: Haig assumes mediation role

10 April: EEC approves trade sanctions against Argentina. Haig in Buenos Aires for talks with Galtieri

12 April: The 200-mile maritime exclusion zone comes into effect

17 April: Haig has talks with Argentine military junta

19 April: Haig returns to Washington after breakdown in mediation talks

22 April: Pym flies to Washington

23 April: Foreign Office advises British in Argentina to leave

25 April: Royal Marines recapture South Georgia. Submarine *Santa Fe* attacked and disabled

30 April: US openly sides with Britain after failure of peace efforts. Total exclusion zone comes into effect

1 May: Harriers and a Vulcan attack Port Stanley airfield. Three Argentine aircraft shot down

2 May: Argentine cruiser *General Belgrano* sunk by submarine HMS *Conqueror* with loss of 301 crew

361

4 May: Destroyer HMS *Sheffield* hit by Exocet missile, set on fire and abandoned with twenty lives lost – later sinks. Harrier shot down

5 May: Peru drafts peace plan

6 May: Two Harriers lost, believed to have collided

7 May: UN enters peace negotiations

9 May: Falklands bombarded from sea and air. Two sea Harriers sink trawler *Narwal*

11 May: *Cabo de los Estados* – Argentine supply ship sunk by HMS *Alacrity*

12 May: Three Argentine Skyhawks brought down

14 May: Three Argentine Skyhawks shot down. Prime Minister warns that peaceful settlement may not be possible. Special forces night raid on Pebble Island; 11 Argentine aircraft destroyed on the ground

17 May: Peacetalks continue at UN as Mrs Thatcher speaks of 'one last go'

19 May: UN peace initiative effectively collapses

20 May: Mrs Thatcher accuses Argentina of 'obduracy and delay, and bad faith'

21 May: British troops establish bridgehead at San Carlos. HMS *Ardent* sunk by air attack. Nine Argentine aircraft shot down

22 May: Consolidation day at bridghead

23 May: HMS *Antelope* attacked and sinks after unexploded bomb detonates. Ten Argentine aircraft destroyed

24 May: Seven Argentine aircraft shot down

25 May: HMS *Coventry* lost and *Atlantic Conveyor* hit by Exocet (sinks 28 May)

28 May: Second Battalion, Parachute Regiment, take Darwin and Goose Green. Death of Lt. Col. H Jones. More air-raids on Port Stanley

29 May: Warships and Harriers bombard Argentine positions: 250 Argentines killed, 1400 captured; 17 British killed

30 May: Shelling continues as British troops advance: 45 Commando secure Douglas settlement; 3 Para recapture Teal Inlet

31 May: Mount Kent taken by British troops

1 June: Britain repeats ceasefire terms

2 June: British troops take Mount Kent

4 June: Britain vetoes Panamanian–Spanish ceasefire resolution in the UN Security Council

6 June: Versailles summit supports British position on Falklands

8 June: Argentine air attack on landing craft *Sir Galahad* and *Sir Tristram* at Bluff Cove, resulting in the loss of 50 British lives

12 June: British forces seize Mount Tumbledown and other key positions

14 June: Final stages of battle. White flags raised over Port Stanley. General Menendez surrenders

15 June: Entry of British forces into Port Stanley

Appendix III

NOP interviewed 1,076 respondents, in 54 constituencies across Britain, using an interlocked quota sample. The constituencies were chosen to be representative of the population as a whole in terms of geographical spread and political affiliation. Within no constituency were area controls set. Quota controls were set by age, sex, and social class, based on figures for the population as a whole, and these controls were fully interlocked in an 18-cell matrix, details of which are shown below. Interviewing was carried out in-home, on 10 and 11 January 1983 and involved 59 interviewers.

Age	Male			Female		
	ABC1	C2	DE	ABC1	C2	DE
18–34	6.1	6.1	3.9	6.7	6.7	3.3
35–54	6.1	6.1	3.3	6.7	6.1	3.9
55+	5.0	5.6	5.0	6.1	5.6	7.8

Index

ABC (American Broadcasting Company), 68
academic production, 95
accreditation, 12–16
accuracy, 127, 205
Adie, Kate, 7
Adley, Robert, 230
age: and expectation of war, 298; and opinion
  on Task Force sailing, 301–9
Ajax Bay, 174, 187, 188
Alport, Mr, 256
Andrew, Prince, 18, 19
Antelope, 97, 109–10, 181
anti-war cinema, 348
Archer, Peter, 18, 22, 23, 24, 26–7, 33, 50, 67,
  107–8, 180
Argentina: boycott of, 244; British film from,
  260; jamming of World Service broadcasts,
  248; news coverage, 279–80
Argentinian claim: journalists on, 97; public
  opinion on, 286–309
Argentinian film: categories of, 265–6; use of,
  231, 238–40, 265–6, 342
Argentinian propaganda, 216–17, 229–30, 265
Argentinians: news of use to, 337–9; point of
  view portrayed, 339–42
Army: information handling, 189, 202;
  relations with journalists, 25, 46; vetting
  procedures, 188
Ascension Island, 168, 248
ashore, getting, 49–58
Associated Press, 4
Association of Broadcasting Staffs, 249
Atlantic Conveyor, 53, 120, 215, 310
atrocities, question of, 122–3
audience: response, 284–344; social
  composition and subtleties of attitudes,
  342–4

balance in broadcasting, 272, 330–1
Barrett, Robin, 27, 139–40, 142–3
Barron, Brian, 7
Barton, Brian, 91, 149–50
Battle for the Falklands (Hastings and
  Jenkins), 115
bayonet incident, 84, 154, 156, 157–8
BBC (British Broadcasting Corporation):
  attacks on, 227–38, 351–3; and pooling,
  61–2, 93; problems in news coverage,
  163–70; relations with ITN, 70–1; self-
  censorship, 221–5; traffic system, 176–8

BBC External Services, government
  treatment of, 246–57; *see also* World Service
BBC Radio, 16; *see also* Fox, Robert
BBC TV, 2, 16; *see also* Hanrahan, Brian;
  Hesketh, Bernard; Jockell, John; Singleton,
  Mark
Beach, Sir Hugh, 345–6
Belgrano, see General Belgrano
Bell, Martin, 7, 65
Benn, Tony, 230
Benyon, William, 241
bias, 95–6, 284–5, 344
Biffen, John, 197
Bishop, Patrick, 16–17, 19, 26, 31, 50–3, 61,
  65–6, 67, 74–5, 82, 84, 98, 145, 150, 154,
  187–8
Black, Captain Jeremy, 21–2, 23, 28–9, 39–40,
  43–4, 46, 132–3, 147–8, 185–6, 213
Blaker, Peter, 218
Bluff Cove, 55–7, 115, 119, 177, 181, 197,
  202–6, 268, 282; pictures, 224
bodies, repatriation of, 223
Bolton, Roger, 223
Braine, Sir Bernard, 223
Brazier, Ken, 243, 252–3
briefings, off-the-record, 22, 197–202, 218–19,
  246
British Forces Broadcasting Service, 248
Brixton riots, 227
broadcasters: compared with print journalists,
  41–3; difficulty of getting action footage,
  92–4; friction among, 70–2; independence,
  105; received feedback, 87, 176
broadcasting, attack on, as symbolic protest,
  350–6
broadcasting culture, 344; threat to, 350–6
Broadcasting House, 174, 175
broadcasting organizations, self-censorship,
  221–5
broadcasting unions, 249
Broadsword, 180
Bruce, Ian, 7, 13, 17, 21, 29, 42, 60, 62, 66, 73,
  74, 76, 77, 79–80, 83, 86, 87, 90, 96–7, 99,
  100, 103, 104–5, 109–10, 112, 119, 129, 160;
  bayonet incident, 84, 154, 156, 157–8; on
  censorship, 147
Buck, Sir Anthony, 218
Burne, Christopher, 21, 42, 107, 161
Bush House, 175
Buxton, Cindy, 162

364